The Ancient Sun Kingdoms of the Americas

THE ANCIENT SUN KINGDOMS of the Americas

AZTEC · MAYA · INCA

VICTOR WOLFGANG VON HAGEN

317 illustrations in photogravure, 16 colour plates

THAMES AND HUDSON · LONDON

PRINTED BY DUMONT PRESSE COLOGNE WESTERN GERMANY

THE MAPS AND MODERN DRAWINGS IN THIS BOOK ARE BY
ALBERTO BELTRÁN

Contents

INTRODUCTION: *'The Newe Founde Worlde'* 9

I A GOD-TORMENTED PEOPLE: THE AZTECS 17

1 THE CONQUERORS FROM THE NORTH 18
A land of extremes · The Aztecs come to Anáhuac · The city of wonder The conquered peoples: Olmec, Zapotec, Mixtec, Totonac The myth of Quetzalcoatl · The 'Place of the Gods'

2 THE FARMER AND HIS FAMILY 33
The peasant-warrior · 'Excellent women, full of grace' · A language that still lives · Rank without class: the clan system · The marriage brokers Trumpets at dawn: the daily round · Training the children · Punishment

3 WORK, PLAY, AND PERPETUAL WAR 44
The all-important maize · War to bring rain · Weaving: the women's art 'Sixty thousand people bartering and selling' · Barbaric festivals: music · The ball-game · Penalties for crime · The Undead

4 'ONE WHO SPEAKS': THE KING AND HIS COUNCIL 67
Priest-king and demigod · The Great Moctezuma · The pomp of power Luxuries of trade and conquest · Tenochtitlán: the crowded city on the lake · A palace of splendour

5 THE ENDURING LEGACY 81
A great city destroyed · The temple-city of the Toltecs The Place of Flowers · Composite of cultures: Monte Albán · The Place of the Dead · Lost beauty in feather and gold · Sculpture of terror

6 THE WILL OF THE GODS 100
A religion fed with blood · The rites of human sacrifice · Divine time and solar time: the five empty days · Waging sacred war · Merchant princes The return of Quetzalcoatl · The fall of the Aztecs

II CITIES OF THE JUNGLE: THE MAYAS 119

7 THE MISSING YEARS OF MAYA HISTORY 120
A beginning deep in the past · The empire in the jungle
Abandoned and forgotten cities: the 'Great Descent' · Renaissance on the plains
'The Land of the Turkey and the Deer'

8 THE MAYA MEN AND WOMEN 133
The people of the soil · Dress and decoration: flattened heads and crossed eyes · Sex and marriage · Maize, chocolate and meat
The dread of drought: its cost in human sacrifice

9 A PEOPLE OF CRAFTS AND COMMERCE 147
The perished art of the looms · Pottery a key to early history
The great market of Xicalango · Traffic in slaves · The days of rejoicing: dance, music and drama · The rites of death

10 THE LORDS OF THE MAYA 165
The state's 'father and lord' · His splendour · His wife and concubines
Choosing a successor · The great city-states: a complex social life
The rise of Mayapán · Struggle of the dynasties

11 AN ART RULED BY THE GODS 172
Stone to cut stone · The jungle remains: strange craftsmanship and astonishing achievement · Tikal, Copán, Palenque · Cities of the plains: the new Chichén Itzá · Intricate and beautiful sculpture · The painted walls of Bonampak

12 THE CULTURE THAT DIED 210
The glorious panoply of battle · Blood for the gods · Thirteen heavens and nine hells · 'An extraordinary preoccupation with time': the calendar
The complex of roads · Maya books · The coming of the Spaniards

CONTENTS

III KINGDOM OF GOLD: THE INCAS 225

13 THE PAST THAT THE INCAS 'FORGOT' 226
The three Perus · The Cat God of Chavín · Brilliant potters: the Mochicas Figures in the sand · The Weeping God of Tiahuanaco

14 BROAD BASE OF THE PYRAMID: THE WORKER 240
'Most fair and good looking' · Dress and daily life · The labours of the months Source of half the world's foods · Llama, alpaca, vicuña

15 PRODUCTS AND PLEASURES OF THE PEOPLE 256
A long history of fine weaving · The language of pottery · Markets of barbaric pageantry · Holidays · Penalties for misconduct · Demons and gods

16 THE ROYAL INCA 269
A king from the sun · Sister-wife and sub-wives · A life of ritual and splendour · 'Grand and stately Cuzco' · The Golden Enclosure

17 'SWEAT OF THE SUN, TEARS OF THE MOON' 281
Fortress-cities of the Andes: Machu Picchu · 'The Hawk's Sanctuary' Cyclopean walls of polished stonework · The fabulous gold of Peru

18 THE HIGHWAYS OF THE SUN 301
The Chosen Women · Roads of a vast empire · The Bridge of San Luis Rey The counting strings · Waging war · The final perfidy

CHRONOLOGY 329

SELECT BIBLIOGRAPHY 337

SOURCES AND ACKNOWLEDGEMENTS 339

INDEX 342

For Victor Weybright Litt. D.
In gratitude and affection

Introduction: 'The Newe Founde Worlde'

WHEN the news of Cortés's exploits in Mexico suddenly burst upon the world in 1519, man in Europe had almost forgotten the very existence of an America. This was understandable. During the years that had passed since its discovery America had provided only false hopes. It had been expected that new foodstuffs would pour out unrestrainedly from the 'spiceries' to relieve the monotony of European diet. Broadsides affixed to walls had proclaimed the discovery and books had told of 'Joyful Newes out of the Newe Founde Worlde', of 'rare and singular vertues of divers Herbes, of Trees and Plantes of Oyles and stones . . .' Even the discoverer of it all, Cristóbal Colón, now Admiral of the Ocean Sea, had fed the illusions by talking without stint of gold, rubies, and silver, which were to be found there more abundantly than in King Solomon's mines.

In anticipation of such riches, a convention between Spain and Portugal early in the discovery had, with the Pope's blessing, divided the Americas; the New World was to be shared between them in exclusivity. The King of France, witty François I, asked to see '. . . that clause in Adam's will which allowed the kings of Castille and Portugal to divide the earth between them . . .' But his irony availed him nothing and these two kingdoms soon settled themselves into the New World. Europe had waited with a certain breathlessness, one gathers from reading the contemporary accounts, and people expected the floodgates of plenty to open up. But, at best, the opening was a timorous settling; the Portuguese merely touched Brazil, and the Spanish confined themselves for the first twenty years to a small piece of the Isthmus of Panama and to the islands of the Antilles. Here was found nothing of the riches so highly vaunted by the original discoverers. Europeans dismissed 'America' as yet one more instance of Spanish braggadocio—until there arrived in Seville, on December 9, 1519, the first treasure ship from Mexico.

Its arrival caused a tremendous sensation. Cortés had sent four fantastically attired Totonacs from the Mexican coast to accompany the treasures, and in the golden cache there were bells and jewels, earrings and nose ornaments of exquisite workmanship, and feather ornaments mounted in jewels, and there were even 'books such as the Indians use.' But that which stirred most was a golden wheel 'seventy-nine inches in diameter, of a thickness of four reales,' an Aztec calendar swarming with strange designs hammered out in *repoussé*. From the documents now extant one can still feel the contagious excitement of those who saw these treasures for the first time.

They so impressed Charles V that he took them to Ghent. Albrecht Dürer saw them in Brussels and wrote in his diary (August 27, 1520): '... I have never seen anything heretofore that has so rejoiced my heart. I have seen the things which were brought to the King from the new *golden land* ... a sun entirely of gold a whole fathom broad; likewise a moon entirely of silver, equally large ... also two chambers full of all sorts of weapons, armour, and other wondrous arms, *all of which is fairer to see than marvels* ... these things are so precious that they are valued at 100,000 gulden, I saw among them amazing artistic objects that I have been astonished at the subtle *ingenia* of these people in these distant lands. Indeed I cannot say enough about the things which were before me ...'

The Italian humanist Pietro Martire d'Anghiera himself could not say enough about 'the two books such as the Indians use.' He remained 'wrapped in astonishment,' for to him the 'books' were a greater index to the quality of this new civilization than the gold. 'The Indians of the golden land write in books,' he said in his letters to other humanists as he analyzed the technique of the book and the hieroglyphics '... which almost resemble those of the Egyptians ... among the figures of men and animals are those of kings and great lords ... so it may be presumed that they made report of each one's deeds ...'

Unfortunately, while the learned debated the Aztec civilization, speculating as to its origin, it was already being overwhelmed and destroyed. Thousands more of these golden Aztec objects, brought to the king as his royal fifth, were melted down and minted into coin to pay off his immense debts incurred by European wars. As for other Aztec 'books,' and exquisitely made golden ornaments, as well as these other objects of Aztec culture, they perished in the Conquest. In the process of being taken, Tenochtitlán, the Aztec capital was utterly destroyed. 'One of the most beautiful cities in the world,' wrote Cortés, his eyes brimming with simulated tears as he walked through the stench of the fires and singed flesh. In the end that which survived

'No description and no drawing *can give the moral sublimity of the spectacle' wrote Stephens, the American explorer, when he first saw the stelae of Copán in 1842. But this coloured lithograph by his companion, the English architect Catherwood, comes close—closer than any photograph—to conveying the full power and grandeur of these Maya monoliths. There are nine of them in the Plaza of Copán, each carved with an elaborately dressed figure of a priest-ruler or god. They marked intervals of time, being dedicated at the end of the period; this is stele H, erected in* A.D. *782.*

numero de años. LI.
tenuch
tenochtitlan
colhuacan. pueblo.
tenayucan. pueblo

of Aztec architecture was torn down to build churches and mansions for the victor, and what was not destroyed by man was overwhelmed by the insults of time.

Six years later, in 1527, the Mayas found themselves on the agenda of conquest: Francisco de Montejo, the would-be conqueror, promised much to Charles V, his liege lord, more gold than he had received as his royal fifth from the rape of Mexico. At that time Charles V had full need of it; he was at war again, this time with France, and moreover, Sultan Solyman of the Turkish Empire had seized Budapest and was threatening Vienna. At that moment no one in the Spanish court could pay too much attention to the happenings in America.

The Maya conquest went off badly. After conquest and pillage, slavery followed. Those chieftains and priests, 'in whom all learning reposed,' who were not killed took refuge either in flight or silence. No intellectual in Europe ever saw a Maya 'book,' and since there was little or no gold to act as stimulant, the learned of Europe never had any communication about those marvellously contrived stone cities which the Mayas had built. This was not the fault of the participators in conquest nor the priests nor the administrators who followed. They penned voluminous reports; yet they went unpublished.

New Spanish cities were fashioned out of the rubble of Maya ruins; other unruined temples were torn down to supply building material for Spanish churches, mansions, and administrative centres. Ancient Maya Tìho became Mérida, the Yucatán capital 'on account of the singularity of its buildings,' the size of which, said a Spaniard in 1550, 'fills one with amazement.' As mere building material Bishop Landa doubted that 'it will never come to be entirely exhausted.' It was 'exhausted' in two decades. Those Maya structures which survived man's destruction were slowly over-run by jungle verdure until, in time, all of these magnificent cities had vanished.

The title page of the Codex Mendoza, *one of Moctezuma's Books of Tribute, copied by native artists by order of Antonio de Mendoza, the first Spanish Viceroy to Mexico (1535–49). In addition to a history of the early Aztec people, it contains details of crime and punishment, children's education, clothing—an invaluable record. On the title page appears an eagle alighting on a piece of cactus (tenochtli), the arms of Tenochtitlán (Mexico City); about it are various 'kings of Mexico', each with a symbol expressing his name—a speech scroll in front of one (with blue face) indicates that he is talking. The border lists the years, named by a symbol and number (the first is '2-house'). At the foot, Aztec warriors have conquered towns, the temples are in flames. In the upper left-hand corner is the signature of André Thévet, Cosmographer Royal to François I of France into whose hands (by pirates) the Codex fell. He later sold it to Richard Hakluyt for twenty crowns in 1584. It is now in the Bodleian Library, Oxford.*

Peru, the real Kingdom of Gold, appeared on the horizon just as the Maya civilization was in its death throes. On May 16, 1532, Pizarro set out from the coast of Peru with his 130 foot soldiers and 40 mounted cavaliers, following the Inca royal road to seek the capital. In the varied history of man, was this not the most quixotic of journeys—170 men against three million, 170 men dedicated to conquer what was then one of the largest empires on earth? The sequence is known to every schoolboy, how Pizarro seized by stratagem the person of the Inca in the midst of his thirty thousand armed warriors and within one half hour—certainly among the most famous thirty minutes in history—subdued his whole empire.

On January 9, 1534, the galleon *Santa Maria del Campo* wharfed in Seville. Officials there who believed they had seen almost everything to be seen in these last fabulous years could not take in with their eyes the treasures that lay there: gold and silver lay piled on the dock, ingot upon ingot, all stamped with the royal seal. In a separate inventory to the king was a list of objects so beautiful that not even the most hardened conquistador in Peru could commit them to the crucible—thirty-four jars of gold, a golden stalk simulating maize, two golden platters, an idol of a man, life-size, over one hundred silver objects, the largest piece weighing 167 pounds. The total was worth twenty million dollars in bullion, and equal to twenty times that amount in terms of modern purchasing power. Never in history had so much bullion arrived at a single moment in Europe. The effect of that treasure ship on the human imagination never quite wore off; even now in Italy when one speaks of something of fantastic value it is a 'Perú.'

At this golden moment Charles V still had greater preoccupations. He was undertaking the conquest of Tunis, so that ships, men, and money were of supreme importance. This time he did not even stop to look at the fabulous golden ornaments. He did that which for instinctive aesthetic reasons even the most debased of his subjects had not done; he ordered the whole of the Incas' treasure to be melted down into ingots. Of the long ton of original golden ornaments from the Inca's ransom not a single example exists in Spain today.

With that conquest, the animus, the soul, of the Peruvian was forever lost. The physical remains of that immense civilization, the buildings and temples of varying forms and functions that spread over two thousand miles along the Andes and the coast went the way of the conquest. Those which were not destroyed then were later toppled by the civil wars fought between the conquistadors over the carcass of the Inca Empire. As with the Aztecs and Mayas, so with the Incas—churches were either built out of the rubble or were set over the temples; Inca buildings were torn down to provide the stone to build manorial dwellings, and administration buildings were set up among the ruins. The lands being depopulated, a road system nearly as fine as that of the Roman Empire went into decay. The *tampu* resthouses which had appeared along the entire length and breadth of the network were reclaimed by the earth, and the suspension bridges which had spanned the awesome canyons along the route rotted and fell. The ingenious *acequias,* which had conducted water for irrigation into the desert, were neglected. The land was reclaimed by sand.

It was the Age of Reason that brought about a renaissance of archaeological interest in the Americas. In 1773 the Maya ruins of Palenque lying in the tangled tropical forests of Chiapis, Mexico, were discovered. Its discovery was brought to the personal attention of Charles III of Spain. He ordered his officials to explore the ruins carefully, to make drawings and preserve all the artifacts found so that they could form the basis for an *Ancient History of America.* Italian scholars were sent from Spain to Mexico to seek out ancient documents in order to prepare such a history. In 1777, a Mexican, Antonio Alzate, found the ruins of Xochicalco, and a few years later, in 1790, while excavations were going on to alter the foundations of the Cathedral of Mexico City, the workmen came across a gigantic monolith—the Aztec calendar stone. Carved out of a single piece of volcanic trachyte, it was eighteen feet in diameter with its centre dominated by the figure of Tonatiuh, the sun god, sculpted in large dimensions; ringed about it were symbols of calendric day-signs. In a previous time the archbishop would have ordered it to be smashed and worked into church masonry; now it was brought intact to the museum.

In Mexico those whose vocation was the antique hopefully believed that the Aztec calendar stone might be another Rosetta stone; such a speculation was still current when Alexander von Humboldt arrived in Mexico City on April 18, 1803. Already well known—his letters to scientific associates in Paris had been published in various journals—Humboldt had, since 1799, travelled and explored in South America with his friend, Aimé Bonpland, botanist and physician. The Spanish viceroy, José de Iturrigaray, himself welcomed Humboldt and let it be known that since Humboldt carried the King of Spain's rubric whatever he wished to see in Mexico was to be placed at his disposal.

Humboldt has been fully and rightfully extolled for his immense contributions to botany, geography, geology, astronomy, geophysics, meteorology, oceanography, and zoology; yet there is more to him. It was he who brought the buried American cultures into focus. His volume on American archaeology was contained in one large folio and published in Paris in 1810 with the title of *Vues des Cordillères et Monuments des Peuples Indigènes de L'Amérique.* This gave the world for the first time a panorama of ancient American history, displayed as never before in accurate scale drawings of Inca buildings, calendar stones from Colombia, bas-reliefs of Aztec sculptures, coloured engravings of pages of the Maya *Dresden Codex*; and drawings of the Aztec calendar stone with detailed explanations and numerous illustrations of Aztec, Zapotec and Mixtec manuscripts with learned commentaries. Under this immense authority America was seen as a civilization with its art placed on the high levels of culture. That volume went through four editions in eight years.

During the 19th century various fantastic theories were elaborated. Viscount Kingsborough, for instance, devoted his life and fortune to proving that the American Indians were Jews. His eight huge folio volumes, the *Antiquities of Mexico*, were published between 1830 and 1848.

Such attitudes were still popular when, in 1840, William H. Prescott began to write the *History of the Conquest of Mexico*. Few then believed that the Aztecs had reared the buildings ascribed to them; few accepted the fact that the American Indian had ever been capable of producing the civilization described by the early Spaniards. So Prescott went to the original unpublished records that lay in Spanish archives. With the appearance of his *Conquest of Mexico* in 1843, the evidence he had amassed was so formidable and the style of his writing so impressive that Prescott in that one book succeeded in giving America back to the Indians. At the same time, his friend John Lloyd Stephens, a New York lawyer who had travelled 'for his health' through Egypt, Arabia Petraea, Poland, and Russia, was then exploring Central America and helped to provide factual evidence. Frederick Catherwood, an architect, was his companion. Catherwood had taken part in some of the earliest English expeditions to Egypt and, being thoroughly immersed in the art of the Old World, he was prepared to evaluate what had been discovered in the new. His accurate drawings with the dramatic overtones of Piranesi illustrated wonderfully well the text of Stephens; together they authored publications which were then avidly read and which time has made into classics of archaeology; *Incidents of Travel in Central America* (1841) and *Incidents of Travel in Yucatán* (1843) continue even now to be republished.

It was Alfred Maudslay who, in 1880, began the modern phase of American archaeology. His explorations, excavations, and recording of all that was then known of Maya texts (on monuments and buildings) gave

A seated rabbit in jade, *carved by an Aztec sculptor. The eyes were inlaid obsidian; a broad belt is adorned with skull and crossbones; at the front, probably attached to the belt, is a head of Tonatiuh (High Flying Eagle), the Sun-God.*

On a ridge of rock *stands Pisac, a natural fortress guarding the upper Urubamba River twenty-five miles from Cuzco. Here the Inca engineers constructed an amazing series of defensive works, tunnels, walls, gateways and (on the right) agricultural terraces which stretch away down the mountain. The stonework, much of it fitted into the living rock, still bears witness to their craftsmanship and precision.*

scholars throughout the world a firm basis on which to assault the mystery of the Maya hieroglyphs. He was the spiritual successor of Stephens.

After Maudslay's publications, interest in the Aztec, Maya, and Inca civilizations quickened. Archaeologists of many nations were drawn to these lost civilizations, and each in his own way, peculiar to the intellectual background of his native land, made his contribution. More and yet more lost cities were rediscovered; and the problems which each new discovery posed grew in number and profundity as the literature mounted.

What, after all, is this search for ancient man in the Americas? It is basically a tremendous and fascinating mystery. With the absence of written records such as occur in the Old World what do we have to go on? We have a profusion of strange-sounding names—Toltec, Mixtec, Chibcha, Cuqisnique. We have a scale—the vastness of the American milieu. We have an enigmatic plot. Who was this mysterious Plumed Serpent god that permeates the whole of Mexico? Why did the Mayas suddenly abandon hundreds of their cities? Why were the Incas and the Mayas unaware of each other's existence? We have sets of clues from which deductions can be made, clues which might well puzzle a Sherlock Holmes. And there is continual novelty: the finding of tombs, such as that of a warrior god in a beautifully wrought underground sanctuary at Palenque, where a tomb was not supposed to be; or the finding of barbarically beautiful murals, such as those at Bonampak in the jungle, unseen by any other human eyes since their abandonment a millennium before. More than a mystery, the quest is also a dream . . . a dream of every archaeologist that someday in the hushed sanctity of the forest he will find a place, a city, a ruin which no other explorer has ever seen. This is a fundamental human instinct, for life exists for the sake of newness. So archaeology is endowed with suspense; it combines the excitement of treasure hunting with romance. Potsherds and mummies, liths and skeletons are all clues on the road of cultural history.

Every technique that objective science offers is used by the archaeologist. The work demands exacting excavations, the study of so unromantic a theme as the shapes of cooking pots, the interpretation of contradictory data about time sequences. These are the minutiae out of which archaeological history is often shaped. In itself it does not make fascinating reading. The high romance of research loses something of its mystery, and with it, its patina of suspense, as the archaeologist cleans, repairs, and catalogues his material. This is the dreary part of the business. Still 'the archaeologist,' as the late Dr. Earnest Hooton insisted, '. . . remains inwardly a romanticist.'

I have made a sincere attempt to remain objective, yet I know that to say this is to deceive; one cannot fail to leave the imprint of one's own prejudices and personality on any work, whatever its nature. So this book is tainted with subjectivity. How can a historian decide what is and what is not a fact? He does so according to his own character and idiosyncracy, his own taste and fancy; in a word, he does so as an artist. Still I have trod the jungles on and off for three decades, felt the persistent sting of the insects, have gone through the usual diseases, climbed the Andes wretched with mountain sickness, been tossed off mules, sat in jails because of understandings or misunderstandings. All this has had an effect on the sharp edges of the romantic agony; they have been smoothed off by plentiful rubbings in the stream of life. When I wanted to know about, let us say, the life habits of the quetzal, that fantastically beautiful bird which yielded its long plumes to Maya chieftains and its name to the Plumed Serpent, I climbed the rain forests and sat it out for six long months, time enough to know its life history, and even essayed its capture in order to gain some insight into how the Mayas were able to supply such fantastic amounts of its plumage without making it extinct. When the origins of Maya and Aztec paper were questioned, I did not content myself with merely inhaling the dust of libraries but set off to the jungles to collect the paper-making plants and run the gamut of the usual physical inconveniences which one always encounters in research such as this. The microscope, history, and the library only confirmed what was found at the source. Since 1930, then, I have journeyed on many expeditions, large and small, and have lived in all of the lands that formed a part of the Sun Kingdoms of the Americas. Neither the Noble Savage nor his antagonist has prejudiced these materials. There *are* prejudices here; yet my varied activities in the field of ethnography, which have carried me far and wide, have given me some knowledge of local geography—and my selection and interpretation of the material is, in, a sense, a qualified *praejudicium*.

Beyond the archaeological and historical literature, which is fully acknowledged in the Bibliography and Sources, I have called upon much else that is not technical to give me the phrases which help me to take these people out of the flow of the purely archaeological and put them back into the human stream of life. I have borrowed much from the original chroniclers to liven up and reshape that which would be merely chipped and dulled if I did not give it a covering of humanism to clothe its bare archaeological bones.

VICTOR WOLFGANG VON HAGEN

The Eagle Knight of the Aztecs: *a warrior's head in stone, framed within a decorated helmet in the shape of an eagle's mouth. It was the ideal of the Aztec warrior, and the motif appears often in Aztec art. The Knights were chivalric orders, who fought both in battle and in ritual gladiatorial combats. The fight between the Eagle Knights and the Jaguar Knights symbolized the conflict between day and night.*

I A God-Tormented People: THE AZTECS

1 The Conquerors from the North

ALL MEXICO is divided into two parts: the mountainous and the flat.

The land is one of extremes: the contrasts of the volcanic wastes, the high *mesetas* of thin air, the aridity of deserts, the lush parts folding one upon another, exiling valley from valley, have made this land the love and despair of man.

Mexico has extremes in climate, and, even though half the land lies in the tropical zone, altitude is more important than latitude. The eastern coast is broader and fiercely rained on by the trade winds; it is more lush, and it was the ground for early civilizations—the land of the Olmecs, Totonacs, Huastecs. The western coast has a narrower fringe of coast line: nature here is not so prodigal and this is reflected in the early cultures; they are threadbare compared to those on the 'other side.'

The Mexican land rises up from these two shores, sometimes abruptly, sometimes gradually, to the high plateau which is the bulk of the geography of Mexico. Orizaba, a snow-topped mountain (the Aztecs called it 'Citlaltépetl': 'Mountain of the Star'), rises out of the verdured jungle to dominate at 18,000 feet the 'cold lands.' Here there is the naked misery of soil that the first Spaniards found: '. . . three days' march through a desert land uninhabitable on account of its barrenness, lack of water, and great cold. . . . Oh! the thirst and hunger suffered by the men assailed by whirlwinds of hailstones and rain.'

This high mesa land, varying between 3,000 and 10,000 feet, is classic Mexican soil, where Mexico City, ancient Tenochtitlán, lies at 8,000 feet.

Rain defines the seasons. On the high tableland it falls, the gods willing, between June and September; the rest of the months are dry except for a caprice of nature, and then it falls out of season and may even snow in Mexico City, an event which might be recorded by the Aztec in their glyph history of unusual events.

The gifts of sun and rain not being equal, much of the land has been inhospitable to man. So while Mexico is vast, much of it in ancient times was empty of man and the empty places were where the soil was naked and sterile. The really fertile areas had been occupied since the earliest times, especially that incunabula of cultures, the valley of Anáhuac, the 'land on the edge of the water,' where Mexico City lies.

The high mesa land of Mexico, *the classic land of Mexican culture, marked by bare mountains, forested valleys and thrusts of sterile reddish lava covered with thickets of chaparral, cactus and mesquite. The ancient capital, Tenochtitlán, now Mexico City, lies at 8,000 feet.*

By the time the Aztecs emerged as a tribe (circa A.D. 1200), the best lands were already occupied. They called themselves 'Tenochas,' descendants of northern tribes. In their search for land they had to run the gauntlet of numerous other peoples, already settled, who disputed passage with them. The hard necessity of war breeds men; peoples grow by and against other peoples to inward greatness. And the Aztecs were landless. They were, as others had been before them, far-ranging animals wandering from necessity—certainly in search of land but also perhaps just out of the 'primary microcosmic urgency to move.'

So into the lakes of Anáhuac in their year Ome-Acatl (2-Reed), moved this god-tormented tribe, this 'Aztec' people who were to systematize rapine and war into a form of state and forever leave their impress on the Mexican land.

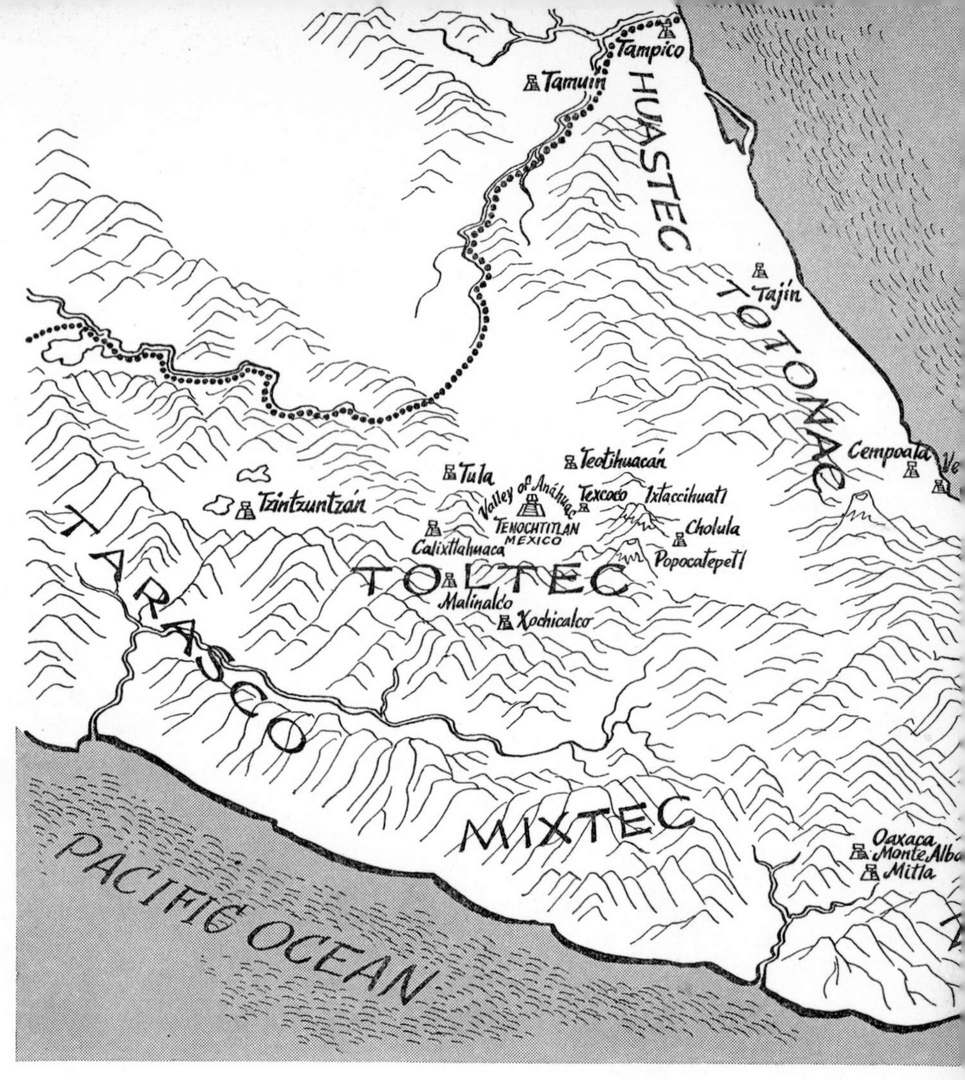

Peoples and places of Mexico *on the eve of the Conquest, with a rough indication of the distribution of the pre-Aztec cultures. The approximate limits of Aztec domination are shown by the dotted line.*

In or about 1168 A.D. the Tenochas, called by us 'Aztecs,' entered the lakes of Anáhuac from the north-west. Landless and friendless and already eyed with dismay by the other tribes settled about the lakes because of their readiness to offer human hearts to their gods, they had little of the outward trappings of human culture. A tribe small in numbers, composed of contending clans and forced out of one settled region after another, they finally selected several islets two miles out in Lake Texcoco and, carrying their god's image before them, they began in 1325 to build their city-state.

Within two centuries they were the overlords of Mexico, and Tenochtitlán, the 'Place of the Tenocha,' was the most sumptuous city ever raised by indigenous man in the Americas. The Spaniards, who had arrived to make its conquest and add its land titles to those of their Emperor-King, Charles V of Spain, entered 'the great city of Tenochtitlán, Mexico, on the 8th of November . . . 1519.'

'Gazing on such wonderful sights,' wrote Bernal Díaz del Castillo remembering it vividly after fifty years, 'we did not know what to say or if what appeared before us was real.' They proceeded along a 'Causeway . . . eight paces in width' which ran 'two miles from the mainland to the city . . . so crowded with people that there was hardly room for them all . . . the towers were full of people . . . canoes [came] from all parts of the lake.'

Being close to the entrance of the city, they were met by the 'king's' entourage: the Great Moctezuma got down from his litter and, supported by others, continued 'beneath a marvellously rich canopy of green coloured feathers with much gold and silver embroidery and with pearls and [jade] suspended from a sort of bordering, which was wonderful to look at. The Great Moctezuma was richly attired . . . many other lords . . . walked before [him], sweeping the ground where he would tread and spreading cloths on it . . .'

As they entered the city they were hardly able to believe their eyes. Bernal Díaz remembered that he 'could [not] count the multitude of men and women and boys who were in the streets . . . in canoes on the canals, who had come out to see us. It was indeed wonderful, and, now that I am writing about it'—he was then eighty-four—'it all comes before my eyes as though it had happened but yesterday.'

Later Bernal Díaz del Castillo accompanied Cortés and looked at the stored treasures of this tribute-state and into where Moctezuma 'kept the accounts of all the revenue . . . in his books which were made of paper which they call *amatl,* and he had a great house full of these books.' And they saw the storehouses of cereals and maize, beans and peppers, brought in as tribute, other storehouses full of war dress, 'many of them richly adorned with gold and precious stones,' and arms and shields and 'a sort of broadswords . . . like to hand-swords set with stone [obsidian] knives which cut much better than our very own swords,' and bows and arrows stacked to the high ceiling and 'artful shields . . . made so that they can be rolled up . . . and quilted cotton armour.'

Then there were those who polished precious stones and jades and 'the great craftsmen in feather work, and painters and sculptors . . . the Indian women who did the weaving . . . who made such an immense quantity of fine fabrics with wonderful feather work designs . . .'

The public markets, of which there were four in the city, were dominated by the great market place at Tlaltelolco, and 'we were astounded at the

The Tenochas, called by us Aztecs, *came to the lakes of Anáhuac from the north-west. This drawing, from an Aztec codex, represents their migration. The four tribes (each shown by the tribal emblem) make towards Tenochtitlán, symbolized by the glyph. Footsteps indicate movement.*

'The Great Moctezuma', *wrote Bernal Díaz of Castille, 'was the chieftain of all Mexico, of good height and slender ...'. This meeting with Cortés was drawn about 1560 by an Aztec artist trained by the Spaniards. Moctezuma, supported by three generals, brings gifts of maize, birds and game. He is indicated by his glyph; Cortés' guard is shown above him (the Aztecs did not understand perspective), and behind, interpreting, stands Malinal, known by the Spaniards as Doña Marina, whom the Indians called 'the tongue'.*

number of people and the quantity of merchandise that it contained, and at the good order and control that was maintained.'

'Truly, my Lord,' wrote Hernán Cortés, continuing the description of this fabulous city when eloquence had failed Bernal Díaz 'Truly, my Lord ... the great city of Tenochtitlán ... built in the midst of this salt lake, two leagues from any point in the mainland, is connected by four causeways ... twelve feet wide ... the city is as large as Seville or Cordova ... as for the whole, it is so large I am unable to find out exactly the extent of Moctezuma's kingdom ...'

All this—despite its rather Arabian Nights unreality—the Spaniards found, a luxuriant form of life of a kind which no other peoples in the Americas had ever attained.

Who were the Aztecs and whence did they come? As we have seen, the Tenochas were the last of the tribes to arrive at the valley of Anáhuac. By 1000 B.C. the great migrations were over. Peoples filled the fertile lands and were beginning to build temple-cities. In central highland Mexico, throughout the hotlands of Vera Cruz, and in the highlands of Guatemala, they laid down their city centres. Man became sedentary; he had developed agriculture and he knew leisure. During the same period in the 'other lands,' the Phoenicians were devising the alphabet, the Greek-Dorians were arriving in the Peloponnesus, and Europe, thinly populated, was coming out of raw savagery.

One tribe was already evident: the Olmecs (800 B.C.–A.D. 600?), who lived in the hotlands of Vera Cruz and Tabasco. It was long suspected that the Olmec might prove to be one of the earlier cultures and now radiocarbon dating from the Olmec site at La Venta has confirmed the evidence that Olmec structures 'appear to have been constructed and used during . . . four centuries . . . 800–400 B.C.' In recent times the great Olmec stone heads have been unearthed, by Dr. Matthew Stirling. At Tres Zapotes he found one colossal head, seven feet high, flat-nosed and sensually thick-lipped. The carving is sensitive and realistic; the style is found among no other people and once seen will never be forgotten or confused with any other. Other colossal heads have been found; in similar style there are carved masks, heads in smaller scale, and votive axes, all exhibiting the same squat figures with perforated noses, pronounced Mongoloid features, and narrow slits for eyes. These have been found in widely scattered areas. The Olmec large-scale monuments, however, are found mostly between Vera Cruz, Tabasco, highland Guatemala, and Oaxaca—this is definite Olmec land. A stele found at Tres Zapotes and numbered by the bar and dot system, bears what is by far the earliest recorded 'American' date: 31 B.C.

The art of the Olmecs is unique—simple, direct, forceful. There is nothing quite like it in all Mexico. Yet aside from this 'art' they must have possessed certain social dynamics to stamp their pattern on Mexico's cultural history.

The Mayas, who also appeared early, had a great influence over the development of culture in Mexico and were the longest-lived. For what length of time they built their temple-cities before their first calendar was set up is not known. The earliest stele, at Uaxactún, is dated A.D. 320.

Enormous stone heads, seven feet high, *flat-nosed and sensually thick-lipped, are striking remains left to us by the Olmec culture. These mysterious people are first known as early as 800* B.C. *in the tropical hotlands, Vera Cruz and Tabasco. The name Olmec derives from 'olli' (rubber).*

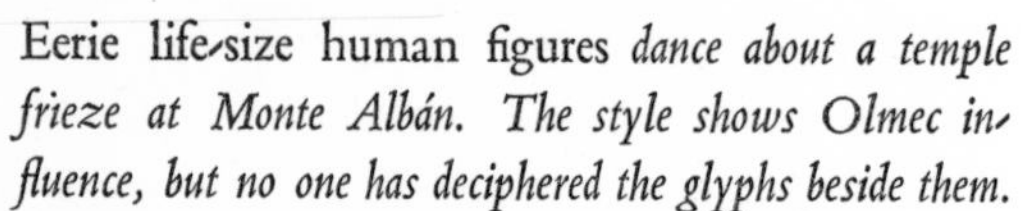

Eerie life-size human figures *dance about a temple frieze at Monte Albán. The style shows Olmec influence, but no one has deciphered the glyphs beside them.*

Tarascan culture *is known for its* genre *pottery—realistic ceramics which show many features of daily life. But here a traveller uses fish for shoes.*

From the earliest times there was much cultural interchange among all these peoples. A large trading area at Xicalango in Campeche was the Maya contact centre for the outside world where, under terms of peace, things of their lands were exchanged with Central Mexico. Possessed of large and traditional tribal lands, the Mayas were free of any large-scale outside invasion until the twelfth century. They perfected their calendar, glyph writing, and stone carving, and evolved the complex temple-cities which can still be seen today. Their influence on the other cultures in the high Mexican plateaus was very marked.

Monte Albán (500 B.C.–A.D. 1469), a Zapotec ceremonial centre and temple-city, lies in Oaxaca atop high treeless hills overlooking the valley and the present-day Spanish city of the same name. One of the oldest in Mexico, its occupation continued from the earliest preclassic period, perhaps as early as 1000 B.C., until the coming of the Spaniard in 1522. This immense time period of twenty-five hundred years is divided into five archaeological horizons. Its beginnings are shrouded in mystery. Dr. Alfonso Caso, who first uncovered it and has worked on its problems continuously for twenty years, believes that its formal structures date as far back

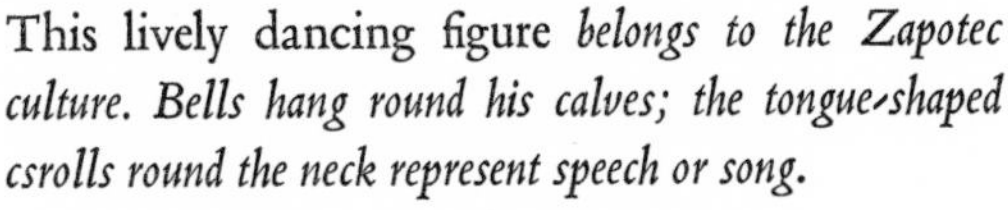

This lively dancing figure *belongs to the Zapotec culture. Bells hang round his calves; the tongue-shaped csrolls round the neck represent speech or song.*

From Tabasco *comes this terracotta figure of* Quetzal*coatl, the plumed serpent god. It was from these shore that he was said to have made his fabled sea-voyage.*

as 500 B.C. Even as early as this they had already developed glyph writing, a calendar, and a complete cosmogony.

Who were the early builders of Monte Albán? From the beginning it seems it was a city of the gods, although not habitable, visited by men and women alike. Before the city (its original name is unknown) took on its Zapotec character, it had from the earliest times a temple with a frieze of dancing figures done in the Olmec style, a 'powerful and mysterious archaism of expressive monsters.' These Olmec-styled figures and stelae, with the still indecipherable glyphs, are the primary mystery of Monte Albán.

One will grasp how really early all this was if one remembers that in the same period of world history Nebuchadnezzar was destroying Jerusalem and carrying off the Jews to their first slavery; by the time the people of Mexico were beginning to set up their temple-city states, Xerxes had conquered Egypt and was setting off to invade Greece. Although the American man had none of the stimulation of the Fertile Crescent of the Near East —which brought the wheel, iron, and the alphabet to the world—he was advanced in city planning, writing, and sculpture.

At about A.D. 300 Monte Albán moved into a transition period, threw off its Maya influence, and turned to its own sources—the Zapotec. For the four hundred years that followed, the great plaza was enlarged, and temples, pyramids, ball courts, and the frescoed tombs were constructed.

The Mixtecs (668–1521), whose capital city was Cholula (the present-day Puebla), occupied a geographical buffer zone between the coast and the highland; they were subject to all the recurring waves of conquest, first from the coast (Olmec), then from the highlands (Toltec). Later they became conquerors; after 1350 they extended south into Monte Albán, only in turn to be overrun by the Aztecs after 1450.

Their mythology was colourful and complex. Quetzalcoatl was a demiurge, priest, and ruler, conceived by virginal birth years after his father's death (his mother was made pregnant when she swallowed a piece of jade); he was ruler of the Toltecs for twenty-two years. He lived in Tula, lost a civil war, fled with a good-sized Toltec force, reached the Coatzacoalcos River on the day of 1-Reed in Aztec reckoning (the sign under which he was born), and set sail into the open sea with the prophecy that he would again return on the recurrence of that date.

The Totonacs, 'discovered' by the collectors of modern art because of their non-representational art styles, also appeared during the preclassic period. The Totonacs had, so far as it is known, an uninterrupted cultura

The 'laughing faces' of the Totonacs *are in striking contrast to the gross and sensual sculpture of their neighbours the Olmecs, and are among the finest and most sophisticated examples of pre-Columbian art. They seem to depict dancers or possibly sacrificial victims. The mysterious smile—the head thrown back in a state of rapture—perhaps expresses religious ecstasy rather than happiness.*

A Totonac head, *sensitively modelled, from the same region as the 'laughing faces'. The rendering is more naturalistic than is usual in early Mexican art.*

continuity in central Vera Cruz from approximately 500 B.C. until the arrival in 1519 of Hernán Cortés. They formed a sort of linguistic 'sandwich' between the Olmecs and the Huastecs, who were of Maya stock and speech. Totonac country has yielded for many decades some of the 'finest and most sophisticated specimens of Indian art'—the freehand clay figurines always in laughter; the 'laughing heads' and life-sized stone heads attached to a tenon, meant to be placed in walls as an architectonic motif; the strange U-shaped objects as large as horse collars and resembling them in size and shape, carved from polished green or black stone, exquisitely decorated and made for an unknown purpose. This art, gay, sybaritic, a contrast to the austere Maya or Aztec form, is a Totonac characteristic. They also left behind an impressive number of temple-cities which, although covered by jungle and eroded by the centuries, still retain their form, so that Mexican archaeologists are able to restore them. All this culture which had been nurtured for a thousand years was at the disposal of the Aztecs.

In the valley of Anáhuac, in the central Mexican plateau, after 200 B.C., the Toltecs learned better management of their agriculture and produced a social surplus. With that, Teotihuacán came into being.

Toltec-Teotihuacán (200 B.C.–A.D. 900), 'Place of the Gods,' thirty-two miles northeast of Mexico City, dwarfs in magnitude all else in Mexico and Middle America (save perhaps Tikal in Guatemala); the remains of the great ceremonial city alone cover an area of eight square miles. It challenges the imagination how the Toltecs at so early a period could have marshalled so many people to build and maintain so enormous a religious centre. So renowned was Teotihuacán that it served as model for all subsequent temple-cities, and the Toltecs remained—even when monuments were covered and were only a vague memory—the master builders, and thereafter all artisans who were masters, especially painters and *tlacuilo* writers, were called 'Toltec' even down into Aztec times.

When Toltec history emerges through the myths that surround it, it follows a pattern. A priest-astrologer guided them through Mexico until they found a fertile valley. There they built their city of Tollan or Tula. The chronology of their kings, which must have been chanted for centuries, was etched into the memory pattern, so that when repeated to a double-languaged scribe and set down in the sixteenth century, it gave the names of their rulers. It told of Toltec dominance under their eighth ruler, a rule which embraced all the land between Jalisco to the north and Cuernavaca to the south; it told of the elaborate ritual of their polytheistic religion and it mentioned in detail the woman known as *Xochitl* (pronounced 'sho-chitl'), who made popular the beverage now called 'pulque' by fermenting the juice of the maguey plant.

Like their rivals of the same period, the Toltecs of Teotihuacán had ideographic writing, tribal records, *amatl*-paper books which pictured their bewildering cosmogony; they also had the fifty-two-year cycle, magical *tonalpohualli* (the numeration of fate), a system of prognostication based on a period of 260-day count, and a lunar calendar for everyday use. And they built the awe-inspiring temple-city Teotihuacán.

Teotihuacán endured from 200 B.C., the approximate time of its shadowy and tenuous beginnings, until about A.D. 900. Its period of slow decline is revealed in its pottery. Here is reflected the gradual change that came over a tribe that lost its political power but kept its respect among others. Another tribe, the Chichimecs, moved into the Toltec domain and took up the remains of 'empire' but found themselves swallowed up in the chaos between the years 1100 and 1300 that followed the break-up of the 'age of cultural unity.' Meanwhile the Toltecs, now migratory, developed two other cultural areas, Tula and Xochicalco.

Tula (A.D. 900–1116) is of the greatest importance. Tula, which was once regarded as pure mythology—prompting an ironical remark by one writer about the 'vague science of anthropology and the exact art of myth'—has been confirmed by archaeology. The very close resemblance of its architecture to the cities of Mayapán, principally Chichén Itzá in Yucatán, confirms the trek of the Toltecs to that region in the twelfth century. Is this

The Sun-Temple of Teotihuacán, *the Place of the Gods, dwarfs all else in Mexico and Middle America. This massive truncated pyramid, almost as large as anything Egyptian, became the standard form of temple where Indians could display the dignity of the gods. Teotihuacán, the ceremonial centre, covers eight square miles.*

Tula, the legendary 'Tollan' as described by the padre-chronicler Sahagún, the beautiful city 'of rich palaces of green jade and white and red shell, where the ears of corn and pumpkins reached the size of a man, where cotton grew in the plant in all colours and the air was always filled with rare birds of precious feathers . . .'? If Tula is Tollan, eight centuries have changed the land. It is now dry, parched and dust-filled.

And yet the description of the city is not as mythical as first believed. Archaeologists found elaborately carved and painted walls, a stepped pyramid with the remains of a temple at its summit, with the symbol of Quetzalcoatl—two stone-painted serpents fifteen feet high—acting as caryatids for the elaborate façades of the temple; carved pillars for the temple of the warriors; immense stone-carved figures; and that sculptural idea which travelled farthest, the reclining figure of Chac-Mool looking blankly into space and holding a stone tray on which palpitating human hearts were placed as food for the gods. This same frightening figure, without any change, was to be carved and set up in the capital of the Aztecs, and was to find its way eight hundred miles south into Yucatán.

All the cultures listed here—and there are many more— were established on Mexican soil as long as twenty-five hundred years before the Aztecs made their appearance as an organized tribe. By the time they put in their appearance close on to A.D. 1200, the tides of these earlier cultures had swept back and forth across the face of the land, devastating one another, at the same time developing all the varied aspects of much of that which we call civilization.

And to all this the Aztecs were the heirs.

The hauntingly horrible figure of Chac-Mool. *It looks blankly into space, turning its stone head away from the lap on which palpitating human hearts were placed, as food for the gods.*

2 The Farmer and his Family

THE BASE of the Aztec society was the plebe who was called a *macehualli*; he was definitely not an automaton, but he was in current labour vocabulary part of the rank and file. He was a member of a clan and part of an earth cell, a sort of mutual-aid society; he was, in summary, an able-bodied, taxpaying Indian. First and foremost he was a farmer, in European terms a peasant, but he was also a warrior, part of the agrarian militia.

Like most men in Mexico, he was short—between 5 feet 1 and 5 feet 5—broad-headed and thickset. He was tireless, used to walking since childhood and could carry a load of seventy-five pounds, fifteen hours a day. His arms were long and feet broad in proportion to his height; his gait straight and inclined to be pigeon-toed. The head was characterized by the jet-black eyes, hair dark and coarse, abundant except on his body and face. He was relatively beardless, and face hair was deemed objectionable, so that mothers used tweezers to pluck it out and applied hot cloths to stifle the hair follicles. They were 'beardless,' even though Cortés said that the Tlascalans had 'barbers to shave you.' Their colour varied from dark to light brown and their faces could assume a fierce mien and often great dignity.

Aztec women were naturally smaller. Yet they bore children easily, followed their men on long marches and carried their share of the load, including the inevitable baby. Many of them were of striking appearance; the Spaniards thought so, married them and found them attractive. Doña Marina, 'The Tongue', an Indian girl who helped talk the Spaniards into victory over Moctezuma, was declared to be an 'excellent woman . . . full of grace.'

Dress was simple and expedient; the same raiment was worn night and day. All wore the loincloth, a cincture that was passed between the legs and brought about the waist, its two ends hanging in front and back and usually embellished. In this they worked on marches when they carried cargo. The mantle (*tilmantli*)—in today's usage, the *manta*—was a rectangular piece of woven cloth tied over one shoulder, made at first from the coarse fibres of the maguey and later, when contact with the hotlands was general, from cotton. They used neither buttons nor pins. When the *tilmantli* was sufficiently flowing, it covered the whole body when seated. Many of these often were beautifully woven; of this however we have little or no evidence except their own pictures and the descriptions by their conquerors. The common Indian mostly walked with naked feet until he grew in social importance; then he travelled in sandals made from animal skin or maguey fibres. For the chieftain or demigod, they were of gold.

Hair styles had some variation: in everyday use the hair hung in bangs and was cut at the back by barbers with an obsidian knife — *Pagenkopf* the Germans would call it—or it was allowed to grow long and braided into a thick pigtail. In wartime it was decorated with turkey or eagle feathers.

Woman's dress in this plebeian class, while of only one cut, varied greatly in design, colour, and pattern, for women were the principal weavers. The woman wore an underskirt of ankle length and often magnificently embroidered; when abroad she would put over this a poncho-like dress, a rectangular piece of cloth with a slit through which the head passed, the sides sewn except for armholes—a prosaic description of some of the finest weaving in pattern and colour found in the continent, which Bernal Diaz, then an impressionable young man of twenty-three, found 'rich and beautifully ornamented.' Her sandals, lighter than those used by men, she wore only on journeys or if her social position demanded it. Her hair, long and lustrous and black, grew to full length; it was braided with ribbons for festival days, allowed to hang when about the house; it was gathered and wrapped about the crown of the head when she worked in the fields.

The Aztec dressed for the climate; *the peasant wore a breechclout, and a sort of poncho, and mostly walked with bare feet. If he grew in social importance, his clothes were more richly decorated and he travelled in sandals. These drawings are from the Codex Florentino, a series made by Aztec artists working for Friar Bernardino da Sahagún.*

Women dressed with dignity, *as this small Aztec carved stone shows. They wore an underskirt varying greatly in colour and pattern, and over this a magnificently embroidered rectangular piece of cloth called 'huipil'. Their hair was left long and lustrous, and was braided and intertwined with ribbons.*

Nahuatl was the language of the Aztecs. It was neither invented nor brought to perfection by them, since it was spoken by many other tribes including the Toltecs and the Chichimecs. But the Aztecs did extend it by their conquests until it was used as far south as Nicaragua. Later, after the Aztecs had themselves been conquered, it became the *lingua franca* of Mexico, and later still, when reduced to Spanish orthography, a further extension of it was made by the Church, which used it and translated the Christian catechism and other religious manuals into it.

Nahuatl is a living language. Thousands still speak it, there are books and musical records in it, some of Mexico's foremost scholars converse in it; it is very graphic and plastic. The language was as compounded as the Aztec ideographic writing and capable of expressing great feeling and poetry, and although the early Spaniards found the suffix *-tl* very bewildering, sixteenth-century savants who mastered the tongue found it clear and harmonious, with an extended vocabulary.

The speech of the Aztec *macehualli* had the same earthiness as the soil man's everywhere; practical and with careless speech habits, he fashioned his talk out of that usage stemming from need which is the living morphology of any language. Ordinary men were careless about the meaning of an affix, of the flections of person, number, case, gender; but in the *calmecac* schools of Mexico-Tenochitlán, where good Nahuatl speech was taught, corrected, extended so that high-placed persons could speak properly to the gods or impress visiting chieftains, this traffic of speech was carefully studied. It must have been. Those informants who worked with the first Spaniards in setting it down *knew* the grammar of their speech.

The early native American societies were democratic, there was rank without class. The community, not the individual, owned the land, and most decisions were made by voice vote. An Indian was born into a clan or *calpulli*. A *calpulli* was a group of families forming a clan which owned certain lands communally. A married man was lent his piece of land directly from the clan. No one had title to the land he worked, he was allowed only the produce of it; if he died without issue or the land was neglected or he was 'drummed out' of his clan, the piece reverted back to the holding corporation. So exact were some of these, that records were kept on *amatl* paper of the various land tracts along with a rebus drawing of the holder's name. According to their records there were seven original *calpulli*; once they settled on Tenochtitlán these were enlarged to twenty.

Each of the clans owned, or held by treaty, land on the mainland. At first agricultural land was very limited; when a *calpulli* had none, its members industriously made *chinampas*, the so-called 'floating gardens.' These were the reed-woven baskets, eight feet in diameter, filled with earth and anchored in the shallow waters. Roots penetrating the basket bottom eventually firmly fixed them to the lake bottom. By this laborious method, a *calpulli* could enlarge its production and extend its clan holdings. Yet as their war conquests proceeded and more alien tribes were forced to yield terrain on the mainland, land grew plentiful and was divided proportionately among all the clans that formed the Aztec tribe. This system of land tenure was, as V. Gordon Childe calls it, 'the fatal limitation of . . . Neolithic economy . . . the sole outlet for an expanding population was to annex more land for cultivation and suitable land was not unlimited.'

The Aztec clan system was not as rigid as the Peruvian system of the *ayllu*, which was over-organized. Yet it was so arranged that the whole group-family, the *calpulli*, moved as a social unit. 'Mexican society,' observed Dr. Vaillant, 'existed for the benefit of the tribe and each member was supposed to do his part in preserving the community.'

An Indian born into a clan could not lose his clan rights nor his right to a piece of clan-held land of a size sufficient to feed the numbers in his family; no one except the duly elected clan chieftains could force an Indian to forfeit these rights by expulsion for crime or other antisocial acts.

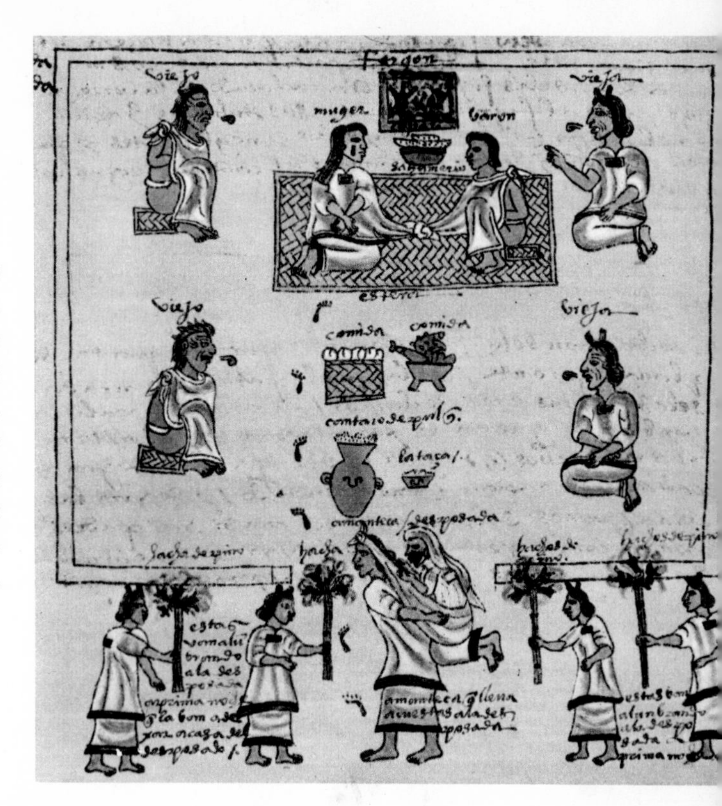

Marriage was consummated *when the girl was sixteen, the man twenty. Old women were the marriage brokers and on the bridal night they carried the bride to the groom's house on their backs. The couple then sat on a mat, their cloaks tied in symbol of union, while they listened to long-winded homilies from members of the family. (From the Codex Mendoza).*

'Tied together' was not merely a figure of speech in Aztec society. Marriage was symbolized by the actual tying together of the edges of the *tilmantli* cloaks of bride and groom.

A man married at twenty, a girl at about sixteen. In this society there was not a prohibition against bachelors as there was among the Incas. But economic factors and especially the preparation of food made it impossible for a man to live without a woman—corn-cakes, the irreplaceable staff of life, made twice daily, took two hours for each preparation and this was a woman's task.

Old women were the marriage brokers. On the night of marriage the bride was carried to the groom's house on the back of one of them. All the principal members of the family involved as well as the headmen of the clan sat on mats facing one another and listened or dozed over the long-winded homilies—'here we are present . . .'—and between the periods of discourse a servant would be at hand to pour out generous portions of intoxicating *octli.*

Once the torrents of speech ended, the man and girl seated on their grass mat had the knot tied, and they were united. There was no fixed rule whether the man went to live with the woman's clan or she moved to his.

The Aztec woman had rights, although they were not as far-reaching as the male's. She could own property, go to the council for justice, and if she was cruelly treated could obtain a divorce. If divorced, she could marry again; if widowed, she could only marry within the clan of the deceased husband. Sterility was her greatest dread, the one thing a woman feared, for if she bore no children her man could peremptorily divorce her.

Once married, the couple built their own house. Like all else it was a communal affair. This was as true within Mexico-Tenochtitlán as it was without. The type of house the *macehualli* built depended on where he was and what he was. Finished, it reflected the peasant-tribesman. Even the greatest Aztecs temples and palaces had their origin in the simple native house. The Mayas knew this and immortalized such a peasant house as an element in the decoration of the south wing of the Nunnery Quadrangle at Uxmal. Dr. Vaillant confirms that 'the great cities of the Aztec had their origin in the simple villages of sedentary tribesmen. . . . These were huts with thatched roofs resting on walls of wattles smeared with mud . . .' On

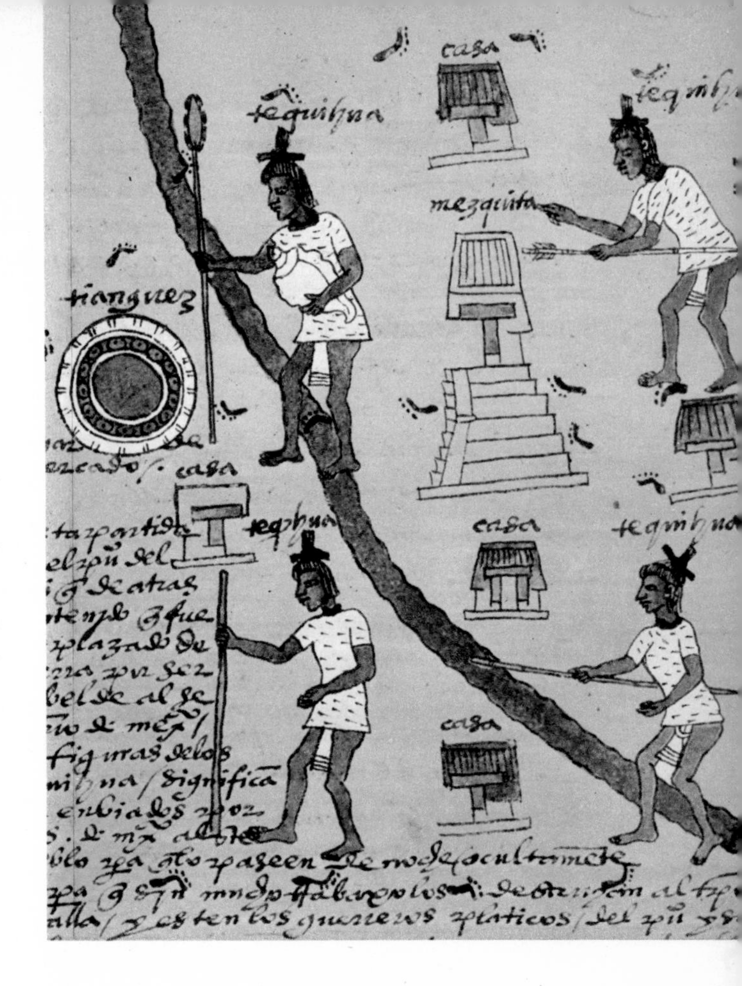

Houses of the common man *were built of wattle and daub and thatched with grass. None have survived, but these pictures in the Codex Mendoza give the essentials. The large building in the centre is a temple, and the diagonal line a stream.*

The steam bath, *taken before dawn, was part of the ritual of Aztec daily life. It was built of rock and mud-cement and attached to the side of the house; the steam was produced by direct fire or by throwing water over hot stones.*

the mainland, in the temperate zone of Anáhuac Valley, such houses persist to this day.

Within the city in a clan division, this house might be of adobe, sealed with adobe cement and painted. We know little about it—all has been destroyed. There is nothing left here as there was at Machu Picchu or Ollantaytambo in Peru, where one can follow the evolution of the *cancha* type of native house into the complexity of the Inca palace. In Mexico and in the Maya country there remain only the temples, pyramids, ceremonial ball courts; the link of evolution between peasant house and florid temple has dissolved.

The interior was partitioned between kitchen and sleeping-living portions. This can be clearly seen in the fragment of Aztec codex that gives the genealogy of the *tlatoani*, hereditary chiefs of Azcapotzalco, with its illustration of a typical Aztec house compound. At one end the fire and kitchen —not a fireplace as we understand it, but rocks of uniform height sunk into the beaten mud floor which merely contained the wood. There was no chimney, no window, no fireplace; the smoke found its own egress through the interstices of the grass thatch. The fire was banked at night and blown into life in the morning by the huff and puff of the women.

Before day's break the Aztecs throbbed to life with the beat of the wooden-tongued drums from the great temples, as each of the smaller *teocalli* throughout the city took its cue from the largest. As Venus, the morning star, appeared to them at about 4 A.M., day was born and the shell trumpets blown by the priests added to the din as all other temples responded in counterpoint. Fires that had been banked were blown to life and all over the city of Mexico-Tenochtitlán the pale smoke arose to a windless sky.

The Indian, as farmers do everywhere, rose at this hour before the sun. He went to the steam bath, tossed water on the heated rocks, passed through the vapour, dipped into the canal—rich man, poor man, little man, chief, all responded in like manner to the rhytm of Aztec life. Even Moctezuma rose at the same time.

People newly married or too poor to have a slave, or too lately wed to have children to help them, had to prepare the corn mass for the tortillas twice daily themselves. There were no short cuts. Dry corn was steeped in lime, then boiled and the corn skin pried loose; then it was brayed on the stone *metatl* with a grooved stone roller. This technique of corn preparation is so old that these artifacts appear among the first (as well as the last) archaeological objects to be found in the yielding earth. The unleavened cornbread, pancake-shaped, was baked on a flat ceramic dish. This was the unvarying base food of their lives. In addition there were beans, chili pepper, fish, sometimes meat; maize could be made into tamales or *atolli*, a gruel made of maize flavoured with honey and chili pepper. The culinary day began and ended with the same food. There were no cattle, goats, pigs, horses until white men brought them, thus no milk or cheese. There was nothing in all Mexico such as the maté used in Paraguay. Chocolate (cacao bean) was imported from the hotlands and only the well-provided had it. There was no grease for frying—everthing was baked or boiled. Food was washed down with the mild intoxicant *octli*.

Maize was the base of life. All the tribes from Nicaragua to Arizona predicated their lives on it; all the temple-cities reared their economy on it. One's day began and ended with maize, and no matter how exotic were the foods of the Aztec leaders—which so surprised their conquerors—the base remained the simple corncake. No other plant has played so large a role in the development of cultures.

At night before dusk the workers were home again and once more there was the business of making maize-cakes. There were available in the market turkey, duck, deer, beans, squash, *camotli*, and such like; the eve-

The goddess of childbirth, *Tlazolteotl, carved in jade, is seen actually giving birth. Like generation itself, mother-love was a commandment and a second condition for the perpetuity of life. The Aztecs needed children.*

ning meal, the largest, took place between four and five o'clock. The man or men squatted on the reed mats, helping themselves with their fingers from the pots of food brought to them. Women ate apart.

At night the room was lighted by pine splinters. By this light the women spun or worked their loom or prepared the pulque intoxicant; the men made paddles for canoes, grass mats, split their knives, arrowheads, and fish needles from obsidian, or chipped out stone querns; these they would trade in the market. When children began to make their yearly appearance, they were first placed in a cradle, and then as soon as they could move they became a part of this fabric of life.

As soon as the woman was pregnant, she was put under the protection of the god Tezcatlipoca. There is a pictured history in the *Codex Mendoza* of the birth, naming, rearing, discipline of a child, of the details of swaddling and the type of cradle. When the child was born, a magician was brought in by the parents from their own local clan temple. He consulted a horoscope, a sort of book of fate, which was unrolled to its twenty-foot length. This was to determine if the child had been born under good or bad auguries. The naming was important, and if they found that the day was unlucky, the naming was put off till a better moment—the avoidance of misfortune itself is the enjoyment of positive good. 'What's in a name?' To the Indians, everything. Many primitives have two names, social and personal. The personal was known and used only by the immediate family in the belief that if used too often, it might lose its power. In times of illness, the witch doctor used the real name to call the dying back to life. Boys were called after their fathers or grandfathers, usually dynamic names, as 'Smoking Crest' (*Chimalpopoca*), 'Obsidian Serpent' (*Itzcoatl*), 'Speaking Eagle' (*Quauhtlatoa*); girls, who seem always to evoke a sense of poetry, were named after flowers, stars, birds, as 'Ibis' (*Atototl*), 'Green Flower' (*Matlal-xochitl*), or 'Rain Flower' (*Quiauh-xochitl*).

Schooling of a sort was given at the clan's house for boys. Each clan maintained a number of these under the administration of a master. In charge was either a well-known warrior or an elder; here boys learned their own mytho-histories, rituals, and, above all, the use of war weapons.

On the whole, training of the child remained in the parents' hands. Learning was by mimicry. One can follow the manner of this training in the recorded picture history. At three years of age, the child is allowed one-half tortilla per day—the tortilla being a foot in diameter; at thirteen he is eating two such outsized tortillas per day. The boy mimics the father; at first he carries a small bag suspended from his neck, for he must be his own draft animal; this is increased monthly until, like his father, he can carry sixty pounds. He fishes, plants, makes dugout canoes; he gathers rushes, weaves *petlatli*, makes sandals, carries, walks, runs. All of this is recorded in detail with word and picture.

Punishment was not always proportionate to the wrongdoing. For some infractions the father held the child's head over smoke; for others he was hand-pricked with a maguey thorn until the blood flowed. Since in these pictures the father is seen talking the while, admonishing while he is punishing (one sees by the speech scroll in front of his face that he is talking), the boy is being trained.

Children's training, *from eleven to fourteen, boys on the left, girls on the right. The age is given by the rows of dots at the top of each section, together with the number of maize-cakes ('tortillas') eaten daily. Age 11: Boy and girl being punished by being held over smoke and forced to inhale it. Age 12: Boy being punished by lying naked and bound on the damp ground, girl sweeping the floor under her mother's eye (the sign above this scene represents night). Age 13: Boy carries rushes and punts a canoe, girl makes maize-cakes. Age 14: Boy learns fishing, girl is taught to weave on the back-strap loom.*

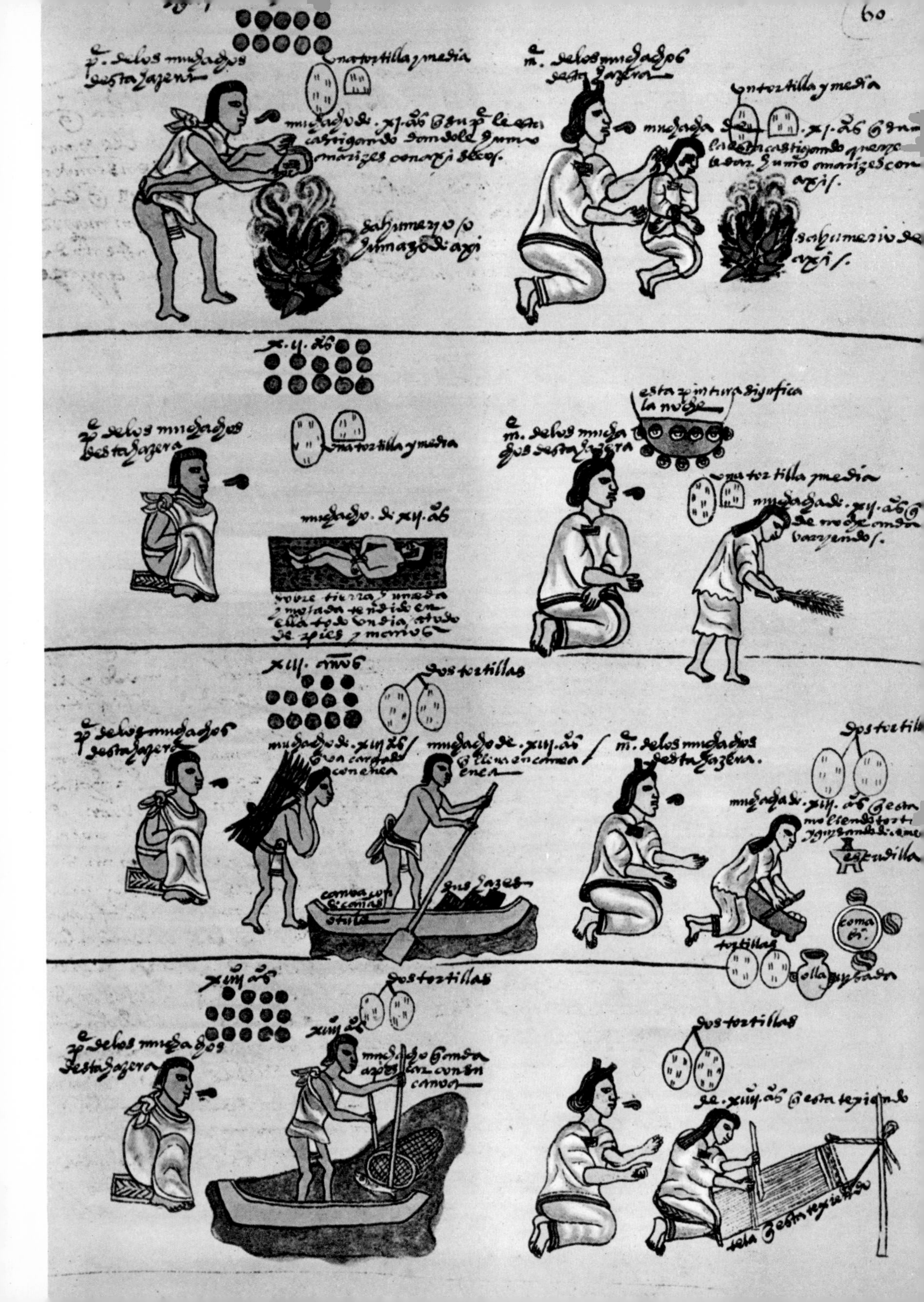
delos muchachos desta hazera
una tortilla y media
sahumerio de aji
delos muchachos desta hazera
una tortilla y media
sahumerio de aji
una tortilla y media
muchacho de xi. años
esta pintura significa la noche
delos muchachos desta hazera
una tortilla y media
xiii. años
dos tortillas
delos muchachos desta hazera
canoa con
delos muchachos desta hazera
dos tortillas
escudilla
tortillas
olla
xiiii años
dos tortillas
delos muchachos desta hazera
dos tortillas
tela

3 Work, Play, and Perpetual War

AZTEC LIFE revolved around the *milpa*—the maize field—and for good reason. No other civilization that has left its footsteps on the road of time has been predicated on the use of a single plant such as Indian corn (*centli*). Earlier than 3000 B.C., the cultures of the Middle East—Assyrian, Sumerian, Egyptian—were cultivating such leguminous plants as pulses, peas, lentils, vetches, whose high protein content made storage easy in semi-desert lands. As for cereals such as wheat, 'that most important extra-tropical grain,' it had been cultivated in India since Mesolithic times. 'Wheat . . . barley, rye, millet, panic-grass' were all part of the diet and economy of all who flourished in the Fertile Crescent. None of these civilizations depended solely on one plant as did those of Mexico and Yucatán.

The Egyptians, to give one pertinent example, according to the Harris Papyrus (Dynasty XX, *c.* 1200 B.C.) knew over thirty types of bread—the Aztecs had one. The Egyptian's diet was varied: peas, lentils, watermelons, artichokes, lettuce, endive, radishes, onions, garlic, leeks. They had beef, honey, dates, as well as milk and cheese and even butter, which was unknown to the Aztecs until A.D. 1525.

Maize made settled life possible in Mexico. Since these people had but one such grain, it is understandable why it played so great a part in ritual

The maize-field, the milpa, *was the centre of the Aztecs' life. The Codex Florentino gives a picture history of its cultivation: a) The seed is planted, after holes have been made by a digging-stick. b) The corn comes up and the ground is hoed. c) The corn ripens, and the cobs are harvested.*

and in practice. The origin of this grain is enveloped in botanical controversy. Although some geneticists believe that the greatest diversity of varieties comes out of Mexico, this is disputed. Paraguay is suggested as the point of dissemination by some, challenged by others. For the moment, 'present evidence points to a dissemination in all directions of the early forms from an unknown centre.'

Milpa culture has remained unchanged for three thousand years. What is true of Aztec farming technique is true of all others in this milieu. Milpas were located two to fifteen miles from the dwellings. If the land was forested, trees were ringed a year before and felled with axe-shaped stone celts. The bush and trees being burned, the ash was turned into the soil; larger trees were allowed to rot with time and provide humus. The earth was turned over and prepared by means of a digging stick. March was the planting time. Corn kernels were placed in holes four to five inches deep; in temperate zones beans and squash were put in at the same time; corn, growing faster, acted as host plant for the vines. April brought rain, and if the desired rain was withheld by the gods, sacrifice was made to Tlaloc, the rain god. Of the eighteen months of the Aztec year, almost every one had its ceremonies and dances connected with the growing and harvesting of maize. The corn ripened in July and there was a feast for the Goddess of Young Corn. In August the rain which had been petitioned in April had to be held back; the Aztec somehow had to cajole the gods not to send rain which would spoil the harvest. So, another sacrifice, this time to a mature woman representing the Goddess of Ripe Corn.

What did all this yield the Indian in food? An Aztec family had a yield of two hundred bushels of corn yearly, or 11,200 pounds. To fell, plant,

Amaranth was a crop important ceremonially. *a) The shoots are picked, and b) tied into bundles and the seed shaken out. c) Seed and dried shoots are stored in jars. In ancient Greece amaranth was supposed to have special healing properties and was a symbol of immortality.*

weed, and harvest this land with the aid of his wife and, say, four half-grown children, the Aztec farmer would have to expend about two hundred days. In the same field he would also plant beans, squash, pumpkins, adding to the yield of the field and also to be included in the produce of these two hundred days. With a surplus of 165 unused days unless he was called to battle, the Aztec could use these in his particular craft, making grass mats, fibre sandals, canoes, weapons, etc. These he bartered for needed things at the markets.

Maize was 'basic.' What else? Beans were grown in the same milpa, using the maize-stalks for support, and squash and pumpkins, all of the genus *Cucurbita*, as well as the crooked-necked variety were planted in between. The Aztecs never had the other 'basic,' the potato, which nourished half of prehistoric South America; as a cultivated plant it was unknown throughout Mexico *until it was brought to them by the Spanish*. They did, however, have the sweet potato; it grew in the warmer valleys below 6,000 feet. An *ipomea*, a tuber-bearing Morning Glory, it is one of a great family of over one hundred species found throughout the world.

The preparation and working of the milpa was collective. Members of the clan assisted one another, and when a farmer-warrior was away to the wars, his fields were cultivated by others of his clan. While the number of plants under cultivation seems impressive, agriculture was not as advanced as among the Incas. They did not prepare elaborate terracing as was done in the Andes; they were not soil-makers, except in the expedient of the *chinampas*. They had no fertilizer other than their own faeces, where the Incas had bird guano and llama offal. Irrigation was casually developed because of the nature of the land; the run-off of the rain could not be harnessed as was done in Peru. Irrigation techniques, which are inseparable from a developed agriculture, were of a poor order. The Aztecs' dependence on rain is the 'reason why' for the ceaseless preoccupation with the appeasement of the gods and with conquests, the wars for more tribute and for more sacrificial victims in order to cajole the rain god into proffering the withheld gifts of rain. As the good will of the rain god could only be sustained by a diet of human hearts, and as these could only be provided by taking prisoners in battle, a long peace was a disaster. Only in perpetual war was there safety.

It was a nightmare.

Even in such a moneyless society as the Aztec, everything, unfortunately, had to be paid for; taxes were paid in service and seem to have been assessed through the clan. 'The tribal council divided the land among the clans and the leaders of each in turn apportioned its share among the heads of families justly and equitably.' Sections were also reserved for the maintenance of the chief of the temple staff, for war supplies, and for the payment of tribute.

A page from Moctezuma's Tribute Roll. *The Aztecs conquered other tribes and forced them to yield tribute. In Moctezumas's time there were three hundred and seventy-one such tribute-regions. This Roll, copied in 1535, was one of many. On the left margin are the glyphs of the tributary village, with the names written above by a Spanish commentator. On the right are the things to be contributed: delivered twice a year, six consignments of mantles for lords, tunics and skirts for women (the feather means 400 in each—one is shown twice, i. e. 800); delivered once a year, one live eagle, two war dresses and two shields; four bins full of corn and seeds.*

Other portions of this land controlled directly by the clan were worked communally and the yield—whether corn, beans, or agave fibres—was paid as tribute-tax to the central tribal council for the maintenance of religion, war, the 'king' and his various non-taxpaying staff, (priests, army, craftsmen, concubines, keepers of the royal aviary), and for the engineering works in and beyond Mexico-Tenochtitlán and all the other paraphernalia of state, with which we today are so fully familiar.

In addition to the foodstuffs which were sent to the central granaries and noted down in the account books by the Tribute Recorder of the Chief Speaker, the clan group was also called upon for levies of manpower to build public buildings. Under direction from architect-builders, who were tax-exempt, dikes, aqueducts, roads were built. The 'king' of the Aztecs also had lands which were cultivated by clans in rotation, and the yield of this also went into the official deposits.

It is obvious that the directing class themselves did not personally consume all that poured into Mexico-Tenochtitlán. The surplus was used

Weaving was the woman's task. *Like all occupations, it had its own goddess (Xochiquetzal) and its own vocabulary. Cotton fibres (they had no wool) were hand-spun on a spindle with a pottery whorl (on the right). Their cloth looms were pulled tight by a strap around the back.*

'Eight damsels, *all eight of them clothed in the rich garments of the country, beautifully ornamented' were presented to Cortés.*

to compensate the specialists. It was also stored for general use during crop failures. Since accounts had to be kept, some archaeologists believe this was one of the factors which brought about the invention of writing.

Weaving was one of the functions that belonged wholly to woman. She gathered the fibre, prepared it, spun, dyed, and then loomed it; no male interfered. Theirs was also an ephemeral art. None of the millions of pieces loomed has survived and all we know of Aztec design is that which has come down to us in the Book of Tributes or else what was painted on pottery and on murals.

The Aztec backstrap loom was simple. The type is known, with little variation, throughout all the Americas. Two wooden rods are fastened, one to each end of the warp, to stretch the cloth to desired length; the lower one is attached to the back of the weaver (hence the name 'backstrap'), while the upper is tied to a post or tree. Three feet wide, the warp was loomed by means of a shuttle woven between the strands of the stretched yarn: that simple. And yet from these looms came, if one can trust the enthusiasm of the conquistadors, some of the finest weavings they had ever seen. 'Eight damsels, they were,' wrote Bernal Díaz, 'all eight of them clothed in the rich garments of the country, beautifully ornamented . . .'

Cotton fibres were spun on the traditional spindle, a slender wooden stick ten to twelve inches in length, balanced at the lower end by a pottery whorl. Colour was more than colour, it was symbolism, and, to the Aztec, very real. If red was used as blood, it became the actual equivalent of blood; it *was* blood. Black represented war because black obsidian glass was the cutting edge of battle swords; it was also the symbol of religion: the priests dressed exclusively in it. Yellow was food because it was the colour of corn; blue meant sacrifice; and green was royal, because it was the colour of the quetzal plumes used only by chieftains.

Design had no horizons—everything was allowed, everything permitted. Protected by the goddess Xochiquetzal, the weaver expressed anything that she felt. Of nature and realism, there were the things of the earth—sun, fish,

'Petrified weaving'. *These ornamental motifs in stone at Mitla seem clearly derived from textile designs. Mitla, where they are extremely well-preserved, dates from a time before the Aztecs had emerged as the conquering tribe.*

snails, cactus, bird feathers, tiger skins, even falling snow were used as motifs; there were geometric designs, highly stylized animals, transformation of representational art into allover patterns. All this is suggested in the designs taken from the Book of Tributes and redrawn from the actual weavings delivered to Mexico-Tenochtitlán.

For themselves women wove the skirts ankle length, elaborately bordered, and for the top part of the costume the well-known *huipilli.* Their art sense ran riot. The striking effect of the women's dress was not exaggerated by the conquistador. Consider this description by a padre during the festivals of the month when the women, especially the beautifully dressed concubines, danced with the soldiers: '. . . and all were well clothed, beautifully adorned, all had wonderfully wrought skirts and pretty *huipilli.* The skirts were decorated with designs representing hearts, others a fish motif, others with spirals or leaves, some were of a simple weave; they all had frames, hems, and fringes . . . As to the blouses, some had loose dark adornments, others motifs representing smoke or black stripes and some with houses or fishes . . .'

Eight Damsels. *A modern artist reconstructs the appearance of three—the designs are authentic.*

Aztec pottery *ranges from simple utilitarian vessels to fine ceramics. Above right: Toltec ware, a threelegged pot from Teotihuacán with red and white incised decoration. Below right: A beautiful example of 'Aztec I', a bowl from Azcapotzalco, conventional black ornament on a buff ground. Below left: A 'cajete'—a bowl with roughened surface for grating peppers. Above left: 'Aztec IV': late work, with graceful spiral pattern.*

Pottery, like weaving and housebuilding, was part of the Aztec cultural equipment. All made pottery in one form or another even if all did not make *fine* pottery. This self-sufficiency is what prompted Aldous Huxley in his Mexican travels to cite 'the primitive's human wholeness.' Pottery making confirms the point that 'a primitive is forced to be whole—a complete man, trained in all the skills of the community . . . if he is not whole, he perishes.' All of the tribes were pottery makers, those of Cholula being especially famed for their red and black ware. It was mostly a craft industry done at home with the leisure time allowed from agriculture. A number of pottery makers who rose in public esteem as artisans left agriculture entirely and organized the guild of pottery makers. Utilitarian pottery, coarse-grained and designed for heavy duty, was used for cooking. Three-legged pots, the large *cumal* which was a flat disk-shaped griddle for baking tortillas, bowls with roughened surface to act as graters for braying chili peppers—these, with pottery goblets for pulque, were part of every household.

The finer pieces of delicate pottery almost as thin as good china, the beautifully decorated kind the archaeologists find in graves, were for the dead.

There was more to pottery than mere pots and drinking bowls. Spindle whorls, which weighted the spinning distaff like a flywheel, and spinning sticks too, were made of clay. Ceramic dolls were made with jointed arms. Toys were made with wheels, although the idea of putting the wheel to any other use never occurred to them. The little clay gods, gods of fertility and corn, were mass-produced in clay forms; the cult figurine was dropped by the farmer into his cornfield to conjure the good will of the local genii for a better corn crop.

The Aztec market astonished the Spaniards when they first saw it. 'When we arrived at the great market place,' remembered the chronicler, '. . . we were astounded at the number of people and the quantity of merchandise . . . and at the good order and control that was maintained . . .'

A market, as the Aztecs must have known it. *The village square of a west coast tribe, portrayed in pottery, showing, in an expressive free-clay moulding, Indians buying and selling with much animation. In the foreground a woman buys maize for 'tortillas', while in the interior, to the left, a kitchen and details of food preparation are shown.*

'Yes,' agreed Hernán Cortés after visiting the same market, 'there are daily more than sixty thousand people bartering and selling . . . the square is twice as big as Salamanca . . . every kind of merchandise . . . is for sale . . . There is a street of game [partridges, turkeys, quail, pigeons, parrots, owls, kestrels] . . . There is a street of herb sellers . . . roots and . . . medicinal herbs . . . and houses of the apothecaries in which they sell the medicines from these herbs . . . There are barber shops where you may have your hair washed and cut.' And, as if they vied with each other, Bernal Díaz recalled 'other wares,' i.e., 'Indian slaves both men and women [brought in] as the Portuguese bring negroes from Guinea . . . tied to long poles . . .' Next there were 'traders who sold great pieces of . . . cotton, and articles of twisted thread . . .' Much in evidence was the coarse cloth spun from the fibres of the maguey and used by those who carried cargo on their backs, and the sandals made of the same fibre. Cortés wrote of the various animal skins for sale and the pottery 'of very good quality'; and his companion asked that they not forget the 'paper' offered for sale, '. . . which in this country is called *amatl,* and reeds scented with *liquidambar* . . . and tobacco . . . much cochineal . . . I am forgetting those who sell salt and those who make the stone knives . . .' There were 'dealers in gold, silver [this would have been impossible in Peru where the Lord-Inca 'owned' all metals], and precious stones, feathers, mantles . . .' And along with all this commercial activity, there was order. 'A very fine building,' Cortés assured his liege, Charles V, 'stands in the great square and serves as a kind of audience where ten or twelve persons are always seated, as judges, who deliberate on all cases arising in the market and pass instant sentences on wrongdoers.'

The Aztec market, which included tribute in its wares, differed little in the beginning from the usual 'American' system of war tribute. Yet the Aztecs systematized it, and every six months 371 vassal cities yielded tribute of products so varied and vast that elaborate account books were needed to keep track of it. The market was further fed by the activities of its wandering merchants. Bernal Díaz himself said: 'But why do I waste so many words in recounting what they sell in that great market?—for I shall never finish if I tell it all in detail.'

The festival followed the market. So many were there that the early Spaniards at first thought that fun and frolic were almost continuous. It is not easy—in this pathos of distance—to separate what was purely festive from what was, in fact ceremonial; what was sacred from what was secular. It is, however, not difficult to find a parallel in times not far distant when hangings and garrotings were always an occasion for holidays, and to realize how, in affairs of this kind, festival entertainment and sacred ritual were interlocked.

Ceremonial cannibalism—
as shown after the Conquest by a native Mexican artist who drew vastly upon his imagination. The extent to which the eating of human flesh was practised is debatable, but it is known that priests sometimes symbolically consumed a piece of human flesh of a sacrificial victim, or went through the gesture of eating it.

Like all other advanced tribes, the Aztecs had a calendar, divided into eighteen 20-day months; every one of these eighteen months had ceremonies and festivals. Months had descriptive names. The first month was Atlcoulaco ('want of water') and there were ceremonies, parades, and sacrifice. The second month was Tlacaxipeualiztli ('boning of the men'), when for sixteen days there were ceremonies and parades with priests dancing in the flayed skins of sacrificial victims.

The third month, Tozoztontli, began with 'fasting,' and if this did not touch the heart of the rain god, Tlaloc, another festival, the flayed-skin dance to Xipé, was performed by the priests. The fourth month brought the people into the city from the fields to celebrate the worship of the new corn; altars in their houses were festooned with cornstalks. This was a bloodless time and young girls gave virginal blessings to the seed corn. By the fifth month (May 3–22) rain was full upon them; there were god-impersonation ceremonies, and they sacrificed children to the rain god to thank him (they had sacrificed children in the third month to bring on the rain). Bernal Díaz wrote: 'I have heard it said that they were wont to cook for Moctezuma the flesh of young boys.' If that occurred at all, it was a ceremonial cannibalism.

The seventh month (June 12–July 1) was marked with the mimic dances of the salt workers, who leeched salt from the lakes of Anáhuac. The eighth month (July 2–21) was a joyous one—the adoration of the eating of the corn, an eight-day feast which could not get under way until the priests had dispatched a slave girl, beautifully attired to impersonate the Goddess of Young Corn. The ninth month, Tlaxochimaco ('birth of flowers'), brought feasts which lasted some days and was unusual in that the two sexes danced together, 'even touching the women.' as an old Aztec explained. It was the rising class of merchant prince (*pochteca*) that gave these feasts, appropriately, for at the end it was to their god, Yacatecuhtli, protector of merchants that they were dedicated.

As an
innocent
child
*the god Xipe
stands
sculptured in
stone—tidy
hair, neat bows
at the back.
It is a thing of
horror, for the
'neat bows' tie
the skin flayed
from a living
victim, the face
stretched until
the mouth
gapes. At the
side, a hand
dangles.
In the Aztec
second month,
the priests
danced and
paraded in the
fresh skins
of the sacrificed.*

Human hearts were the food of the gods, *and without them the world could not continue. When the great temple of Huitzilopochtli was dedicated in 1486, the Aztecs amassed more than 20,000 sacrificial victims who lined up, waiting their turn of the knife.*

Above: Four men hold the victim over a stone, the priest cuts deeply with a flint knife, pulls out the palpitating heart and offers it to the Sun-God. Still warm and quivering, it is deposited in the lap of the recumbent Chac-Mool. The body of the victim is cast down the temple stairway.

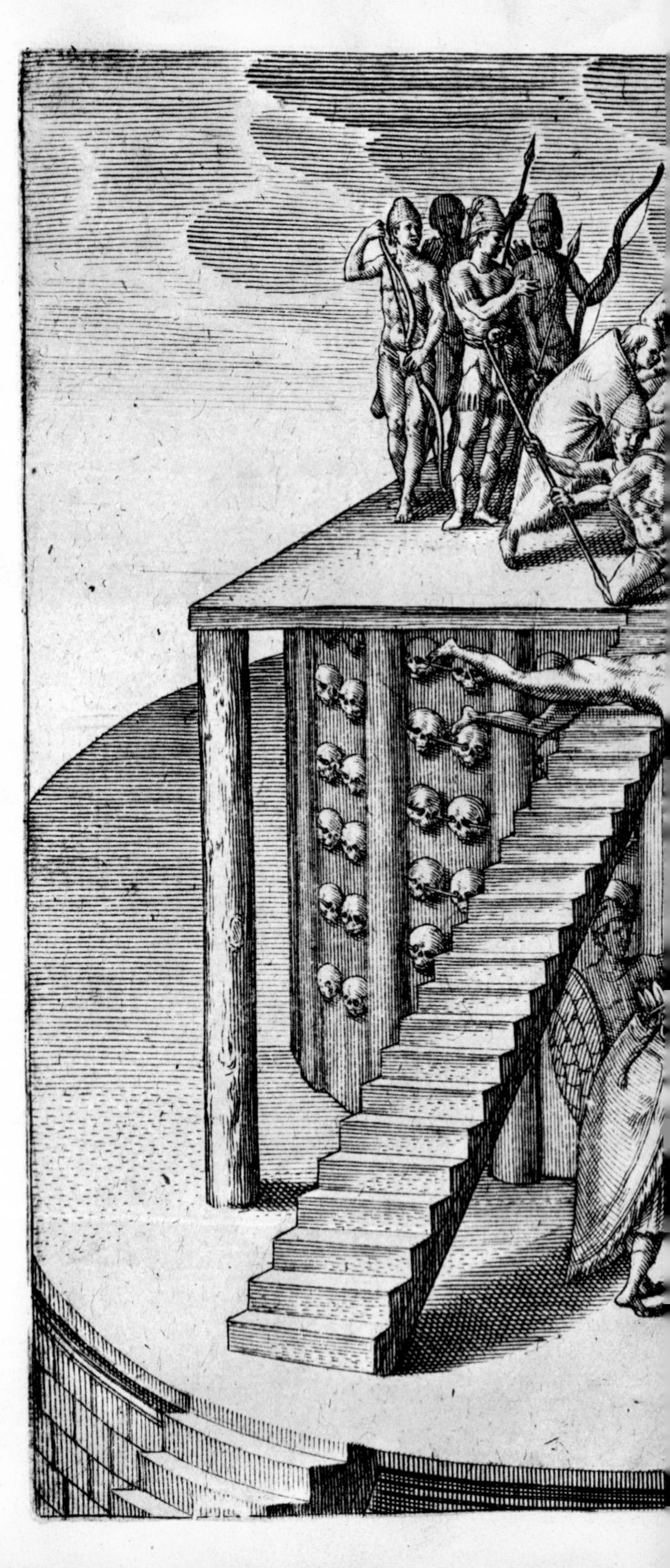

Right: Conquistadors were also sacrificed. They were regarded as supermen and their death on the altar was held to be especially beneficial (an imaginative engraving by de Bry).

The tenth month (August 11–30) was ostensibly to celebrate the 'fall of the fruits.' The people poured in in a festive mood, much as they once did in Europe to see someone drawn and quartered or, even better, beheaded. Prisoners of war danced together with their captors and then, according to Dr. Vaillant, ascended to the top of a platform where *yauhtli* powder, an analgesic, was blown on their faces to anesthetize them somewhat during the next minutes. The half-awake prisoners were whirled about a dazzling fire and then dumped into the coals, fished out while still alive to have their still palpitating hearts cut out to be offered to the gods. There followed, after food and libations of intoxicating *octli,* a competitive climbing of a pole about fifty feet high to retrieve various paper insignia on top of it.

The eleventh month, from the end of August until September 19, was Ochpaniztli ('month of brooms'), with, of course, the usual sacrifices. It was also a military month with a review of all the clans parading with new arms, their own insignia on their shields; there was a procession of the knights of the Eagle and the knights of the Jaguar (who wore the animal skins as battle dress), a phalanx of warriors with special privileges; the festival ended in a gladiatorial contest.

The twelfth month, Teotleco, marked the return of the gods to earth (*teo,* 'god,' *tleco,* 'return') and good fun for young and old, for ceremonial drunkenness was the rule of the day.

The thirteenth (October 10–29) had to do with Tlaloc, the demanding rain god. The fourteenth involved a general penance for four days; men were expected to abstain, with ceremony or without it, from their wives. Panquetzaliztli ('feast of the flags'), which was celebrated as the fifteenth month, honoured the war god first with mock battles; then, says Sahagún, 'the women sang and danced . . . intermingling with the men . . .' They poured jugs of water over their heads—much as was done in the carnivals in Lima—took off their wet clothes, dyed their arms and legs blue, and dressed in *amatl* paper. The people marked for sacrifice also dressed in paper. It was raining again by the sixteenth month (December 9–28), and the month's name, Atemoztli, meant 'fall of waters.' The people prepared themselves by fasting five days previous to this feast.

The seventeenth month brought the cold—it was the end of December. Now they tried to touch the rain god's heart, to persuade him to give them the withheld gift of rain. First the women wept, then the men; the men pelted their women with straw-filled bags to hurry on the tears. The eighteenth, the last month of the year, was to Izcalli. It was a time of mass sacrifice. The women who were to be immolated were dressed in *amatl* paper clothing, and after that they repaired to Cuauhtitlán, where prisoners of war were lashed to scaffolds and killed with arrows.

Sacrifice by the arrow ceremony: *(above) a contemporary Aztec illustration. The victim is tied to a ladder and arrows are shot at him until his chest 'looks like a hedgehog'. Blood from the wounds is then smeared on an idol. This type of sacrifice was widespread. It was practised by the Aztecs, the Pawnees (Plain-dwellers) and the Mayas—for it was drawn also on the walls of ancient Tikal.*

The Volador, the fly-wheel, *a game ceremony in which men dressed as birds hung from ropes, is shown on the right. The two beams where the men are sitting were really on the same level, meeting in the shape of a cross. The men are about to jump off and be swung in a circle when the whole apparatus is rotated. It was supposed to give the effect of birds in flight and is still performed in remote parts of Mexico. The drawing is on Aztec 'amatl' paper.*

In all, the eighteen 20-day Aztec months accounted for 360 days. The imagination could not encompass more. It was satiated. There followed the *nemontemi,* the 'five empty days' (February 7–11). One did nothing . . . no fire, no music, no love . . . one sat huddled waiting, waiting . . .

Aztec music—indeed all primitive American music—was tied up with dancing; any 'pure' music has disappeared. What remains suggests that Aztec music was strong in rhythm but lacking in tone. This, at least, is what one infers from the instruments: the large upright drum, skin stretched over wood frame, was beaten with the bare hands and some control was exercised on the beat and quality of the tone; a smaller counterpart was hung around the neck and beaten with both hands, but contact with the body spoiled the resonance; the two-note wooden drum was beaten with rubber-tipped beaters, sonorous but monotonous. The conch shell gave out an impressively deep blast: a chorus of them were used early in the morning with the rising of Venus to arouse the people out of sleep. They also had flutes shaped like Panpipes, in clay or of reed, and whistles, and in addition to the rattles, seed-filled gourds, and the seed or shell attachments on the ankles that kept the beat. These are still used by the present-day Yaqui people. There were also notched bones, usually human femurs, which, rasped with a stick, suggest modern *musica Cubana.* The thing to note was

An Aztec 'orchestra' *at work, supervised by the patron god of music (from the Aztec Codex Magliabecchi). Drums, rattles, gourds and shells kept the rhythm, while flutes carried the melody.*

A wooden two-note drum—*a single piece of wood carved in the form of a coyote. It was struck with rubber beaters. Aztec music was strong in rhythm but lacking in tone.*

that the music was rhythmic, not melodic; its outward effect was cadence to the dancer, its inward effect, hypnotic.

Games, even though performed seemingly for fun, were in fact for them endowed with seriousness; they were ritualistic and magical. The passions which man displays in games were best seen in a game played from Honduras to Arizona and known as *tlachtli*. It began as a sport; it ended up as ritual. No one can say precisely where or when it began, except that the Olmecs who lived in the hotlands of the Gulf Coast, where rubber grew, had the game as early as 500 B.C.—a ball court was found in their temple complex at La Venta—and their name was derived from the word for rubber, *olli* (*Ol-mec*: 'rubber people').

Tlachtli was then already formalized. Yet the expressive pre-Aztec clay figures of tribesmen playing a variant of the game show it was as popular and ritualistic as baseball. It was played in a court shaped like an *I*; walls of tiered seats were on either side. In the middle of this was the 'basket,' a stone or wooden ring set, not horizontally as in basketball, but vertically; the object was to put the rubber ball through the ring. The ball was hard, not inflated. The players were allowed to strike it only with legs or hips or elbows; they were padded like a goalie in ice hockey.

Although many played it, *tlachtli* was essentially a religious game performed before the rulers of tribes. In Mexico-Tenochtitlán, the ball court stood in the sacred enclosure in front of the racks of skulls of those who had been sacrificed at the main temple.

The Friar Bernardino de Sahagún wrote of the game: 'the balls were about the size of bowling balls [i.e., six inches in diameter] and were solid, made of a gum called *ulli* . . . which is very light and bounces like an inflated ball.' In playing, both players and spectators placed enormous bets, 'gold, turquoise, slaves, rich mantles, even cornfields and houses . . . at other times the lord played ball for his pastime ... he also brought with him good ball players who played before him, and other principal men played on the opposite team, and they won gold and *chalchiguites* and beads of gold, and turquoise and slaves and rich mantles and maxtles and corn-fields and houses, etc. [feathers, cacao, cloaks of feather] ... the ball court ... consisted of two walls, twenty or thirty feet apart, that were up to forty or fifty feet in length; the walls ... were whitewashed and about eight and a half feet high, and in the middle of the court was a line which was used in the game ... in the middle of the walls, in the centre of the court, were two stones, like mill stones hollowed out, opposite each other, and each one had a hole wide enough to contain the ball ... And the one who put the ball in it won the game. They did not play with their hands, but struck the ball with their buttocks; for playing they wore gloves on their hands and a belt of leather on their buttocks, with which to strike the ball.'

In other games also the Aztecs were certainly as 'punctilious in play as in serious matters.' *Patolli,* something like backgammon or parchesi, was a less sanguine sport and was played on a marked board or paper, with beans for counters. The object was to travel about the board and return 'home' to win. It is doubtless the same game that Cortés used to play with Moctezuma when he was the Spaniards' captive in his own palace. Bernal

The ball-game, *called 'tlachtli', was played throughout Mexico. In this animated piece of Tarascan pottery is shown a simple version of the game, with two players in action, spectators along the sides of the ball-court and a judge at the end.*

Warrior or ball-player? *This clay figure from Jalisco wears a helmet and a heavy protection around hips and neck. The 'bat' suggests that a ball was struck, but there is no other information about such a game.*

'Patolli' was a gambling game *played with a board, which resembles ludo; beans were used for counters; the speech scrolls (wagging tongues meaning speech) suggest a controversy over the score. The patron god, Macuil-xochitl, watches over the game.*

Díaz called it *totoloque*. It was a gambling game, as he said, played 'with some very smooth pellets made of gold . . . They toss these pellets some distance as well as some little slabs which were also made of gold . . . In five strokes or tries they gained or lost certain pieces of gold or rich jewels that they staked.'

There were only two players but each had his own official scorekeeper. Cortés had Pedro de Alvarado (called 'the Sun' by the Aztec because of his white-blond hair), and Moctezuma observed that Alvarado always marked more points than Cortés gained and 'courteously and laughingly he said he was being done ill because Cortés was making so much *yxoxol* in the game,' i.e., he was cheating.

Aztec society, as do all societies, existed (in theory and mostly in practice) for the benefit of its component parts. The Aztec ideas of justice were ancient. Stealing to them was an aberration, for which restitution in kind was the usual penance. For things that could not be restored, there was death or else expulsion from the clan (the same thing) or into slavery. Adultery brought death, although this varied much with the circumstances of the people involved. Punishment to tribesmen who misused the 'king's way,' the Aztec road, was severe; robbery of merchants carrying on 'sacred business' was death by stoning—commerce and the royal way were sacrosanct. The penalty for murder naturally was death.

The most heinous were religious crimes. The robbing of temples, an offence that might provoke the disfavour of the gods, or doubting the efficacy of prayers, in short to blaspheme (to blame) anything that might bring disaster on the whole tribe—this brought immediate death. Witchcraft was the deadliest of crimes. Obsession with it is interwoven in the deepest fibres of the primitive mind, especially if it was directed toward someone of one's own clan. It was the worst crime that one could commit, and to cause death by witch-craft was considered worse than murder—it was anthropophagy, i.e., the eating of kin's flesh. The sentence of death was carried out only after protracted torture.

The administration of justice was designed so that the Aztec people would live in harmony among themselves. It was not designed for their neighbours, as all other men were enemies.

'It is a fact,' wrote Thomas Mann, 'that a man's dying is more the survivors' affair than his own'; it certainly was a fact to the Aztec. Death complicated everything. The survivors had to do penance in many ways for the unsocial act of their kinsman's dying. The dying man had to confess and the sorcerer was called in to attend to it; invocations were made to the gods so that he would die like an Aztec of good sense. Then they prepared the body for burial. First in his mouth a greenstone to take the place of his heart. It was not like the obolus which the Greeks put into the mouth of the dead to pay the passage across the river Styx; rather it was a heart symbol—the 'Heart of Jade'—for his journey to the unworld. Food was prepared, drink put in bowls, and the mummy bundle made complete. The next step was either burial or cremation. Cremation was general except where those of elevated rank were concerned; the leaders were entombed. The 'Anonymous Conqueror' found one of them after the rape of Mexico-Tenochtitlán. He found a mummy sitting with a painted symbol of his personal device, sword, and jewels amounting to 'three thousand castellanos.'

The departed went to those tutelary genii who had protected them in life; the

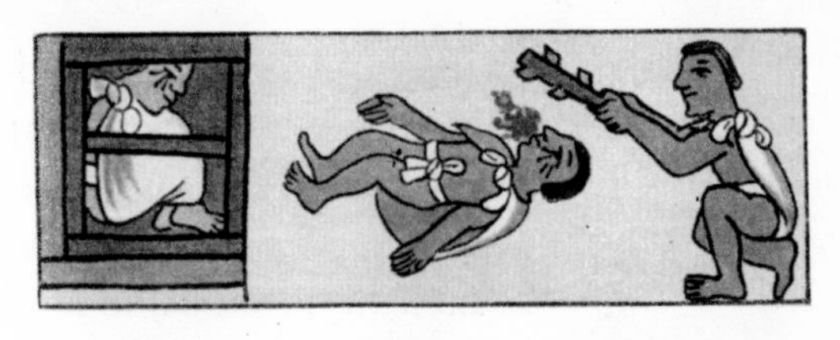

Punishment fitted the crime—*Aztec artists working for Sahagún depict the operation of the old laws. At the top an errant musician is being punished by being shut in a box and by blows on the head. Music was magical. It was intended to soothe the gods, and a missed beat might wreak havoc. Middle: a punishment for a minor crime—perhaps petty theft—was puncturing the skin with sharp agave-spines. Bottom: the death penalty. An official has been condemned for a serious crime. The judge watches his execution by strangling.*

knights of the Eagle, warriors, and valiant women (considered the same as warriors) went to the land of Tlaloc, the rain god; he also cordially received those souls who died by drowning, since he was the god of water. How one acted or did not act in life had no relation to one's degree of immortality; conduct in life did not determine the soul's place in the shades. When the soul arrived at the realm of the Lord of the Dead, he was assigned to one of the nine hells; the piece of greenstone tied to the mouth when the cadaver was swathed was left as a pledge in the seventh hell.

Meanwhile, the living must go into mourning for eighty days. There were a variety of impositions and taboos on food, dress, and indulgence in sex; sustenance had to be regularly placed at the death urn, prayers given, blood offered from cuts made in the ears and tongue. All must be done to obtain the good will of the recent dead; their displeasure could have dire consequences and could expose the living to twofold retribution: from the justly offended recently dead and from fellow clan members, who collectively would have to suffer the consequences of the dead's anger. After eighty days the taboo was lifted. It was repeated on and off for four years: 'For . . . it is a fact that a man's dying is more the survivors' affair than his own.'

Death and burial: *the dead man is swathed in cloth and surrounded by the things that he used in life—food, drink, copper bells, arms and a complete ocelot skin.*

4 'One Who Speaks': the King and his Council

THE RULER of the Aztecs was 'One Who Speaks.' He was elected, thus William Prescott was not entirely incorrect in calling their form of government an 'elective monarchy.' The leader was not absolute, as in Inca theocracy—he did not claim ownership of the land, the earth, the people, as did the Inca—the Aztecs were in theory democratic. Each family was a member of a soil community; a cluster of these families formed a clan, of which twenty made up the tribe of the Tenochas. Each clan had its own council and an elected leader; of these the oldest or wisest or more experienced were selected to make up an interclan council, the link between the clans and the tribe's governing body. This council was narrowed down to four principals, who were advisers to the leader of state and, as well, electors of the 'king' (functioning, to pursue a convenient analogy, as did the electors of the Holy Roman Empire), since 'kings' were not such by primogeniture but could be selected by the *tlatoani* from the brothers of the previous ruler, or, if he had none, from his nephews. These *tlatoani* were the key figures in Aztec government; they chose that 'noble' descendant who in their mind was most distinguished in valour, war, knowledge. Such a one was Moctezuma, who was 'crowned' in 1503.

'Moctezuma himself,' wrote Cortés, 'came out to meet us with some two hundred nobles . . . They came forward in two long lines keeping close to the walls of the street . . . Moctezuma was borne along in the middle of the street with two lords, one on his right and left. . . . Moctezuma wore sandals, whereas the others were barefoot.' 'The Great Moctezuma was about forty years old, of good height and well proportioned, slender and spare of flesh, not very swarthy, but of the natural colour and shade of an Indian. He did not wear his hair long . . . his scanty beard was well shaped and thin. His face was somewhat long, but cheerful . . . He was very neat and clean and bathed once every day in the afternoon. He had many women as mistresses, daughters of Chieftains, and he had two great Cacicas as his legitimate wives. He was free from unnatural offences [i.e., sodomy]. The clothes that he wore one day, he did not put on again until four days later [the Lord-Inca never wore the same garment twice]. He had two hundred Chieftains in his guard . . . and when they went to speak to him they were obliged to take off their rich mantles and put on others of little worth . . . to enter bare-

Acamapichtli
1375–1395

Huitzilhuitl
1395–1414

Chimalpopoca
1414–1428

Itzcoatl
1428–1440

Moctezuma I
1440–1469

Axayacatl
1469–1481

foot with their eyes lowered to the ground, and not to look up in his face . . . And they made him three obeisances . . .' (The Lord-Inca imposed a similar ritual.)

Moctezuma became a demigod. For although elected, with leadership he took on semidivinity. He was high priest, supreme commander of the army, and head of state, a plenary ruler, advised by council, with his power only held in check by ancient mores. Moctezuma was the ninth in succession, the nephew of the last ruler, Ahuitzotl, and grandson of Moctezuma I (surnamed 'the Wrathy'). As an Aztec ruler-aspirant he was trained like all such in the 'religious' schools, the *calmecac* ('house of the large corridors'). There, with the image of Quetzalcoatl painted on the wall, he learned by means of glyphic charts the history of the Tenochas. He was taught to read glyph writing, to remember the list of dates of rulers and history.

He studied the use of Aztec arms, swords, slings, and arrows, for it was expected he would be a military leader; once he knew and understood ideographic writing he learned about the stars, astrology, the calendar, and through constant reading of the *tonalamatl* (used as an aid in memory) he learned the rituals and interpretation of phenomena. As a youth Moctezuma had taken a very active part in the wars; later he devoted much attention to religion, 'scrupulous in his attentions to all the burdensome ceremonial of the Aztec worship.' José de Acosta also said that he was 'grave and staid and spake little, so when hee gave his opinion . . . then he was feared and respected. . . . Hee marched with such gravitie . . . they all sayd the name of Moctezuma ['Courageous Lord'] agreed very well with his nature.'

Moctezuma was 'crowned' with a sort of mitre; the colour symbol of his power was blue-green. Immediately after coming to power he turned out the rankless people about him, commanding that 'only the most noble and most famous men of his realme shoulde live within his pallace,' thus severing the democratic base of Chief Speaker; it had been the custom to have people of all shades and hues about the royal rooms ever since the time of 'king' Itzcoatl, who had been born of a slave concubine in his father's house. Moctezuma seems to have taken on some of the prerogatives of a god; whether this was done before by other Chief Speakers is not clear.

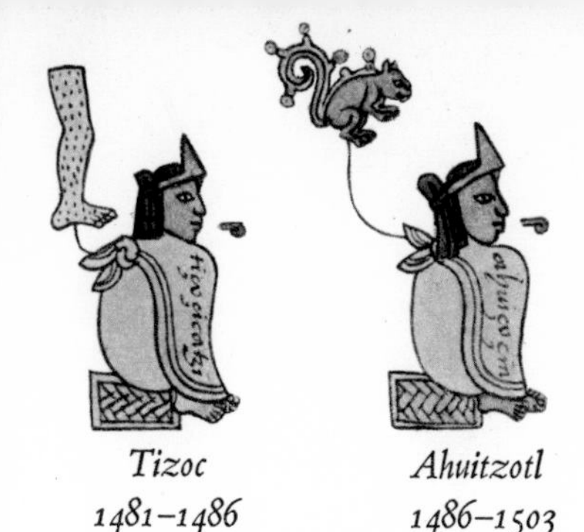

Tizoc
1481–1486

Ahuitzotl
1486–1503

The Aztec kings, *their names and name-glyphs. The ruler of the Aztecs was the 'Chief-Speaker' who was chosen or elected by a council of four.*

Moctezuma (Courageous Lord) *1503–1520 (right), was king at the time of the Spanish conquest. He was a warrior and priest 'grave and staid . . . feared and respected, giving scrupulous attention to all the burdens of ritual'.*

Dress for Moctezuma was as the lower man's except that it was more elaborate. He wore the breechclout, elaborate sandals, the manta (*tilmantli*), and all the other accoutrements so highly praised by the conquerors. These descriptions by the Spaniards, which were later dismissed by eighteenth-century historians as inspired by the heady fumes of war, have been confirmed by archaeology. Few—outside of the Maya kingdom—lived as sumptuously; the apparent overdrawing is no exaggeration of the real splendour of it all.

His numerous progeny were trained for office. This is true of all polygamous marriages; the Inca used his enormous offspring as sources for leadership in the realm and the Aztec practiced a similar nepotism. Nezahualpilli, 'king' of Texcoco, allied to Mexico, 'had more than two thousand concubines.'

Moctezuma ruled effectively. He spread the realm farther than all others before him; tribute was collected from 371 towns; justice in particular was well organized by him. 'If there were any excesse of defect he did then punish it rigorously. . . . And also to discern how his ministers did execute their officers he often disguised himselfe . . . if they offended, they were punished. Besides that he was a great justicier and very noble, he was very valiant and happy . . . and he obtained great victories and came to his greatness.'

Omens and symbols of ill-luck *appeared prior to the coming of the Spaniards. (a) Moctezuma consulted the auguries by viewing the magical bird whose head was a mirror . . . this showed him hordes of strange armed men. (b) A two-headed man was seen. (c) A new comet appeared. (d) One of the temples burned mysteriously and for no obvious reason. (e) Snow fell on Tenochtitlán. (f) A tongue of fire rose out of the earth and threw up new stars.*

But the times were out of joint; the heavens and the hells rose to plague him. What we would call natural phenomena, to them was evil omen: it snowed in Mexico; the volcano Popocatépetl, which had lain quiescent for a long time, became active. A child was born with two heads; the 'king' of Texcoco (he of the two thousand women), who was a 'greate Magitian,' came over one day 'at an extraordinary hour' to tell him that the gods had revealed that he, Moctezuma, would lose his whole realm. To give it all a sense of history, Quetzalcoatl, that God who had declared against human sacrifice and was the cultural hero of these lands, had sailed away in exile into the Atlantic saying that he would again return in the same year of his birth to 're-establish my rule.' His birth had been in the Aztec year of 1-Reed (Ce-Acatl); in the Aztec calendar this fell in the years 1363, 1467—and 1519. For years Moctezuma had all but given up the military direction of his government and was surrounded by a corps of astrologers, augurs, necromancers, and mediums from whom he sought, by the interpretation of signs, symbols, and observation of the portents, to learn what to do to win back the favour of the gods.

What had happened was simple enough: white men had reached America's shores. In 1502, one year before Moctezuma's coronation, Cristóbal Colón, on his fourth and last voyage, had made contact with the Mayas; it did not take long for this event to boil over from the Maya councils and be carried over the trails from people to market and from tribe to tribe. Later, Yañez Pinzón and Juan Díaz de Solís skirted the shores of Yucatán, and once again rumour sniffed the breeze, as it were, travelled over the jungles, and somewhere was set down by a glyph writer to be sent to

Moctezuma: strange bearded men in large boats have come from out of the ocean-sea.

No 'king' in Aztec history had so terrible a problem to cope with as Moctezuma.

The rule and organization of Tenochtitlán was activated through the system already outlined: the 'king,' Uei Tlatoani, gave his desires to the 'council of four'; they in turn conveyed them to the larger body of clan heads, then down to the clan body, where another official, who enforced peace and was the clan leader during a war, gave to members of the clan the programmes promulgated from the higher reaches.

This clan, the basic unit of the system, enforced clan peace, organized for war, rounded out clan taxation; orders through these methods reached down to the very last rung of the social ladder. It seems that the Aztecs did not administer the affairs of conquered peoples. Perhaps they were not interested in doing so. The Incas in Peru had a system of sending *mitimaes,* a 'safe' population of Quechua-speaking peoples, into newly conquered lands and removing

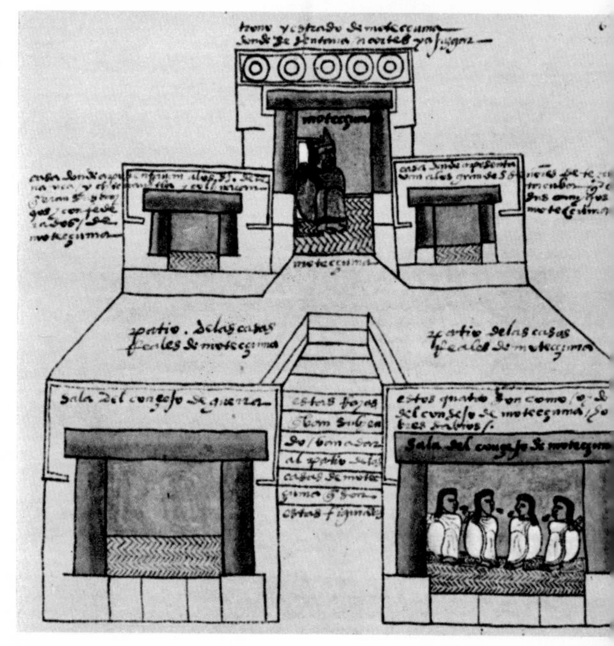

Moctezuma's palace *stood where the Mexico city-hall now stands. It was an immense place, two storeys in height and honeycombed with rooms. This view, from the Codex Mendoza, shows the courtyard and steps to the 'throne room'. Moctezuma sits at the top; bottom right is his council chamber, with the 'council of four' in session. There were also sumptuous quarters for the chieftains of states allied to Mexico.*

the unsafe of the newly conquered. By this system the Incas conquered and amalgamated that which they conquered. The Aztecs had no such system. They imposed a tribute, not excessive, except for sacrificial victims, a contribution which fitted into the conquerors' economy. This was brought every six months to Tenochtitlán. Still the Aztecs won no friends and forged no empire.

They went through all the typical social evolution of Neolithic states everywhere: they moved from the land, where at first all worked at agriculture, to the city which became a temple-city, where a social surplus produced non-farmers—specialists in architecture, and sculpture, lapidaries, and priest-craftsmen, people who themselves no longer grew food. Then their society passed into the city-state with satellite towns, and Tenochtitlán developed an extended priestly class who exacted 'first fruits' for the temples. Then lastly it became the conquering and finally the tribute city.

There were enough reasons for this. The Aztecs were fighting people. They had no luxuries on their land: cotton, brilliant bird feathers, chocolate, gold, rubber were not of their earth's bounty. If they wanted these things, they got them by conquest. Moreover, as they became specialized they manufactured and traded. It was difficult enough: each region was hostile to every other; there were few natural avenues; imbroglios had to be called off so that trading could be carried on. There was a great lack of unity even among towns nominally Aztec. As Tenochtitlán, the conquering city, widened its horizons, new products, new ideas came into it, and gradually luxuries were converted into necessities.

Trade became vital to Mexico. War was continuous; tribute, the result of conquest, poured in from many far-flung places and was distributed among the clans. As this gave people more leisure from the fields, leisure was devoted to manufacture, which in turn produced articles they traded for luxuries at the market.

A new class of merchant (*pochteca*) came into being—a phenomenon in ancient America—traders who had their own guilds, their own gods, and were above the laws that applied to most. They set out from Mexico periodically with long trains of human carriers, sixty pounds on their backs, preceded by the lordly *pochteca*. Protected in disputed terrain by soldiers, the human caravans penetrated into southern Mexico, into and beyond Guatemala, down as far as Nicaragua. They traded Aztec manufactured goods for the raw products of the hotlands: emeralds, which slowly found their way from Muzo in Colombia (the only place they were found in pre-Hispanic America), gold from Panama, feathers from Guatemala, jaguar skins, eagle feathers, cotton, chocolate, chicle, rubber, live birds for the royal aviary in Mexico (the source of plumage for the feather weavers).

The 'floating gardens' of Tenochtitlán. *As agricultural land was limited on the two islets, it was extended by filling reed-woven baskets eight feet square with earth and anchoring them in shallow waters. These 'basket gardens' were held in position by stakes and on 'land' thus formed plots were tended. Thousands of these 'chinampas' clustered round the city and enlarged it.*

Roads of a sort were opened; Aztec garrisons were placed at strategic places or among the newly conquered. The *pochteca* moved freely.

There is a natural limit to conquest and the Aztecs had no definite plan of assimilation. Conquest often followed trade as the Aztecs got information on riches and defences brought back by the merchants; sometimes the process went the other way: villages, city-states, subjected to sharp wars of conquest, were made to yield tribute. The number of these expanded until at the time of Moctezuma there were 371.

So during the growth of Aztec power all the riches of all these cultures were pouring into their capital.

Mexico-Tenochtitlán was an island and a watery city.

It was something like Venice; there were the same type of *calli* and *campi,* with hundreds of meandering streets, filled with canals, bridges, and dikes. This Tenochtitlán began, as Venice, not out of 'feelings of men' which oft-times founded cities, but out of safety. Just as the primitive Venetians took possession of the tide-washed sandbanks in the Adriatic and turned this undefined swampy tract into a city with its canals and waterways, so did the Aztecs, fleeing the mainland, seek safety on the two marsh-bound islets three miles from shore on Lake Texcoco.

The oval-shaped valley of Anáhuac at 7,244 feet altitude, 30 by 50 miles, held the waters of the lakes, which were identified by five separate names although they formed a continuous body of water that varied from fresh to saline. The largest of the lakes was Texcoco. Directly out from Chapultepec forest, three miles more or less ('seven leagues' said Hernán Cortés), there were two islets, rock outcrops surrounded by mudbanks and reed-fringed. This was the base of Tenochtitlán.

'The great city of Tenochtitlán', *wrote Cortés, 'is two leagues to any point on the mainland.*

Four causeways lead to it, some twelve feet wide'. It covered an area of about 2500 acres.

The first buldings were structures of wattle and daub, the 'immortal' house even today of the upland peasant. Then followed the temple, which, rebuilt from century to century, grew into the awesome Temple of Huitzilopochtli (the present site of Mexico's Cathedral). While developing the two islets the Aztecs apparently maintained by treaty some foothold for cultivation on the mainland, augmenting this by the ingenious *chinampa,* the 'floating garden,' and the space between these formed the canals. Centuries of these operations enlarged the original mud flats until 'Greater Mexico-Tenochtitlán,' that is, Tenochtitlán and Tlaltelolco, formed a city 1¾ miles square and containing upwards of 2,500 acres. This was a sizable area: Rome's walls at the time of Marcus Aurelius enclosed a city of only 3,500 acres; London town in the time of Samuel Pepys was scarcely any larger.

'The great city of Tenochtitlán,' wrote Cortés, '. . . is two leagues [five miles] . . . to any point on the mainland. Four causeways lead to it . . . some twelve feet wide.' The one which he took to enter the city in 1519 began at Ixtapalapa ('. . . we saw so many cities and villages built in the water and other great towns on dry land and that straight and level Causeway going towards Mexico . . .' says Bernal Díaz). This causeway ('as broad as two lances and broad enough for eight horsemen to rode abreast') went for about a mile and there made junction with another causeway coming from the city of Coyoacán. Here there was a fort with battlements and a drawbridge; then the causeway went on some two miles directly north to the city. It was much used, 'but broad as it is, it was so crowded with people that there was hardly room for them all . . .' The second was an auxiliary causeway with aqueduct, which arched in a curve connected with some part of the mainland and entered this main causeway close to the entrance of the city. The third went westward toward Chapultepec (branching off to Tlacopán), i.e., Tacuba. This carried the aqueduct to the heart of the city. 'Along . . . [this] causeway two pipes are constructed of masonry, each two paces broad [6 feet) and about as high as a man; one of which conveys a stream of water very clear and fresh.' The other one lay empty to be used when the first was being cleaned. As the causeway had at intervals removable bridges in case of attack, the fresh water conduit, as explained by Hernán Cortés, 'flows into a kind of [ceramic] trough as thick as an ox [twenty-five-inch conduit], which occupies the whole of the bridge.' The fourth and last causeway, the shortest, not much over a half-mile in length, connected the city with the mainland at Tepeyac.

This system of causeways, the greatest engineering feat of the Aztecs, had a twofold purpose: to facilitate communication and to serve as a dike or levee. The lakes were subject to rise and fall; rain could raise the level

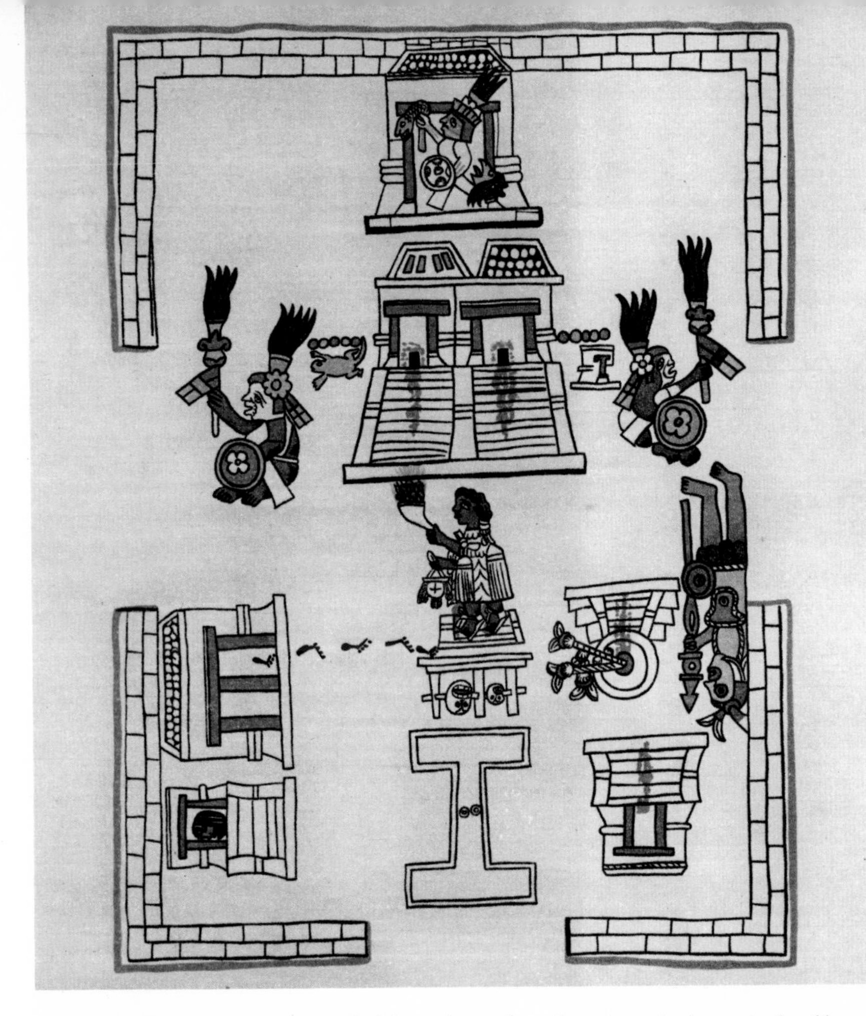

The heart of the city—*a 'picture-plan' from the Codex Florentino. At the top is the old temple of Huitzilopochtli, below it the twin shrines of Huitzilopochtli and Tlaloc, flanked by the God of Flowers with dates Five Lizard (left) and Five House (right). Below stands a priest (having come from the priest's quarters, note the footprints) above a skull rack and the ball court. To the left are also the Eagle Knights' quarters and to the right the sacrificial stone, the god Xipe (upside down) and his temple. The sacred area is enclosed by walls.*

rapidly (there was no outlet); wind could raise huge waves that lapped up to and over the city, which was subject to frequent inundations (as it is still today).

The city, like Cuzco, capital of the Incas in Peru, was divided into four sections, corresponding to the causeways, which entered the city from three of the four cardinal directions. Each formal entrance to the city proper had a roadblock, where taxes were collected. House styles varied with the rank of the owner. Those of the lower class were constructed with walls of wattle and smeared with mud, grass-thatched; those of rank were raised on a stone platform (in case of flood), made of sun-dried brick, plastered over, and brilliantly coloured. The ordinary house, invariably one-storied and with a pitched straw roof, had its postern to the street, a patio garden within, and by a narrow canal, which was its street, was the entrance. There was also a jetty for the dugout canoe. The principal houses were two-storied, made of *tezontli* stone, with flat roofs. The city 'had many wide and handsome streets.' Many if not most of these 'streets' were waterways, canals such as in Venice. Each dwelling had a small plot of earth, a garden; this is evident in the fragment of an Aztec map showing very clearly the individual houses, ground plots, streets, and the great waterways.

The stone-paved great plaza measured, as do the boundaries of the central square of present-day Mexico, 520 by 600 feet, and within that square there was the great *teocalli* with four lesser pyramids on its several sides: the Temple of Quetzalcoatl, a rounded structure entwined with green, open-fanged serpents; a raised dais on which gladiators fought; the sacred ball court, with, on one side, the residence of the officiating priests and, on the other, the house of the military order of the Eagle, an élite warrior class. The skull rack, on which hung the craniums of the sacrificial victims, was close to the ball court. Three causeways terminated in the main square (just as in Cuzco, the capital of the Incas, the roads of 'four quarters' that ran the length and breadth of their land terminated or began in the main plaza). The water entered the city at the great square and was from there either piped off to other sections or was collected in water jugs.

The other half of the great square was the market. At one end was the sacred stone of war where the captains met before going off to do battle; at the other end was the calendar stone. In front of this was the new palace of Moctezuma. It was an immense structure, as large in area as the plaza, a virtual city in itself and honeycombed with rooms. There were sumptuous quarters for the 'kings' of the city-states of Texcoco and Tlacopán, to which the Aztecs were allied. There were other rooms for at least three hundred accompanying guests, always coming and going. Below there were the tribunal rooms, the public repository where all the tribute from the 371 tribute towns was delivered and stored for distribution. It is to one of these rooms that Bernal Díaz was conducted to see the tribute: '. . . his steward was a great Cacique . . . and he kept the accounts of all the revenue that was brought to Montezuma . . . Montezuma had two houses full of every sort of arms . . . and in other quarters, cotton, foodstuffs, chocolate, feathers, gold, jewels, all that was part of the tribute-economy.' In other sections were the rooms of the administrators who kept record of the economy of the theodemocracy.

On the second floor were the rooms of Moctezuma's wife, his 150 concubines and their offspring, his hundreds of guards and attendants.

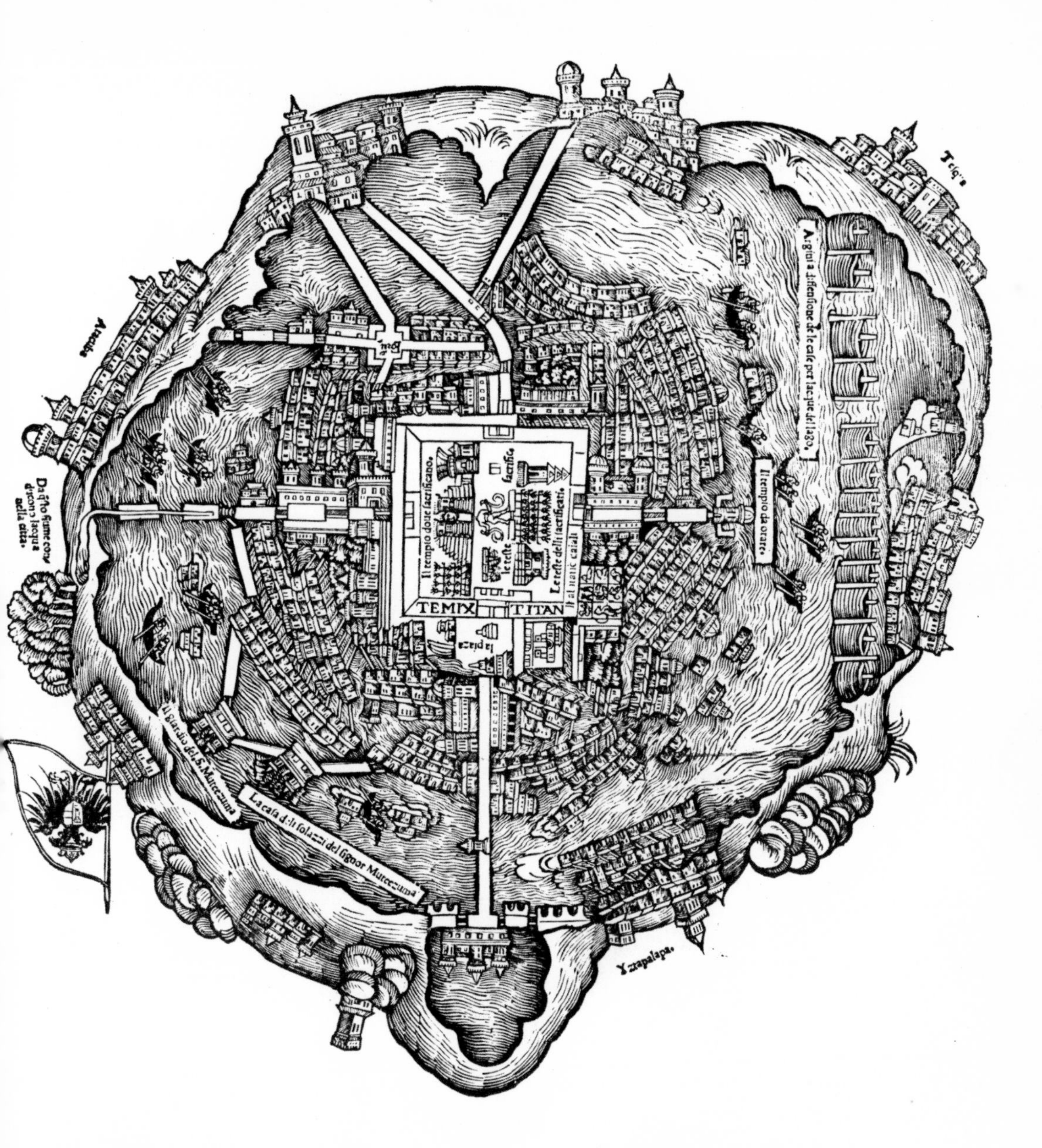

The first plan of Mexico-Tenochtitlán *was made by its conqueror. Hernan Cortés drew and then had redrawn this 'Plan of Tenochtitlán' to illustrate his 'Letters', two of which were published in Nuremberg in 1524. The map itself is said to have been done by Albrecht Dürer (who saw and commented upon the Aztec treasures) or by one of his brothers. The map shows the principal features: the twin cities Tenochtitlán (centred on the large square) and Tlaltelolco (centred on the small square); the causeways leading to the city and the aqueduct (on the left) which brought in fresh water from the forests of Chapultepec. The clustering of houses, the streets, waterways and bridges, can be clearly seen.*

Attached to the palace, or within it (for it was full of patios), was the royal aviary. This astounded the conquistadors, for there were no zoos in Europe—they were unheard of. 'There were ten pools of water in which they kept every kind of waterfowl known in these parts . . . and I can vouch for it to Your Majesty,' wrote Cortés to Charles V, fearful that if he described such a thing as an aviary the king would think him mad, 'I can vouch that these birds, who only eat fish, receive some 250 pounds daily.'

How large was the city, how large the fief of the city-state of Tenochtitlán? No one knew. Cortés admitted that he was 'unable to find out the exact extent of . . . the kingdom.' He thought it 'as large as Spain.' Certainly, even taking natural exaggeration into account, it was one of the world's largest cities; few of the temple-cities in the Old World seem to have been as large.

How populous was ancient Tenochtitlán? The conquistadors said there were from seventy to a hundred thousand inhabited houses on the island kingdom; if each house had between four and ten inhabitants, averaging six to the house, the population would have been about one half million. Cortés' small army of one thousand men, even with his Indian auxiliaries, could not have beaten down *that* number. One historian gives thirty thousand for Mexico-Tenochtitlán. A modern French authority falls back on the old figures; he says that the city had 'a population certainly more than five hundred thousand and probably inferior to one million.' The truth is that Mexico-Tenochtitlán had no more than ninety thousand inhabitants. Even 'reduced' it was still one of the largest cities in the world: at that time London had no more than forty thousand, Paris could boast sixty-five thousand.

Although the Aztecs were not an empire (as the Incas were an empire), although they did not have what most regard as the essential elements of civilization—metal, the wheel, draft animals, the rotary quern—they had a form of organization, an intensification of older native techniques, which made possible the achievements that follow and stamped indelibly all things they touched with the word 'Mexican.'

The skull of an Aztec sacrificial victim, *overlaid with turquoise mosaic. Skulls of prominent and powerful chieftains were kept as amulets; in the great plaza of Tenochtitlán there was a huge rack of them. But in this barbaric piece, one of the treasures of the British Museum, death has been transformed into something macabrely beautiful.*

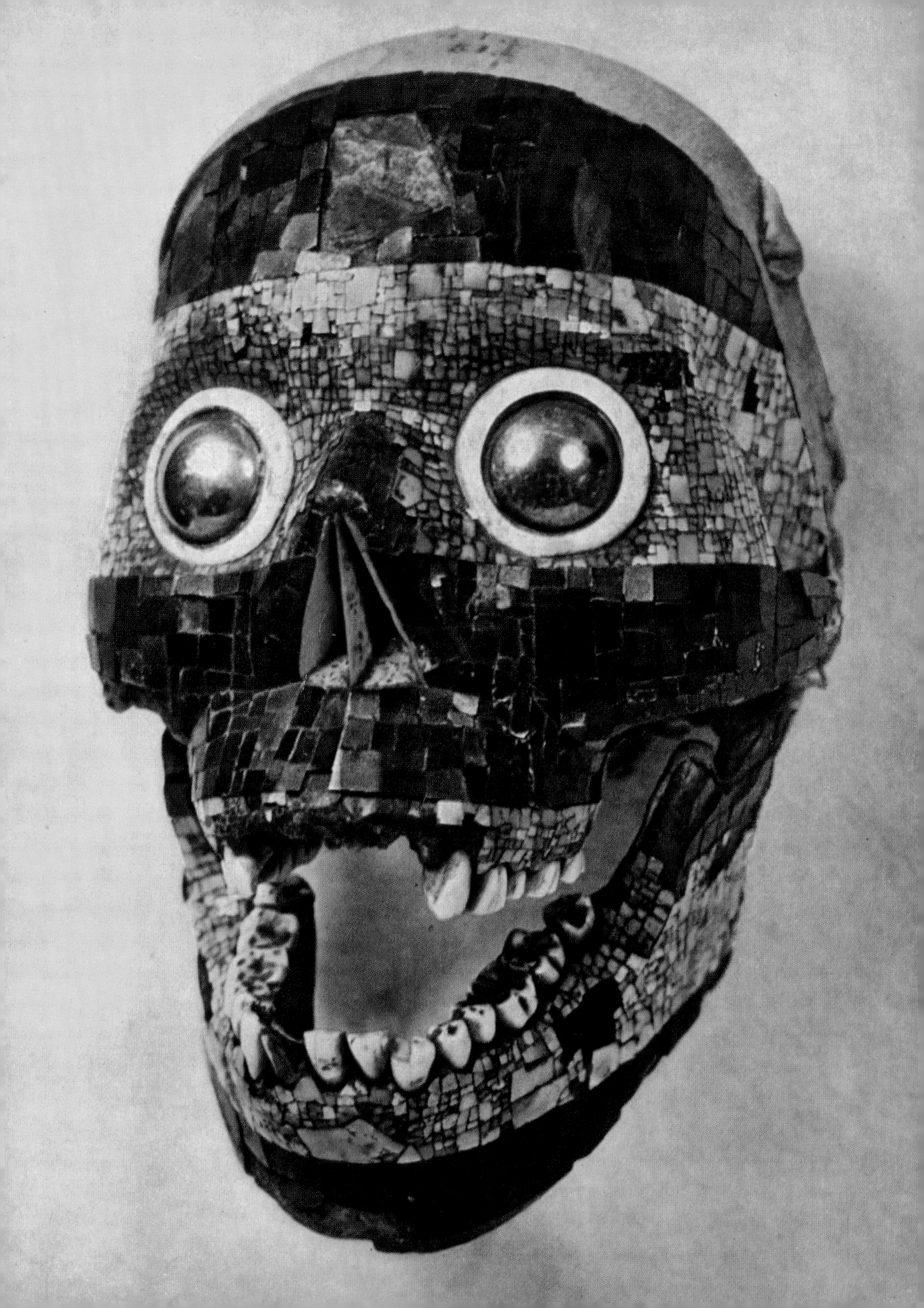

The Aztec shrine to the War God, *at Xampala, one of the few to survive into modern times. It stands more or less as depicted here by Castañeda in 1805.*

5 The Enduring Legacy

AZTEC ARCHITECTURE perished with the conquest. Most of it lay about the immediate vicinity of the lakes, dotted like satellites around Tenochtitlán. It is all gone. Yet enough has been found in the descriptive literature developed out of archaeology to attempt its reconstruction.

Tenochtitlán appears to have had one of the best planned urban centres of all ancient American cultures. It had not, to be sure, the mechanistic perfection of Cuzco, capital of the Incas, but its attention to human comfort for all the population, its zeal in transporting water through aqueducts, its hedonistic approach to life—often absent in the austere Inca city—doubtless surpassed all others. The only city-state to which it can be compared, where much of this luxuriousness obtained, was that of Chan-Chan, capital of the Chimú Empire in the desert coast of Peru and contemporaneous with the Aztec capital.

Religion was the dominating factor in Aztec life and Tenochtitlán was 'divine.' The whole of it was, in its essence, religious; everything important within it was dedicated, in one form or another, to religion.

The symbol of it was the pyramid. The great *teocalli* stood in the plaza encircled by a high wall fashioned as writhing snakes, and hence its name, *coatepantli*. It measured at its base 150 by 150 feet and rose to about 160 feet high at its truncated apex, which was 70 feet square; on it rested two temples dedicated to the principal gods. It commanded the city, the main road led to it, and it could be seen in the clear atmosphere miles away. 'The temple capped the substructure and was the culmination of a harmonious series of ascending planes, calculated to increase the illusion of height by emphasizing the effects of mechanical perspective.' The religious, administrative, and social aspects of life in the city were grouped, as previously explained, about the temple; this architectural pattern was repeated over and over again, throughout the city. The houses tended to be like squares on a chessboard and formed the basic plan of rectangular rooms set about a patio.

Water was kept potable by flowing through ceramic pipes and was distributed through the city to fountains. The small channels were kept open, the larger constantly cleaned; the engineering works and dikes to prevent the overflow of lake waters and the long causeways to provide access from the mainland to the island temple-city, the removable bridges and sluice gates, all were only part of city planning.

Sanitation was far in advance of anything in Europe until the end of the eighteenth century. So as not to pollute the lake, excreta was collected and brought to the mainland fields in canoes, to be used as fertilizer; urine was preserved as a mordant for dyeing cloth. Public latrines were seen by the conquistadors all along the causeways.

Calixtlahuaca, located near Toluca in the state of Mexico, and within the traditional boundaries of Aztec dominion, is an Aztec structure only by courtesy; it was captured by them in 1476 under the reign of Axayacatl and then destroyed by them in 1502. It is so ancient that it has seemingly no precise beginnings; its pottery reveals that the principal temple was begun about A.D. 500. The highest placed site in Mexico, 9,517 feet in altitude, it is famous for its Temple of Quetzalcoatl, which was circular, like the convolutions of a seashell, with doors leading into sealed labyrinths within; outside the traditional stairway mounted.

Malinalco, also in the present state of Mexico, is the only site indubitably Aztec that lies outside of the immediate vicinity of Mexico-Tenochtitlan. The monuments and architecture, which date from 1476, during the reign of Axayacatl, were built sixty miles from the city, close to the village of Tenancingo. It is the only temple-city that is partly hewn out of the living rock. It is not, to be sure, a Petra, but for America it is unusual enough. Malinalco, (from *malinalli,* 'grass') is self-contained, an architecturally composite site of six larger structures and a number of smaller ones. The principal building is hewn round out of the rock ledge, guarded by squatting pumas. At its entrance is a flight of fourteen steps cut out of the living rock. These lead to a temple, whose door once was the open mouth of a fanged snake head. This gives access to a circular chamber where eagles with furled wings and puma heads are carved in the natural rock wall. In another temple there are the remains of an impressive fresco of marching warriors, typically Aztec, with shields and spears 'at ready.' It is believed by Dr. García Payón, who carried on most of the excavations, that Malinalco was reserved for the rituals of the military orders of the Eagle and the Jaguar, the two élite corps of warriors. A beautifully carved wooden drum found at this same Malinalco confirms this theory; around it circles a lively dance of Jaguars and marching Eagles, the symbols of the war cult.

That ends the melancholy parade of what is known of Aztec ruins, places which even in Bernal Díaz's time were razed into nothingness, for he wrote: 'Of all these wonders that I then beheld, today all is overthrown and lost, nothing is left standing.'

It shows also how utterly incorrect is the term 'Aztec Empire.' Theirs was not, like the Incas' or as the Mayas', a homogeneous empire, tribe and state; they had domination—not dominion—over the conquered lands. Held only by troops; there was no political or architectural unity. For instance, the number of Inca structures along the two-thousand-mile stretch of their empire is incalculable, there are so many. And the number of temple-cities in the old and new Maya empire reach beyond a hundred; each year sees more and more sites revealed out of the jungle. Unlike these, the Aztecs had no political method of ab-

sorbing the conquered populations into their system and imposing upon them an architectural formula. Theirs was essentially a tribute state. For this reason, to grasp something of Aztec architecture, which had its centre in Anáhuac and which was destroyed by the Spanish Conquest, we must turn to those from whom the Aztecs borrowed and adapted.

Teotihuacán, the temple-city of the Toltecs, dwarfs in magnitude all else in Mexico and Middle America. It was in ruins and nameless when the Aztecs knew it. Its Temple to the Sun, 216 feet high and covering ten acres of ground, has no peer; all subsequent pyramids, including the great *teocalli* in Mexico-Tenochtitlán, were stylistically based on it. The remains of

The great wooden drum of Malinalco, *with an extended drawing of the design running round it. Malinalco is a late Aztec site, built about 1476. The very fine carvings on the drum show the dance of the Jaguar and Eagle Knights. Similar motifs appear at Tula, and also at the Maya centre of Chichén Itzá, having been brought there by the followers of Quetzalcoatl.*

The round temple of Calixtlahuaca, *an ancient site known to exist from* A.D. *500.*

Monte Albán: steps facing the huge plaza. *This great temple-city on the borders of Aztec territory was a complex of cultures, continuously changing—Olmec, Maya, Zapotec, Mixtec and Aztec.*

Façade of a building at Mitla. *These buildings, low horizontal masses of an austere grandeur, 'strangely unlike any of the other pre-Columbian ruins', are the work of the Zapotec culture.*

Teotihuacán, capital of the Toltecs, *which in magnitude dwarfed all else in Mexico and Middle America. A vast area, three and a half miles long and two miles broad, was devoted to the gods. It was a ceremonial centre, not a living city. Dominating the remains today are the Pyramid of the Moon (bottom left) and the even larger Pyramid of the Sun. Other imposing buildings lined the central road running south from the Pyramid of the Moon.*

this great ceremonial city and centre, which alone covers an area of eight square miles, date back to as far as 200 B.C. It continued up to 900 A.D. In this vast extent of time the immense Temple of the Sun, and its heavenly companion, the Temple of the Moon, rose to dominate the long avenues of religious structures which are part of Teotihuacán.

The Toltecs, famed as architects, craftsmen, knew how to handle mass; their buildings are impressive. The decoration, especially in the well-known Temple of Quetzalcoatl, with its great feathered heads as the dominant motif, has a massive awesomeness. Murals uncovered in the temple of agriculture show all the cultivated plants being grown—meaning that every domesticated plant had been developed one thousand years before the Aztecs appeared; the 260-day calendar, great monthly markets, writing, even the familiar Aztec speech scroll—the human tongue wagging in front of the speaker—had already been perfected long before A.D. 500. All were well-worn cultural elements, taken in the whole or inherited by the Aztecs.

Cempoala is utterly unique. We have a good description of how it appeared to the Spanish in 1519 to compare with the structure as it has grown out of its present-day restoration.

In 1519 the Spanish were following the ancient coastal road on the way to Cempoala; they passed, says Cortés, 'a few large towns very passably laid out. . . . The houses in those parts which can obtain stone are of rough masonry and mortar, the rooms being low and small, very much after the Moorish fashion. . . . Where no stone can be got they build their houses of baked bricks, covering them over with plaster and a rough kind of thatch. . . . Certain houses belonging to chiefs are quite airy and have a considerable number of rooms . . . we have seen as many as five inner corridors or patios in a single house and its rooms very well laid out around them. Each one of the chief men has in front of the entrance to his house a large patio and some as many as two, three, four, sometimes raised a considerable way off the ground with steps leading up to them and very well built. In addition they have their mosques, temples . . . all of fair size.'

Cempoala was twenty miles north of the modern port of Veracruz. As they approached it and saw the whitewashed buildings rise out of the green jungle, barbarically coloured and vibrant, 'we were struck with admiration,' said Bernal Díaz. 'It looked like a garden with luxuriant vegetation, and the streets were so full of men and women who had come to see us. . . . Our scouts . . . reached a great plaza with courts . . . and it seemed to be white-washed and burnished . . . one of the scouts thought that this white surface which shone so brightly must be silver . . .'

Archaeology has confirmed all that Cortés and his minions said of Cempoala. The temple-city alone with its surrounding houses had a population estimated at about thirty thousand; the walled plaza—which has been measured and in some parts restored by Mexican archaeologists—had an over-all measurement of 251,000 square yards. The general aspect revealed by research was that it was stone laid with soaring temples. There were fifteen, large and small, within the plaza, the ceremonial centre surrounded by one-storied houses, gaily painted and grass-thatched. Dr. J. García Payon, who directed the excavations, found eight large groups of such buildings.

An Aztec garrison was close by. The *pochteca* merchants made frequent visits and the tribute collectors paid semi-annual calls for tribute. Five of them were there at the time of Cortés' arrival, and they were 'full of assurance and arrogance,' writes Bernal Díaz. 'Their cloaks and loin-cloths were richly embroidered, and their shining hair was gathered up as though tied on their heads . . .'

In the southern highlands of Mexico there are other cultural centres which influenced Aztec architecture. The one that has been the longest known and yet is still the least known is *Xochicalco,* 'Place of Flowers' which lies twenty miles south of Cuernavaca. It squats lonely on the highest hills, overlooking two fresh-water lakes two miles distant, in a strongly fortified position. The hills were artificially flattened and terraced, with strong points for defence. Four roads radiate in the four cardinal directions and march up through the impressive buildings into the principal plaza, where the famous Temple of Quetzalcoatl stands. Another temple is reached by a paved ceremonial road sixty feet broad.

Xochicalco was a ceremonial and, in addition, perhaps an administrative centre; all the familiar edifices are here: palaces, temples, the ball court, and, when finally excavated, there will be found a house complex within the temple-city—the famous temple to the Plumed Serpent, which has one of the finest façades in all Mexico, has been uncovered. The handling of the figures would suggest Maya were it not for the fire snakes, which are a symbol of the Mixtecs; the glyphs and dates seem Mixtec and other features suggest Toltec.

Monte Albán lies southeast of this city in Oaxaca, isolated from the Mexican plateau by a range of mountains sufficiently difficult to prevent an Aztec invasion until 1469. A composite of cultures, Olmec, Maya, Zapotec, Mixtec, and Aztec, it was perhaps one of the longest continuously inhabited temple-cities known to us (500 B.C.–A.D. 1469). Located on top of the bald hills, 1,500 feet above the level of the valley, although 5,000 feet above the sea, the site has been modified numerous times. There were five marked periods of occupation: Olmec art adorns the early buildings and this links it to the coastal cultures. There followed a period of Maya influence until the Zapotecs exerted their control; this lasted the longest, from

The plumed serpent *that decorates the façade of the Temple of Quetzalcoatl at Xochicalco, 'Place of Flowers'. This is a complex site, only partially excavated and something of a puzzle, for the features suggest Maya, Mixtec and Toltec. It seems to have been built about* A.D. *900.*

Geometric patterns *on the walls of a temple at Mitla, manifestly inspired by and based upon textile designs. Mitla lies only twenty-five miles from Monte Albán and is part of the same culture. Its name in Zapotec means 'Place of the Dead'.*

The skull-altar *of the rain-god Tlaloc at Calixtlahuaca. It suggests either that the cult of death was pre-Aztec, or that this temple was altered by the Aztecs after the conquest in 1476 to conform to their own religious concepts.*

Tula *was another large sacred city of the Toltecs. This is a detail of the outside wall of the temple, showing in the middle layer of the frieze a stylized version of the plumed serpent, symbol of Quetzalcoatl, disgorging the skeleton of a man it has swallowed.*

A.D. 534 until A.D. 1125. The fourth period found it under the sway of the Mixtecs, who brought new art, new gods, a variation in the calendar, tombs, murals, urns; it was they who made the superbly beautiful goldwork discovered by Dr. Caso in one of the unopened tombs.

The fifth phase of Monte Albán was its last; Moctezuma I, surnamed 'the Wrathy,' set out to conquer Oaxaca in 1469. The Aztecs needed it in order to give their merchants passage down to the Isthmus of Tehuantepec, from there to reach the untouched markets on the western Pacific side of Guatemala and into Central America. They won the temple-city, lost it, and finally, under the next to last leader of the Aztecs, captured it and held it until the arrival of the Spanish. It was well known to the Aztecs and there is definite evidence that they were influenced by its urban planning.

Mitla, called in the Zapotec language *Yoo-paa,* 'Place of the Dead,' is part of the same culture; it lies twenty-five miles directly south of Monte Albán and is not only one of the best-known sites in Mexico but also the best preserved. There are five groups of buildings, extending to both sides of the usually dry Mitla River, all of them constructed with the same basic plan which, Dr. Vaillant has emphasized, characterizes all Mexican structures: rooms formed around a rectangular patio. A cross section of one of the buildings at Mitla suggests how similar Aztec structures were roofed with giant wooden beams. The architectural façade is unique here, although used by the Mayas in Yucatán; the handling of its lines and proportions is unusual. The structures do not stand on pyramids; they are low horizontal masses and have a fortuitous beauty of proportion. There is an austere grandeur in their massive outlines. Aldous Huxley found them 'strangely unlike any of the other pre-Colombian ruins . . . the walls of the temples . . . are decorated with geometric patterns . . . all are manifestly inspired by and based upon textile designs. . . . petrified weaving . . .'

All of these temple-cities, and there are many more, were the source of Aztec architectural ideas and Aztec urban planning. It is cause for regret that so much is gone. Yet, if the history of Aztec architecture is so fragmentary it is because there was so little. There was not, architecturally, any such thing as an 'Aztec Empire.'

Sculpture was the greatest Aztec contribution to art.

A work of art should be measured by its impact, and if one looks at the powerful and awesome goddess Coatlicue, her head of twin serpents, her necklace of human hands and hearts, her arms claw-handed, and her skirt a mass of writhing serpents, it has the same terrible impact that the Assyrian bas-reliefs had on one explorer: 'My hair alternately stood up and flattened down upon seeing them. . . .'

Realism was the high quality of Aztec sculpture. Delicacy is often combined with terror—as in the lifesize scull cut from a piece of almost flawless quartz which grins at the visitor who chances upon it in the British Museum. There are masks carved out of obsidian and then polished; a woman is seen grinding maize, a superb piece chipped out of volcanic basalt. Aztec sculpture had an uncanny vitality and unself-consciousness that makes it appeal to the modern eye, and is somewhat unusual in primitive American art in that it is made to be seen from all sides.

Sculpture was closely linked with architecture. Almost in every structure extant one sees how closely allied were these two functional things—there were sculptured friezes, enormous stone-carved caryatids, columns; sculpture was not a superficial element as in our concept, but a fundamental part of architecture. All of their art was purposeful, functional, and it belonged to religion. Art was purposeful and hieratic; religion was life and life was religion, and sculpture along with all their crafts was tied to it. This is equally true of almost all the art forms of the other tribute states, Babylonia, Assyria and Egypt.

Metalwork arrived late in Mexico, coming up slowly from South America.

None of the early cultures worked metal; it does not appear at Teotihuacán, which was already a memory when the technique of gold and copper working reached Mexico. It was unknown to the early Mayas. It was not practiced in Mexico much before the eleventh century.

Colossal warrior figures, *over fifteen feet tall, supported the roof of one of the main temples at Tula. Here is the carved back of one; originally there were many, each carrying an atl-atl in one hand, an incense bag in the other.*

The mask of Xipe, *the 'Flayed God'. The front view shows the face with open mouth and blank eyes; the lobes have been enlarged to receive the ornamental ear-spool. The back view shows a priest dressed in the flayed skin of Xipe, with elaborate head-dress and surrounded by symbols of the god. It is carved out of black basalt.*

The Mother of the Gods, *Coatlicue. This terrible figure, eight feet tall, with its head of twin serpents, necklace of human hands, hearts and a skull, skirt of writhing snakes and claw hands and feet, must have inspired awe and dread in the people.*

The mosaic serpent, *a double-headed rattlesnake carved of wood, and set with thousands of pieces of turquoise. The bite of a rattlesnake affects the nerves of the spine and causes the dying victim to jerk his head up and down spasmodically—a circumstance which was considered 'God-touched', and which was one of the reasons why this snake was paid such high, almost divine, regard by the Aztecs.*

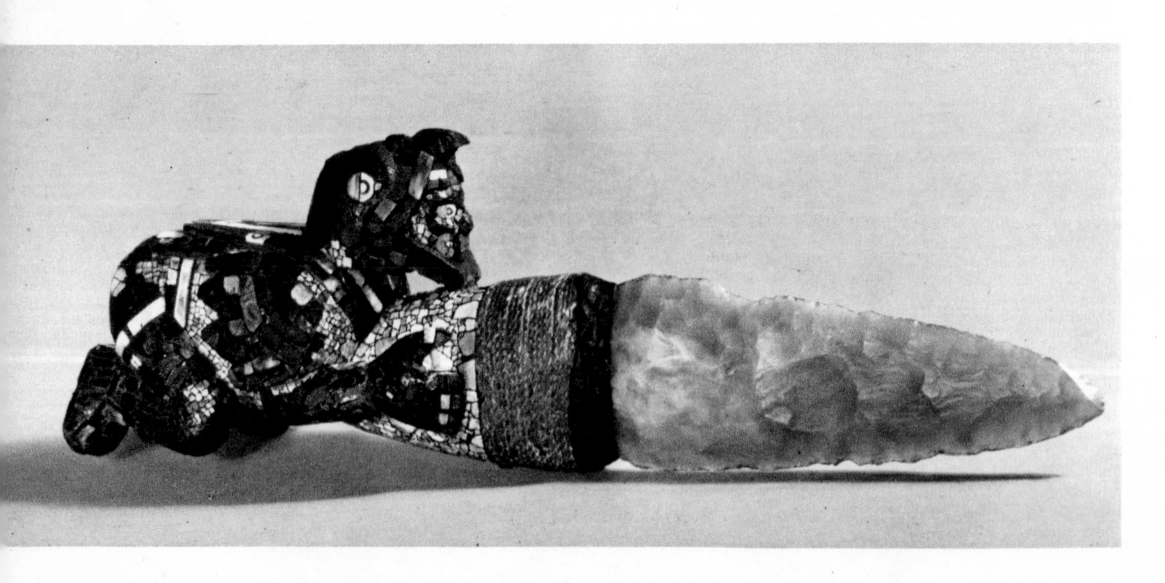

With this knife *Aztec priests cut out the hearts of sacrificial victims. The blade is flint, the handle wooden, carved with a crouching figure and head of a Knight of the Eagle and set with a mosaic of turquoise and carnelian.*

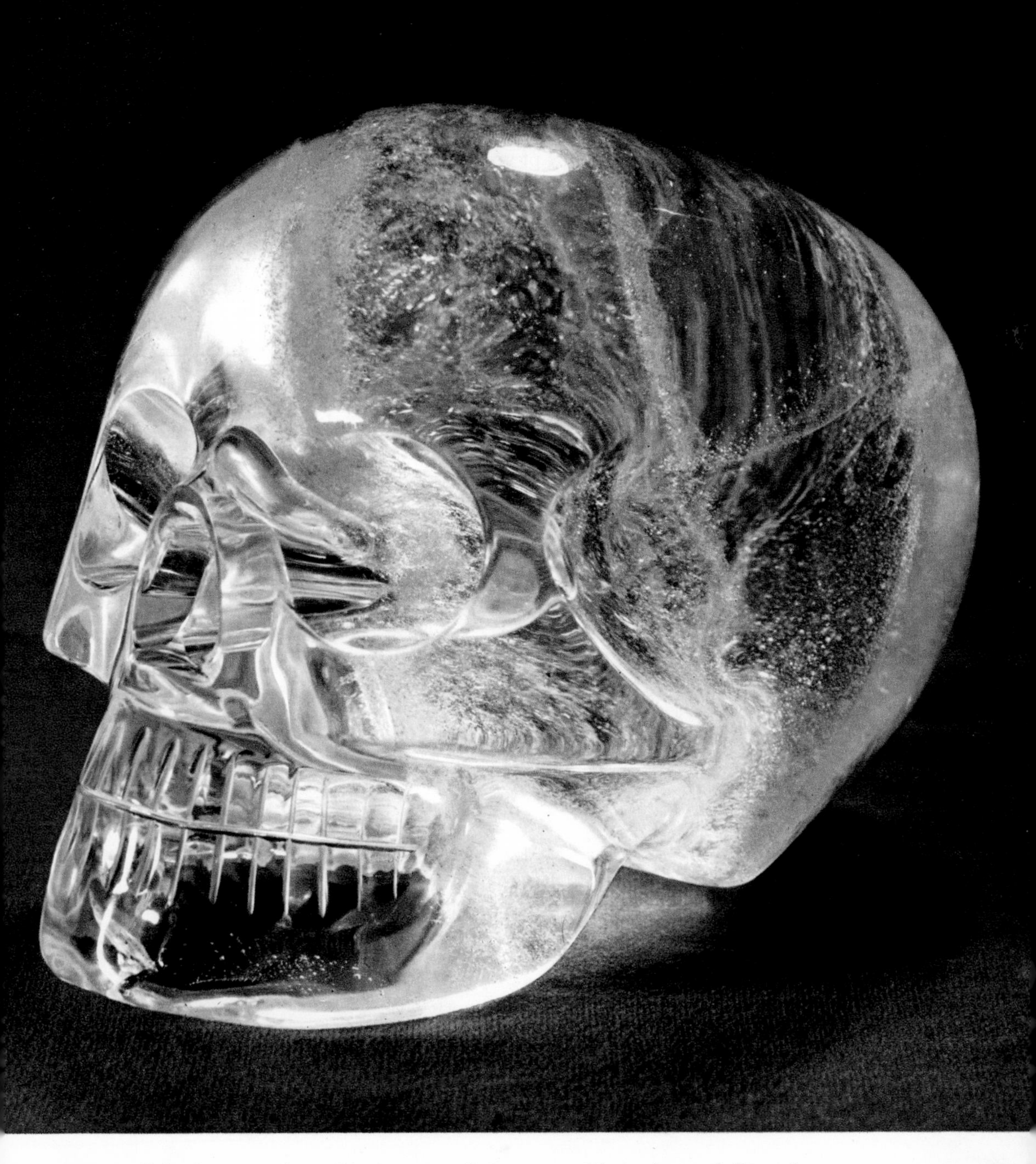

Beauty and death *join together in this masterpiece of Aztec art: a life-size human skull carved from a solid piece of crystal. It is utterly amazing how craftsmen achieved such delicate work when nearly all their tools were of stone.*

Gold was panned or collected in nuggets; silver, which seldom occurs pure in nature, was more of a problem and was less used. Gold is a metal of great ductility, for a single grain can be drawn into a wire five hundred feet long. It was worked by the simplest of techniques. It was melted in a furnace heated by charcoal, draught being supplied by a man blowing through a tube into the charcoal embers. There are few implements extant but we have been left illustrations of goldsmithery. They worked the gold by means of hammering, embossing; plating, gilding, sheathing. Out of this simple, almost crude technique came gold pieces which excited more than the cupidity of the conquistador. There were 'three blow guns,' said Bernal Díaz, 'with their pellet molds and their coverings of jewels and pearls, and pictures of little birds covered with pearl shell.'

Most of the gold extracted from Moctezuma, some 600,000 pesos weight of it, was melted down into ingots; some of it they thought too beautiful to destroy, like the pieces they received at Vera Cruz at the beginning of the adventure: 'a wheel like a sun, as big as a cartwheel, with many sorts

Mixtec-Aztec gold work: *a buckle-ornament representing the Flayed God Xipe—found in Monte Albán. Goldsmiths formed a guild and were attached to Moctezuma's palace. They were freed from work-service tax.*

The head-dress of quetzal plumes, *which Moctezuma thought he was sending to Quetzalcoatl. Cortés received it, with considerable gold treasure, and transmitted it to the Emperor Charles V, who was then in Brussels. On July 12, 1520, Charles gave it to his son, Archduke Ferdinand of Tyrol, who placed it in Schloss Ambras in Innsbruck. It was found four centuries later and identified as one of the few such pieces that escaped war and the insults of time. It is now displayed at the Museum für Völkerkunde in Vienna.*

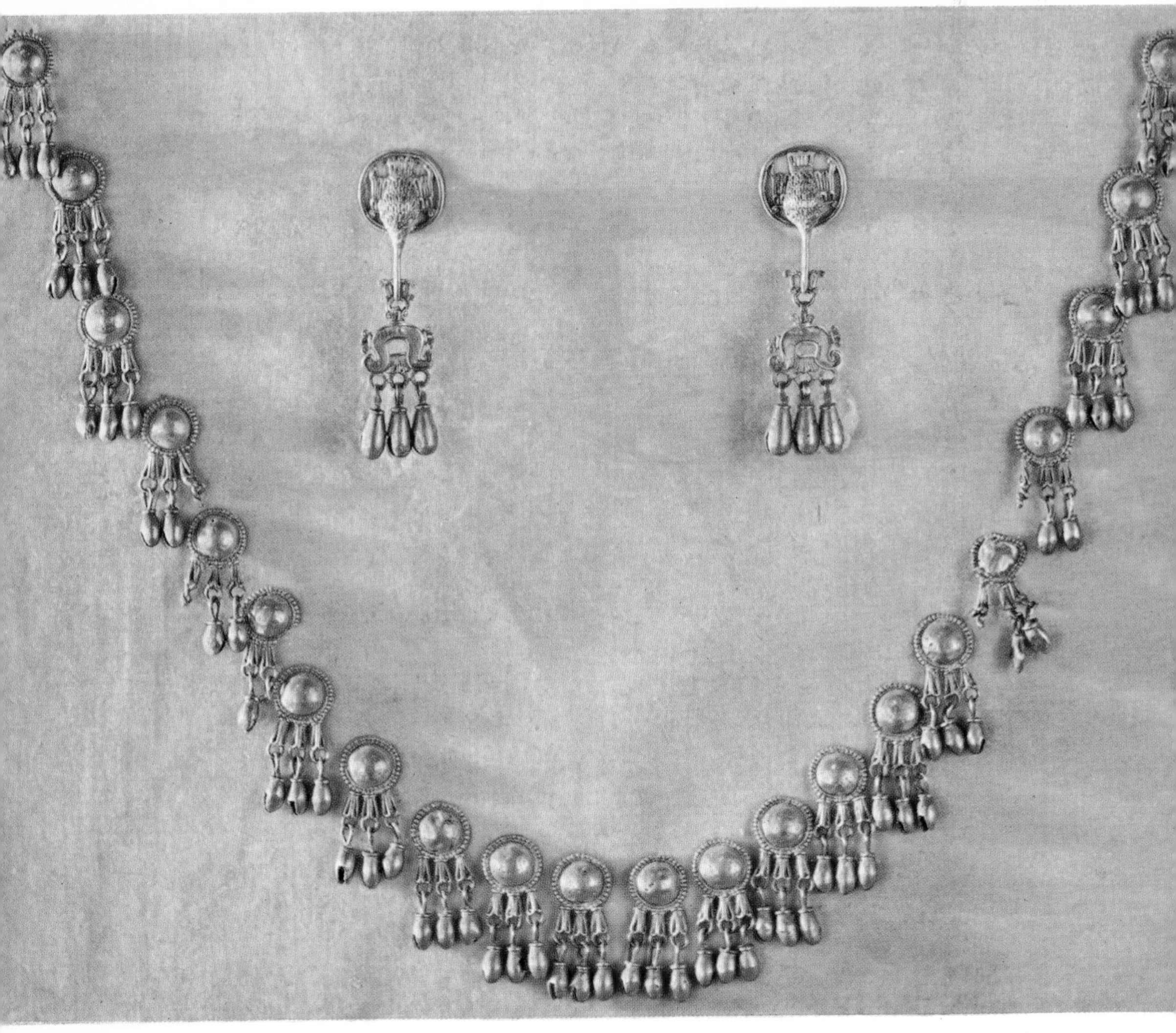

Mixtec gold necklace *found in a tomb at Monte Albán. Although pre-Aztec it gives an idea of the delicacy, workmanship and quality of Aztec gold. Metal came late to Mexico, arriving by slow degrees from South America. Yet Cortés extracted some 600,000 peso-weight of gold work from the Aztecs and a conqueror has recorded what a wonderful thing it was to behold, '... twenty golden ducks, beautifully worked and many other articles of fine gold ...'*

of pictures on it, the whole of fine gold; and a wonderful thing to behold . . . Then another wheel was presented of greater size made of silver of great brilliancy in imitation of the moon . . . Then were brought twenty golden ducks, beautifully worked and very natural looking, and some [ornaments] like dogs, and many articles of gold worked in the shape of tigers and lions and monkeys . . . Twelve arrows and a bow with its string . . . all in beautiful hollow work of fine gold.'

It was only in 1931 when Dr. Alfonso Caso found the undisturbed tomb of a Mexican chieftain at Monte Albán, containing superbly beautiful necklaces, earplugs, and rings, that historians realized that the simple, honest Bernal Díaz was making a magnificent understatement.

Goldsmiths had a guild. Those attached to Moctezuma's many-roomed household were nontaxpayers. They were supplied with placer gold and busied themselves making pieces for Moctezuma and other officials. Bernal Díaz speaks of the 'workers in gold and silver . . . and of these there were a great number in a town named Atzcapotzalco, a league from Mexico.' Since the gold was sold in the market, presumably any craftsman who had enough to barter for the goose quills of gold dust could work it up into jewelry for himself or else for trade.

Lapidaries, workers in precious stones, were many, and like the others: 'skilled workmen Moctezuma employed.' Foremost of the stones was jade. It was an article of tribute and the glyph for it is found in the Book of Tributes. Masks, with their expressionless slit eyes and swollen lips, were sometimes made of it, and were a feature among all of these cultures. Some are exquisite, others are 'vulgar,' stereotyped through constant repetition.

Turquoise came by trade from the north. It was much in demand. The Aztec exacted turquoise as a form of tribute and it so appears from eleven towns on the tribute rolls; it was used with other materials for the making of mosaics on masks, knives, and even walls.

Obsidian glass was an Aztec speciality; it was exported as raw material and as finished product. Found close by, a product of volcanic action, obsidian was used for knives, razors, lip plugs, mirrors of high polish, and other objects of immense beauty.

The feather weaving was another of the Aztec accomplishments. Examples of it have disappeared completely because of conquest and climate. The only examples of real magnificence of this art are preserved by mere accident of history. The rest has perished.

Feather weavers formed a guild and were of the professional class. In feather weaving, quills were inserted into the web, each quill was hooked over a thread and secured by a knot in the second row, leaving only the colour part of the feather visible on the other side. The colour pattern had to

The making of feather mosaics *was a highly developed art among the Aztecs. The Codex Florentino, written by Friar Bernardino de Sahagún and illustrated later, describes how the feathers were gathered, dyed and made into ornaments. Two methods were used, glueing and weaving. In these pictures: a) the design is drawn b) the feathers are dyed c) the glue is applied d) the feathers are fixed to the pattern e) For weaving, the frame is prepared.*

be carefully arranged as a mosaic before the feathers were applied. Shields, headgear, cloaks, banners, totem emblems were all done in feather weaving.

Since colourful birds were limited in the altitudes of Mexico-Tenochtitlán, there was much activity on the part of the merchants to obtain bird feathers when the local supply did not meet the demand.

Birds of all climes were brought alive to Mexico and their habitats simulated; the waterfowl alone had separate pools, as attested by Hernán Cortés: 'ten pools of water in which were kept every kind of waterfowl known.' There was no such thing in Europe until Padua in 1545 erected a zoological garden. The type of food and water depended on the bird. There were three hundred men employed to look after them and 'each pool was overhung by balconies cunningly arranged from which Moctezuma would delight to watch the birds.' In another part were cages for the land birds, wooden trellises cleverly made, 9 feet high and 18 feet around; there were another three hundred men to look after these. Bernal Díaz could not even name all of the various species that he saw in that aviary: 'birds of

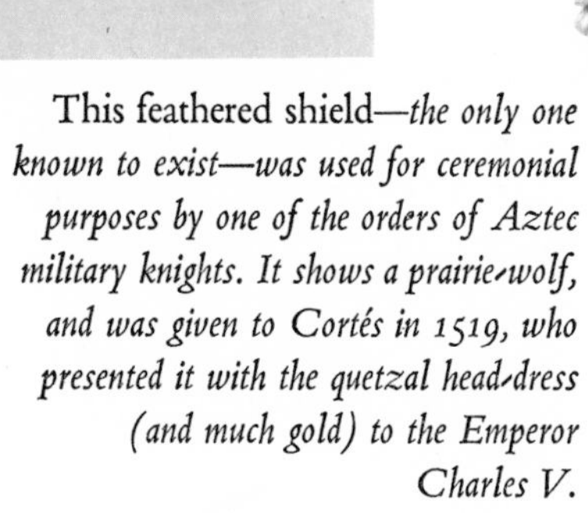

This feathered shield—*the only one known to exist—was used for ceremonial purposes by one of the orders of Aztec military knights. It shows a prairie-wolf, and was given to Cortés in 1519, who presented it with the quetzal head-dress (and much gold) to the Emperor Charles V.*

great size, down to tiny birds of many-coloured plumage . . .' The birds bred in the cages, too. As they moulted, the feathers were gathered, selected, graded, and brought to the feather weavers.

Let no one doubt the magnificence of this art. One piece has been preserved, the headdress sent by Moctezuma to Hernán Cortés when he first landed at Vera Cruz and was believed to be Quetzalcoatl returning to reclaim his empire. This was sent in turn to Charles V, who passed it on to his fellow Habsburg, Archduke Ferdinand of Tyrol; it was long preserved in the castle at Ambras. When discovered and its history made known, it was sent to Vienna, and there today it rests in a burst of golden-green iridescence in the Museum für Völkerkunde—a double assurance, if that be needed, of the Aztecs' sense of beauty.

6 The Will of the Gods

WAR AND RELIGION, to the Aztecs, were inseparable. They belonged to each other. 'It is no exaggeration to say,' observes a recent writer on the subject, 'that the government of [Aztec] Mexico was organized from top to bottom so as to be able to sustain, and thereby mollify, the unseen powers with as many human hearts as it was possible to give them.'

The object of Aztec religion was to attract favourable forces to it and repulse or at least mollify those which were not. They knew that nature moved in a series of rhythmic patterns. They put all their powers of observation to work to discover what these rhythms were and to harness them, not alone for their own good but for all mankind's survival.

Sun worship was an essential part of Aztec religion, and there were gods of the four cardinal directions, each symbolized by his own colour.

There were personal gods, each plant had its god, each function its god or goddess, even suicides had one. Yacatecuhtli was the deity of the merchants. In this polytheistic world all gods had clearly defined traits and functions. So the pantheon grew more complex as the people took to worshipping the different manifestations of the gods.

All this was beyond the pale of mere man. He kept to the little gods. The image of the corn goddess he purchased at the market—a stamped clay figure which he buried in his *milpa* field with prayers and tears. There were household gods set up in some remote corner. There was the goddess of the maguey, Mayahuel, whose spirit was evoked when he drew the sweet syrup and converted it into an intoxicant.

These earth gods were their life. The complicated religious pattern they left to the priests, who told them when to weep, when to get drunk, when to rejoice, when to die. The people seemed content to resign themselves to those who spoke of the unknowable with so great a certainty.

Huitzilopochtli, the Hummingbird Wizard, was the Aztecs' own. He was the sun, the ever-youthful warrior who fought battles with the other gods for man's survival. Each day he rose, fought the night, the stars, the moon, and, armed with sunbolts, brought on the new day. Since he fought these battles for them, the Aztecs could only repay him by nourishing him for his eternal wars. The proffered food could be neither the watered-down intoxicant pulque, nor corncakes such as mortal man ate—the god must be nourished on the stuff of life: blood. It was the sacred duty of every Aztec—for all were part of an agrarian militia—to take prisoners for sacrifice in order to obtain for Huitzilopochli the nectar of the gods—human hearts and blood.

War, eternal war, then, was bound up with religion. How else could human hearts be obtained? A long peace was dangerous, and war thus became the natural condition of the Aztecs, for if the beneficent gods were not nourished they would cease to protect man from the other gods, and this might lead to the total destruction of the world. When the great temple pyramid to Huitzilopochtli was dedicated in Mexico in 1486, 'King' Ahuitzotl, after a two years' war campaign in Oaxaca, amassed more than twenty thousand prisoner victims. These were lined up in rows waiting to be spread-eagled over the sacrificial stone. Their hearts were cut out and held briefly to the sun, then, still pulsating, deposited in the heart urn of the recumbent Chac-Mool figure. The priests directed the intellectual and religious life of Mexico. Two high priests (*quequetzalcoa*) lived in Mexico. Under them was another who administered the business end of tribute tithes and who supervised the schooling of new priests and the establishment of the faith in the newly conquered villages. There were, it is said, five thousand priests attached to the temples in Mexico-Tenochtitlán alone. They dressed in black, their *tilmantli* were ornamented with a border of skulls and entrails. Bernal Díaz said that the priests had 'long robes of black cloth and long hoods like those of the Dominicans . . . The hair of these priests was very long and so matted that it could not be separated or disentangled . . . and [it] was clotted with blood.'

Gods of the Aztecs. *Tezcatlipoca, the great Sky God; Huitzilopochtli (Hummingbird Wizard), the War God; Yacatecuhtli, God of the Travelling Merchants; Tlaloc, the Rain God.*

Day-signs of the Aztec calendar. There were twenty altogether.

13 dog *1 monkey* *2 grass* *3 reed*

They elaborated cult rituals, taught in the religious schools, helped train those who traced out rituals, worked with the *tlacuilo* artists, taught and extended the knowledge of hieroglyphic writing and the symbols of the complicated mathematical and astronomical computations. They intervened with the unseen powers, remembered and chanted the historical events until they became fixed in human memory. This theocracy pervaded everything in Aztec life.

The calendar was at the base of every action of the Aztecs.

There were two calendars, the ritualistic one (*tonalpohualli*), a parade of 260 days; and a second which was a form of solar calendar. The latter consisted of eighteen 20-day months, a lunar reckoning of 360 days plus five uncounted days, the empty *nemontemi*.

The first calendar was magical and sacred; it bore little relation to astronomical observation, and the origin of the cycle has never been satisfactorily explained. It was very ancient; the Aztecs gave it nothing, for it had been known to the Mayas under the name of *tzolkin* for fifteen hundred years. The divinatory cycle consisted of twenty periods of thirteen days. There were twenty day names—*calli* (house), *coatl* (snake), *malinalli* (grass), *tochtli* (rabbit), etc.—which, combined in sequence with the numbers one

Year signs, *confined to four.*

1 house

2 rabb

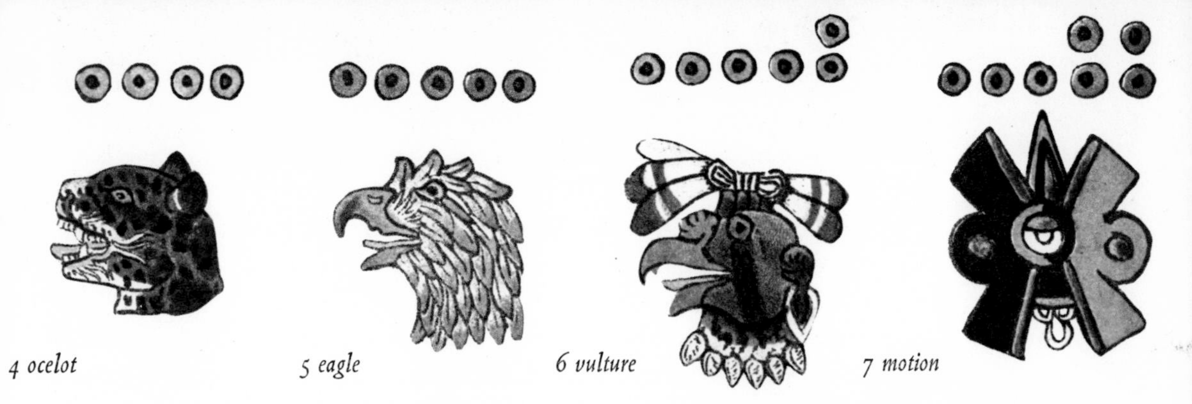
4 ocelot 5 eagle 6 vulture 7 motion

to thirteen, designated the days, such as 1-Grass, 2-Reed, 3-Ocelot, etc., to 13-Lizard, when the next period began. In this example, the name 'Grass,' coming up in its regular position, would coincide with the number 8 in this next period, followed by 9-Reed, 10-Ocelot, etc., to 13-Motion. This pattern recurred again and again in a continuous fifty-two-year solar cycle, or 18,980-day period, in such a way that no day could be confused with any other, since the name of the day and its associated number precluded repetition within the fifty-two years. Each year was named after the day on which it began; thus a year known as 1-Reed would recur every fifty-two years.

The most impressive monument to the system is the Aztec calendar stone. Two years in the carving (1479–81), it stood thirteen feet high and weighed twenty-four tons. It embodies 'a finite statement of the infinity of the Aztec universe,' with the face of the sun god Tonatiuh in the centre and twenty names of days circling it; it is filled with symbols of previous world epochs, symbols of heaven and colour—a grandiose conception of the universe.

The solar 'year-bundle' (*xiuhmolpilli*), as the Aztecs called it, consisted of 365 days, divided into eighteen months of twenty days each. The remain-

3 reed

4 knife

ing five, 'the empty days' (*nemontemi*), were the unlucky days and neither named nor counted, just as in New York City many buildings do not have a thirteenth floor.

The least common multiple of 260 (20 by 13) and 365 (whose primes are 5 and 73), as Franz Boas graphically explained, is 18,980 days. This was the fifty-two-year cycle; after this period the same divinatory combination repeated itself. In another form the Aztec astronomer-mathematicians, or those from whom they obtained this most complicated, ingenious calendar, determined that seventy-three years of the divine calendar (20 by 13 by 73) resulted in the same 18,980 days, making again the magical fifty-two-year cycle.

Why this extraordinary preoccupation with time? Did they find the endless continuity of time so appalling even though they marked it into spatialized periods with rituals and festivals? No one knows. The dominant note was the fifty-two-year cycle; the whole of the tribe's intellectual forces were put to work long before its advent to allay the wrath of the gods.

The priests had to calculate ritual by most involved methods; they had to know the precise interconnection between each particular god and 'time' as given on the calendar. All the developed intellect of the Aztec was turned toward one thing: how to propitiate the right god at the right time. So sacrifice was not mere butchery, it was a parade of elaborately conceived ritual with only one object in view: to preserve human existence.

For the Aztec was threatened not only at the end of each fifty-two-year cycle; when the priests announced the end of each year there came the dreaded *nemontemi*, the 'five empty days.' Fires were extinguished, fasting was general, sexual intercourse ceased; artists left off their work, business lay idle. The same thing occurs in the Austrian Tyrol when the *Föhn*—the warm south wind—blows: important business grinds to a halt. No transactions on these days have legality. On the dawn of the fifth day, when the priest-astronomers, consulting their calendar books, observed the Pleiades rising in the heavens and knew the world would not end, they reached out, and found a sacrificial victim, slashed open his chest, pulled out his heart, and in the freshly weeping wound kindled a new fire; from it all the fires in the temples were rekindled; and from it people all over Mexico-Tenochtitlán gathered the new fire for the new year.

All was right once more with the Aztec world. War was related directly to religion (captives for sacrifice). It was related to economy (supplying tribute for the tribute state). War was an Aztec preoccupation; it was sacred; it had a mystic religious quality which made it all the more ferocious. Every able-bodied man was a warrior, part of an agrarian militia; the only professional army in the Aztec confederation was the small coterie of well-born

The gigantic Aztec calendar stone, *13 feet in diameter, representing the history of the world as conceived by Aztec cosmology. In the centre is the sun. The twenty day names, enclosed by glyphs, circle the sun. Two large serpents, whose fanged mouths meet, are symbols of time. This stone was found in 1790 when the Cathedral of Mexico City, built over the Aztec temple, was repaired.*

warriors who formed the bodyguard of the Chief Speaker. The Aztecs had national military service hundreds of years before Napoleon returned to nature by using a mass army without regard to losses (instead of the artificial manoeuvres with small bodies of troops favoured in Baroque times).

War as a branch of politics began with the pow-wow. Ambassadors, called *quauhaquauh nochtzin*, were sent to the village or tribe to persuade them to join the Aztec 'commonwealth'; trade and road protection were offered. With the compact came the demand that the Aztec national god Huitzilopochtli be placed alongside their local deity. They were to be allowed to

The Stone of Tizoc. *Upon this stone, chieftains were supposed to have taken the oath to Tizoc, and in later years the leaders gathered in front of it when war had been decided. Carved during*

keep their own dress, manners, and chieftains; they would yield tribute every six months. Negotiations were long and involved; they were given the length of a lunar calendar month to capitulate.

When war was decided the leaders gathered in front of the stone of Tizoc in the great plaza. Set up during the reign of Tizoc (1481–86), the large cylindrical block of trachyte, eight feet in diameter and carved with figures in low relief, shows Aztec warriors capturing others in battle, symbolized by the warrior grasping a lock of the enemy's hair. It was set up facing the great *teocalli*; there or near to it the final act of war was set in motion.

Tizoc's reign (1481–1486) the bas-relief shows Tizoc, dressed as Huitzilopochtli, capturing enemies by their hair, which was the symbol of conquest, as in ancient Egypt.

Aztec warriors, *showing their weapons, elaborate headgear (intended to overawe the enemy), shields and face-painting, all part of war equipment. The round shields, made of wood covered with*

The war lord held office only the duration of a particular campaign. He was generally related by blood ties to the Chief Speaker. His war dress was elaborate. It was impossible not to discern him in battle and one of the prime objects was his capture. The élite of battle, the military order of the Eagle, wore a mimicry of an open eagle's beak and feather weavings of eagle feathers; the military order of the Jaguar dressed in jaguar skins; the soldiers, other common warriors from the clans, wore distinct tunics. Their shields also bore a totemic device of their clan. Before they set off, priests had to consult the *tonalamatl* to divine if the moment was propitious for victory.

The Aztecs, in comparison with the European standards of 1519, were lightly armed. Headgear when worn was more decorative than protective. They wore quilted cotton tunics, soaked in brine; as Bernal Díaz observed,

animal hide, are decorated with the crests of the clan. Obsidian blades are fixed into the spear-heads. The warriors wore quilted cotton tunics, soaked in brine—armour superior to the Spanish.

they 'wore armour made of cotton reaching to the knees.' For the hot country it was superior to Spanish armour. All carried shields made of wood covered with animal hide, many extremely decorative, with the totemic device of the clan. The closing-in weapon was the *maquahuitl*; it was of hardwood edged with blades of obsidian sharp enough for a warrior to sever a horse's head. The bow with obsidian-tipped arrows, they used with deadly effectiveness 'and great skill,' confesses Bernal Díaz, who received many in his time; 'the first flight of arrows wounded fifteen soldiers.'

The nature of the land conditioned strategy. Wars had to be of short duration, for since there were no beasts of burden, everything had to be carried on the backs of the men themselves. There was no system of supply such as the Incas in Peru set up along finely developed roads. Siege wars under these conditions were almost impossible. Besides, the Aztec plan was not to slaughter unnecessarily or destroy; death and destruction would imperil tribute, which was the primary aim of the battle, along with the need for sacrificial victims.

The watery defence of Mexico-Tenochtitlán was a deterrent to any save the Spanish, for in general there were no fortifications. Fighting was in the open. All had the same type of arms; what counted most in battle was surprise, ambush, morale. Battle began with a war of nerves: there were military promenades to overawe the enemy; warriors came with drums, conch-shell horns (the type seen in the Maya murals at Bonampak). The Spaniards in their first encounter got the same treatment; the Indians were 'drawn up in battle array whistling and sounding their trumpets and drums.'

Before the campaign got under way, ambassadors had to be sent to towns and villages, subject or not, to arrange for supplies. It was almost impossible to hide intent in a major undertaking. In some instances the Aztecs deliberately refrained from use of surprise, not only giving their enemy time to arm, but sometimes even sending them arms, to develop the premise that the outcome on the battlefield was, in truth, the will of the gods.

When at a distance of an arrow flight from each other, the opposing warriors released their shafts over the heads of their forward forces; then they hurled rocks, accurately enough, from plaited cotton slings. Spears followed, which really wrought havoc, then in a welter of noise and fearful shouting they fell on each other with the *maquahuitl*, the closing-in weapon. The object was to capture the leader. Often this alone was enough to decide the issue—a single battle could suffice; again enmities could be protracted over the years. Slaughter was only to cause a rout; when that happened prisoners were taken. In token of victory the Aztecs burned the temple, for that was the symbol of conquest in their glyph writing. Then the tribute tribunal fixed the amount and kind to be yielded every six months. The warrior-prisoners were sent to Tenochtitlán to be held for sacrifice; if the tribe was unreliable, an Aztec garrison was placed close by and their chieftains were sent as hostages to the Aztec capital. No attempt was made at absorption of the newly conquered into Tenochtitlán.

The guilds of 'commercial travellers,' the *pochteca*, were a law unto themselves. They had distinct prerogatives. They lived in their own wards or *calpulli* (Pochtlán was one), guild rights passed from father to son; they paid no taxes; they had their own gods; and they were not subject to the ordinary law tribunals.

The *pochteca* were a rather late development in Aztec society. Their own chronicles said, 'commerce began in Mexico-Tenochtitlán in the year 1504'; assuredly it was earlier. It rose out of the great social surplus piled up in the city as a result first of tribute and then of the manufacturing activities of a people somewhat relieved from constant attention to agriculture. In and about the city the manufactured cotton cloth, rabbit-fur robes, obsidian and copper mirrors, cosmetics (a tincture of cochineal with grease) for face painting, medicinal herbs, flower pastes as a base for perfumes. Salt, which they leached out of the lakes, and other stuff that was light enough for long journeys, were also in the list. In return for these things the directing classes and the common man alike wanted from the hotlands cotton, feathers, precious stones, chocolate, rubber. The *pochteca,* like the early traders of the Old World, were purveyors of luxuries.

Trade was their monopoly. Days, weeks, months were spent by them acquiring the articles for trade at the various markets; they then assembled carriers who were capable of carrying sixty pounds on their backs, and the human caravan set off. In regions where conditions were not fully secure they were accompanied by Aztec warriors. Trade has always been sacrosanct. The way to bring down swift reprisal was to plunder them. If one of their numbers died in a far-off land he was given the same rites as a warrior slain in battle.

Aztec trading colonies under the *pochteca* penetrated to Guatemala, going down the Pacific Coast (which was not controlled by the Mayas) as far south as Nicaragua. Their caravans were often gone for a full two years. They also left colonists behind, small 'islands' of Nahuatl-speaking peoples called *pipil,* who, even now, show their Nahuatl origin in their designs on pottery and weaving and their use of the symbol of Tlaloc, the Aztec rain god.

Merchants on the road. *Man was the carrier in Mexico. There were no dray animals such as llamas; slaves, or tribesmen who had lost status, were employed as carriers; more often than not merchandise was carried from one village to another by tribesmen selected by the village cacique.*

Merchants report to Moctezuma. *They brought him luxuries from the hotlands.*

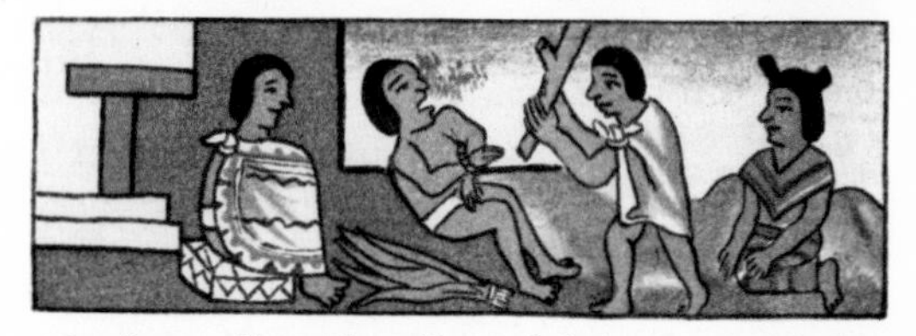

Merchants formed a class of their own *with their own laws—a closed group, highly respected. Here we see a merchants' court in session and (below) a merchant being punished. If a merchant died in a foreign land he was given the same rites as a warrior killed in battle.*

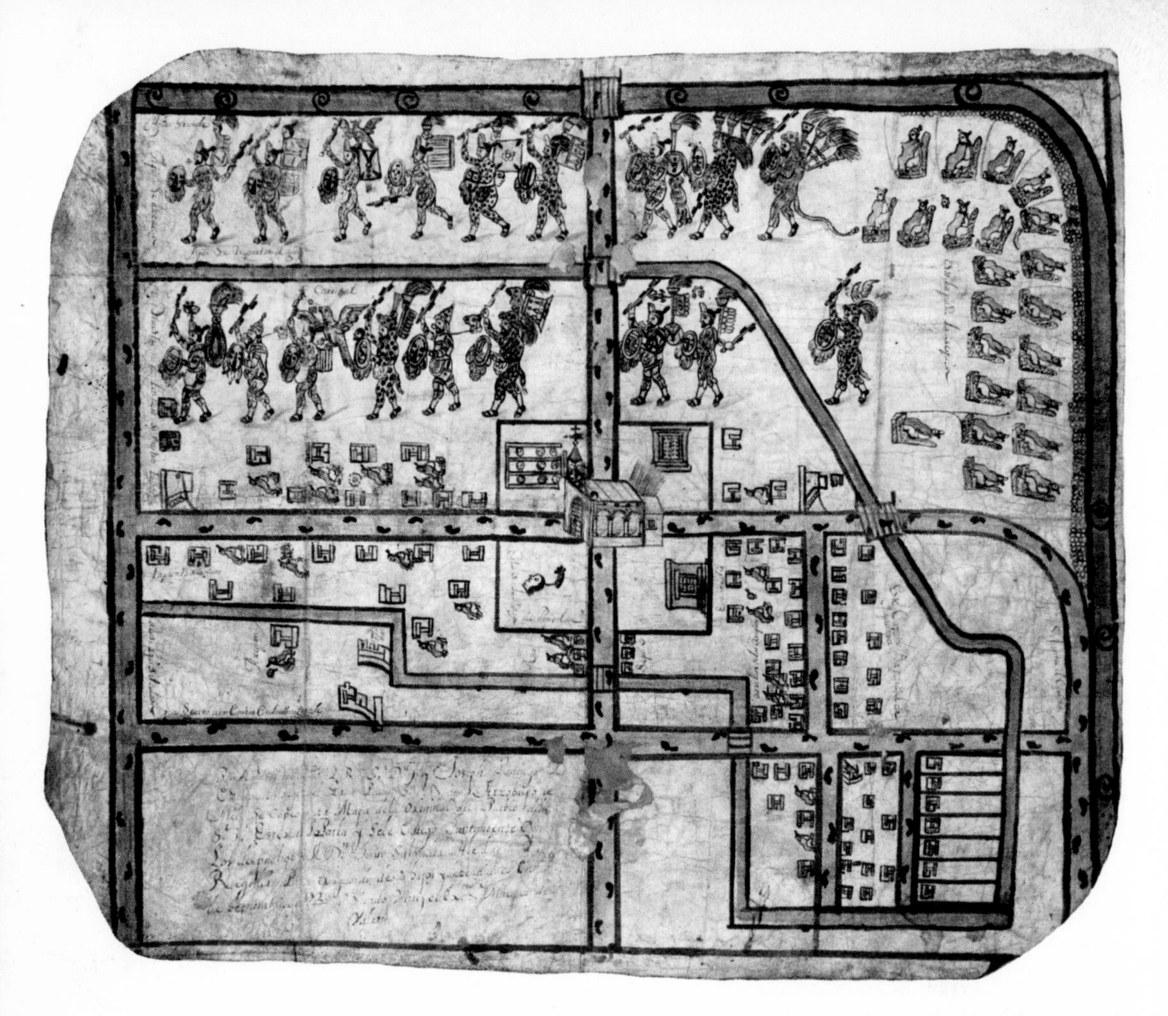

Aztec roads leading through a village—*the footprints indicate that they have been recently travelled—with symbols for houses, and a company of warriors dressed for battle. This example is post-Conquest (note the Christian church in the centre), but Cortés had used maps very like it.*

Little is known of Aztec roads or communications. That there *were* roads and good communications must be assumed. Yet there have been no connected studies of Aztec roads such as have been made of the network of the Maya *sacbeob*, nor has there been such an extensive survey as the von Hagen expedition study of the Inca highways on the west coast of Peru.

The best-known Aztec road, since it was the one that Cortés and his small army followed from the hotlands to the uplands of Mexico, was that which ran from Vera Cruz to Mexico-Tenochtitlán; the precise route has been identified.

The wheel, except as used in children's toys, was totally absent in Mexico. The whole principle of the wheel as arch was unknown, as was the potter's wheel and the rotary quern. Even if the wheel had been known, it is doubtful that it could have served much without draft animals. Instead the Aztecs used the litter. This conveyance for the exalted was universal in the Old World as well as the New; few advanced cultures were without it. The Aztecs seem to have considered it only a ceremonial device and not, as among the Incas and the Chimús in South America, a mode of transport. To the Spanish, Moctezuma first appeared being carried in a litter along the great causeways out of the city. There is no mention, however, of the litter being used beyond this; when Cortés took along the unfortunate last Aztec 'king,' Cuauhtemoc, on his expedition to Honduras, he walked as did the rest of the Indians.

Water transport was limited to the lakes. The Aztecs constructed dug-out canoes—almost everyone seems to have had one in this Venice-like city. Much of the lacustrine commerce was carried on by water. Canoes brought in produce. They removed the excreta from the public toilets so as not to pollute the city and used it for fertilizer.

The Aztecs used no other type of boat larger than the dugout; when Cortés built two moderate-sized sloops on the lakes of Mexico, he took the

The Mexican did know the wheel *in various forms, but it was used mostly in a non-utilitarian manner, as this children's toy. Wheels as a means of moving heavy objects or as rotary querns for grinding were utterly missing from all American Indian life.*

Litters *were used when men of the highest rank travelled. Here Moctezuma himself is carried on the shoulders of two men, while a third blows a conch-shell in front of him.*

Paddling a canoe. *Water transport was limited to the lakes, and canoes were only as big as the tree-trunks from which they were made. From the Codex Mendoza.*

captive Moctezuma for a sail to a distant isle, skimming over the wind-swept waters, so that 'Moctezuma was charmed and said it was a great thing this combining sails and oars together.'

Couriers were employed on the roads to carry messages. Beyond the fact that they existed there is little more reference to them, whereas those Spaniards who went from Mexico to Peru were astounded at the Inca system of *chasquis*, who, running in relays, could cover a distance of 1,250 miles in five days.

Pictographic communications were put into a forked stick. It is not known for certain but it is probable that an artist accompanied the runners on important missions. At Vera Cruz Cortés was amazed upon receiving an embassy from Moctezuma who 'brought with them some clever painters ... and ordered them to make pictures true to nature of the face and body of Cortés and all his captains, and of the soldiers, ships, sails and horses ... even of the two greyhounds; and the cannon balls ...' Later he found when in Mexico that Moctezuma had known every action of theirs since they touched the shores of Mexico.

Thus the Aztecs had roads, wayside rest houses, roadside gods, couriers, and, through their pictographic writing a good form of communications. The Europe of 1519 had not as much. 'To journey in Europe,' wrote Awaliyal Effendi in 1611, '... is like a fragment of hell.' Roads in the sixteenth century were paved like hell in the proverb, and many the complaint that travel was a purgatory 'in little.' To move over Europe's roads one had

to have 'a falcon's eye, an ass's ears, a monkey's face, a merchant's words, a camel's back, a hog's mouth, a deer's feet.'

It is small wonder that the conquistadors praised the Aztec roads.

All advanced civilizations (with the amazing exception of South American cultures such as the Inca, Chimú, Mochica, and Tiahanaco) had some form of paper, some form of writing, and some form of literature. In all these phases of culture the Aztecs excelled. Paper (*amatl*) was an article of tribute. On the tribute lists of Moctezuma one reads: 'twenty-four thousand reams of paper are to be brought as a tribute yearly to Tenochtitlán.' Twenty-four thousand of these reams would be 480,000 sheets and judged by any standard this is an enormous consumption of paper.

A form of paper was made in Yucatán and Mexico. There is no manner of dating its appearance, but probably it was used as paper among the Mayas as early as 1000 B.C. The Mayas folded their *huun* paper and made polychromic books of it. The paper prepared from the inner bast fibres of the wild fig trees was, in use and appearance, like true paper. There are only three such Maya 'books' or codices left of those that escaped the 'burning of the books' in Yucatan by Bishop Diego de Landa.

All of the advanced cultures in Mexico had paper and writing. The Toltecs had glyph writing and the same graphic techniques; they are credited with having an encyclopedic *teoamextli*, a divine book compiled in A.D. 660; neither it nor others like it have survived. The Mixtecs at Cholula had paper and writing; several of their codices are extant. So did the Zapotecs in Oaxaca and the Totonacs in Vera Cruz. Bernal Díaz saw piles of books near the Totonac city-state of Cempoala: 'Then we came on some towns ... [and] found idol houses ... and many paper books doubled together in folds like Spanish cloth ...'

Paper and writing, then, were not an Aztec invention; the Aztecs, however, perfected them.

The fact that the Indians had books and writing greatly astonished the conquistador: 'There is so much to think over,' said Bernal Díaz, 'that I do not know how to describe it, seeing things as we did that had never been heard or seen before or even dreamed about.' So much so that they sent back to Spain, along with the first gold collected, two of such books. Fortunately these fell into the hands of the Italian humanist Pietro Martire d'Anghiera, who was then in Seville; he, corresponding with the learned, wrote about 'books such as the Indians use.'

The Aztec glyph for *amatl* was a roll. Yet there were other types. A yellow paper always sold in sheets came from the town of Amacoztitlán on the Rio Amacuzac in the state of Morelos; it derived from the fibres of the yellow wild fig, the *Ficus petiolaris*. This whole area, in a tropical setting of under 5,000 feet, was *the* paper manufacturing centre of ancient Mexico. Itzamatitlán, a village in Morelos on the Rio Yuatepec, was the source of yet another type of paper.

The greater bulk of the paper was used to keep the genealogies, trial records, land records, for each ward or *calpulli* had its land registers and tribute rolls. There were hundreds, perhaps thousands, of such 'books.' Bernal Díaz thumbed through them when he wandered into the endless rooms of Moctezuma's palace; he followed an 'accountant' and he saw 'all the revenue that was brought ... [and recorded] in his books which were made of paper which they call *amatl*, and he had a great house full of these books.'

Like all early writing, Aztec writing was nonphonetic. It was not capable of any general statement nor could abstract ideas be expressed. Aztec writing, in 1519, was still pictographic: a wrapped mummy figure was a symbol of death; migrations or movements along the road were expressed by footprints; seeing was expressed by an eye projected beyond the viewer; speaking was a wagging tongue; a mountain was symbolized so obviously that even one untrained in reading Aztec glyphs would know it.

There was naturally no alphabet to this system, yet the Aztecs did combine a series of pictorial elements, often abstract, to give complicated meanings; by these methods as well as by puns, colour, position, they produced a staggering amount of records.

Their literature was mostly history, annals of ancient times, year counts, books of the day and the hours—even diaries. There were observations of planetary events, eclipses, movements of stars, observations of celestial phenomena which had affected or might affect their present. There was much out of the past; for their mythopoetic faculty was well developed. They were poets and most delighted when writing and singing of the past—for only the past is really poetic. One of their chief concerns was this; their 'histories,' recorded on paper, showed the migrations, the stopping-off places, the wars, conflicts, founding of cities. Their sacred almanacs were scarcely literature nor were their tribal records, land registers, lines of descent, and tribute charts.

The rise and fall of Mexico is a tale that no matter how often retold never seems to lose the patina of romance. The Spanish who took active part in it felt the historicity of the moment: Hernán Cortés penned his famous *Five Letters* even while wading through the sea of Aztec blood. Three other Spaniards who participated left their impressions as well, including that wonderful Bernal Díaz del Castillo, one who even at the age of eighty-four could not forget its impact: '. . . it all comes before my eyes as though it had happened but yesterday.'

Hernán Cortés arrived at a psychological moment in Mexico (just as in Peru Francisco Pizarro came when the Incas had just gone through a civil war). A god, Quetzalcoatl, was expected from the east. Columbus made contact with the Mayas in his fourth and last voyage in 1502. This amazing bit of intelligence, enlarged every time it was told and retold, came to the ears of Aztec merchants who were trading near Yucatán at the ancient market of Xicalango at that time. Moctezuma came into power in 1503. During his reign white men continued to appear and disappear along the Gulf shores. Quetzalcoatl, the culture hero of these Americas, who was expelled from his land, vowed as he sailed away into that selfsame Gulf sea that 'on the date of my birth which is Ce-Acatl, the year of 1-Reed—*I will return.*' According to the Aztec calendar this year 1-Reed could only fall, in the Christian calendar reckoning, in the years 1363, 1467, or 1519. In 1519 Hernán Cortés appeared on the shores of Vera Cruz, and one of the first gifts sent to him by Moctezuma was a magnificent headdress of quetzal plumes. Long before this the Aztec people had gone through years of tribulations; they felt their insecurity as their priests searched the heavens and the earth for portents of disaster. Long columns of sacrificial victims were taken from tribute villages and immolated on the sacrificial block so that the gods might bring them answers to their questionings about the strange creatures that were appearing and disappearing on their shores. It was natural that these demands upon other tribes for sacrificial victims would alienate them; even those tribes who had been friendly for two hundred

Cortés and his army attacking Xolloco. *This illustration is by a native artist working thirty or forty years after the event, and in a style much influenced by his Spanish conquerors.*

years were desperately angry over the drain on their own kin; bonds between conqueror and conquered were loosened. But the Aztecs in fear and uncertainty increased the pressure.

Then Hernán Cortés appeared. He came with new weapons, horses, steel armour, and new gods. Two different worlds, two different human natures, met. The Aztec had no concept of himself as a separate absolute entity; he thought in terms of clan. The Spaniard believed in his own person; the most real reality of his world was his own individual soul.

On Saint Hippolytus' Day, August 13, 1521, in the stench of a thousand fires, the Spanish Conquest was complete and the Aztec civilization passed into limbo.

The mask of Izamal. *In 1842 Stephens and Catherwood explored this Maya site. Catherwood's romantic drawing shows the ruins by moonlight; it is the only record we have of the colossal mask on the step pyramid which is now wrecked.*

II Cities of the Jungle: THE MAYAS

7 The Missing Years of Maya History

AN AIR of mystery hangs still over Maya civilization, a mystery which it has had ever since its chance discovery by Christopher Columbus in 1502. Despite the fact that for the four succeeding centuries, conquistadors, priests, historians, geographers, archaeologists, engineers—with a fair sprinkling of picaros—have tried to push aside the veils of the Mayan Isis most of the fundamental facts about them remain unknown.

Much, if not all of our knowledge of the ancient Mayas—those that existed before 900 A.D., when the great Maya cities were built—is based on deduction, because a preliterate people can only be seen through their art. They are otherwise inarticulate. From the vague Maya beginnings, somewhere around 2000 B.C. down to A.D. 987 there are no tangible records and no traditions, nothing but the evidence of their existence—and this in an overwhelming degree—contained in the remains of buildings, sculpture, murals and pottery. What the Mayas were really like as human beings is known only through inference.

Maya history with some degree of certitude begins after 900 A.D. when these people began their 'great descent', that is when they abandoned the large population centres, such as Copán, Tikal, and Palenque and 'descended' into the peninsula of Yucatán. From this day forward the Mayas have 'books', glyph-written illustrated books, which deal with mythology, astronomy (or rather, largely astrology) and a kind of history which, however vague, has confirmation by oral and 'written' traditions outside the Maya area.

After the fall of the Aztecs in 1521, it became the turn of the Mayas. They had been by-passed by Hernán Cortés, in 1519, since that very worthy conquistador did not believe that they offered much in the way of golden loot. His instinct proved to be true. The Spanish conquest of the Maya had neither the impact nor the dramatic finality of that of the Aztec. Francisco de Montejo who began it lived to regret it; in point of historical fact he died in his regret. There was no precise centre or capital of the Maya and the conquest was long and costly in human lives. It dragged on from 1527 to 1546—and then only was won through a combination of factors—annihilation, plague, weariness. Final and complete victory was not assured until 1697.

Christopher Columbus, *on his fourth and last voyage in 1502, landed on an island off the coast of Honduras. There he met an Indian trading party in an immense dugout canoe. When asked from whence they came, the Indians replied 'from a certaine province called Mayam'. This old engraving shows Columbus arriving in America, accompanied by interested sirens and Father Neptune.*

However after 1542, when Yucatán settled down under its yoke of peace, and Spanish cities were raised out of the rubble of Maya culture, the padres began their spiritual conquest of the defeated people. It is at this point that Maya history becomes alive, for much of the detail that we know of Maya daily life, as well as an outline of their mythology, religion and history, comes out of the reports of these God-inspired men. They wrote these in a form of *relaciones,* informal histories which were intended to guide and instruct the Spanish court. The most important for Maya history is that of the Franciscan Diego de Landa, whose small manuscript *Account of the Things of Yucatán,* is the source of most of the informative quotations in this book. Arriving in Yucatán in 1549, he quickly became adept at the Maya language; his interests remained broad; his Mayan informants were of the best and considering the nature of his task—to blot out their ancient ways and make them accept new ones in their place—he remained amazingly objective. The great historical value of his work—which although written in 1566 was not discovered and published until the 19th century—is attested by the numerous editions of the *Things of Yucatán*.

Meanwhile, the insults of time blotted out the great Maya cities from human memory; those that were not purposefully torn down to provide building material for the new Spanish settlements were reclaimed by the land. In time the jungles wove about them a verdure that hid them from human sight and therefore memory. There was, to be sure, an occasional chance discovery, such as occurred in 1576 when Copán was found by Diego Garcia de Palacio. Unable to believe that the Indians could have built it he ascribed it to the Romans and speculated in a report to his King just how the Romans got there . . . 'I shall try to find out . . . what people lived there . . .' But that was all. Maya archaeological history began at the ruins of Palenque. It was in 1773 at the time when the Old World was reviving its interest in the 'Antique' that Palenque was discovered. In the mid 1st millennium A.D. it had been one of the great ceremonial and population centres of the Mayas but in the 9th century it was abandoned; after 900 no-one was even dimly aware of it until an Indian chanced to come across it. He told a priest, who wrote a report and this in time reached that intellectual monarch, Carlos III, who sent out Italian architects all the way from Spain to prepare reports and collect its art so that it might illustrate that which he felt necessary for a proposed *Ancient History of America*.

Since that time, some of the greatest names of archaeology have been connected with the unravelling of the Maya mystery: there was Humboldt, who first printed pages of the famed Dresden Maya Codex; Waldeck, the amazing Jean Frédéric de Waldeck, who lived to be 109 years of age and regarded himself at the time of his death as the most noble ruin in Paris. The gently mad Irish aristocrat, Edward King, Viscount Kingsborough, gave his fortune and eventually his life to compile the monumental 'Antiquities of Mexico'; Prescott adumbrated something of the Mayas in his 'Conquest of Mexico'—but it was the New York lawyer John Lloyd Stephens who really discovered them with the aid of his friend, the English-born architect Frederick Catherwood, one of the finest archaeological architects, in both worlds, Old and New, ever to appear on this variegated earth . . . Men of many nations and many interests have worked, pondered and written about the Mayas and so they have not remained anywhere the exclusive concern of any one nationality. And now, even the Russians, although lately arrived in

The land of the Mayas, *now Yucatán, Guatemala and British Honduras. The chief Maya sites are shown; many more lie in the jungle and forest lowlands, unsurveyed and unexplored.*

N

GULF OF MEXICO

Cape Catoche

Ekab

Buct-zotz

Dzibilchaltún

Tho (Merida)

Izamal

Chichén Itzá

YUCATÁN

Cozumel I.

Cobá

Mayapán

Yaxuná

Xelha

Soliman

Tancah

Tulum

PUUC

Maní

Uxmal

Labná

Kabah

Jaina

Sayil

Kewic

Holactún

QUINTANA ROO

Champotón

Santa Rita

Chetumal Pen.

CAMPECHE

CARIBBEAN SEA

Xicalango

L. de Términos

Calakmul

BRITISH HONDURAS

ASCO

Uaxactún

San José

Tikal

Palenque

Lake Petén

Piedras Negras

Usumacinta

CHIAPAS

Yaxchilán

Bonampak

Nito

Omoa

Quiriguá

GUATEMALA

HONDURAS

Copán

Santa Lucía

SALVADOR

Maya history, claim attention; Dr Yuri Knorosow claims to have the 'key' to the Maya enigma.

However, the simple Indian, creator of all this civilization, should not be allowed, as he often is, to disappear wholly in technical discussions of time and tide, number and astrophysics; the Maya was human, all-too-human. Who he was and what he was and how he came to be will be the essential theme of this chapter.

In the beginning Yucatán was not called 'Yucatán'. When Spaniards following the spoor of Columbus's earlier visit chanced upon numerous Maya buildings dotting the coastline, they landed peacefully enough and in time enquired, in Spanish, naturally, who they, the Mayas, were. They answered: 'Ci-u-than'. It meant, actually, 'We don't understand you', but the Spaniards took this for an answer and in time, those words 'Ci-u-than' became 'Yucatán'. Yet when Bernal Díaz de Castillo, conquistador and historian appeared, he tried as usual to preserve 'a true history of things'; he soon discovered that Yucatán was not its true name . . .'The Mayas . . . now say their country is 'Yucatán' and so it keeps that name, but in their own language they do not call it by that name.' Instead they called it 'The Land of the Turkey and the Deer'—suggesting that it was a land of milk and honey, and so it must have seemed to them.

Yucatán physically appears to be as some gigantic thumb projecting itself northward into the Gulf of Mexico. It is a peninsula of pure limestone, covered by a dry forest. As the land of the Mayas recedes inwardly, the rainfall increases and so does the jungle. The land gradually rises until it is transformed into towering mountains, the Pacific ranges—over 13,000 feet. Of volcanic origin, these yielded a basalt stone, out of which the Maya fashioned *metatls,* grinding stones; and on these they brayed their maize, to make their bread. The volcanic mountains also yielded obsidian, from which knives, mirrors, razors were made. Other geological formations yielded jade—a stone which seemed almost as important to them as life itself. In the high mountain-forests lived red and green guacamayos, important for Maya ritual, and as well, the quetzel bird—who gave its long jade-green tail feathers to deck the headgear of Maya chieftains.

In the lowland areas where the great temple-cities were located—Tikal, Uaxactún, Yaxchilán, Calakmul—is El Petén. Here rain forests alternate with depressed areas, which are seasonal swamps called *skalches*; and high bush with alternating savannas of tall grass. It is the least likely place one would choose for developing a culture, yet it is precisely here that the earliest-known Maya cities are found. The lowland jungles are set upon plateaus of limestone and are amazingly fertile, yielding valuable trees and plants which were of great use to the Maya economy. Giant cedars were

Above the thick forests of El Petén *rises the leafy summit of Pyramid I at Tikal. Lost in impenetrable thickets and covered with vegetation so that they look like natural hills, Maya ruins are still often discovered by accident.*

fashioned into outsized canoes eighty feet long for navigation on the Caribbean. Copal, an odoriferous resin, as essential to the Mayas as amber was to the Greeks, was a commodity of 'very great business for them'; it was burned on all priestly occasions. There was the brazilwood, used for dyeing Maya cloth; and the sapodilla, or 'chewing-gum tree,' which yielded a fine-tasting fruit as well as the chicle sap. Lignum vitae, as hard as iron, was 'a specific against syphilis and buboes.'

The tropical jungles thin out and disappear in the 'thumb' proper, which is the present state of Yucatán. This limestone zone, low and flat as a tortilla, characterizes the whole northern part of the peninsula. 'It was a country,' remembers Diego de Landa, 'with the least amount of earth I have ever seen. . . . it all seems to be one living rock . . . this because there is only a small cap of earth over the limestone and in many places it is less than six inches in depth.' Despite its apparent flatness, the land is broken up into limestone outcrops and depressions with a profusion of loose stones—*dzekel,* the Mayas called these hillocks of limestone rubble. It was doubtless a good source of rock for the inner core of their buildings, yet most difficult for traffic. It is because of this that the Mayas built their famed *sacbeob,* or causeways, in order to make trade and travel easier.

In the interior maize fields were cultivated, and supported other subsistence crops in addition to corn. Stingless bees were bred in tree hollows; 'the land abounds in honey used for sweetening and, more important, for a meadlike intoxicant called *balche*.' There was much cotton, which was spun and woven into mantas. Cacao, the seed which when dried, toasted, and ground is chocolate, was the Maya elixir.

In the northwest of the base of the Yucatán peninsula was Campeche, a rolling country of forests and rivers, and west of it the lushly tropical Tabasco, covered with swamps and quagmires, a network of bayous, creeks, rivers. The land was made for cacao plantations and the Indians planted little else, depending on the exchange of cacao for cloth, salt, and corn. South, at the other extreme of the Maya domain, was Hibueras—Honduras—also possessed of rivers. On the banks of these rivers there were 'wide roads bordered with cacao trees.'

Water, however, was the one element the Yucatán Mayas could not command. Although water was everywhere, there was often not a drop to drink. Great quantities of rain fell, varying from 39 inches a year in the driest parts of Yucatán to over 150 inches in the wetter zones. During January and February there were light rains. June through August were heavy rain months, and even September brought light rainfall. The temperature varied with the seasons, as low as 45 degrees in December, as high as 105 degrees in April. Still, there was no way to hold the rain. There are no rivers on the Yucatán peninsula.

To meet the water problem the Mayas constructed reservoirs and cisterns. At their greatest city, Tikal, they hollowed out an immense reservoir between two temples, cementing the porous limestone so that it would hold water. In northern Yucatán, where all the rain water percolates underground, Maya cities developed around natural wells. (These wells were formed by the collapsing of the friable limestone shelf, which exposed the subterranean water table. Some of these natural *cenotes* are two hundred feet in diameter, with the water one hundred feet below the surface.) At Chichén Itzá there were two of these, one for drinking, the other for watery sacrifices. Where the natural *cenote* (Maya, *dzonot*) did not occur and they wished to build a city, the Mayas in Roman fashion made underground cisterns. These were called *chultunes*.

'God provided openings in the rock *which the Indians call 'cenotes'', wrote Diego de Landa. One of the largest and most impressive is that of Bolonchen, shown here in Catherwood's superb drawing. It was a dramatic setting, 'the wildest that can be conceived', said Stephens, 'men struggling up the huge ladder with earthen jars of water strapped to back and head, their sweating bodies glistening under the light of the pine-torches.' The great ladder is now in ruins.*

Water, or the lack of it, was the curse of the Maya paradise (it was equally so to the Aztecs), and drought and its disastrous consequences play an important role in native Maya literature.

Apart from their periodic droughts, the Mayas lived in a land which might be characterized by the Biblical phrase 'flowing with milk and honey.' No other tribe in the Americas had so balanced a wealth of natural resources. Although the Maya society was Neolithic (the Mayas had neither metals nor the wheel nor draft animals, and needed none), they had a soil and climate that gave them maize in such awesome quantities that it allowed them leisure. A rich and varied flora and fauna yielded all they needed for food, clothing, and medicine. Limestone rock for temples and dwellings was easily quarried, even without metal tools. The same stone was burned and easily reduced to lime. The material for a durable stone-mortar masonry was everywhere available.

Sometime, circa 2000 B.C., these people who were to be the 'Mayas' filtered slowly into this land. Once in possession, they were to hold it for thirty-seven hundred years, in continuous cultural sequence, before the last city was subdued.

The history of the land before 2000 B.C. is still very uncertain. A longheaded people, in thinly scattered tribes, lived there. We know little more. They were rudimentary farmers and were perhaps the proto-Maya. Tribes using Maya speech were widely scattered along the hotlands of the Mexican Gulf Coast, from Yucatán to Tampico, and doubtless inland into the low, flat Tehuantepec isthmus, and certainly in the high hinterland, since they followed the Rio Usumacinta along the fringe of the tropical highlands of Chiapas.

At this theoretical date, 2000 B.C., the intellectual equipment of the Mayas was certainly no better than that of any of the other tribes about them. Their agriculture was the same. Society was primitive and agricultural techniques were on the same level. Their safety depended on the beneficent gods. They counted the stars in their balance, watched the seasonal rising of planets, noting the portents in the sky for rain or sun, and in this way gradually roughed out their primitive calendric system.

What these people did, said, and wore can only be inferred. At the moment all we have of early Maya man is a collection of potsherds. These are fragments of a utilitarian pottery which is called *Mamom* ('Grandmother'); the term was suggested by the *Popol Vuh,* the sacred book of the ancient Quiché Maya. Their houses, circular and thatched with palm leaf, were of wood. A crude flat stone was used for braising the maize for the unleavened corncakes. Open woven bags held beans and squash. Their crude beds, over which rush mats were thrown, rested on stilts. Until cotton

An immense Maya city, *with beginnings as far back as* 1500 B.C., *has been recently explored at Dzibilchaltún ('where-there-is-writing-on-flat-stones'). The stele is not carved, but inscriptions may have existed in stucco or paint. The Temple of the Dolls in the background is the first of the restored buildings; crude in concept, it illustrates the beginning of Maya architecture.*

was developed and the loom perfected, clothes were beaten from the bast of wild fig fibres. The fire-hardened planting stick (never improved upon by the Mayas in 3,700 years) they already possessed, and their weapons were spears and arrows tipped with flint or obsidian. For hunting they had the barkless dog.

From these people to the Mayas the cultural sequence is missing. Suddenly archaeology reveals mounds and small pyramids; there is a developed pottery and much other evidence of the formed Maya type of social organization.

These Mayas are revealed as people with wit, passion, and interest. Superbly painted polychromatic pottery depicts the already formed upper classes, a stratified society where inequality is stressed. Man has set bounds to his fields, and he wars, hopes, fears.

Population centres, small, compact, and self-contained, were springing up over all these areas during the long formative period, i.e., between 1000–300 B.C. Trade, language, and common culture rather than political ties held them together as 'Maya.'

El Petén is the name given to a region which is composed of vast swamps, jungles, and savannas, with a medial chain of lakes, and grassland surrounded by tall tropical forests. It is here that the people begin to show the characteristics of their culture which define 'Maya.' The potters depict human forms on their bowls; painting and colouring is rich, imaginative, and polychromatic. Much of the pottery is dated with glyphs. Thus far no one has traced the evolution from utilitarian pottery into aesthetic ware. It appears suddenly, full-born.

Maya epigraphy once suggested that the Tikal-Uaxactún region was the immediate birthplace of Maya civilization; the art, architecture, and ceramics of the two cities also seemed to lead to the same view. But recent research has modified it. By A.D. 200 Uaxactún is already on its cultural way; the oldest stela there is dated A.D. 328. Eleven miles west is Tikal, another temple-city. After this there is a quickening of building throughout the entire length and breadth of the land. The cities can be listed by their dated stelae in the order of their appearance in Maya history.

This was not a unique performance. There was a florescence of cultures throughout Mexico and Middle America. The perfection of the calendar, the progress of glyph writing, the perfection and use of paper, the ritualistic calendar, and dated monuments were common to all advanced peoples. Cultural exchange of ideas and techniques through trade had gone on since the beginning. So far as is known now—although this concept is subject to re-evaluation at any time owing to new and continuing discoveries in the Maya area—the early Maya city-states had a common trade, a common language, and similar cultural traits. There was a cultural union but not a political one. There is no known centre or Maya capital. These cities endured between the extreme dates of 500 B.C. and A.D. 1000.

It is believed that they ceased to function after the year 1000. The archaeological evidence gained through the superb deductions of the epigraphers would indicate that after this date the Maya tribes within the area of what is called the 'Old Empire' no longer raised dated monuments, and so far as is known now, the cities ceased to function. This does not imply that the temple-cities disintegrated at once; it was perhaps a long, slow process. The explanations for the decline and fall have been many but none is convincing.

To us it seems illogical that a people numbering no less than three million would abandon stone cities which took them centuries to build. Yet the archaeological evidence shows that city-states as widely separated as Copán and Tikal 'ceased to erect monuments at the end of successive periods—one of the fundamentals of Maya life,' and gradually melted away.

These Maya temple-cities (numbering several hundreds) were not in most cases abandoned because of conquest. The temples, the priestly houses,

Frieze of marching jaguars and eagles, *on the temple at Tula. The same motif is repeated on the wooden drum from Malinalco (Aztec) and at Chichén Itzá (Maya, below).*

Squatting Jaguars *on the pyramid temple of Kukulcán, Chichén Itzá. The influence from Tula is inescapable. It is thought that Toltecs from Tula (a march of 1000 miles), and Itzás dispossessed from Chichén Itzá, reoccupied the city in the 10th century* A.D.

the pyramids, and the dated stone monoliths stand as they were left. There is no evidence of any cataclysmal climatic change nor of diseases that had not appeared elsewhere in the Americas, nor is there evidence of large-scale wars. The cities, some of the most impressive monuments built by man anywhere, were just left to be enfolded by the tentacles of the jungle flora.

The Mayas have compounded their own mystery. Their involved glyph writing, even though capable of expressing the abstract quality of numbers, tells nothing about themselves beyond such facts as that a certain building or stela was completed on such and such a date. Of themselves—nothing. They have not left a name, even of a chieftain or a city. Until formulas are found to decipher the remainder of the glyphs which are not concerned with the calendric system, we shall be a little longer in the dark. Even the Incas, who had no writing, left an oral history which, confirmed by archaeology, has at least given us the great names of their kings and the epochs in their history.

Whatever the causes, the cities within a wide range of the humid forest were abandoned. What happened to the people? Where did three million people go? Or did they go at all? We know only that after A.D. 1000 the bulk of the population was concentrated in the Guatemalan highlands and in the north-eastern part of Yucatán, Quintana Roo and Honduras.

This was the time of the Maya renaissance; art and architecture flourished anew. There was an introduction of Toltec motifs throughout the region of the Puuc and around Chichén Itzá, the plumed-serpent caryatids, the prancing jaguar, the eagle with unfurled wings—talisman of the warrior-knights' cult of Toltec origin. A new architecture introduced wooden beams, instead of the self-limiting corbelled arch, and buildings took on new graces. During this time Uxmal, the most beautiful city of the entire region, was built. New or extended rituals came into religion, with human sacrifice and its bloody bath. New weapons made war more fearful. The old causeways were rebuilt and extended. Cities were walled along the coast. Seafaring Mayas moved as far as Panama and up into the Nicaraguan lakes. Trading posts were spread along the coasts, and contact was even made with the Caribs from the isles of Cuba and Jamaica. Maya learning was revived and extended, painted books were multiplied, and the *Dresden Codex,* a beautiful example of Maya draftsmanship, was made into a 'new edition' in about the twelfth century.

8 The Maya Men and Women

LIKE ALL theocratic societies, Maya society was a pyramid with the common man at the bottom. They were maize farmers. When war was upon them they were soldiers. They erected the soaring temples. They built the immense ball courts and terraces. They felled the trees, dressed and then transported the limestone blocks, carved the glyphs, and sculptured the Maya art. They built the raised causeways, the *sacbeob,* that bound city to city.

The community seems to have been organized in clans and each member of such a clan was part of an earth cell. The lower and higher man were both wedded to the soil. One's taxes were paid out of it; either a portion of the crops went to the *batab* (tax collector) or else the cultivation of the fields was in the form of work tax. Agricultural surplus provided leisure that was used in the building of temples, palaces, and roads.

There were more than three million Mayas around A.D. 800. The Maya's average height was 5 feet 1 inch. Still, he was robust and strong. The Mayas were brachycephalic, one of the most broad-headed peoples in the world. Even today their features closely resemble the faces on the ancient monuments. As soon as a baby was born his head was artificially flattened by being placed within two tied boards. This custom, as it was explained to Landa, 'was given to our Maya ancestors by the gods. It gives us a noble air . . . and besides our heads are then better adapted to carry loads.'

Ear lobes were pierced for pendants and so was the septum of the nose. The left side of the nose was also pierced—as is the practice of certain peoples of India—and, the gods willing, a topaz was set into it. The hair was long, black, and lustrous, wrapped around the head, and 'braided like a wreath, leaving the queue to hang down behind like tassels.' Tied to the hair was an obsidian mirror disc. 'All of the men wore mirrors,' but the women wore none, and for one man to call another a cuckold, 'he need only say that his wife put mirrors in her hair.'

The hair on top of the head was cropped short, singed in fact, so that it looked like a monk's tonsure. Facial hair was disliked. Mothers stunted the hair follicles of the young, and therefore beards were scant. Such hair that appeared was pulled out with copper tweezers. Despite this, old men had straggly beards, which are often represented in Maya sculpture.

'They tattooed their bodies . . .' a fact confirmed by archaeology, since quite a few sculptured stone heads show tattooing 'the design being pricked in the skin with a sharp bone into which pigment was rubbed, and accompanied with great suffering.' For this reason, the more tattooing one had the more one was thought brave and valiant.

Maya eyes, dark and lustrous, appear to be more Mongolian than those of most American peoples; the position of the eyes in the face emphasizes the epicanthic fold that gives them their 'slant.' Many were cross-eyed; in fact, to be so was considered both a mark of beauty and distinction. Itzamna, god of the heavens, is always featured as cross-eyed, and so are some of the other gods and personages that appear on the carved monuments. Bishop Landa wrote: 'Maya mothers hung a pitch-ball in front of their children's eyes so close that both eyes focused on it and in this way began to cross.' The practice must have been widespread, for Bernal Díaz, in the early days of the conquest, 'took prisoners . . . many of them cross-eyed.'

Men dressed for the climate. The basic dress was the *ex* (pronounced 'eesh'), a woven-cotton breechclout which the 'women made with great care.' This was wound around the waist several times and passed between

The flattened heads of the Maya *were artificially created to give 'a noble air' and heads 'better adapted to carry loads'. This drawing of stone figures at Palenque is by Count Waldeck, one of the most picturesque figures in the story of Maya exploration. He came to Palenque in 1832 and held the theory that the Mayas derived from the Romans or Phoenicians. In his drawings he invented many features in accordance with this belief; as art they are often superb, as archaeology misleading.*

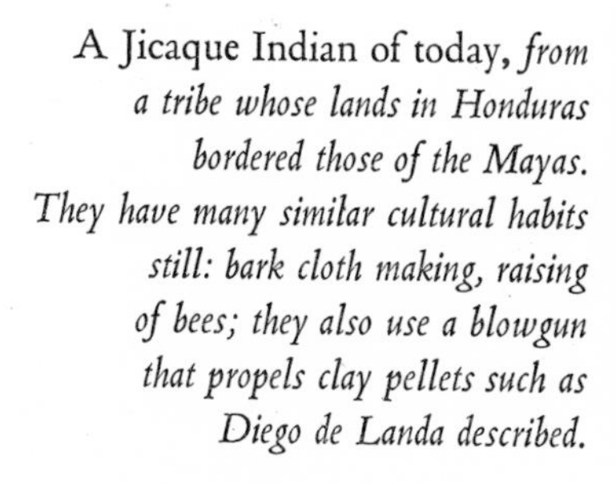

A Jicaque Indian of today, *from a tribe whose lands in Honduras bordered those of the Mayas. They have many similar cultural habits still: bark cloth making, raising of bees; they also use a blowgun that propels clay pellets such as Diego de Landa described.*

the legs. The ends hung down in front and back. This is the most common article of Maya dress and is pictured from the earliest times. Men wearing the *ex* are found on painted pottery, and certain sculptures dated A.D. 600 show the ends of it elaborately embellished and decorated.

Around their shoulders the Mayas wore a covering like a poncho; it was elaborated according to one's life station. The same piece was used as a covering for the night's sleep. Sandals were the final item in the attire of the lower man. Almost all wore them, especially in Yucatán, because of the roughness of the terrain. These *keuel* were made of either tapir or deer hide and tied to the feet by two thongs.

Women's dress was the *kub,* a single piece of decorated woven cloth with holes for the arms and a square-cut opening for the head (the original chemise). The style, which one sees on the famous murals of Bonampak, has survived for two thousand years; it is still worn throughout Yucatán. Underneath, the women wore a lighter white petticoat, decorated and fringed. About their shoulders they draped a stole. They walked barefoot.

'... in this country there is but one language.' Landa, who first studied it, stated this as bald fact, yet time has borne him out. The Mayas did not always fully understand one another, but a lowland Maya generally could understand a highlander, just as a peasant from Naples can understand a peasant from Milan. Since there was common trade between the diverse areas—coast, highland, jungle—and common communications, and the same glyph-written language was used in cities that might be five hundred miles apart, it is presumed that there must have been a basic common tongue. Although more than fifteen dialects were spoken (such as Chontal, which extended across the humid centre of the Mayas, and the dialects in Guatemala, Tzeltal, Ixil, Quiché, etc.), the languages must have been, as Eric Thompson suggested, closely related to one another as are the Romance languages. The modern conclusion is that one can properly speak of only two Maya languages at best, highland and lowland Maya, the dialects being only variants of these.

The precise name for Maya speech is unknown. Mayathan was that language used by the Mayas of the League of Mayapán in the area controlled by them in Yucatán. There was doubtless a certain unity of speech among

Crossed-eyes were a feature of beauty *and distinction to the Mayas. Indeed, 'Maya mothers hung a pitch-ball in front of their children's eyes so close that both eyes focused on it and in this way began to cross'. The god Itzamná (left, a stone head from Copán), chief of the Maya pantheon, giver of food, patron of medicine and inventor of writing, was always represented as cross-eyed.*

Ear lobes were pierced for heavy pendants—*also a feature of distinction. This wild and fearful head is a detail from a relief on a richly ornamented stele at Bonampak.*

the lowland Mayas as there was among the highland Mayas; even so, the fact that the name glyphs were uniform throughout the country did not mean that the language itself was without variants. Diego de Landa admitted that there were some differences in usage between the speech of the coastal inhabitants and that of the inlanders, and that 'along the coast they are most polished in their language and behaviour.'

Maya society was composed of a noble class, *ah mehenob,* from which all office-holders—and there were many—were selected, and the mass of the people, as well as multitudes of slaves. This much is certain. Yet it is readily admitted that 'we have no direct evidence as to the type of government and social organization prevalent among the Maya.' The evidence gathered from art, sculpture, murals, and painted vases shows the nobleman in full command. Maya lords are shown being carried in litters. Armies are led by superbly accoutred leaders in panoplies of jade and quetzal feathers. Chieftains are seen laying down laws, the captured warriors being judged and put into slavery. Yet these vignettes refer only to limited aspects of the social organization. The Aztecs had a well-known clan organization wherein the land was communally owned and communally worked. The Incas developed the *ayllu,* which was collectivistic in principle, as their basic social unit. The Mayas are thought to have had some similar form of organization, yet its name and precise form is unknown.

The Mayas were not an empire, as the Incas were. Yet there was a common Maya culture, language, and religion. There was a system of roads, some the finest constructed in the protohistorical Americas, binding coast and highland together. Trade was general and far-flung. Maya society has been likened to that of the city-states of Greece. The comparison is most apt. Although Sparta, Athens, and Corinth had, like the Mayas, a common language, culture, and religion, they were fiercely independent and often warred with one another, sometimes even supporting foreign invasions against other Greek cities.

The organization of Maya temple-cities follows a social pattern similar to most neolithic societies. The first harvests are brought to the temple and offered to the gods. The people know, of course, that the produce does not go directly to the gods. They are aware that it is eaten by the priests. All of the early peoples, who were farmers, believed that they were dependent on the favour of the gods and that they needed the hierarchical priesthood to secure it for them. The priests maintain the temples and are themselves maintained by the products and the service of the farmers. As the local shrine grows into a temple and the temple into a city or a ceremonial centre, houses are grouped about it. The lower man, whose tribute and service help to build the temple-city and maintain it, finds the temple ceremonial centre to be useful. His maize grows better. He is told the time to plant and harvest (the priest is also the astrologist-astronomer), and the nature of mysteries are explained to him.

Out of this develops clan organization. The lower man is convinced that the gods are the owners of the land and that the priests in parcelling it out are acting on behalf of the gods. The various clans are allotted areas of land by the temple-city councillors (among the Aztecs actual maps drawn on *amatl* paper gave the rebus names of the owners), and the councillors presumably officiate at the division of the land. Among the Mayas, each family was assigned a piece of land of four hundred square feet, a *hun uinic,* measured with a twenty-foot measuring tape. We are ignorant of further details. Whether the land was held in trust by the ruler, as among the Incas, and was returned to the clan on the decease of the user to be reallotted, or whether it belonged to the *calpulli,* as among the Aztecs, we just do not know—at least no more than Diego de Landa, who says, '. . . each married man with his wife . . . sow a space four hundred square feet . . . which they call a *hun uinic,* measured with a rod of twenty feet.'

The elaborate head-dress *of this figurine is a typical example of the Maya chieftain's dress. The figure is from the island of Jaina in Yucatán, and is a small pottery whistle—which an artist of high skill has made beautiful in its serene repose.*

Marriage was at once mystical and practical. The Mayas thought it mean-spirited for a man to seek out his own prospective wife; he employed a professional matchmaker, or the father himself arranged marriages for sons and daughters even while they were in infancy. They treated the other family as in-laws long before the formal marriage-rites.

Young men, who lived apart from the old, had in each village 'a large house, whitened with lime, open on all sides,' where they met for amusements, dice, ball and bean games. Their bodies were painted black as was the custom for a man before marriage. They slept together, but, says Bishop Landa in a quick aside, they did not practice the 'abominable sin,' that is, sodomy. They brought public women into their quarters. 'Although the women received pay for it [a handful of cacao beans] they were besieged by such a great number of men that they were harassed almost to death.'

Monogamy was the rule among the lower men. 'The Yucatecans never took more than one wife.' When a young man thought of marriage and his father put the thought into action, he took good care, writes the bishop, to seek a wife in good time and of good quality. A matchmaker was engaged, a dowry and marriage settlements were worked out. To ward off the evil spirit that hung over marriage, they consulted a priest who read the astrologic book of days to determine whether their birthdays, their names, and the date of the contemplated union fell on unlucky days. The mothers-in-law then wove new garments for bride and groom, and the bride's father prepared the house for ceremony and feast.

Divorce was by repudiation. If the woman was barren, or if she did not properly prepare the husband's daily steam bath, she could be repudiated. She might also take similar action against the man; although that was not as easy. When a couple was divorced, the younger children stayed with the mother. If older, the sons went to the father, but the daughters always remained with the mother.

The house of the lower man was like that of the eternal peasant everywhere, simple and practical.

A Maya built first a small house opposite the dwelling of his father or father-in-law. Later his larger house was built with the aid of the community. The house could be constructed round, square, rectangular, or as it is best known in Yucatán, apsidal, rounded at both ends. Its frame was made of withes and rested on a stone foundation. The withes were then covered with adobe. Later the house was colourfully painted. The highpitched roof was made of trunks and saplings and wonderfully thatched, then as now, with palm (guano) 'of very good quality and in great abundance,' wrote Landa. In ancient times (A.D. 500) the house was usually square and mounted on a low substructure. Yet houses, while not always the same, tended to resemble one another in specific areas.

The interior of the house was divided by a wall. One part became the kitchen, and the other contained the sleeping racks. 'They had beds made of small saplings' says Landa, 'laced together by withes which . . . gave way to the movement of the body like a mattress.' This was covered with a woven grass mat. They used their cotton mantas as blankets. Whether the hammock later used by the Mayas was known to them before the arrival of the Spaniards, who brought examples of it from the island of Hispaniola, would seem doubtful.

There was one entrance and it had no door. Across the entrance-way was placed a light string from which hung small copper bells. One brushed against these to give the owner notice of arrival. People seldom entered a house without permission, for 'they considered it a grave crime to harm the houses of others.'

The common man built the houses of the nobles, which were larger and more spacious than the others. Some were made of sculptured stone. 'The slope of the roof comes down very low in front on account of their

The peasants' houses *have naturally not survived, but some of them are immortalized in stone on the façade of the 'Nunnery' at Uxmal. The roof represents a thatch of palm leaf, the walls wattle and daub. Out of such humble beginnings grew Maya architecture.*

love of sun and rain' (as protection against the sun and the rain). The walls of their houses 'were painted with great elegance,' an observation which has been confirmed by archaeological excavation. The single entrance, also without a door, could be closed with a drapery, usually a woven hanging of much richness. Certain structures that are now found in the temple-cities may have been nobles' homes, although no buildings have been found which can be definitely associated with the ruling class.

A house endured for little more than a generation. The excavations of the house mounds reveal a 'complete ceramic period,' As the inhabitants of a house died, they were buried beneath the hard mud floor ('they bury their dead inside or in the rear of their houses,') After several burials the house was abandoned and was then treated as a sacred burial plot.

A Maya day began at about 4 a.m. One of the women rose and roused the dormant fire under the *koben*, the three-stoned hearth fire on which a flat ceramic baking-dish lay.

'Their principal food is maize, from which they make various foods, also drink . . . in the morning all they ate was maize water.' The evening before, the woman, with the aid of daughters or slaves, had prepared the dried maize. It was boiled with ash until softened and then husked, after which it was brayed on a stone grinder until reduced to a thick paste from which the women prepared tortillas.

When the Maya farmer departed in the early dawn for the fields, he took with him several apple-sized balls of ground maize wrapped in leaves. He returned early in the afternoon. The women, by custom, had a hot bath ready for him. In the large centres such as Tikal and Chichén Itzá, there

The peaceful life of a sea-coast village—*a subject rare indeed in Maya art—is the theme of this fresco from the Temple of the Warriors at Chichén Itzá. On the sea are three canoes, each with an oarsman at the prow and two passengers. On the shore men and women go about their daily tasks amid houses, trees, and, on the right, a temple with an outer and an inner chamber; from the inner one rises a feathered serpent while worshippers kneel in the outer. There is no attempt at perspective. Conventional stylization (trees, houses, water, the feathered serpent) exists side by side with a charming naturalism (the human beings, fish and sea-animals.*

were communal steam baths. Where these were not available, the common man contented himself with a crudely made steam bath or hot water in an improvised tub, with a dip later in the local well. Food was varied. Meat dishes included fowl, deer, armadilloes, iguanas and hutles.

Maize, the 'principal sustenance,' was supplemented by several varieties of beans, squash, and pumpkins. The chayote, a vine bearing a squash-like fruit, was found everywhere. The pale sweet potato appeared on the warm coasts. Fruits were many. The avocado was cultivated, as were the

papaya and sapote. Mulberries and melons were gathered, and the vanilla bean of the orchid was found in the jungle. Maya boys ate the fruit of the 'chewing-gum tree' and chewed its gum.

Like the Aztecs, the Mayas were enthusiastic drinkers of chocolate. 'They made it of cacao and ground maize . . . a foaming drink which is very savory.' Since cacao was grown in the humid lands on the periphery of the Maya country, it was expensive, so much so that the beans served as money.

Yet the mainstay of the Maya diet (as with all of the Central American

In the 'Land of the Turkey and the Deer', as the Mayas called Yucatán, meat foods included fowl, deer, armadilloes and iguanas. A huntsman with obsidian-tipped spear brings home a deer.

and Mexican tribes) was—maize. Maize was eaten on every occasion. During the main evening meal each male would consume upward of twenty large-sized tortillas.

The cornfield was therefore their preoccupation; 'the greatest number of them were cultivators . . . who applied themselves to harvesting maize,' said Diego de Landa. These observations are confirmed by another priest in a sixteenth-century document written in the Maya highlands: 'If one looks closely he will find everything these Indians did and talked about had to do with maize. . . .' The grain is ancient; the latest dating through maize finds in the Bat Caves of New Mexico places it as a cultivated plant before 2000 B.C.

Methods of agriculture seem not to have changed much since the earliest times. The Mayas felled trees and brush with a stone axe and burned them during the dry season. The earth was turned with a fire-hardened digging stick. Each Indian was allotted by his clan organization a portion of corn land, a *hun uinic*, of four hundred square feet. Land was communal property: '. . . the land was held in common and so between the towns there were no boundaries or landmarks to divide them except when one [city-state] made war on the other.' The technique of corn culture was the same everywhere in the Americas: the felling of trees, burning, fencing, planting, weeding, bending the stalks at harvest (so as to deter the birds), harvesting, and shelling. The Mayas preserved the corn in storage bins; 'they kept it in fine underground granaries called *chultunes*.'

Water was always a Maya problem. Those in the hinterland built huge reservoirs. At Tikal an immense one was located in a deep ravine, the porous rock cemented and held by a masonry dam. The sites of Piedras Negras, Palenque, and Yaxchilán were located on rivers. Cobá, in Yucatán, was set felicitously between two lakes, but most of the cities in Yucatán had the *cenote* as their only permanent source of water. A Maya farmer tried to locate his milpa as close as possible to the wells. As new fields were needed, there was a tendency for the Maya farmer to move farther from a given centre. This in time doubtless loosened his connection with the city-state. Agricultural decentralization could well have been one of the factors which loosened the social structure of the Old Empire and contributed to the disintegration of cities.

Planting was ritually controlled. Maize, the gift of the gods, was sacred, and planting had to be done with the proper ritual. The rain god Chac was properly propitiated and those days when rain should fall were selected for planting, in order that the newly planted seeds would sprout. Astronomy was mostly astrology. But the almanacs for planting were based on empirical observation; in one of the Maya codices it is stated: 'This is the record of the year-bears of the *uinal*. . . .' Actually, this was weather forecasting based on observation of previous years. In the ninth month, Chen (Moon), and the tenth, Yax (Venus), planting was to be done during certain lucky days. Typical interpretations of the Maya planting almanac were these: 'Cimi, the 5th day of the 11th month Zac [February] . . . bad day for planting . . . with rain incantations there is a good downpour . . . The month and day of 9 Caban [February–March] . . . good day, lucky day, heavy rains, good for planting everything.'

Chac was the rain god. He is represented in the Maya glyphs in books, on sculpture, and in painted murals as the long-nosed god. His eyes, T-shaped, suggest tears and, symbolically, rain. His importance in the Maya pantheon can be gauged from the fact that the Chac name glyph occurs 218 times in the three surviving Maya codices. Chac was a benevolent deity and considered to be man's friend. The Maya farmer always evoked his name when planting. He was *the* god. So in the months of Chen and Yax there were great festivals to honor him.

Planting was simple and effective. All that was required was a bag to hold the maize kernels and a fire-hardened planting stick. A hole was made in the soil, four or five inches deep, and into it three to six kernels were dropped. After that, Chac willing, the Maya waited. September and October brought light rains; they were also the hurricane months. In November, when the weather was cool and dry, the corncob was bent downward to keep it from the birds, and when dry it was harvested.

The Maya cultivated much besides maize. In the same cornfield, using the maize stalk for support, the farmers planted beans; on the ground, squash and pumpkins grew. Chili peppers were grown at the edge of the fields or in the houses as an ornamental shrub. In separate fields in the

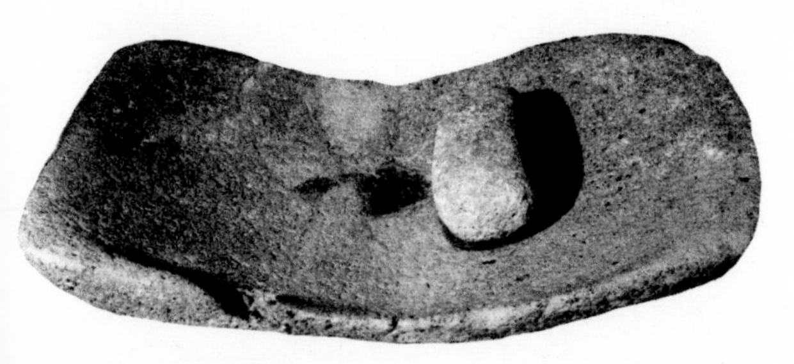

Maize was the principal food *of the Mayas. Preparing it was the women's task. The dried corn was husked and boiled with ash until soft. Next it was brayed on a milling stone (an example with grinder, from Xunantunich, is shown above). The resulting thick paste was baked into the flat tortillas.*

The bee-god, *represented in the form of a bee, comes in to swarm at the hive. Honey and wax played an important part in Maya life.*

warmer areas the Mayas grew the pale sweet potato. The sweet cassava was known, as was *chicham*, a root shaped like a turnip. They had one good green vegetable, the chayote; the fruit of a herbaceous vine that when cooked tasted like summer squash. Around the gardens which surrounded their houses the Mayas planted papayas 'which they esteemed very highly.' The avocado, a 'very large and fresh tree with fruits of great delicacy,' appeared in groves, while the soapberry tree they put near their houses to obtain the roots from which they made a kind of soap.

Droughts were frequent and of great intensity and their 'disastrous consequences play an important role in Maya literature.' Rains were usually heavy, but the greater part of the lowland is only a thin soil cap laid over a limestone outcrop. The rain trickled through the porous limestone and down into natural cisterns. The Mayas tried to combat this; at many of the city-states they built artificial cisterns. During the rainy season water was gathered from the roofs by means of cemented run-offs and was directed into wells, which were elaborately roofed to prevent evaporation in the hot weather. Tikal, although in one of the wettest zones, suffered repeatedly from drought. There the engineers cemented up an entire ravine of porous limestone around the principal plaza, to create giant-sized reservoirs. Over these passed causeways which served as both dams and roads. All this was of no avail for the maize fields. When rain did not fall at its stated interval, the soil quickly dried up, cracked, and became cement-hard.

When this happened (and it is obvious from the frequent appeals to the rain gods that it happened often), the Mayas abandoned their cities, went into the jungles, and were reduced to eating the bark of trees. The old, who were unable to come, were left to die. Human sacrifices to the gods were frequent on these occasions. Other Mexican tribes suffered in the same measure from drought, and the Aztecs sacrificed thousands to the rain gods. For some strange reason they seem never to have thought of irrigating their lands from wells, though water in fact lay not far below the surface.

There was also a mental block against the use of the wheel. None of the practical uses of the wheel, in whatever form, were known: pulley, arch, roller wheel, rotary quern, potter's wheel, or water wheel. Had the Mayas had the latter in that terrible year of 1464, when there was drought followed by a locust swarm so thick that the weight of it broke the limbs off large trees and engulfed the land until 'nothing green was left,' they might have survived and weathered the great hurricane which followed and destroyed houses, trees, and fields. 'After this the land of Yucatán remained so destitute of trees that . . . casting one's eyes over the country from some high point it looks as if the whole land had been cut by scissors. . . .'

9 A People of Crafts and Commerce

IN OTHER techniques, the Mayas were much further advanced. Weaving was carried on both for home consumption and for trade. The women wove *huipilli* for themselves and breechclouts for their men.

The spindle whorl is universal. The Maya spindle was a stick ten to twelve inches in length, with a pottery balance ring three inches from its end. It was spun about in a small ceramic dish. These pottery whorls are all that survive of Maya weaving.

Cotton was 'gathered together in wonderful quantity and grows in all parts of the land . . . there are two kinds of it.' One type was an annual: '. . . they sow it every year.' The other was a perennial, a sort of tree cotton (*Gossypium herbaceum*), as its classification suggests, 'and this lasts five or six years and bears cotton every year.' Tree cotton was known and used by the pre-Inca cultures; it grew in the coastal drylands about Piura.

Dyeing was done before weaving. Colours, vegetable and mineral, were symbolic. Black was the symbol of war, since obsidian tipped arrow and spear; black was obtained from carbon. Yellow, the colour of ripe

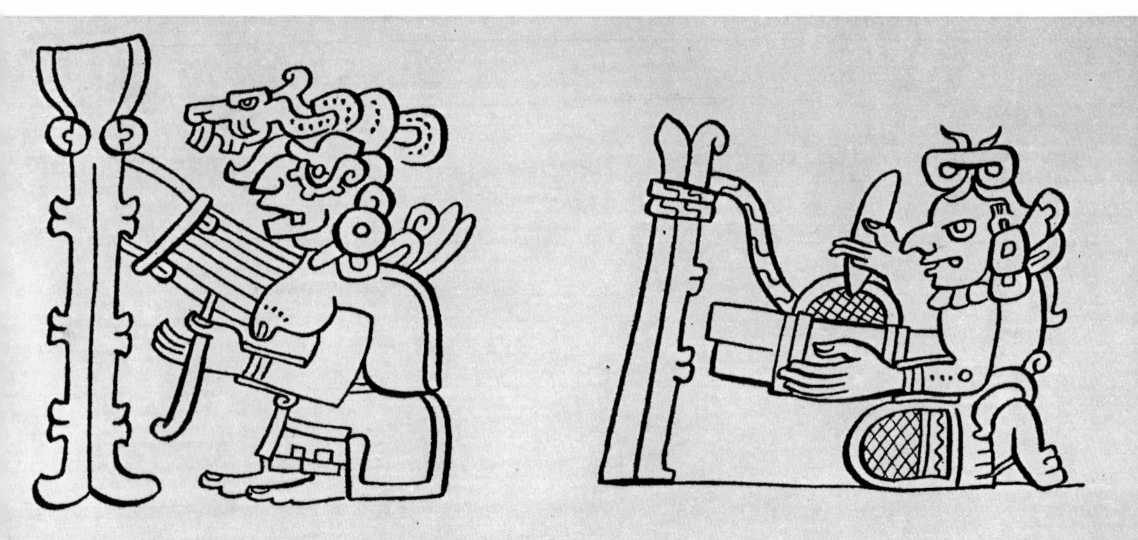

The Mayas were skilled at weaving, *though most of their textiles have perished. On the left, the goddess of weaving works with a backstrap loom; right, a woman adjusts the woof of a weaving by means of a sharp stone.*

corn, was the symbol for food. It was extracted from hydrous iron oxide. Red was a blood symbol; it came from several sources: red iron oxide and, from the vegetable world, *achiote* and brazilwood. Cochineal was highly prized, 'the best in the Indies coming from the dry land.' It was obtained from the insects that Maya boys 'herded like cows' on cactus pads. (In the sixteenth century the insects found to yield cochineal of a good colour were cultivated in Italy and Greece, replacing all other sources of red dye.)

Blue was the colour symbol of sacrifice. That particular 'Maya blue' which one sees so vividly on the murals of Bonampak, came from a mineral which has been identified as a blue chromiferous clay. 'Colours of many different kinds were made from dyes of certain trees.' The Mayas also made them from the wild tomato, the blackberry, and the green-black avocado. The most prized, because it was difficult to obtain, was the deep purple obtained from a mollusk (*Purpura patula*). It is somewhat like the famous Tyrian purple derived from several genera of mollusks, *Murex* and *Purpura*. Dyes were pounded in stone mortars, which are sometimes found in graves. The dry colours were doubtless kept in small bags, which one does not see among the Mayas, but their counterpart in Peru has been preserved.

The Maya loom was identical with that of all the other American tribes. The backstrap loom had a horizontal rod that was attached to a post or tree. The warp was then fastened to the lower wooden rod, which had a thick hemp cord that went around the ample rump of the woman weaver. The designs of the cloth produced from these Maya looms must have been fantastic, judging by the scant evidence which is shown on their murals, sculptures, and vase paintings. There were fabrics made of the imported rabbit-wool yarn from Mexico, others with bird plumage tied in to form feather mosaics, and tough manta cloth padded with cotton and soaked in salt brine for body armour. Designs and colours ran riot, and yet all we know of them are from the scant, tantalizing illustrations. All of the art of those looms has perished with war and conquest, time, and the elements. Except for the fragments found at the bottom of the wells of Chichén Itzá, there is little other evidence. It is a great loss to the history of art, for we know from an analogous source—the weavings of Peru, where dry desert conditions have preserved many superb pieces—how wonderful it must have been.

From the simple manta woven in strips eighteen yards long, used for trade, came the colourful *huipil* for women, the breechclout for men, the robes of the priests and chieftains, the cloth for dressing idols, the portières for temple doors, and the body armour referred to above.

All this has perished.

The Mayas were also pottery makers of the highest quality. The imagination, design, and form is as good as anything of the Greeks, far surpasses the Roman ceramic arts, and is superior to the pottery of almost any of the cultures of the ancient Near East. All of the wonderful Maya pottery forms—too varied to detail—were done without the potter's wheel. Pottery was done by coiling. The technique is almost as old as man. Clay moulded into long coils, a sort of outsized spaghetti, is laid down in successive rings and worked and pressed into a single form with the hands. The clay form is then smoothed with a shard. If the vase is large—and some were gigantic—the potter walks around the vase, becoming himself the potter's wheel. This technique is not limited to the Mayas; all the tribes and cultures covering the wide area of the Americas employed it, and many used it in Africa and the peripheral Asiatic world.

These time-consuming methods have changed little since the earliest Neolithic times. The pottery wheel would have simplified the process, but we have seen that the wheel was almost unknown to the cultures of pre-Hispanic America.

Pottery was turned out in mass. They had moulds for pressing designs on finished pots. Excavations have turned up such moulds with decorations in vertical, horizontal, and pinched stripes for rouletting and comb markings, and moulds of baked clay to impress patterns. There is no technique (other than the wheel) used by the best 'mechanical' potters of the classic era that was not known and employed by the Maya.

After being decorated, the pottery was fired in an open kiln (wood-, charcoal-, or grass-burning) and baked at a heat of 450 degrees upward. All Maya pottery was made in this fashion: simple utilitarian bowls and cooking pots, decorated dishes, pitchers to hold chocolate, beakers to be filled with the heady mead. Braziers were made, to warm a chilly room or to burn copal. There were plates to hold sacrifical urns for the ashes of the dead ('the nobles had their ashes placed in great urns'). The Mayas made man-sized jars, as large as the knotted and corded jars found in Knossos, Crete; they used immense ones for underground water storage. Those found at Tabasco had an elaborate appliqué decoration. Life-sized idols were fashioned from clay, and each of the twenty thousand houses in Mayapán had one such. Even in Landa's time 'they earned a great deal by making idols of clay.'

Decorated with scenes of Maya life, the most beautiful of pottery was made for the dead. The Jaina clay figures already mentioned are freely moulded yet exquisite in detail, showing Maya chieftains elegantly dressed and women richly clothed with necklaces and elaborate coiffures: 'an extraordinary mastery of handling, realistic knowledge of form and movement; they are elegant and refined, majestic and monumental . . . excellent examples of the Maya aesthetic ideal.' Their pottery has left us many details of Maya life, especially the life of the women, which is never indicated in the

The Mayas made pottery of the highest quality, *all without the potter's wheel, which they did not know. They used the coiling method—the clay was moulded into long coils, laid down in successive rings and worked and pressed into a single form with the hands. These examples are from the south Mayan area. The design which was used varied from naturalistic representation of birds and animals and the use of geometric ornament to the depiction of elaborate scenes. Above is a fine example of plumbate ware, the first in the Americas to show signs of glaze and (above right) a piece which shows possible Toltec influence.*

A grotesque demon-god—*old, bearded, almost toothless—was recovered recently from a Tikal tomb, dating from 400–500* A.D. *Of pottery, 14 inches high and originally painted, he sits on three crossed thigh-bones; in his outstretched hands he holds a human head, and more heads are bound to his legs and arms. Especially interesting are the odd three-petalled eyes.*

carvings on the monuments. Clay modelling was in a large sense a secular art; the clay figurines show Maya man as he saw himself. They were the expression of the lower man and the world about him, not an art form designed for the dominating élite, grandiose, elegant and remote. The modelled figures give a picture of appearance and habits, the dress of men and soldiers, houses and games. Figurines which came from the coast of Vera Cruz greatly influenced the later Mayas. They show the Indian as gay; the laughing heads and the soft modelling of bodies emit a sort of contagious happiness and embody sophisticated elements.

When polychrome pottery appears it is already fairly well advanced. Archaeologists have given Maya pottery, and therefore Maya history, five phases and to each (except the fifth) a name drawn from the *Popol Vuh.*

Mamom, 'Grandmother,' pottery (2000–500 B.C.) is strictly utilitarian; it has been discovered at the lowest levels in El Petén (where the earliest dated records begin). Most in evidence are the rounded cooking pots (*cum*) which remain relatively unchanged throughout the length of Maya history. They are simply decorated, grooved, and incised. Naked clay figurines also appear and flat eating dishes.

Chichanel, 'Concealer,' is the Maya formative period (500 B.C.–A.D. 300). There now appears some of the superbly painted polychromic Uaxactún pottery. The human form is treated literally, and it is often glyph-dated. Between this and the Mamom phase there has seemingly been no evolution of form; Chichanel suddenly appears full-born. The Chichanel styles vary widely throughout El Petén and Yucatán. The shapes are low, flaring; bowls have an orange colour, decorated by what has been called the *abatik* process.

Tzakol, 'The Builders' (A.D. 317–650), is the period of the rise of the great ceremonial or temple cities throughout Mayadom. 'Thin-orange,' a very delicate pottery, appears. Widely distributed far outside the Maya area, it was developed from some unknown centre. This period, archeological stratification proves, lasted about three centuries.

Tepeuh, 'Conqueror' (A.D. 650–1000), is dominantly Maya. All the traits that are Maya appear. One senses that the potter has now full control of clay and design, and it turns into decorative baroque. It is an ornate phase in Maya art. There is a change from static to dynamic composition; the richly dressed personages in the sculptures are presented in anecdotal scenes, and there is an unrestrained elaborateness, an exaggerated love of ornament. The greatest temple-cities, Tikal, Copán, Palenque, Piedras Negras, have all been built and there follows what most have called a period of decadence—the mass of building stops and grinds to a halt. There seems to be some relation between this baroque period and the abandonment of Maya cities.

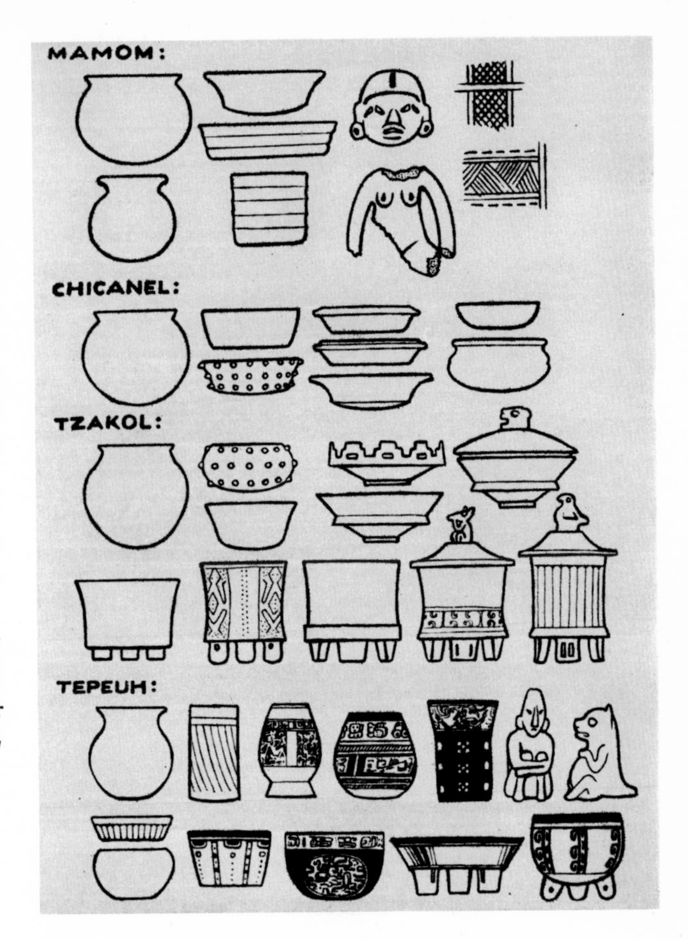

Pottery is a key to early Maya history. *Archaeologists have divided it into four phases, given names from 'Popol Vuh', the sacred book of the ancient Quiché Maya. The first examples, Mamom, date from 2000 B.C. onwards and are strictly utilitarian, with round cooking pots which persist through the centuries. About 500 B.C., Chichanel suddenly appears as if full-born; typical are the low, flaring bowls, orange in colour. Tzakol developed from an unknown centre about A.D. 317 and included a very delicate 'thin-orange' pottery. The final phase is ornate and dynamic. It ended in decadence, at the time of the 'great descent'—the abandonment of the temple-cities of Tikal, Copán and Palenque.*

The ceramic arts, at the same time, show a shift in frame of reference; decoration becomes secular, religious motifs no longer hold, and the artist becomes increasingly concerned with the world about him.

The Mayas were the only one of the three great American theocracies which maintained trade both by sea and land. The trade routes seem to date from the very beginnings of Maya culture. The Guatemalan highlands were linked with both coasts by trails and later by regular roads. These earlier trade-routes have been traced by articles found in Maya graves.

Highland Mayas traded in obsidian; jade, a Maya symbol and passion, came from the highlands (although the geological source has not been found), as did the feathers of the quetzal. Copal, an incense, was an export item, along with flint, alum, and cochineal. These were exchanged with the lowland Mayas for cotton, salt, cotton yardage, honey, wax, *balche*, cacao, dried fish, and smoked deer. New ideas accompanied the march to market—patterns for weaving, deadlier weapons, new foods, all these followed commerce.

The routes are best detailed in Yucatán, for here the Mayas were concentrated in the last centuries of their cultural existence, and here they were conquered by the Spanish, who chronicled the details of their lives. Christopher Columbus, on his fourth and last voyage to the Americas, met a Maya trading canoe on the isle of Guanaja in 1502. The canoes were forty feet long. They brought obsidian razors, copper hatchets, and cotton draperies of many different colours, and the Maya chieftain explained that they had come to this island, which lay twenty miles off the coast of Honduras, to trade for green parrot feathers and crystal.

When Cortés was in Xicalango in 1524, seeking the route to Honduras, one of the Maya traders there gave him a well-made map, painted on finely woven cloth, showing the entire inland routes from Xicalango through Campeche to Nito, on the Gulf of Honduras, a distance of four hundred land miles.

All sea or land communications led to the great emporium of Xicalango which lies a few miles inland from the Laguna de Términos. Into this outsized lagoon debouch four rivers, the largest of which is the Usumacinta. At the northeast end of the forty-mile-long lagoon there is a smaller one, the Laguna de Pom; on its shore was Xicalango. It was strategically placed. To reach it traders coming southward had to use canoes. It was surrounded on three sides by bog and swamp. On the northeast side there was a causeway leading to Vera Cruz and Aztec Mexico. Xicalango was a meeting place of Maya, Aztec, Toltec, Mixtec, and Totonac.

Merchants brought salt, dried fish, cotton yardage, copal, honey, wax, corn, beans, and feathers woven into cloaks, shields, and caps. Certain tribes of the Mayas had a virtual monopoly on salt. 'There is a marsh in Yucatán worth recording,' says Diego de Landa, 'more than seventy leagues long and entirely of salt. . . . here God . . . has made the best salt.' The lagoon began at Ekab, a large commercial trading centre with an extensive canoe trade dealing mostly in salt. Only certain Maya clans were allowed to gather the salt, and the lords of Ekab demanded a royalty on it.

Fish, turtles, turtle eggs, and large conch shells (used for trumpets and for making cement lime, the shell also became the symbol for zero in Maya arithmetic) were brought into Xicalango. Cotton mantas were widely exported. Maize was sent in sacks. The Mayas lacked metal, but flints were used for knives and were a large trade item. 'God,' said Landa, 'provided them with many outcrops of flint . . . and so flint served for metal.'

Merchants, called *ppolms*, belonged to an honoured profession. Like the Aztecs' *pochteca*, they were counted among the more important people. They had their own god, Ek Chuah, and their own rules of social conduct. They were non-taxpaying; they had special social privileges.

The merchants operated canoe fleets, and maintained warehouses for exchange along the Gulf Coast, as well as deep into the interior of the country. Hernan Cortés, in 1524, found evidence of stone-laid roads with 'resthouses along the entire way,' and beyond Lake Petén he captured a high-placed Maya who told him he was a merchant trader and that he with his slaves had voyaged to these parts in his ships.

At Xicalango large, palm-thatched, stone-built warehouses awaited the cargoes. The merchants gave and extended credit, solicited terms and payment dates. Contracts were oral; there were no written documents. Deals were closed by public drinking, emphasizing 'legality through publicity,' a failure to pay or dispute over oral terms often led to wars. Trade was on a truly vast scale. Post-Hispanic tribute lists record that twenty-six villages in the Maya province on Maní paid an annual tribute of 13,480 cotton mantas, each 16 yards long by 24 inches wide. This was 215,680 yards of cotton fabric from this small area alone!

There was a considerable trade in luxuries—cacao, stone beads, green stones called *tuns*, 'emeralds', topaz nose beads, cochineal for dyeing, alum, and, from the distant Maya-speaking Huastecs, bitumen, which those tribesmen gathered from oil seepages around Tabasco, now Mexico's primary oil fields.

After cacao, slaves. An excellent market for slaves was in Tabasco, near Xicalango. It was here in 1518 that Cortés on his way to the Conquest of Mexico was given the famous woman Malinche, 'The Tongue,' later honored by the Spaniards with the title of Doña Marina for her part in the taking of Aztec Tenochtitlán. She was 'from the town of Paynama, eight leagues from Cotzacoalcos in Tabasco,' writes Bernal Díaz. Her father had been the chieftain of the town. When her mother remarried, her presence was found inconvenient and she was given into slavery.

Slaves were big business. The Mayas trafficked widely in them. The basic cost of a slave was one hundred cacao beans. They were used for heavy manual labour, as fishermen, paddlers, and cargo carriers. Women slaves helped to draw water, grind maize, and dye cloth. Men slaves had their hair cut short and were given ragged mantles to wear.

Of all the market places known to the Spaniards, Chichén Itzá was the greatest. This city, with its sacred wells and imposing buildings of Toltec-Maya origin, was a place of pilgrimage with an extensive market. 'Pilgrims came from foreign parts to trade as well as to worship.' Within the court of the 'thousand columns' of the Temple of the Warriors is a large area which Landa called the *mercado*. Open on four sides, it had a thatched roof supported by tall stone Doric-like columns, which still stand. There are also remains of a stone dais, on which the official sat to administrate sales and trad-

POP

ing. In the open courtyard, squatting under white cotton awnings, men and women bartered the goods that they created in the surplus time allowed them by the cultivation of maize. In appearance it probably did not differ from the Aztec market so often described. Each product had its place. There was a section where fish, deer-meat, and birds were sold. Cloth and cotton dealers had their precise area, as did those who traded in plumes, arms, and the other items of commerce.

UO

The lords who had accumulated a surplus of maize, beans, shells, salt, and cotton, through tribute tax and 'gifts,' offered these things in trade to merchants who brought cacao, gold, obsidian, feathers, or jade, things the lords needed to uphold the dignity of office or to adorn their persons. Local merchants traded their surplus for the things of other lands, principally slaves and cacao. They did business in gross. The goods in turn were traded to the lower man, who then resold or traded them under the shadow of the cotton canopies.

ZIP

'Cacao was the gold of this country . . . and it serves for money in the plaza . . . of Chichén Itzá,' wrote Bishop Landa. The cacao tree grew on the periphery of the Maya territory, for it had need of much rain and thick jungle loam. It is a thick-trunked, low-growing tree that produces oval pods the size of small papayas. The pods when matured are allowed to rot and the seeds ferment. Cacao seeds are almond-sized and almond-shaped; dried in the sun they become dark, chocolate-coloured, with a parchment-like skin. It is these beans that were used as money. A rabbit was worth ten cacao beans, a pumpkin four, a slave one hundred (the amount of cacao that would make about twenty-five cups of chocolate), and so on. Maya public women, always around the markets, 'gave their bodies for a price. . . . he who wants them for his lustful use can have a run for eight or ten cacao beans . . .'

ZOTZ

Festivals were religious in nature; much, if not all, that the Maya did had a magical or religious purpose.

TZEC

XUL

YAXKIN

MOL

CHEN

The name-glyphs of the eighteen months *into which the Maya year was divided. Each was twenty days, leaving an extra five-day unlucky period, Uayeb. Each month had its special festivities:*

The month of Pop, which would fall in our calendar in July, was the Maya New Year. It was the time for renewal. People put on new clothes, destroyed their old pottery and fibre mats. There was a sense of re-dedication. It was a solemn occasion.

Uo, the second month, was a period of festivals for all the special patron gods, those who served the fishermen, hunters, travellers, and so on. The Maya gods seemed innumerable to the Spaniards, for most gods had different aspects. Uo was the month of vocational festivals; it ended in drink, dance, and fornication.

Part of month five, Tzec, was the bee god's turn. All those who kept bees—and there were many—joined the festival. The object was obvious; they wanted to cajole the bee god into increasing the flow of honey.

So it went, month to month. Each had its special festivities. In Chen, the ninth month, new idols were finished, paid for, and presented. Yax was the renovation month. All over the land hunters made amends for shedding the blood of the animals they had killed. To the Mayas all animals possessed soul force, and when they were killed the hunter had to show them respect. If this was not done, other animals of the same species as the one insulted would not allow themselves to be killed.

In the last three divisions of the Maya year, the months Kayab and Cumhu, and the five-day *uayeb,* there were also festivals, except that most pleasures were of a private nature. There was much drinking and—judging from the frequency with which it is discussed—considerable adultery. 'They had no fiesta,' says Landa in clerical disgust, 'in which they did not get intoxicated, drinking a kind of mead into which a certain root was added by which the wine became strong and stinky.'

Maya music was group music, and percussion instruments were important, since there were no string instruments in pre-Hispanic America; music and song were one.

Drums gave the group a hypnotic feeling of oneness. The *tunkul* was an

Pop, the New Year, which fell in July, was the time for new clothes and new resolutions; Pax had a very different meaning from the Latin—in it war was celebrated.

upright kettledrum, coming up to the beater's chest. It was made of a hollow log of light decorated wood, with a deer membrane stretched across it. It was beaten with the hands. Another rested on the ground and the drummer sat on it while it was beaten. A third was like the Aztec *teponzatli,* horizontal and hollowed out of wood, with two wooden tongues; it was beaten with 'beaters tipped with rubber.' If beaten when the wind was right, the drums could be 'heard two leagues off.' When dancing the Mayas held a small drum, called *pax,* which they played with the hand and there was another drum made of hollow wood with a heavy, sad sound.' Still another type of drum was made from the shell of the small land tortoise, the carapace carved and lacquered. This same type of tortoise drum is used by many other Mexican peoples. 'They strike it with the palm,' wrote Landa, 'and the sound is doleful and sad.'

The Mayas also used an ingenious ceramic drum shaped like two connecting vases; across one end was stretched a membrane. This type of drum still exists among the primitive Maya-speaking Lacandons, who call it a *kayum.* That it is very ancient is confirmed by its appearance in the *Dresden Codex,* where an illustration shows musicians playing about the head of the corn god; one of them plays the *kayum,* and musical speech-scrolls pour from the mouth of the drum.

Trumpets were of various kinds. The large conch shells found abundantly in the waters of Yucatán were made into trumpets that emitted one

The great procession of Bonampak, *part of the frieze, painted in brilliant colours, which covers four walls of one room in the temple. These are the musicians; they can be seen blowing*

full awesome sound and were used to call down the gods. Similar horns were used by the Incas as well as the Aztecs.

Trumpets carried 'melody.' The largest of them were of wood or ceramic, five feet in length. One can see these instruments painted in the murals of Bonampak. They were always made as twin trumpets and blown in unison, although each part was set in a different key.

Flutes were of wide variety. The six-note flute was made from a human leg bone, a deer's femur, reeds, or baked clay ('they had whistles made of the leg bones of deer—and flutes made of reeds'). The five-note Panpipe, almost identical with the Old World type, was known to the Mayas; it also was extensively used in South America. The place of its origin is unknown.

Bells of copper and of gold or silver, tied on legs, waist, or wrist, gave sound to the dancer's prance. There were *raspadores,* various grating instruments similar to those used widely in present-day Cuban music.

In the vivid murals of Bonampak is depicted a twelve-man orchestra. The music is being played by two matched ceramic trumpets, one kettledrum, three turtle-shell drums, and five musicians shaking gourd rattles.

Landa saw fifteen thousand Indians come from miles around to attend the dances. There were two dances which he thought 'worthy of seeing': *colomche,* the 'Dance of the Reeds,' was performed in a large circle of 150 dancers, who moved to the rhythm of drum and flute. At a signal from the

matched pottery trumpets, scraping hollowed-out turtle shells, beating a tall kettledrum and rhythmically shaking gourd rattles. Among them are figures wearing grotesque masks.

leader two performers leaped into the centre of the living wheel; one was the hunter, the other the hunted. The hunter threw rubber-tipped reed lances at the other, who caught them 'with great skill.' All the while the circle moved and kept time to the music. The other dance, which Landa does not name, was performed by eight hundred dancers carrying cloth, paper, and feather streamers. The choreography was based on a deliberate, warlike step. They kept time (punishment was meted out if they did not), and danced the whole day without stopping, for food and drink was brought to them without their breaking formation.

For the most part men danced with men, women with women. The only dance which men and women performed together was the one that Landa thought 'not very decent.'

Dance was a mystical communion between participants and the onlookers. The object of the dance was by group participation to gain victory over the unseen powers. To the Mayas, drumming, singing, hand clapping, and ululation exercised a mystical influence, formed a social bond in which they all felt in contact with the supernatural.

Dramatic presentations in which actors took part, their actions set to musical stresses, were also performed by the Mayas. Landa tells us that 'their players act with a great deal of wit,' and he unhesitatingly says that there were 'professionals.'

Stages were both indoor and outdoor. At Chichén Itzá in 1560, Landa saw 'two stages built of stone with four staircases . . . and paved on top; here they recite their farces . . . and comedies for the pleasure of the public.' These two-stage platforms, now restored, can be seen at Chichén Itzá. One is the Platform of the Cone, a twenty-foot-high stage with four stone stair-

The Mayan use of rubber *is shown in an interesting form by this effigy, recovered in 1961 from the sacrificial well at Chichén Itzá, after 500 years under water. About 4 inches high, it suggests a dancer's pose and features deliberately grotesque, but its purpose is still obscure. It is one of the oldest rubber objects in existence.*

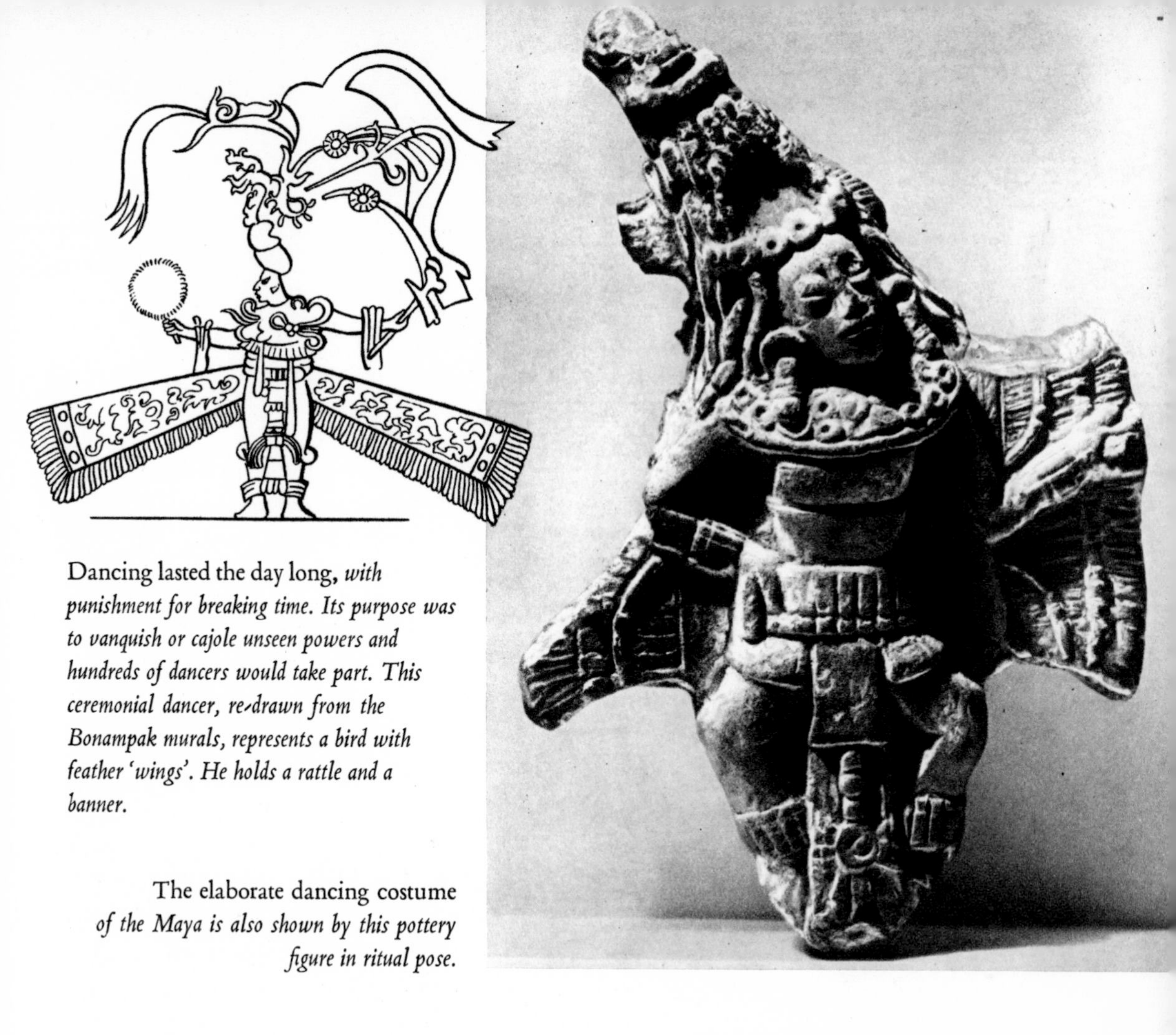

Dancing lasted the day long, *with punishment for breaking time. Its purpose was to vanquish or cajole unseen powers and hundreds of dancers would take part. This ceremonial dancer, re-drawn from the Bonampak murals, represents a bird with feather 'wings'. He holds a rattle and a banner.*

The elaborate dancing costume *of the Maya is also shown by this pottery figure in ritual pose.*

cases on a direct line between the pyramid-temple and the *sacbe* roadway. It has a flat space on top for performances. The other referred to by Landa is the *Tzompantli* stage, decorated on all its sides with, as its name implies, stone-sculptured human skulls. It is in front of the Great Ball Court.

The passion of the Maya, and one that they shared with most Central American Indians, was the game of *pok-a-tok,* it was not unlike the modern basket-ball. No one seems to know where the game began. Presumably, as it was a rubber ball that was used, and rubber came from the Mexican coast, the Olmecs (regarded by some historians as even older than the Maya) were the inventors of it. The word for rubber was *olli,* and the name Olmec means 'rubber people.' All of the larger Maya temple-cities that have been found have their ball court. Those who have visited the ruins in Mexico or those of Copán or Chichén Itzá will remember the ball court's appearance: long and rectangular in shape, like an *I,* with tiered seats on both sides for the spectators. In the exact middle on either side of the court, often as high as

'Pok-a-tok', *the ball-game of the Mayas, is reconstructed in this modern drawing. The players wore special padding on arms, body, knees and head.*

The immense ball-court of Chichén Itzá *as it must have appeared to the players: 545 feet long, 225 feet wide. High on the walls on each side can be seen the stone ring, set vertically, through which it was the purpose of the game to butt the rubber ball—a feat which, understandably, seems to have been rare.*

thirty feet from the floor, a stone ring is set, not horizontally as in basketball but vertically.

Because *pok-a-tok* was no longer being played by the Mayas in Landa's time, we must fall back on the description of the game as played by the Aztecs, written by the friar Bernardino de Sahagún. No such detailed description of the game as played by the Mayas has come down to us, but the *Popol Vuh* chronicle refers briefly to the sport:

'Let us play ball, said the lord of Xibalba.

'Then the lords seized the ball and butted directly at the ring of Hunahpu.'

Chichén Itzá had seven ball courts. The largest one, the greatest seen in any temple-city in the Americas, is one of the exciting features of the site. It was built by the Toltec-Mayas and decorated with motifs derived from Tula, eight hundred miles away. It is 545 feet long, 225 feet wide, and the millstone 'basket' is decorated with an open-fanged snake, thirty-five feet above the playing field. It is so high, in fact, that the rule of the game cited by the friar—that the player could not use his hands, but only butt the ball through the 'basket' with elbows or hips—cannot possibly hold for this court. As in Aztec Mexico, the Maya lords wagered high on the game, and if the player put the ball through the hole—a feat that seems rare enough—he had the right to demand as forfeit all the clothing and jewels of the spectators present.

Maya houses had no doors, no locks, only a drapery or a string of bells to inform the owner that someone had entered. For theft the punishment was slavery. The thief had to 'work off' the theft; or should his immediate relations feel the social defilement brought on by his enslavement, they paid off the debt. There was no social atonement for theft. The thief did not pay society, the Mayas having no form of imprisonment except for sacrificial victims; the culprit paid the victim.

Homicide even if accidental, carried a death penalty—unless the relatives were willing to pay the victim's survivors. There was no such thing as accidental death; homicide was treated as willful murder. 'The penalty of homicide,' says Landa, 'even when death was accidental, was to die in the snares set by the victim's survivors.'

To their mystic mentality (this is true of primitives everywhere) there was no such thing as chance or accident; what we call accidental was to them purposeful. It revealed that evil influences were at work even before the 'accident' and that the intended victim had been 'selected'; it was a sign of malignant influences.

Any form of death was defilement. The greatest social uncleanliness came from the shedding of blood. The Mayas even had to atone for the killing of an animal. That is why the hunter hung up some part of the animal and usually pierced his own tongue and/or penis and spread a few drops of his own blood over the recently killed animal. Killing an animal gratuitously was the same as homicide, and anyone who took life and shed blood brought about social defilement; he was subject to tribal discipline.

Loss of property by accident was treated in the same way as if it had been caused deliberately. If an Indian knocked over another's beehive, he had to pay the owner. If it was proven that an Indian committed suicide because of blameful commission or omission on the part of another, the latter had to pay.

Adultery brought death. The only legal loophole was that one had to be caught *flagrante delicto.* If so caught, the wife's paramour was brought bound to the judges, was heard, sentenced, and then handed over to the husband, the offence being not so much a violation of virtue as of property. The adulterer was summarily executed by the husband, who 'dropped a large rock on his head . . . from a great height.'

When a Maya died he was wrapped in a shroud, usually his own manta. Into his mouth was placed ground maize with a few jade beads, 'which they also used for money so that they should not be without means to get something to eat in the other life.' The lower man was buried in the hard mud floor of his house with the things of his life; if he was a fisherman, nets and harpoons, if a warrior, shield and lance. All had pottery filled with drink and food.

Houses were abandoned after a generation of burials, becoming in effect family shrines. The possessions of the dead man were usually taboo, and most of them were buried with him.

The noble dead were buried in the plazas of the temple-cities. In Chichén Itzá the high priest was found in a sumptuously appointed stone-lined grave. Around what had been his neck were baroque pearls brought perhaps back from Venezuela by the seafaring Maya tradesmen. A chieftain's tomb found recently under a temple at Palenque is as elaborately splendid as anything found in the Old World.

In Yucatán, nobles were cremated and their ashes placed in an urn (made of ceramic or wood) which portrayed their features. Portrait statues were made of deceased people of position. The back of the head was left hollow and the ashes of the dead placed in it. 'They preserved these statues with a great deal of veneration.'

The Mayas believed in immortality and a form of heaven and hell. Those who kept the rituals, that is, 'the good,' went to a place shaded by 'the first tree of the world,' and drank their fill of cacao under it. As everywhere, the survivors had their taboos. They were socially defiled; by the clan custom they must keep the rituals or the dead would come back and claim something from the living. Privations of various kinds were imposed upon them. Her husband's death made a widow 'unclean,' and so long as the tie to the dead was unsevered, the uncleanliness persisted.

10 The Lords of the Maya

AT THE HEAD of the Maya city-state stood the *halach uinic.* He was *the* man, the 'real man,' the 'true man,' endowed with plenary powers and restrained only by a council who were presumably related to him by blood ties. He was absolute and, as in all theocracies, a demigod.

He surrounded himself with suffocating ritual, and was, said the Spaniards, trying to define him, 'the [state's] father and lord.' His skull was flattened so that it reached a narrow peak at the top, and his face was tattooed, actually scarified. He remodelled his nose with putty, making it a hooked beak to 'conform with the concept of beauty.' The prominent nose is the dominant feature of many stone bas-reliefs. His hair was allowed to grow long and into it were braided various ornaments. Ears were perforated and gradually enlarged, and enormous ornaments were passed through the lobe. (This custom recalls that of the Inca nobles, the 'Big Ears,' whom the Spaniards called *Orejones.*) The nose septum was pierced and a jade ornament passed through the perforation. The left side of the nostril was perforated and kept open by wooden plugs, replaced on festive occasions with a topaz that the Spaniards called 'amber.'

The Mayas' horror of empty space caused their art to be confusingly luxuriant; every part had to be covered with ornament. Their bodies were similarly treated; heads flattened, ear lobes widened until they would admit a turkey egg, the nose perforated and artificially deformed, the eyes purposely made crossed, facial hair pulled out, teeth filed and inlaid with jade, face and body tattooed. Finally, even the penis was transmogrified; this was often so cut that the glans looked as beribboned as a tassel. They sported jade rings on their fingers and toes; wrists and ankles were cuffed with ornaments. Sandals were often as gaudy as their loincloths. The Maya lord put over his breechclout a long skirt, often ankle-length; sometimes the skin of a jaguar was attached to it.

The headgear of the Maya lord was monumental. Often it was as large as himself. The headpiece was a mask, symbolizing the rain god or the sun god, and carved of wood or made of wickerwork. On this framework was elaborated a superb feather ensemble topped with swirling masses of iridescent green quetzal feathers.

He dressed differently for each of his various offices, religious, military, or civil; for each he carried a symbol of authority. As a war leader he wore a sort of body armour and carried lance and shield.

The glorious headdress of the Maya lord, the focus of his attire, was in contrast to the simple cloth 'crown' worn by Moctezuma and a far cry from the 'crown' of the Inca, which was a mere *llautu,* a sling worn about the head to which was added 'royal fringe.' A scene in which headdresses are being made ready appears in the murals of Bonampak. Detachable feather ornaments, mounted on winglike wooden elements are attached to the belt of the chieftain.

The *halach uinic* had one legitimate wife. Her title is not known. He also had his concubines, although there are no figures as to their number. (Moctezuma had 'many women as mistresses,' and the Inca rulers had a ménage of royal concubines (*pallas*); one of the last of the Lord-Incas had, in the male line alone, five hundred descendants!) Whatever her title, the wife of the Maya lord was herself 'lordly.' She was held in high respect, as can be seen from the superb modellings in clay of women of the upper classes. In the Bonampak murals the wife of the *halach uinic* can be seen with head flattened and ears pierced, wearing earrings and a necklace. Her hair is tied up and made into a swirling coiffure. A white *huipil* hangs off the shoulder, and a red stole is draped carelessly around her arms. Her hand holds a folding fan. So modern is her appearance—except for the flattened head—she could walk right out of the murals, which were painted in A.D. 800, and take her place in modern society.

The office of the Maya *halach uinic* was neither elective like that of the Aztec ruler, nor selective like that of the Inca, but hereditary. The office descended from father to son. 'If the lord died . . . it was the eldest son who succeeded him.' However, if the sons were not fit to rule, a brother of the ruler became head of state; and if no one was available for succession, a capable person was chosen by the council, probably a relative of the late lord, with the same patronymic.

How well did such a theocracy work? Diego de Landa thought it worked very well: 'Before the Spaniards had conquered that country, the natives lived together in towns in a very civilized fashion. They kept the land well cleared of weeds, and planted very good trees. The manner and order of their towns was as follows—in the middle of the town were their temples with beautiful plazas; all around the temples stood the houses of the lords and the priests, and then came the houses of the most important officials. Next were the homes of the rich men, and then those of the merchants who were held in the highest estimation, and at the outskirts of the town were the houses of the lower classes.'

The immense city-states built by the Mayas presuppose a high degree of

Buried for centuries in the jungle, *the Maya monuments are now yielding up their secrets. The huge Temple I at Tikal, rising to a height of 229 feet, is seen here in process of excavation. Vast labour must have been required to build the core of the pyramid, with its long steep flight of steps. At the top the temple proper occupies a space of only 150 square feet. Tikal survived until* A.D. *869.*

Chichén Itzá *lay near the tip of Yucatán. In this reconstruction by Tatiana Proskouriakoff the sacrificial well (cenote) is in the foreground; a wide ceremonial road leads to the Pyramid of Kukulcán, which dominates the whole area. On the right is the ball-court, in the rear centre the round Caracol, and on the left the Temple of the Warriors, with the corridor of the thousand columns below it. Behind this is the market. The old city can be seen in the background.*

social organization. A city structure must be planned. Manpower has to be organized and close at hand if the buildings are elaborate, as most Maya temples were. Artisans had to be trained and available. The earliest and the greatest of Maya cities was Tikal. It was so immense that its full size has not yet been determined. At present it is calculated to cover over twenty-five acres of jungle. The great court, lying roughly in its centre, is 400 by 250 feet in size. About it are its tallest pyramids, the largest of which towers 229 feet above the plaza. There are many other such and hundreds of structures, from small plazas to enormous reservoirs, broad causeways, ball courts, and a still undetermined number of lesser monuments. Each of these large pyramids contains something like 260,000 cubic yards of filling. It would require something like 100,000 manhours merely to place the core.

The Maya temple-city was a civil as well as religious centre. The reason one finds no evidence of city housing at such sites as Copán, Tikal, and Palenque is that the dwellings were made of very perishable materials and have vanished, leaving nothing behind except the remains of post-holes.

Mayapán was the only known organized Maya capital. The evidence of its existence is authentic—a written glyph history, a long tradition, and the proof offered by archaeological excavation. Since it is the only Maya site that has all these, it is the site that one must examine to form some idea of the structure and function of the Maya city. Mayapán was founded in 987 (or 941) after the Itzás, with the aid of the Toltecs, had taken possession of Chichén Itzá and the surrounding areas; it was, however, not really functional as a capital until after 1200. The Itzás were Maya-speaking, using Chontal, a Maya dialect. They came, it is believed, from Tabasco, the lands that produced much of the cacao-chocolate which was a Maya obsession.

Mayapán gave its name to the league of city-states in which it was, according to tradition, associated with Chichén Itzá and Uxmal. The league probably controlled much more than this. A Spanish report states that Mayapán 'conquered all these provinces,' and time and exploration in this area will reveal through the roads that lead to Mayapán that it was specifically erected for the purpose of controlling most of the north of Yucatán.

The towns, villages, and city-states controlled by the league were so many, said Diego de Landa, 'that the whole land appeared to be one town.' In 1194, as victor in a war with Chichén Itzá, Mayapán became the major power in northern Yucatán.

It was administered jointly by two tribal dynasties, the Cocoms, who claimed the closest descent from the Toltecs, and the Tutul Xius, who, through the Itzás, believed themselves claimants to the rule left by Kukulkan. 'These lords of Mayapán,' explained Diego de Landa, 'held the entire country in subjection and the natives of it were tributary to them. All the citizens and inhabitants who lived within the walled enclosure of Mayapán were exempt from tribute tax and in it dwelt all the nobles of the land. ... the lands were held in common so that between the towns there were no boundaries or landmarks. ... salt beds were also held in common [which bears out the author's contention that the League of Mayapán extended beyond the three cities] in those provinces on the northern sea coast which supplied all the inhabitants of the land.'

Though founded very late in Maya history, Mayapán is as 'early' as the capitals of the other theocratic Sun Kingdoms of America. Cuzco, the celebrated capital of the Incas, was not the capital before 1100, and the island capital of the Aztecs, Tenochtitlán, was not even founded until 1325.

In 1194, this 'dual monarchy' of Mayapán, after two hundred years of joint administration, exploded in violence. Chichén Itzá, one of the cities of the League of Mayapán, was held by the Tutul Xius, the hereditary rivals of the Cocoms. Since the strength of each of them was almost equal, the Cocoms went to Xicalango and hired a small army of Toltecs who had gathered there, for in 1156 Tula was burned and destroyed by the Chichimecas and this forced more of the Tula-Toltecs to migrate (as had Quetzalcoatl and others in the last part of the tenth century). Their bows and arrows and spears, with the deadly atl-atl, the throwing device, were for hire. Hunac Ceel, leader of the Cocoms, introduced the Mexicans into Yucatán. All sources, for once, agree on this; the very same names given for their chieftains is Mexican. Their capture of Chichén Itzá is pictured on the frescoes, the bas-reliefs, and even on the golden disks that were thrown into the *cenote* and dredged up in the nineteenth century. The contrast between Mexican and Maya, in dress, person, and weapons, is easily discernible. With the rivals of the Cocoms expelled from Chichén Itzá, this city was rebuilt.

Mayapán was now the dominant city, and the Cocoms the ruling element. The other contending dynasty, the Tutul Xius, were not fully quiescent; they nurtured their hate for two hundred and fifty years. In 1441 (or a date within ten years of that) a chieftain named Ah Xupán of the Tutul Xius, in conspiracy with others within the walled city of Mayapán, engineered a

'If this country had gold', *wrote one of the early Spaniards, 'it would be this well'—the 'cenote' of Chichén Itzá—'that would have the greater part of it, so great was the devotion which the Indians showed for it.' In 1905 these words were abundantly confirmed, when a treasure of sacrificial offerings was brought to the surface, among them this disk of sheet gold. It shows Tula-Toltec warriors extracting the heart of a Maya captive. Recently many more objects have been dredged from the 'cenote'.*

carefully arranged revolt. It was planned to occur when all the ruling members of the Cocoms were within the city walls. When the slaughter occurred, all of the chieftains were killed, save one who at the time was off on a trading expedition to Honduras.

There are native records of the fall of Mayapán, for it was a live and throbbing story when the Spaniards arrived seventy-five years later. It was the end of the only known capital of the Mayas.

11 An Art Ruled by the Gods

MAYA ARCHITECTURE differed from that of the other Sun Kingdom civilizations because of the use the Mayas made of lime mortar. Their buildings, said one writer, 'are essentially monoliths of rubble and lime with an exterior veneer of cut stone.'

Stone was quarried, shaped, and sculptured with stone celts. Neolithic peoples used thin-butted, polished-stone blades, and a reconstruction of such axes shows them to be empirically effective; a large tree can be felled within one hour. The cutting edges of stone axes are almost as sharp as steel, and they can be sharpened by rechipping. Similar stone hammers and chisels were the tools of the Maya builder.

Plans for Maya buildings were made on either paper or wood, and there must have been a unit of measurement, although no one has succeeded in discovering it. They doubtless had, like the Incas, professional builders or architects, that is, non-taxpaying specialists. Yet as great as is Tikal, not one architect's name has come down to us.

The *na,* the simple fascine house daubed with mud and thatched with palm leaf, was the humble origin of Maya architecture. The Mayas acknowledged this on one façade of the finest building in the Puuc, the Nunnery Quadrangle at Uxmal, where some sculptor depicted a series of these houses as decorative motifs.

Inca architecture also evolved from the simple native house, in their case the *wasi,* built of field stone and adobe cement. The Vitruvian theory, which holds that features of stone temple construction derive from wooden house prototypes, can apply to many cultures.

Stone hammers and stone chisels *were the tools with which the Mayas fashioned their building blocks and carved in the round and in low relief—thousands of intricate patterns, figures and glyphs.*

A stone mosaic, intricately carved, *cut in the façade of the finest building in the Puuc, the 'Nunnery' at Uxmal. In it will be seen one of the series of replicas of the simple peasants' house which the sculptor incorporated, and out of which Mayan architecture developed.*

Out of this house of the 'eternal peasant,' the Mayas shaped the most distinctive feature of their architecture, the corbelled arch. In this, the stones are placed so that each projects beyond the one below it; eventually the walls meet and a vault is formed. To support this type of arch, a weight mass was necessary. This developed into the roof comb, an overhang to act as cantilever to the vaulting, that became for Maya sculpture a façade on which to lavish intricate and swirling design. The Mayas have been known to raise a massive pyramid with an estimated 260,000 cubic yards of fill, only to place at its pinnacle a building of less than 150 feet square. Aware of the self-limiting aspect of the corbelled arch, the Mayas later used massive wooden beams and wooden lintels as well; these were made of sapodilla, a metal-hard wood. They counted on everything but the termites.

The sheer number of Maya remains is staggering. No one has yet tried to give them a precise figure. Those ruins which have been surveyed and photographed run into the hundreds while those which have been merely noted total even more. It can only be surmised that the scrub jungles and the rain forests yet hold hundreds more from man's sight.

Apart from cities and ceremonial centres, there is in the Maya architectural vocabulary a variety of other specialized constructions—ball courts, gateways, sweat baths, vaulted bridges, and raised platforms where plays were performed. Much of this the early Spaniards saw while it was still in its pristine form.

So many of these stone cities were there that Landa said 'the whole land appeared to be one town.' And so many are the remains of these cities today that neither this nor any one book could hope to cover all in full detail. Besides, to say everything is to say nothing. Here then is a selection of Maya cities with brief accounts of their form and function.

Tikal (A.D. 416) was the largest of Maya cities. Although it is only thirty-five miles from Uaxactún (they were connected by a causeway), its format is different. Tikal rests on a gigantic limestone outcrop. The surrounding forest is as thickly treed as the Amazon. Cedars, mahogany, palms, and the strangler *ficus* are dominant. Jaguars, tapirs, and snakes prowl the jungle floor, while monkeys and a variety of birds rule the treetops. It is here that these machineless men built their greatest city.

On an artificially levelled tongue of lime-rock, between two ravines, the centre of Tikal, civil and ceremonial, was built. Since there was a lack of dependable water supply, even with a high incidence of rainfall, the two ravines were converted into reservoirs and spanned by a raised causeway that is also a dam. There are five separate groups of buildings all connected by wide causeways, covering a square mile. Beyond this in every direction Tikal stretches out for several miles. So immense is the site that no one has yet even attempted a definite calculation. Since 1956 the long-held dream of archaeologists has been in the process of realization: the University of Pennsylvania is now at this moment of writing excavating and restoring the ruins.

Tikal is best known for the number of its monuments; thus far eighty-three stelae and fifty-four altars have been found. The city has the finest wood carvings known in the entire Maya area, twelve doorways and lintels carved on sapodilla wood, of which the first and the finest was carried off to a Swiss museum.

The pyramids of Tikal, which push their verdure-covered heads above the jungle, arrogantly towering above all else, were, one may well assume, its pride. Interior space was sacrificed to height and grandeur. In the great court, in the centre of Tikal, two of these massive pyramid-temples face each other. In the plaza, which measures 400 by 250 feet, stands a structure not unlike a Mesopotamian ziggurat; it rises to 229 feet. A stone staircase follows the setback structure to its apex. There, with decorated roof crest, is the temple—three dimly lit rooms with a gross space of less than 150 square feet. It is for this that Maya labourers worked incredibly long years to carry on their backs enough limestone rubble to fill 260,000 cubic yards. It is estimated that twenty-five thousand manhours were required merely to build up

The most distinctive feature of Maya architecture *is the corbelled arch, in which the stones are placed so that each projects beyond the one below it, until a single stone can rest across. This great arch is at Kabah, at the entrance to the ancient Maya road to Uxmal; it underlines the extraordinary failure of the Mayas to discover the principle of the true arch.*

the core of one of these pyramids. To cut, set, and finish the stone of the surface and rear the temple, with its florid and decorated roof crest, cannot be easily calculated. This must have cost the skilled masons twice as many man-hours as were required to build the inner core.

Next, lime mortar had to be made. It has been estimated that one sixteenth of most Maya structures is lime mortar. To reduce limestone to cement, which was done by burning, required four times as much wood, by volume, as limestone. For every twenty-one cubic yards of lime cement, a cord of wood was consumed. The immense labor service needed merely to fell trees with stone axes, then carry the wood to the lime kilns, can be grasped if not precisely calculated.

At Tikal there are eight such immense temple pyramids. Lesser structures—palaces or habitations—total ten times this number. There were acres of stucco surface to cover, and many of these structures are covered with glyphs. The mind reels at the thought of the organization required merely to supply labour to a city such as Tikal.

According to its own records, Tikal survived from A.D. 416 until 869, though it is possible that it was reoccupied briefly in the fourteenth century by the Itzás. Its existence was made known to the outside world in 1696, when a Franciscan monk, Andrés de Avendaño, on his way to 'reduce' the remaining Mayas about Lake Petén, stumbled upon 'a number of ancient buildings which although they were very high and my strength very little, I climbed.'

Copán (A.D. 460) the most southern of the great Maya cities, lies at an altitude of 2,000 feet in what is now Honduras. It was bound to those cities already mentioned by sea road and land road. Copán was built at the edge of the Copán River, which flows into the Motagua River, which in turn debouches into the Gulf of Honduras near Omoa, in ancient times a large Yucatán trading post. The region was known for its cacao and obsidian, its fine Ulúa marble vases.

Copán covers seventy-five acres; beyond this rather vast acreage lived the people. It is the second largest of Maya cities and composed of five main plazas and sixteen subgroups. The enormous main plaza, surrounded by tiers of stone seats, has been likened to the Roman Circus Maximus. The compact acropolis, overlooking the Copán River, is an amazingly wonderful complex of temples. In the eastern courtyard are tiers of stone seats and, at one end, the Jaguar Stairway, flanked by the stone jaguars from which its name is derived. The animals are rampant, one forepaw outstretched, the other akimbo. Their coats were spotted with rounded pieces of inlaid obsidian. The architects of the temple that dominates the courtyard made use of a squatting stone Maya figure to support a panel that is obviously alle-

The serpent god, *a grotesque head, with snakes writhing around the mouth. It is one of the two guarding the so-called Reviewing Stand at Copán, a flight of five steps, fifty-five feet wide. The date, given by a glyph at the top, is A. D. 771.*

gorical—a cacoplastic *mélange* of arms, gnomelike figures, dragonlike heads, a design that is mobile, moving out into space, formless yet form-consuming.

In the western court is the Reviewing Stand, which is dominated by a god entwined by a snake, in the fashion of Laocoön. From the same courtyard rises the famed Hieroglyphic Stairway, thirty feet in width and sixty-three treads in height. Each tread is decorated with a running commentary of glyphs. The dates, which alone have been deciphered, show that it was dedicated in A.D. 756. It is calculated that there must be twenty-five hundred glyphs in the stairway. Stephens hoped that when read they would reveal the 'entire history of the city,' but since only ten treads were found in their original positions, the restoration, completed in 1942, is at best tentative and conjectural.

Beyond this is the great plaza, at one end of which is a small temple. Carved and dated stelae, the most beautiful in the Maya lands, are scattered throughout this area.

Copán was no isolated city. Near by is Quiriguá, which is believed to have been intimately connected with its history. Northeast of it are several other known Maya sites.

Palenque (A.D. 642) is 280 miles northwest of Copán. No direct trade contact between the two cities has been established, but their art, sculpture calendric system, and glyph writing are similar. The two cities are separated by rivers, high mountains, deep ravines, thick jungles, and almost three hundred miles. Geography did not prevent the interchange of intellectual ideas between independent Maya city-states. Despite political disunity, there was a cultural unity.

The city is barely visible in a sea of jungle. Set at a 1,000-foot altitude in the Chiapas forests, near a small river (the Otolum, a tributary of the Usumacinta), Palenque by river travel is less than eighty miles from Xicalango, the great trading centre, with which it had trade connections. The city became known in 1773, when an Indian brought it to the attention of a priest who, amazed by all he saw, drew up a report. It was later visited by a Spanish captain of engineers, who wrought havoc there with his battery ram techniques. He was accompanied by an Italian architect, Antonio Bernaconi, in the Spanish service. When these reports were brought to the personal attention of Charles III of Spain, a ruler of the Enlightenment, he ordered that all antiquities found at Palenque be well preserved so that they could illustrate an *Historia antigua de América.*

That part of the site thus far uncovered consists of two groups of eight structures divided by a small ravine with river water that has been canalized to flow through a corbelled-arch sewer (an unusual Maya engineering feature). On the west bank is the Palace, an irregular rectangular structure 340 by 240 feet and sixty feet high. It is thick-walled and many-chambered, and has an interior court from which rises—unique in Maya architecture—a tower four stories in height with an interior stairway. At the entrance to the Palace are archaically carved stone figures, and the sides of the edifice are decorated with stucco figures in high relief, regarded by all as the finest anywhere. Within, there are carved stone panels with a remarkable series of well-preserved Maya texts. Four of the other structures, the temples of the Cross, the Sun, the Inscriptions, and the Foliated Cross, are outwardly similar—an artificially raised pyramid, with a single structure atop that is crested by an immense, decorated roof comb. The engineering purpose of the latter is to act as a cantilever to the corbelled arching beneath. All are decorated on the exterior with figures and ornaments in stucco, which were once brilliantly painted. Each of the large rooms has an altar and a carved wall panel. In one, the Temple of the Foliated Cross, are two life-sized figures (Maya dimensions) holding a mannequin up to the gaze of a bird which despite embellishments is the sacred quetzal. There are many inscriptions on the tablet. On the altar of another, the Sun Temple, the two figures stand upon the bodies of prostrated men. In the centre is the symbol of the sun, the face which some have likened to a Gorgon's head. Once again mannequins are held up in reverence. The Temple of the Inscriptions, which lies near the Palace, has lost its roof comb. It retains its decorations. The date that has been deciphered is A.D. 692.

In 1951 the Mexican archaeologist Alberto Ruz Lhuillier was assigned to restore some of the structures at Palenque. When his investigations

The creeping jungle *still covers much of ancient Palenque. Only the palace (left), the Temple of the Foliated Cross (centre) and the Temple with the Altar stand out in this aerial view. At the right foot of the large mound the roof-comb of the Temple of the Sun reaches above the trees; four other structures, including the Temple of the Inscriptions, are hidden.*

brought him to the Temple of the Inscriptions, he noticed in the inner room a large slab set neatly into the floor, with finger holes in it so it could be raised. He raised it, and following a narrow corbelled stairway downward, first in one direction and then another, he reached another large slab poised horizontally, sixty feet below the surface. In front of the door were the skeletons of six Mayas who had 'elected' to remain as guardians of the tomb. Beyond the stone door, a few steps down, was the tomb. When discovered it was a veritable fairy palace. Through the centuries the dripping water, lime-saturated, had formed into stalactites.

Over the tomb was a beautifully carved slab in relief. A portrait with hieroglyphics, it weighed five tons. Within was the skeleton of the 'true man,' bejewelled with enormous jade earrings, a jade necklace, and a pear-shaped baroque pearl. It had been long held that the Maya pyramids were built solely to support temples and did not contain the tombs of important personages, as pyramids do in other lands. The findings at Palenque changed this attitude.

Bonampak (A.D. 540) was an architectural satellite of Yaxchilán, some eighteen miles from the other city. Since it was recessed in the jungles away from the river, no one ever heard of Bonampak before 1946. In Maya the word means 'painted walls.' Giles G. Healy, a photographer pursuing a Maya chase for unknown ruins, pressed the search for Bonampak when he heard the Indians say 'painted walls.' He was led to the city on May 21, 1946. Hidden in the innermost recesses of the Lacandon jungles, Bonampak proved to be one of a constellation of unrecorded sites. There Healy found a local ceremonial centre, with eleven buildings and part of a carefully laid compact plaza 270 by 370 feet. Here were several dated stelae and decorated, carved, and dated altars. On a slight rise were several structures; one had three doorways. Its façade revealed marvellously moulded figures in stucco. (All of the sculpture found here is superb; it much resembles that of Yaxchilán.) Within this building Healy found the murals. Painted in A.D. 800, these rank as art with anything of similar antiquity, be it in Crete, India, China. As history they are one of the best sources of information of Maya life patterns, showing warfare, dress, musical instruments, religious ceremonies, sacrifice, and above all, the attitudes and expressions which make possible a new analysis of Maya social organization.

Uxmal (A.D. 987) lies in the Puuc of Yucatán, a range of low hills, rolling limestone ridges, with alternate pockets of soil. It is not only the most uniform of Maya cities; it is also the most beautiful. It has history, written, recitative, and traditional. Uxmal was part of the League of Mayapán. It even has a date in the literature: 'In Katun 2 Ahau [A.D. 987] the Maya Lord Ah Suytok Tutul Xiu was established in Uxmal.'

Higher than all else at Uxmal *rises the 'Temple of the Dwarf'. It is next to the 'Nunnery', which was probably the living quarters of the priests serving the temple. 'The 150 steps', wrote a Spanish friar in 1586, 'are difficult to ascend, for they are steep and, from their being very old, very dilapidated.' Its oval plan is unusual in Maya architecture.*

The luxurious palace of Sayil, *five miles north-east of Kabah, had a hundred rooms arranged in three storeys, the second and third set back so as to form terraces. Sayil dates from about* A.D. 800. *Dignified and simple, with columns oddly reminiscent of pre-classical Greece, it has none of the over-powering profusion of ornament typical of later Maya architecture.*

Open to the waves of the Caribbean *lies Tulum, a walled city dating at least from* A.D. 564, *showing the influence of the Toltecs and still inhabited when the Spaniards arrived in* 1519. *The wall is pierced by five gateways—the ruins of one of them occupies the foreground. Further away, overlooking the cliff, is the 'Castillo', the largest structure at Tulum, twenty-five feet high and with a square temple on the top. Tulum is one of the remotest sites in Yucatán.*

The 'thousand columns' of Chichén Itzá *stood in front of the Temple of the Warriors, and to the south of it (right) surrounded a square of four and a half acres. Outside this were three ball-courts and a sweat bath; inside it (off the picture) was the market. The columns supported carved wooden beams. Their builders were probably Toltec, the whole complex dating from the eleventh and twelfth centuries* A.D.

The temple of Kukulcán, *the largest building of Chichén Itzá, as it appeared in 1842; it has since been largely restored. There were four stairways, one for each side, the balustrades terminating in huge open-mouthed plumed serpents, one of which is lying in the foreground of Catherwood's picture.*

Traces of paint, *wrote Stephens, were still visible on the stucco ornaments in the square niches flanking this gate at Labná. The entrance is formed by a fine corbelled arch. Catherwood drew his lithograph in 1842.*

Count Waldeck may be trusted *in this view of the tower at Palenque in 1832—part of the Palace, four storeys in height and with an interior stairway. The sighing of the night-wind through the taut tree roots, he said, sang like a deep Aeolian Harp. The Indians would not go near it.*

Elegance was not always a quality in Mayan art, *but the several small pyramid-temples of Palenque show that it could be achieved. The Temple of the Sun is typical of the group—a simple structure set on an artificial mound, the surfaces covered with figures and ornament in stucco, once brightly painted, and the whole topped by an immense decorated roof-comb.*

Labná, which is dated from A.D. 869, *shares many of the characteristics of its neighbours—Uxmal, Kabah and Sayil. Here, on the ruins of its rubble-built base, is the Temple of the Figures, so called because the niches in its façade were once filled with life-sized carved figures of men and gods.*

The greatest of Maya observatories *is that at Chichén Itzá. It is a round tower forty-one feet high, standing isolated on a vast terrace. Near the top is an observation chamber with openings which follow certain astronomically important lines of sight—that through the west wall exactly bisects the setting sun at the vernal equinox.*

Maya baroque—*the façade of the Palace of the Masks at Kabah. The trunk-like ornamental motif repeated over and over again is the long nose of the god Chac. It covers the whole surface of this 150-feet building.*

'The single most magnificent building in the Americas'—*the House of the Governor at Uxmal. The lower half is plain, the upper covered with a dense mass of decoration, a masterpiece of precision and craftsmanship.*

Uxmal is fifty miles from the sea and a hundred from Chichén Itzá. It is the main city of the Puuc; about it are scores of cities, small and large, all of a similar style. The site of Uxmal is unusual because it was built near a *cenote*. The region has rich soil and plenty of rainfall, but no wells. So, as the Romans did at Capri, the builders of Uxmal relied on underground cisterns that collected the run-off of rain from roofs. It has been calculated that the plaza of Uxmal if used efficiently as a cistern could have kept six thousand people in drinking water throughout the year. All the Puuc cities provided themselves with underground cisterns, an engineering feat which would have brought encomiums from the Romans themselves.

There are eight groups of buildings at Uxmal, covering an immense area. The House of the Governor and its related structures stand at what is considered to have been the secular administrative centre of the city. Mounted on an artificially constructed mound, fifty feet high and reached on all sides by stone steps, the group covers five acres of ground. The palace itself is 320 feet long, 40 feet wide, 26 feet high, and it is the single most magnificient building ever erected in the Americas. The whole is covered with a veneer of ornamented stone, the joints fitting as perfectly as a mosaic. Each stone is an element in this immensely beautiful facade, which is a masterpiece of precision and craftsmanship. On an altar in front of it rests a double-headed jaguar, heads fore and aft. In front of the main flight of steps was an enormous stone phallus, which is broken in half and for 'moral' reasons never restored. It stood ten feet high when in its pristine state.

Around the House of the Governor are pyramids, other palaces, and the House of the Pigeons, so termed by someone because the roof comb resembles a dovecote. Close upon the palace, on the same raised plaza, is the House of the Turtles (the decorative motif on the façade is a parade of realistically carved box tortoises). South of this, where the great *sacbe* causeway passed (it ran directly in front of the House of the Governor and led to Kabah), there are other buildings, now mostly amorphous except for the Temple of the Phalli, where there are enough reminders of the worship of the ithyphallic to make even Aldous Huxley change his assertion, 'There is no sex in the art of the Maya. . . .'

The ball court is north of the palace, and beyond it is the second group of buildings: the Nunnery Quadrangle and the temple-pyramid of the Dwarf. The latter is an oval-shaped pyramid. On one side a broad flight of stairs mounts at an almost perpendicular angle 125 feet high to the temple, which had as its motif Chac, the open-mouthed god, patron of rain. Immediately below the pyramid, so close that in the late afternoon it shadows it, is the Nunnery. This is a somewhat irregularly shaped quadrangle, enclosed by a low range of buildings, each with a different motif. Like the

Governor's Palace, the whole is faced with a veneer of cut stone set into designs which 'project'—the white stones are set so as to create a chiaroscuro of light and shade. One of these buildings is multi-storied, a temple dramatically set back with intricate ornamentation. On another the corners have the long snout of the rain god as decoration. The third has as its motif the simple *na* house of the common Indian, immortalized in stone. The fourth shows another variation of the fret design, over which stone snakes coil, twist, and entwine. At intervals there are figures of men with abnormally large penes.

Uxmal, although still little explored beyond its immediate confines, has been partially restored. There is much contradiction here. Mentioned in the Maya chronicles as having been built by the Maya-speaking Toltecs, it possesses the least of Mexican architectural traits. Uxmal is supposed to have been one of the triumvirate of the League of Mayapán, but archaeologists suggest that it was abandoned before the league was in operation. It has been called decadent, whereas it has a style wholly its own. Sixteen dated stelae have been found in and about Uxmal. When read, the dates are within the tenth century. The style of the sculpture, ornate and flamboyant, is also decadent, says one writer, in comparison with that of Tikal.

Kabah (A.D. 879) lies nine miles southeast of Uxmal. The ancient Maya *sacbe*, which leads to it, leaves Uxmal in front of the Governor's Palace and goes past the Hacienda San Simón (which belonged to Simón Peón, host to Stephens and at that time owner of Uxmal). Near by is a stone arch similar to the one at Kabah. It stands in isolation and is not related to any other structure. Six miles farther, following the *sacbe*, one comes to Kabah. The main road continues southeast, but a branch of it makes a sharp left turn and comes up and passes under the Great Arch of Kabah. Stephens discovered it and Catherwood made a drawing of it, but later archaeologists, who could not find it, politely smirked at this 'triumphal arch.' Today it stands restored, and is the formal entrance to Kabah.

As Kabah now stands, there are three groups of buildings visible to the eye, and uncovered mounds and temples abound. Around Kabah, in the eleventh and twelfth centuries, was one of the densest populations in Yucatán. The Palace of the Masks—for once rightly named—is Maya baroque; the long-snouted masks of the god Chac are repeated over and over again along the whole range of the 151-foot-long building. The effect of this lavish use of the motif is simply overwhelming. In front of it there is an altar filled with a running commentary of glyphs. Before it and underground is a huge cistern, a *chultun*, which was the depository for water collected from the roofs. Kabah had two dated wooden door-jambs (A.D. 879) showing warriors with spear throwers—an indication of Toltec presence in the Puuc.

Labná (A.D. 869), one of the constellation of cities about Uxmal, is only six miles from Kabah. Its architecture is characteristic of the Puuc. Labná lacks architectural continuity. One feels that the project was larger than the labour supply and that buildings grew by accretion; many structures were left unfinished. There are only two known dates from Labná. One of these, A.D. 869 is carved on the elongated proboscis of the god Chac.

The Palace, imposingly set on an artificial hill, has two immense cisterns, one within the building itself and another that takes up its whole front (the very one into which John Lloyd Stephens lowered himself, despite all warnings, to make sure that it was a cistern). This palace, presumably an administrative centre, was joined to the other group of buildings by a causeway, a ceremonial road 450 yards in length, ten feet wide, and varying between two and eight feet in height. There is here, as at Uxmal and Kabah, a gateway; it is part of a building. As at Uxmal, the native house, the common dwelling of adobe and thatch, is immortalized in stone. Here it is used on either side of the gateway as a decorative motif.

Sayil (A.D. 800) is the oldest of the group. The dating is based more on its style than upon any dated stelae. Its centre of interest (there are many other structures in ruins about it) is its palace of a hundred rooms arranged in three stories. The second and third are set back, leaving terraces as rest areas for the occupants. A great stone staircase beginning at the bottom leads to all three terraces. It is 210 feet long and seventy-five feet wide; it has magnitude, proportion, order, and sensibleness. The style is massive and simple and has the classic qualities of Greek Doric architecture. Around its façades is the ubiquitous mask motif. It has, wrote Tatiana Proskouriakoff, 'a freedom from the oppressively monotonous intricacy of ornament that mars many *Puuc* structures.' There are so many late Maya cities within the Puuc, each with something individual about it, that we can mention only the more important: Xcalumkin; Chacmultun, with its interesting murals; Holactun; Almuchil; Kickmool; Keuic, visited by Stephens, who spelled it 'Kewick'; Huntichmool; Sabacche; Yache; Xcalumpococh.

Chichén Itzá, thrice founded (A.D. 432, 964, and 1194), was the greatest of the Maya cities near the Yucatán tip. On a plain so flat that its great pyramid can be seen for miles around, Chichén Itzá was joined by road to Izamal and to the seacoast at Polé, in direct line with Cozumel Island. Important in the history of the city are its two enormous natural wells, one of which was used for human sacrifice and the others as a source of water.

The first founding of the city (A.D. 432) was by immigrants from the Old Empire during the 'Little Descent.' They formed their city around the salubrious Xtoloc well, where they built two masonry stairways descending precipitously sixty feet to the water's edge. The architecture of old Chichén is reminiscent of the Puuc style. Many of the buildings have almost identical

The tall columns of the Temple of Warriors *at Chichén Itzá are covered with decoration and glyph inscriptions. Behind is a plumed serpent, characteristic of Toltec and later Mayan cultures, its open mouth on the ground, poised tail aloft. In the centre sits Chac-Mool, the Rain God, awaiting on its lap the hearts of human sacrifices.*

motifs, masks, colonnettes, and frets, especially the building named the *Abab dzib*. Traditions and dates give this further proof. The rounded 'astronomical tower,' certainly one of the most interesting in the area, is dated A.D. 900.

Chichén the 'new' was founded at the north end about the sacrificial *cenote*. This well is 190 feet in diameter and now contains thirty-six feet of water, green with algae, and forty feet of detritus. Its water level stands sixty-five feet below the surface. The 'new' part of Chichén Itzá was occupied by the Itzás between the years 987–1194. There were two distinct Mexican invasions into Yucatán and Chichén Itzá. The first was peaceful, of Maya-speaking Itzás who, although of apparent Mexican origin, had an understanding with the Toltec leader, Quetzalcoatl, who had been exiled from Tula with an army of his followers. They jointly descended upon Chichén Itzá, then unoccupied. It was the period in which many people, both in the Mexican highlands, and throughout the Maya country, were in mass movement. Famine, drought, or disease may have been the concomitant causes. Tikal, Palenque, Piedras Negras, and doubtless hundreds of smaller inland Maya cities were putting up their last time-markers and passing into cultural silence. This was the time of great dispersals almost everywhere in this part of the Americas. Among the Mayas it was known as the 'Great Descent.' It is recorded in their traditions.

Chichén Itzá was apparently unoccupied when the Itzás with the Toltecs of Quetzalcoatl took it over. Some time after 900 (there is a confusion of time sequences between archaeological and native history) they built the first large truncated pyramid at Chichén. This was discovered when archaeologists of the Carnegie Institution while restoring the pyramid-temple of Kukulcán, found a smaller one underneath it that served as core to the larger. It was Maya in style, but with Toltec motifs, e.g., marching jaguars such as are found at Tula in central Mexico. A secret stairway led to the Red Jaguar throne room. Here a life-sized effigy of an open-mouthed jaguar, painted a mandarin red, stood guard. Its spots are seventy-three round disks of polished jade.

Chichén Itzá, by a strange concatenation of events, was now bound up with the culture of Tula which lay seven hundred and fifty miles to the northwest. This ruined city, near Mexico City, had been the capital of the Toltecs, after the collapse of ancient Teotihuacán. Between the years 900 and 1156 it was again the centre of Toltec culture. The temple of Tula had the

Man of the Maya. *A pottery figurine from Jaina, in Campeche, showing the breechclout (originally painted red), the cloak with its strange spikes, not yet explained, the cowl head-dress, necklace of beads and tattooed chin. The figure is in fact a whistle, 8½ inches high, with mouthpiece under the left knee.*

Into this pool were flung gold and jewels, *images (some of rubber), works of art—and human beings. It is the sacred 'cenote' of Chichén Itzá, a key point in the huge ceremonial plan. Today the author looks down on a calm weed-covered pond, though its original shape is still clear and it still holds 36 feet of water.*

plumed serpent motif, an immense snake rampant, formed into fifteen-foot-high caryatids. Inside the temple were immense warrior figures as colonnades. About the lower portions of the temple were motifs of marching jaguars and rampant eagles. Above all else there appeared the terrible figure of the Chac-Mool, a prone stone figure with a vacant expressionless face. Its hands held a stone dish, and into this freshly torn human hearts were flung during sacrifices.

Some time in the tenth century, Chichén Itzá was occupied for the second time and those who came with the Itzás were of Toltec origin. Archaeology, history, and tradition, except for precise dates, are for once in full agreement; 'it is believed,' wrote Landa, '. . . that with the Itzás who [re-] occupied Chichén Itzá, there reigned a great lord named *Kuk* [quetzal] *ul* [feather] *can* [serpent], and that the principal building, which is called Kukulcán, shows this to be true.' This temple, called the *Castillo* by the Spanish (because a conquistador once mounted his cannons at its pinnacle), the temple one now sees, was erected over the first; its ninety-one steps rise on all four sides and terminate at its truncated summit with an elaborate temple. The Toltec builders under Huanc Ceel, the conqueror of Chichén Itzá in 1194, introduced carved wooden beams to provide larger space, since Maya rooms were severely restricted by the use of the corbelled arch. The walls had murals which still survive to show many aspects of Toltec-Maya life. An open-mouthed plumed serpent is on the balustrade on each of the four stairways ascending the pyramid. On top, at the temple, the serpents appear again, this time as sculptured columns—precisely like those at Tula. To make doubly certain that people knew it was the Temple of Kukulcan, the top of the building is decorated with the symbol of the sky god, Quetzalcoatl.

The square where the temple rests is a huge, roughly trapezoidal walled square, 1,600 by 1,400 feet. Within this is a gigantic ball court (its tribunes carry architectural motifs derived from Tula). There are low platforms, 'theatres,' reached by stone stairways (Landa refers to 'two small stages of hewn stone where they gave farces . . . and comedies for the pleasure of the public'). Near by is a thirty-foot-wide ceremonial causeway, leading nine hundred feet to the sacrificial *cenote*.

The Temple of the Warriors faces the great square. Its corridor of the 'thousand columns' is below, within another walled enclosure. This,

The Toltecs who invaded Chichén Itzá *left a powerful impression on its sculpture and architecture. Compare this Toltec figure from Tula of the terrible Chac-Mool with that seen through the columns of the Temple of the Warriors at Chichén Itzá (facing page 192). In both a dish awaits the human hearts and a vacant, brutal face turns away.*

smaller than the great plaza, has at one end another group of buildings, one of which is called the 'Market.'

The Temple of the Warriors in many of its features resembles the Toltec temple at Tula: the plumed-serpent columns, fanged mouths open and tails rampant; the motifs of marching jaguars and eagles, symbolizing the military orders of highland Mexico; the dwarfed figures at the temple's edge that held feather banners; and that Tula fixture, the reclining figure of Chac-Mool. Finally, the 'thousand columns,' which once supported carved wooden roof beams, bear the same martial motifs as those at Tula: armed spearmen with helmet and body armour of Mexican origin.

Tula, near Mexico City, lies seven hundred and fifty miles in a direct line to Chichén Itzá, but as man then had to move through mountain passes, swamps, jungles, high mountains, not to mention hostile tribes, all of which necessitated wide détours, the distance was actually more than a thousand miles. 'The extraordinary fact,' states Eric Thompson 'is that nowhere between central Mexico and Yucatán have buildings or sculptures [such as the Temple of the Warriors and the temple at Tula] in this distinctive style been found.'

Tulum (A.D. 564) is a walled city lying on the open Caribbean sea coast opposite (and twenty-five miles from) the extreme southern tip of Cozumel Island. The present-day Mayas have in their folklore a tale that in ancient times Tulum was connected to Cobá, Chichén Itzá, and Uxmal by *cuxan san*, a road suspended in the sky. This *cuxan* (living) *san* (rope) is based on considerable archaeological fact; stone-laid causeways at one time did connect these cities.

The beginnings of Tulum, anciently called Zama, stretch back into the earliest time. It was being added to during the late Toltec period in Yucatán, and it was populated when the Spaniards in four ships under command of Juan de Grijalva sailed along the coast in May, 1518. The chaplain, Juan Díaz, reported seeing 'three large towns separated from each other by two miles. There were many houses of stone . . . we perceived a city or town so large that Seville would not have seemed more considerable. . . . there was a very large tower; on the shore was a great throng of Indians, who bore two standards which they raised and lowered to signal us to approach.' There were really four towns—Xelha, Soliman, Tulum, and Tancah—situated so close to one another as to give the impression of one continuous city. At that time the chieftain of Tulum was the captor and master of the Spaniards Aguilar and Guerrero.

Tulum is the largest and most impressive Maya city on the east coast of Yucatán. It is mounted on the summit of a limestone cliff forty feet high, lashed by waves of the open sea, and covered with a cheval-de-frise of cactus

With fanged mouths open and tails rampant, *these plumed serpents of the Temple of the Warriors at Chichén Itzá show clearly the influence of the Toltecs who built the temple of Tula. A thousand-mile journey through difficult country separates the two.*

and thorned plants, a veritable barbed wire. On its other three sides the city is protected by a great wall, thirty-six hundred feet in length and averaging fifteen to twenty feet in height. It is pierced by five narrow gateways, each of which will admit only one person at a time. Guardhouses are placed at the western end. Beyond is a solid mass of vegetation growing out of swamps that stretch for many miles inland. The northeast gate was the sally port to the causeway that led to Xelha, six miles distant, and somewhere near it was the turnoff for Cobá and thence to Chichén Itzá.

Most Maya sculpture was an integral part of the building, but sometimes it stood on its own as an art form; this sculpture had various voices and various mediums—stone, stucco, wood, and clay.

Most conspicuous, since they are massive and impressive, are the carved stone monoliths called stelae. These large, shaftlike obelisks appear scattered throughout the Maya cities that existed between the dates A.D. 328 and 889.

Fifteen hundred years ago *this stele was carved at Tikal. It was discovered during the most recent excavations, and may prove to be the 'Rosetta Stone' of Mayan archaeology, since it contains an unparalleled series of well-preserved glyphs. The side illustrated here shows a priest, with damaged profile, wearing an elaborate head-dress. His raised right hand (left side of the picture) holds a chain, with heads dangling from it, and he carries another head in the crook of his left arm.*

Intricate ornamentation *from the East Range of the 'Nunnery', Uxmal, with strong reliefs of cut stone dominated by the long snout of the rain god, Chac. The drawing was made by Catherwood in 1842.*

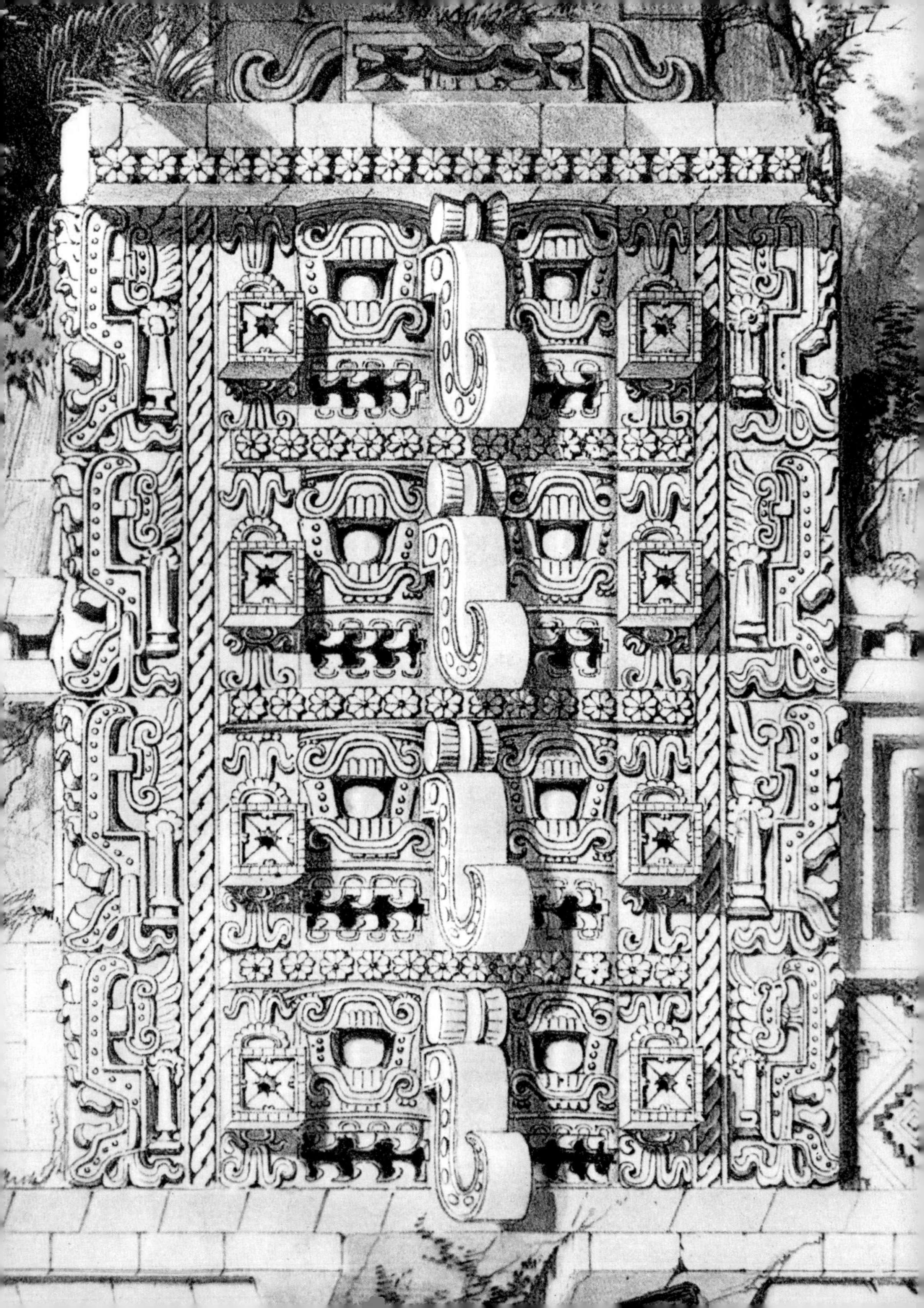

To shed one's own blood *was the most effective way of securing the favour of the gods. Here, on a carved stone lintel from Menché, a worshipper kneels before a priest and pierces his tongue with aloe thorns fixed to a cord. The drops of blood are then caught in the basket in front of him and offered up to the god.*

The Sun-God Pipil *descends for his tribute of a human heart, held up to him by a priest who has just ripped it from the palpitating breast of a sacrificial victim. This bas-relief shows Toltec influence and comes from Santa Lucía, Guatemala.*

Jade was a favourite material *of the Maya artists and they achieved an astonishing range of expression in this difficult medium. It was obtained chiefly from the mountains of eastern Guatemala.* Below: *an ear-ring from Pomona (British Honduras) with date-glyphs inscribed on its surface. Above right: a tiny jade pendant, showing a bearded face, dignified and almost classical. Below right: in complete contrast, a mask whose sensual features recall the huge stone heads carved by the Olmecs. Below: a more typical Maya mask from Chiapas.*

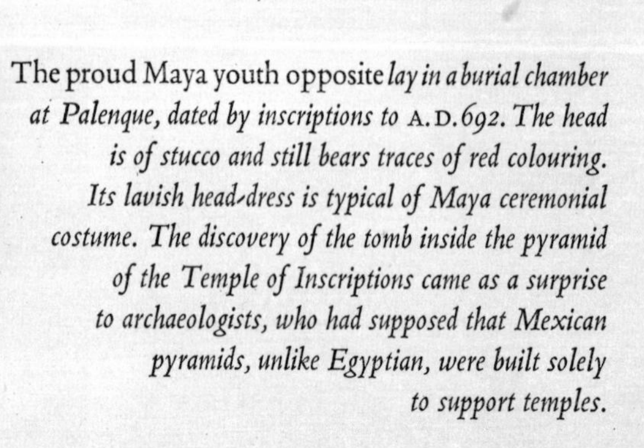

The proud Maya youth opposite *lay in a burial chamber at Palenque, dated by inscriptions to* A.D. *692. The head is of stucco and still bears traces of red colouring. Its lavish head-dress is typical of Maya ceremonial costume. The discovery of the tomb inside the pyramid of the Temple of Inscriptions came as a surprise to archaeologists, who had supposed that Mexican pyramids, unlike Egyptian, were built solely to support temples.*

'The Queen of Uxmal'—*an expressive and sensitively modelled human head, with tattooing on one cheek, emerging from the wide-open jaws of a serpent. It once formed part of the decoration of the pyramid supporting the Temple of the Dwarf at Uxmal. The title is an invented nickname; there is no evidence of a queen at Uxmal.*

The wide range of Maya commerce *is illustrated by the objects found in the cenote of Chichén Itzá. They come from regions as distant as Columbia and Peru, and were offered, as the most precious possessions of their owners, to the gods. This is a gold pendant in the Quimbaya style, from the Cauca Valley of Columbia; its design is a stylization of a man's face and body.*

The obelisks represent portraits of priests or rulers, and are carved in relief or in the round, with glyphs that record their dates. Since they served a hierarchic purpose, the figures are formal, austere, overpowering. Only the backgrounds have freedom, and some are vehemently alive, the sculptor carving animals, birds, and men that flow about the religious format. One such stele at Quiriguá is thirty-five feet high and weighs fifty tons.

The sculptor's tool was the stone celt (either made from basalt or diorite). His usual medium was limestone, which often had the texture of marble. Inexhaustible patience had taught him to transcend the limitations of Neolithic techniques.

Stucco allowed the Maya artist greater freedom than stone and this form of sculpture is found at widely separated areas, from Tulum on the coast to newly excavated Dzibilchaltún, and up to Palenque in the humid jungles. Stucco is a natural outgrowth of hand-modelled clay. As sculpture, it also was closely allied with architecture. It is at Palenque, however, that 'stucco came into its supreme expression. . . . whether frugal or abstract it speaks one idiom. . . . it is highly articulate and technically pre-eminent.'

Clay sculpture preceded stone sculpture and modelling in stucco. The small clay heads made to propitiate the gods are among the earliest artifacts to be found. While Maya modelling does not have the force of the Aztec, it has great merit. The life-sized funeral urns seen by Diego de Landa and dug up in fragments show how large a clay mass the Maya artists could handle with elaborate appliqué decorations.

Figures in sculptured clay have been discovered throughout the Maya area, but the finest are those found in a cemetery on the island of Jaina, off the Campeche shore; these are the jewels of any Maya collection. The Jaina figures are portrait statuettes. Although small, ranging from six to twelve inches in height, they are majestic in concept. Little else in the whole range of Maya art is more sensitively wrought. Of the Jaina pottery the late Miguel Covarrubias, one of the few creative artists who weighed these as art, said: 'it shows an extraordinary mastery in handling, a realistic knowledge of form and movement.' The statuettes reflect the Maya ideal; there are figures of warriors and actors with arms outstretched in dramatic movement, chieftains sitting cross-legged and festooned with elaborate headgear; in a sort of 'Susanna and the Elders' theme, an elderly man caresses a young woman. This is the kind of detail for which a historian searches when trying to construct what the Mayas looked like behind the luxuriant façades of surface decoration. In these the faces are so exquisitely modelled that every nuance of expression can be seen. Calm, defiance, lust, all can be discerned. More than half of the Jaina statuettes found are of women. These meet Huxley's

Amid the ruins of Tikal *were found twelve superb doorways and lintels carved in sapodilla wood, of which this is one. The central design is a rush-mat which stood for 'Pop', one of the months of the Maya calendar. Glyphs on one of the carvings give the date* A.D. 741.

complaint ('the most conspicuous absence from Maya sculpture is that of the female form—*et tout ce qui s'ensuit*'), for here women as subject matter are treated with concern and feeling.

Wood carving was for the Maya only another form of sculpture, except that wood is a more obedient medium than stone. A considerable number of wood carvings have been found in Yucatán, but the finest are those discovered at Tikal.

Before the Maya carved their calendars on stone, they carved on wooden stelae. When they used wooden beams for ceilings instead of stone corbelled arching, the beams were carved. Landa referred to some he had seen as 'great beams standing erect and ornamented with carvings.' At Tikal several of the temple-pyramids yielded, even after a thousand years, wooden panels carved of sapodilla wood. One, with a spread-winged quetzal and a fantastically conceived god, is seven by seven feet; a carbon-14 dating does not disallow the date given on its own glyphs, A.D. 741. Several such have been found at Tikal; they are now all in European museums. Wood carving was practised extensively by the Mayas. They made idols, helmets, ceremonial masks (which were adorned with feathers), masks for actors, intricately adorned wands of office, and carved boards that served as bindings to their 'folded books.' Landa admitted even in his time that the Mayas earned 'a great deal making idols and carvings . . . of wood.'

Yucatán produced neither gold nor copper, but by the early eighth century gold began to filter into the land of the Mayas. After 900, when they were concentrated in the Yucatán peninsula and trade was extended, gold and copper began to appear with some frequency. It was further quickened by the coming of the Itzás. Copper brought from Oaxaca to trade at Xicalango was made into bells; gold plate and leaf brought from Panama was fashioned into ornamental disks and crowns. All that is now known of Maya gold concerns the objects dredged from the *cenote* at Chichén Itzá by Edward H. Thompson. Reposing in the Peabody Museum at Harvard for many years, they have recently been the subject of a splendid brochure. Many of those objects found are in the style of Veragua, suggesting that they were cast there. The gold plates a foot in diameter are interesting for the history of the Mayas, for despite the Maya glyphs that rim the disks, they are decorated in Toltec themes—the ritual of tearing the heart from a sacrificial victim, the scenes of naval battle between Itzás and Mayas—evidence of how late goldwork came to the Mayas.

Maya painting, as revealed in the frescoes, shows a realistic perception and a more advanced realistic style than that of any of those other civilizations numbered among the Sun Kingdoms of the Americas. Art was not for the masses. It was not meant to be educational and rarely designed to commemorate historical events: it was religious, symbolic and it never so completely lost its symbolism as to become purely decorative.

Because art was religious it concerned itself little with the secular. Despite this the Maya artist limned real people in naturalistic poses, there is an emphasis on movement and an attempt at perspective, people are differentiated by head-dress, costume, action. The earliest known mural—that found at the ruins of Uaxactún—depicts what is easily seen to be a conversation between Maya lords (precisely what they are talking over the glyphs do not reveal). It has gesture, colour, movement. Those found at Chacmultun, in the Puuc region of Yucatán, removed by a distance of 210 miles and six hundred years from the one at Uaxactún, reveal the same spirit.

Murals have been found elsewhere in the country, unfortunately in fragments. The narrative quality of the murals at Chichén Itzá, created during the Toltec period, is almost wholly secular. Those within the Temple of the Warriors, which covered a wall space 9 feet high by 12½ feet wide, belie the name of the temple, for they show scenes of everyday life in a coastal village in Yucatán, a type of picture seldom found among the

The Viceroy in his vestments. *The batabob, or territorial governors, gathered for a ceremony, are being dressed. The figure on the right is almost ready: his jaguar skin and magnificently embroidered skirt are on, his bracelets, collar, ear-plugs and anklets. His elaborate head-dress is possibly of pressed fibre, formed into shapes such as symbolic fish and water-lilies. Behind, the great green frame of quetzal feathers is in position. An attendant fastens one bracelet, another daubs his skin with red ochre. It is the apparel of power, on a man to be feared. The scene is a detail from the murals of Bonampak, copied by Antonio Tejeda.*

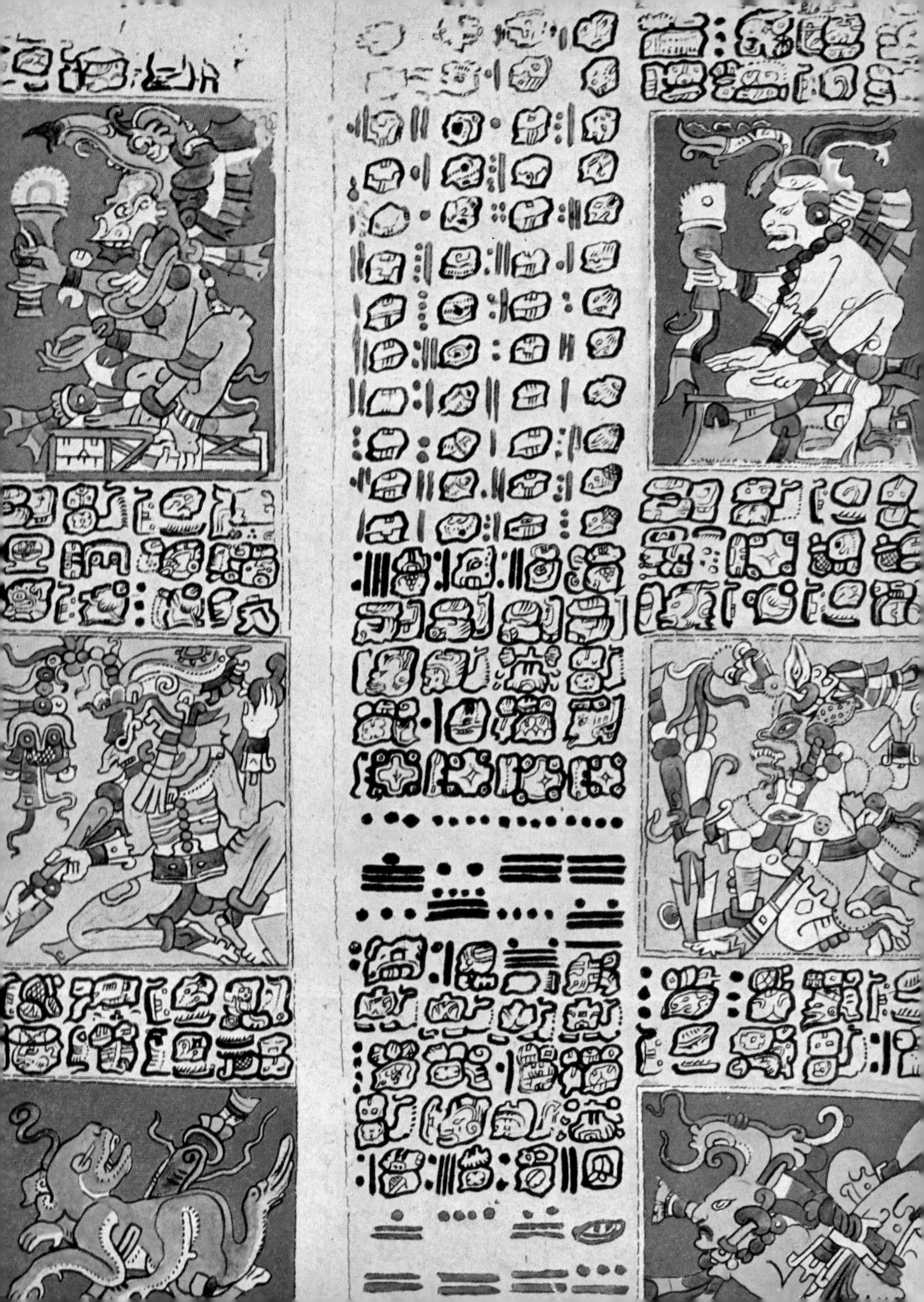

Mayas. Here are realistic and genre drawings of Maya dugout canoes, trees, houses, and even the tall feather-and-wood markers that were used to signal the landfall for sea traffic. The artist here does not depict temples and priests, but shows the simple native house, women at work and at rest, men 'who were the oxen of the land,' carrying their trade goods to market. On the walls of other structures at Chichén Itzá—the ball court, the Temple of the Jaguars—there are animating scenes of battle. Instructive as to Maya armour and weapons, they are also revealing tableaux of dress and postures.

The murals of Bonampak, discovered in 1946, have so revolutionized our earlier concept of Maya society that the literature has yet to come fully to terms with the change. There are three rooms of murals; taken together they form a continuous narrative: a raid on enemy territory, a consultation among the chiefs, a judgment of prisoners, and a festival to commemorate the victory. The figures are almost life-size.

The technique was done in classic fresco. Cement was applied to the walls, and while it was still wet the artist drew his cartoon on it. Then his assistants—and there must have been many—applied the colours. As analyzed by the Mexican muralist Villarga, who aided in the copying of the Bonampak pictures, the whole of the three rooms must have been painted in forty-eight hours. Plasterer and artist have to work together in this medium, and since Villagra could not detect where the plaster was laid, the making of a fresco must have been a continuous process. The palette of the Bonampak artists was rich. The famous Maya blue dominates, and there are yellows and browns and a lustrous black. The colours were mostly mineral; the reds and yellows were oxides; Maya blue came from a blue chromiferous clay; and black was carbon. One authority believes that the ground colours were mixed with the resin of the *pom* tree, from which varnish is now produced commercially. The murals of Bonampak show us the Maya artists' mastery of line and colour, and a passionate movement of figure, a limitless freedom of posture, that has never before appeared in primitive American art. Although the Bonampak murals have disintegrated, they were superbly copied, and the small temple ruin duplicated.

Polychromic pottery can also be considered painting, and there are many superb examples of it. The Maya 'book' itself was only a continuation of the mural. And in turn, many murals, especially those found at the ruins of Tulum and Santa Rita (in British Honduras), would appear to be copies of pictures in the 'books.'

The Dresden Codex *is the best of the three surviving Maya documents. This reproduction is from Humboldt's 'Nouvelle Espagne Atlas' (Paris, 1810), the first copy of the Codex to appear in Europe. It shows elaborate astronomical calculations, recording the rhythm of the planet Venus.*

12 The Culture that Died

THESE ARTS did not flourish in tranquillity; the myth of the peace-loving Mayas has been completely shattered. War was continuous. It could not be otherwise. There were contending city-states with no set boundaries; farmers by the very nature of their agriculture moved back and forth in trespass. Commerce was carried on, then as now, at friend or enemy's expense. Slaves were important, and the only way to get them was in battle. Victims were needed for sacrifice, since an individual was not expected to immolate himself for the gods if someone else was available.

Their primary weapons were the spear, the obsidian-edged war club, and the spear-throwing *atl-atl,* the last a very effective weapon as Bernal Díaz confirms ('our captain was wounded in no less than twelve places by these arrows'). For close-quarter fighting they used a broad-bladed flint knife and a three-pronged claw knife, made out of a large shell, that could work havoc. Slings were used; there is extant a sculpture showing a warrior carrying into battle a basket of stones the size of hen eggs.

The warrior died gloriously. No knight went into battle more panoplied than he. His wooden headgear had a magnificent stream of quetzal and parrot feathers cascading over his shoulders, his face was gaudily painted, and his jade bracelets and necklaces flashed like emeralds under the Maya sun. A marked man in battle, he was its primary object. When he was captured, his warriors usually fled—and he was sacrificed.

War, although continuous, was waged in relatively short battles. They often occurred in October when the farmer-soldier did not have to work his cornfield. Surprise was the desired tactic. When defences were plumbed, the Maya warriors attacked en masse. If the defenders were too firmly entrenched, the Mayas hurled entire hornets' nests into the enemy and set thatch roofs afire. Then in a chaos of sound, drums beating, conch shells and whistles blowing, they fell to. Slaughter was not the primary aim of

War was continuous *between the Maya city-states. This fresco from the Temple of the Warriors at Chichén Itzá gives a vivid idea of a raid. A village is being sacked. Typical Maya houses appear in the middle and far distances. In the centre, warriors seem to be defending a temple against attackers whose sumptuous equipment proclaims their high rank. In the foreground, naked prisoners, painted with horizontal stripes and with their arms tied behind their backs, are being led away to captivity.*

The end of the world. *The last page of the Dresden Codex describes the eventual destruction of the earth by water—a myth which still persists among the Maya of today. At the top of the picture is a dragon, whose body carries the symbols of the constellations and, hanging from its belly, signs of the solar and lunar eclipses.*
From these signs, and from the dragon's mouth, gush streams of water. Underneath, the old Woman Goddess holds an inverted bowl, also with water pouring from it; while at the bottom sits the God of War, with two javelins and a long staff, all turned downward.

warfare. Like the Aztecs, the Mayas wanted prisoners—the distinguished ones for sacrifice, the less worthy as slaves. After a victory the dead were decapitated and their jaws cleaned of flesh 'and worn on the arm'. Shields were heavy, and warriors wore a quilted cotton jacket that was soaked in salt brine to toughen it. The Spaniards later adopted it as better for tropical warfare than their own steel armour.

The defects of Maya warfare were in its ceremonial and ritual characteristics. When the chieftain died, war ended; they did not fight at night. The farming instinct was stronger than the warring. The Inca revolt against the Spaniards in Cuzco in 1536 might have been won had not the soldiers melted away as the planting season came upon them. The Mayas had the same obsession; as late as 1848, during the 'war of the castes' the badly used Indians had Mérida, the capital, surrounded—until there came the time to plant maize.

Religion pervaded the whole of Maya life, birth, death, agriculture, time, astronomy, and architecture.

The Maya cosmos was much like that of the highland Mexicans. It had thirteen heavens and nine hells. The heavens were a number of horizontal layers, one above the other, where the gods dwelled, and they were sustained by four gods who stood at the four cardinal directions and held up the heavens and the world. Each of these four gods had a symbolical colour.

The world of the Mayas, according to them, had suffered cataclysmic destructions four times. When the veil lifts on Maya history they are living in its fifth re-creation. They even had traditions of a flood, and on one of the fascinating pages (page 74) of the

Dresden Codex is a symbolical destruction of the world by a universal deluge, *haiyococab,* 'water over the earth.'

Gods pervaded the underworld, walked the earth, and animated the sky. Itzamná headed the Maya pantheon. He had various attributes, as food-giver, patron of medicine, inventor of writing. There followed all forms and fashions of gods in all walks of life, all crafts, all professions; each had its patron. The beekeeper, the corngrower, the fisherman, the warrior, the traveller, the merchant, even the comedians and the dancers had their own deities.

Yum Kax, *the youthful corn god*

Yum Kax, thought to be the corn god, was youthful and depicted as holding maize cobs. His portrait found at Copán is as moving as anything in Old World sculpture. Death was called Ah Puch and represented as a skeleton; he was the patron deity of the Maya day Cimi. The war god was painted red and black just as warriors were painted when going into battle. Wind, war, death, all had their individual traits and symbolical glyphs. All these were the unseen partners allied with man in the problem of survival. All gods had to be treated with scrupulous respect. Sacrifice had to be offered to them in a prescribed form and at the right time. Since the gods were so numerous and complex, the priests had to observe the rituals with almost legalistic exactitude based on long-observed formulas.

Ah Puch, *the skeleton god of death*

Like any other living beings, the gods had to be nourished, and since the gods proceeded necessarily from the Maya brain, they were imperfect and had human faults. If rain was withheld or disease appeared, it was because the gods were not properly propitiated. Blood and, most of all, throbbing human hearts were cherished by the gods. War yielded prisoners for sacrifice. A victim marked for sacrifice was painted blue, that famous Maya blue which is found on murals and stone carvings.

There were various forms of sacrifice. One was the 'arrow ceremony'. Another was to throw the 'selected ones' into wells. The great *cenote* at Chichén Itzá was the best known depository, and Landa described it. Four hundred years later Edward H. Thompson proved him correct when he dredged that sacred well and found the skeletal remains of men, women, and children, as well as the artifacts that had been thrown with them into this clouded water.

Ixtab, *goddess of suicide, with black spot of decomposition on cheek.*

Blood has for primitives a mystical significance. The folklore connected with it lies so deep in the human consciousness that it has slipped over into most religions. Smearing the body with blood, or with a blood surrogate, increased the vital principle. The Mayas, however, 'offered sacrifices of their own blood.' They pierced their cheeks, their lower lips, 'and their tongues in a slanting direction.' Blood so obtained was smeared on an image of the god that was being propitiated, or onto their own hair and bodies.

The whole of the country of the Mayas with its hundreds of stone cities and thousands of sculptured stones may be said to be one vast monument to their extraordinary preoccupation with time and its consequences. On ball courts and temples, on lintels, sculptured panels, shells, jade, polychrome dishes, on wood, on stone and modelled stucco, the Mayas over a period of a thousand years carved the date when each particular piece was finished or begun, or a date that marked some important event of the past or present. At Copán the famed Hieroglyphic Stairway—composed of sixty-two flights, thirty-three feet wide—has more than two thousand individual glyphs carved on its risers. The dates of completion can be read from these, but little else.

The Mayas believed that time was cyclical, that the same influence and thus the same consequences would be repeated in history.

They had not one calendar but three. The *haab* year was made up of eighteen periods, or months, of twenty days each, plus a terminal period of five days called *uayeb* (the empty or unlucky days). The second was the *tzolkin,* a sacred calendar of 260 days. The Aztecs and Toltecs also had the *tzolkin.* No one knows why they settled on this precise number of days, unless it comes out of some 'crystallized pantheon,' for it has no astronomical significance. The third calendar was the 'long count,' which reckoned the number of days since the mythical beginning of the Maya era, which was dated 4-Ahau 8-Cumhu for reasons unknown (equivalent to 3111 B.C.). What occurred at this date? We do not know. There is no clue, for archaeology reveals that at this time the Mayas as such did not even exist. Still, all of the known calendars of the world hark back to a date which represents the beginning of time.

Twenty *kins,* or days, made up the Maya month (*uinal*). Eighteen *uinals* made the 360-day year (*tun*); this plus the five-day *uayeb* brought the total of the Maya year to 365 days (*haab*). Next came the *katun,* a period of 7,200 days, or twenty *tun* years. Then there was the period of fifty-two years now called the 'calendar round.' Each day of the *haab* year had a name and number, as did each day of the sacred *tzolkin.* The coincidence of any given *haab* day with any given *tzolkin* day occurred every 18,980 (*haab*) days, or every fifty-two years. The Aztecs had a similar obsession with the fifty-two-year cycle.

Maya calendric system was not mere intellectual gymnastics. The farmer had to know when to plant and when to sow. He depended on the priest-astronomer to tell him when rain could be expected. The seafarer had to know when to expect a full moon, an eclipse, or a hurricane.

Every moment of their lives was involved in the position of the planets. They feared that if the gods were not propitiated they would put an end to the world, and that is perhaps the reason for their obsession with having an

The Mayas invented a complex calendar. *The diagram above represents its working by a system of interlocking cog-wheels. The smaller wheel, to the left, shows the sacred year of 260 days formed by combining 13 day-numbers (centre wheel) with 20 day names (outer wheel). It is the day 13 Ahau and the glyph in the centre shows the god of the number 13 preparing to set down the load of Ahau at the end of his day's march. This particular day glyph will not occur again for the 260 days needed for all the combinations of the 13 numbers and 20 names to be completed.*
On the right is the calendar year of 365 days composed of 18 months and the unlucky period of five days. The glyphs for these are shown on the far right. Each month contains 20 days, numbered from 0 to 19. The part of the year shown here gives the end of the month Cumku, the unlucky Uayeb period and the first two days of Pop. To give any day in the Maya Calendar its complete description, it is necessary to have both the sacred and calendar position, so that the day 13 Ahau is, more correctly, 13 Ahau 18 Cumku. As 5 is the only common factor of 365 and 260, the year wheel will have to rotate 52 times before 13 Ahau again falls on 18 Cumku. This 52 year period is called the Calendar Round. There are therefore 52 x 365 or 18,980 different combinations of day name, number and month positions in the Maya Calendar.

almost exact calendar, so that each god at the right moment might have his prayers or the sacrifices meant for him.

Many scholars believe that the Mayas, no matter how widely dispersed, exchanged astronomical data to perfect their calendar and that there was a 'congress' at Copán in A.D. 765 to adjust the calendar and the accumulated errors of the fifty-two years before that time. The month of Pop began their year, and they gathered at Copán to put Pop in order. The presence of the

The sacbe or ceremonial road *leading to the Temple of the Dolls at Dzibilchaltún. It is dry-laid on a wide causeway of limestone which keeps on an even level whatever the depressions of the ground. The actual road-surface was of gravel wetted and trampled down. Roads like this have been traced for upwards of sixty miles, linking the great Maya cities with one another.*

same date on Maya monuments as distant from one another as three hundred miles suggests intimate contacts for exchange of this data.

Diego de Landa was the first to call attention to their calendar. 'They have their year as perfect as ours, consisting of 365 days and six hours. They divided it into two kinds of months, the one kind of thirty days . . . and the other kind of twenty days. . . . The whole year had eighteen of these months plus five days and six hours . . . for these . . . they have twenty days or characters by which they name them.' Landa fortunately had the good sense to copy down the glyphs of the day signs, with their Maya names in Spanish script, and upon these sketches all subsequent study by epigraphers has been grounded.

Early Spanish settlers in Yucatán noted the remains of Maya roads. 'There are signs even today,' says Diego de Landa, writing in the sixteenth century, 'that there was once a handsome causeway from T'ho [now Mérida] to the other city, Izamal.'

And there were other roads (*sacbeob*) connecting various ancient cities. 'There are remains of paved highways which traverse all this kingdom and they say they ended in the east on the seashore. . . . these highways were like the Spanish *caminos reales,* which guided them with no fear of going astray.' Roads were also seen in the jungles.

Maya roads constructed during the classical period (A.D. 300–900) seem to have connected most of the inland cities with those of the coast. A recent aerial oil survey in El Petén has revealed the scars of roads comparable to the known Maya road axis at Cobá. Tikal was bound by a causeway to Uaxactún and thence onward toward rivers which by canoe connected them with the sea in the province of Chetumal. Although there has been one very limited study of a Maya causeway, it may be presumed that many of the Maya centres in classical times were bound together by roads; trade routes have everywhere been reported by the early padre-explorers.

Maya cities in the Puuc, of which Uxmal was the centre, were connected by roads, as Stephens first noted in November, 1841. The writer of this book has explored those roads during his various periods in Yucatán. A causeway fifteen feet wide, varying in height from two to four feet, runs from Uxmal to Kabah (where it still can be seen). One part there makes a 180-degree turn to enter the gateway of Kabah; another leads on to Sayil, Labná, and other cities of the Puuc. Northwest Uxmal was connected with Mayapán and from there to Chichén Itzá. The latter has eight *sacbeob* within the city, and at least two of the roads lead out of its environs toward other Maya centres. Best known at Chichén Itzá is the ceremonial causeway that leads from the Temple of Kukulcán. Nine hundred feet in length and thirty-three feet in width, it goes to the edge of the sacrificial *cenote.* Not so well known are the *sacbeob* that led out from Chichén Itzá. These have been traced by the writer from an air survey. Photographs reveal that a road went from Chichén Itzá toward Chabalam, where it doubtless connected with the well-known (and only really surveyed) road that leads from Yaxuná sixty-two miles toward Cobá.

The ceremonial roads within some of the greater Maya cities are well known. As was mentioned earlier, those of Tikal, built between A.D. 400 and 900, were economic as well as ceremonial. A causeway in the south ravine of the city acts as a dike; the ravine itself, its porous limestone cemented, served as a reservoir. The wide surface of the dike was a ceremonial road which passed from one centre to another. All of Tikal is bound by wide stone causeways. Many other Maya sites have causeways. The one at Labná, six hundred feet long and twenty-five feet wide, is well known; it went from the principal temple to a smaller one famed for its gateway. The newly uncovered ceremonial road at Dzibilchaltún, twice the width of the one at Labná and possibly a thousand years older, reveals the form and function of a Maya ceremonial road.

The only *sacbe* which has been formally explored is the so-called Cobá-Yaxuná axis. It was dry-laid. The Maya engineer first laid down a roughly dressed limestone bed; the stones in this varied in weight from twenty-five to three hundred pounds. On top of this went a limestone gravel which when wetted and trampled down made a hard, smooth surface. The result was the *sacbe,* the white road which the early Spaniards found 'fine, broad and level.'

In its 62.3 miles the Cobá-Yaxuná road makes six changes in direction. There is no topographical reason for this, but the remains of a Maya city lying in the direction of every shift suggest that the road was built to reach towns already in existence.

At stated intervals ramparts cross the *sacbe* transversely; it may well be that these held 'stations of the road.' The Incas maintained rest stations (*tampus*) along the entire length of their royal road, every twelve to eighteen miles. We know from the literature that the Mayas had a similar system, but we have neither its name nor precise function. We know much of the Inca *tampu* system, but nothing of the Maya other than a post-conquest reference to an *alcalde meson* who in each village was designated to keep up the traveller's house and see that wood, maize, and other provisions were always at hand. Markers have been found along the road every five miles. Señor Alfonso Villa, who explored the road, believes them to have been boundary markers rather than distance markers.

This road complex unmistakably indicates that the *sacbeob* were not only ceremonial; they were trade arteries as well.

Having no draft animals, the Mayas carried all produce on their backs. The chieftains were carried in litters. Though no litters survive, there is an illustration of a very elaborate one scratched on the walls of a temple at Tikal; and there are several eyewitness accounts of Maya chieftains being carried 'in large litters decorated with plumes.'

The Mayas alone of all the great civilizations of the ancient Americas were a maritime people, going out in large ocean-going dugouts, travelling over thousands of miles of coastal sea.

The first things that Columbus met when he landed at Guanaja in 1502 were Maya boats. At one of the islands he saw and examined one 'as long as a galley, eight feet in breadth, rowed by twenty-five Indian paddlers,' and laden with commodities—cacao, copper, bells, flint-edged swords, cotton cloth—brought from the mainland, twenty miles distant.

As Spanish voyages began to multiply, others reported seeing immense dugout canoes that held as 'many as forty Indians.' In 1542 at the siege of Omoa, a trading colony in Honduras, fifty war canoes were sent at one time all the way from Chetumal, a distance of over two hundred sea miles, to aid in resisting the conquistadors. Many of the early Spanish accounts mention the tremendous number of canoes and the amount of canoe traffic along the entire coast from Tabasco to Panama.

The Maya canoe was usually made from cedar, and carved out of a single tree trunk often as long as eighty feet. It was built with a high bow and stern more or less as the Mayas have themselves pictured it in the murals of Chichén Itzá. There were several well-known canoe-building areas. The fallen cedars were dragged from the woods over log rollers by means of rope cable and manpower. At the town of Buct-zotz, a little west of Cape Cotoche, there was a special enterprise for cutting cedar and making it into canoes; these were largely used for the salt trade at Ekab.

The whole coast about the Laguna de Términos—where Xicalango was located—was a network of rivers, bayous, and creeks. A Spanish map of the seventeenth century shows inland waterways and describes in detail routes by narrow channels, such as appear on the Florida coast where boats of small draft can move without actually going out into the open sea. This coast was difficult for European ships, which had to stand out to sea, but not for the Maya dugouts.

There were limits to Maya seafaring. There is no evidence that the Mayas had contact with Cuba, even though it is only 125 miles away, perhaps because a bewildering and dangerous current runs between Cuba and Yucatán. Yet there was an occasional accidental, if not purposeful, contact with the Antilles. Bernal Díaz met at Cozumel Island 'a good-looking Indian woman' who—spoke 'the language of the Island of Jamaica . . . As

I . . . knew the language . . . we were very much astonished, and asked the woman how she happened there. . . . two years earlier she had started from Jamaica with ten Indians in a large canoe intending to go and fish . . . the currents had carried them over to this land where they had been driven ashore . . . her husband and all the Jamaica Indians had been killed and sacrificed to the Idols.'

One wonders how far Maya sea traffic extended. There is evidence, archaeological and historical, that these voyages carried them from Tampico down to Panama. Following the coast line, this is over twenty-four hundred sea miles, and it would reach an impressive three thousand miles if they went as far south as Margarita Island, which lies fifteen miles off Venezuela opposite Araya Peninsula and was one pre-Columbian source of pearls. A baroque pear-shaped pearl was found in the tomb at Palenque under the Temple of Inscriptions (dated A.D. 692), and another was found in the tomb of the high priest at Chichén Itzá.

After A.D. 900 the Mayas seem to have extended their commerce to Panama, for from that time on gold frequently appears. Emeralds, if the Mayas had them—and the writer has seen none which are really emeralds—would have come from the same Panamanian source. The goldworking Indians about Coclé, in Panama, traded with the Chibchas of highland Colombia, who exploited the emerald-producing lands about Muzo and Chimor, then the only source of emeralds in the New World.

There is no evidence of any direct Maya penetration into South America. No pottery has been found in South America which is unquestionably Maya. Finally, there is no hint in the traditions of any southern cultures that they were even dimly aware of the existence of the Mayas.

The Mayas had books. These were naturally not our kind of book; they were in effect illustrated glyph texts, but the fact that they had books astonished the Spaniards. When young Bernal Díaz thumbed through them in a Totonac temple at Cempoala, he saw 'many paper books doubled together in folds. . . . it gave me much to think over. . . . I do not know precisely how to describe it.' And, as we have seen, among the things sent back to Charles V along with gold and feather ornaments were 'two books such as the Indians use.' Many of the scholars in Spain were 'wrapped in astonishment' at this proof of high culture. For not only the Mayas but the Totonacs, Aztecs, Mixtecs, and almost all other Indians of high culture had books. The Mayas, however, had them over the longest period of time—perhaps as long as eight hundred years.

Maya paper was made of bark pounded from the inner bast fibres of *Ficus* trees. The bark was pulled from the tree two palms wide and as long as twenty feet. It was soaked first in water to soften it and to extract the heavy

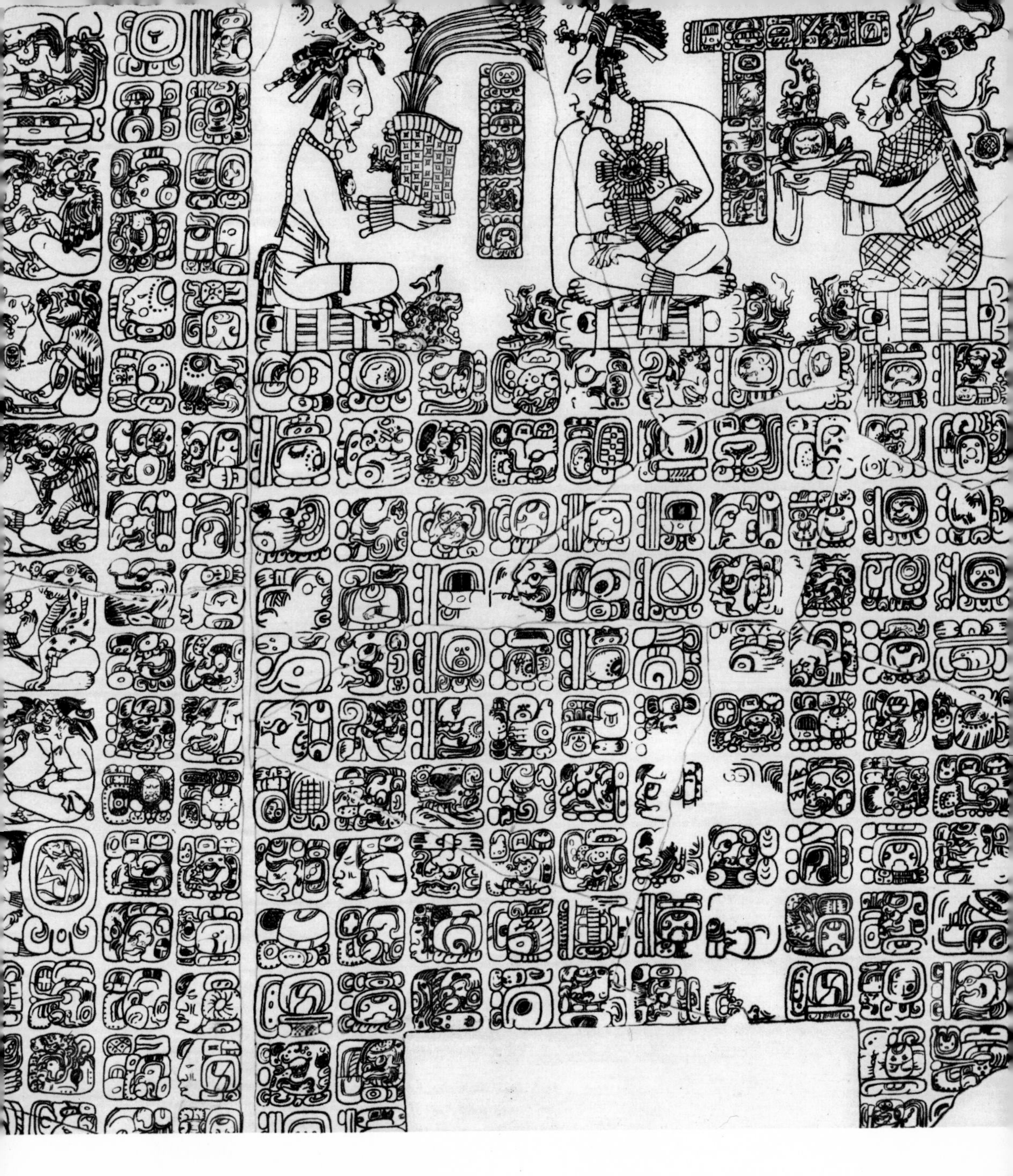

Only one third of all Maya glyphs *can be deciphered with any certainty, though the corpus of material available continues to grow and the riddle may be solved. Palenque has been a fruitful source of examples, some of which are shown here in the form of detailed drawings. Maya writing was ideographic—that is, each sign represented an idea, not a sound. Some scholars, however, believe that it was moving towards a phonetic alphabet. The calendric system has been fully worked out, but what, besides dates, have these mysterious inscriptions still to reveal?*

white sap, then beaten with a ribbed beater. This action stretched the fibres so that a piece of bark twelve inches wide was extended to paper forty inches in width. It was folded into a book by doubling the paper screenwise; each leaf or page measured about three inches wide by eight in length. The ends were glued to wooden boards presumably carved with glyph titles. A Mexican codex that survives is similarly bound and is ornamented with inlaid jade in the manner of the jewelled bindings of Europe's Renaissance. The *Dresden Codex* has thirty-nine leaves painted on both sides, or seventy-eight pages. These pages are the 'folds of the katun,' of which the codices speak. The Maya priest-scribes worked with brushes made from bristles of the wild pig. The colours used were dark red, light red, black, blue, yellow, brown, green, and a lustrous black.

There is no precise date on the beginnings of the Maya book. The Maya after A.D. 889, for reasons unknown, abandoned the practice of erecting dated carved-stone stelae. After this, it is deduced, they kept similar records on a more obedient medium such as paper. Sometime around 889, then, it is conjectured that the first Maya book came into being.

Of the three surviving codices, the *Dresden* is astronomical, the *Tro-Cortesianus* astrological, the *Peresianus* ritualistic; they present almost nothing that can be regarded as history.

The *Dresden Codex* is the finest of the three surviving Maya books, and gets its name from the Royal Library at Dresden, where it was brought from Vienna in 1739. The precise provenance of the book is unknown, but since its latest date corresponds to A.D. 1178, Dr. Eric Thompson believes it was a new edition made about the twelfth century from an original executed in the classical period (A.D. 323–889).

The Spaniards said the Maya books treated 'of the lives of their lords and the common people' and spoke of 'the history they contained.'

But if the Maya books covered fields other than those of the extant codices, we will never know, because the Spanish friars destroyed them. Diego de Landa says flatly, '. . . we burned them all . . .'

It was decreed that idolatry must be stamped out. Diego de Landa himself signed the decree in 1562. As part of the Spanish religious programme, all Maya books were seized and brought to the town of Maní. 'We found a large number of books,' wrote Landa, '. . . and they contained nothing in which there was not to be seen superstition and lies of the devil, so we burned them all, which they regretted to an amazing degree and which caused them much affliction.'

The Mayas, first of the Sun Kingdoms to feel the presence of the white man, were curiously enough the last to fall under that presence. There was no escaping the wave of the future once Columbus noted the presence of a very superior people, the *'Maian,'* in 1502. The Spanish persisted. The relationship was violent from the beginning. The Mayas were fierce warriors; they gave no quarter and asked none. When the report reached the Spanish governor at Cuba—'we have discovered thickly peopled countries with masonry houses, and people who cover their persons in cotton garments'—more conquistadors poured over to break a lance; hundreds left their bodies on Yucatán shores.

When Cortés arrived he gave a practised military eye to the inhospitable shore and, somehow sensing that there was little gold, remained only long enough to pick up the castaway Aguilar. Later, in 1523, after Mexico had been conquered and organized, Cortés sent Pedro de Alvarado to undertake the conquest of Guatemala and dispatched Cristóbal de Olid in 1524 to Central America to sniff out the tribute channels of the Aztecs, but the latter set up an independent government in Hibueras (Honduras) instead. So Cortés set off after him, making the famed trek through quagmires and rivers and jungles. He cut a wide swath through Maya territory, meeting little resistance. The Mayas were in awe of that energetic man who, undismayed by the terrible geography of the land, came down upon them replete with mistress, falcons, buffoons, and jugglers.

In 1527 came the turn of the Mayas. Francisco de Montejo, who had played his part in the Conquest of Mexico (it was he who had carried its treasure to Spain), used this to advantage; he emerged from an audience with the king with a contract to conquer, settle, and convert all the territory of the Mayas. He arrived in Yucatán in 1527 with 380 men, 57 horses, and high hopes. Montejo was, says one who knew him, 'middle-sized and with a merry face. He was fond of rejoicings but was a businessman; and a good horseman. When he came over to Mexico he may have been about thirty-five. He was liberal and he spent more than his income warranted.' The lives he would spend were even more unwarranted. The party settled at Xelha, where skirmish and sickness whittled away his forces. He then moved up the north coast, encountering one large Maya city after another. At every turn the Indians attacked, chewing up his small troop. By 1535 there was not a white man left alive in the whole Yucatán peninsula. Those who had not died or wearied of unsuccessful war had heard the clarion call from Peru, where Francisco Pizarro was engaged in the conquest of the Incas.

Montejo, full of years and scars, resigned his title and authority to his son. Furiously renewing the conquest in 1542, the conquistadors occupied half of the peninsula and founded their capital, Mérida, within the buildings of ancient T'ho. In 1546 they put down with terrible and indiscriminate slaughter those Maya tribes who refused the yoke of peace, and the conquest was over.

The Mayas were engulfed by the waves of conquest. They had known slavery, which was part of their social system, but their new masters improved upon it. Five hundred thousand free men were sold into peonage, ancient Maya centres were destroyed, and the chieftains who did not submit were killed. The priests were disposed of and their books burned. Their learning died with them.

Still the conquest was not complete. After the fall of Chichén Itzá in 1194 to the forces of Huanc Ceel with his Mexican mercenaries, one part of the Itzá tribe moved, en masse, out of Yucatán into the humid area of El Petén. On an island in the centre of what is now Lake Flores, they built their capital of Tayasal. Around the edge of the lake and into the Petén's interior were the houses and cornfields of the people. This was classical Maya territory; the ruins of Tikal lie only fifty miles from the lake. There the Mayas lived unmolested from 1200 until 1618 (except for the brief, friendly visit of Cortés in 1524). The Spaniards became aware of them soon enough. It was a neo-Maya state and its mere existence encouraged rebellion among other Mayas living under the Spanish yoke.

Throughout the seventeenth century there were repeated attempts to enter Itzá territory: they were repulsed. Construction was begun on a Guatamala-Yucatán highway designed to bring two economic units together. The Itzás were in the way, and that decided their fate.

January, 1697, found Martin de Ursua, governor of Yucatán, with his soldiers at the farthest point of the new road. On March 13, a force of Spanish soldiers crossed the lake in a large galley to accept the peaceful surrender of the island capital of Tayasal—or to make an assault on it. As it made its way, a canoe flotilla of two thousand armed Indians encircled the galley. The soldiers were under orders to withhold their fire, which they did even though provoked by accurate arrow thrusts from the Itzás. But near the shore of Tayasal a soldier, wounded to fury by an arrow, fired his arquebus at close range. At this, the other soldiers fired, and the lake soon was strewn with Itzá dead. As the troops landed, the remaining Indians fled. On March 14, 1697, the Spaniards formally took possession, in the name of the king, of the last living city of the Mayas.

They had endured as a cultural entity for thirty-seven hundred years. This is a long time in human cultural history.

The whole Inca story *through European eyes is depicted in this engraving by the 16th century historian Theodore de Bry, with the emphasis, of course, on gold. In the upper part of the picture the Indians are shown digging the ore and washing it. Below is the Inca himself, supported on a litter and seated on a splendid but suspiciously Baroque throne, while in the background is an equally unhistorical version of Pizarro's landing at Tumbes.*

III Kingdom of Gold: THE INCAS

13 The Past that the Incas 'Forgot'

THERE IS not one Peru but three, and all these Perus lie parallel to each other: coastal desert, high mountain, and low-lying jungle. It is these three discordant geographies that the Incas coalesced into an Empire. In few other places in the world have climate and geography been such vital factors in shaping the culture of human lives.

First there is the strange sea. The coast of South America from Antarctica to the Equator is curiously modified by the presence of a cold stream of water, deep and extended: the Humboldt current—a cold mass within a tropic sea which has had marked effect on the land; normally rain never falls and along the extended coast-line the land is reduced to extreme waterless desolation.

Although along the 2000-mile-long desert coast there are more than forty valleys, between each lies a lifeless void of desert. Rivers, some large and perennial, others small and occasional, which have created these valley oases cut through the towering Andes and rapidly descend into V-shaped valleys bringing every year a renewal of fertile silt.

Early South American men filtered into these valleys and formed into tribes; in time they extended these valleys by careful irrigation, increasing artificially and unnaturally the areas of fertility.

Since trees were relatively rare here, the idols of these coastal dwellers were of wood; since mud and sand were the base of their material culture, they built of sun-dried brick, and their most fabulous cities were in reality only plastic mud. Since here the sun was always menacing and was *not* to be appeased, they selected as their principal deity the moon, which controlled the sea.

Yet the Incas did not originate in this environment; they first appeared in a high, treeless tableland, a region of long grass, a land which is seared by the noonday heat and made frigid by night. This was the land of the *Keshwas* (or Quechuas), the 'warm-valley people'; their name in time was to be given to the language of the Incas.

The empire of the Incas *stretched for over 3000 miles down the west coast of South America. It covered coastal desert, high mountain and low-lying jungle.*

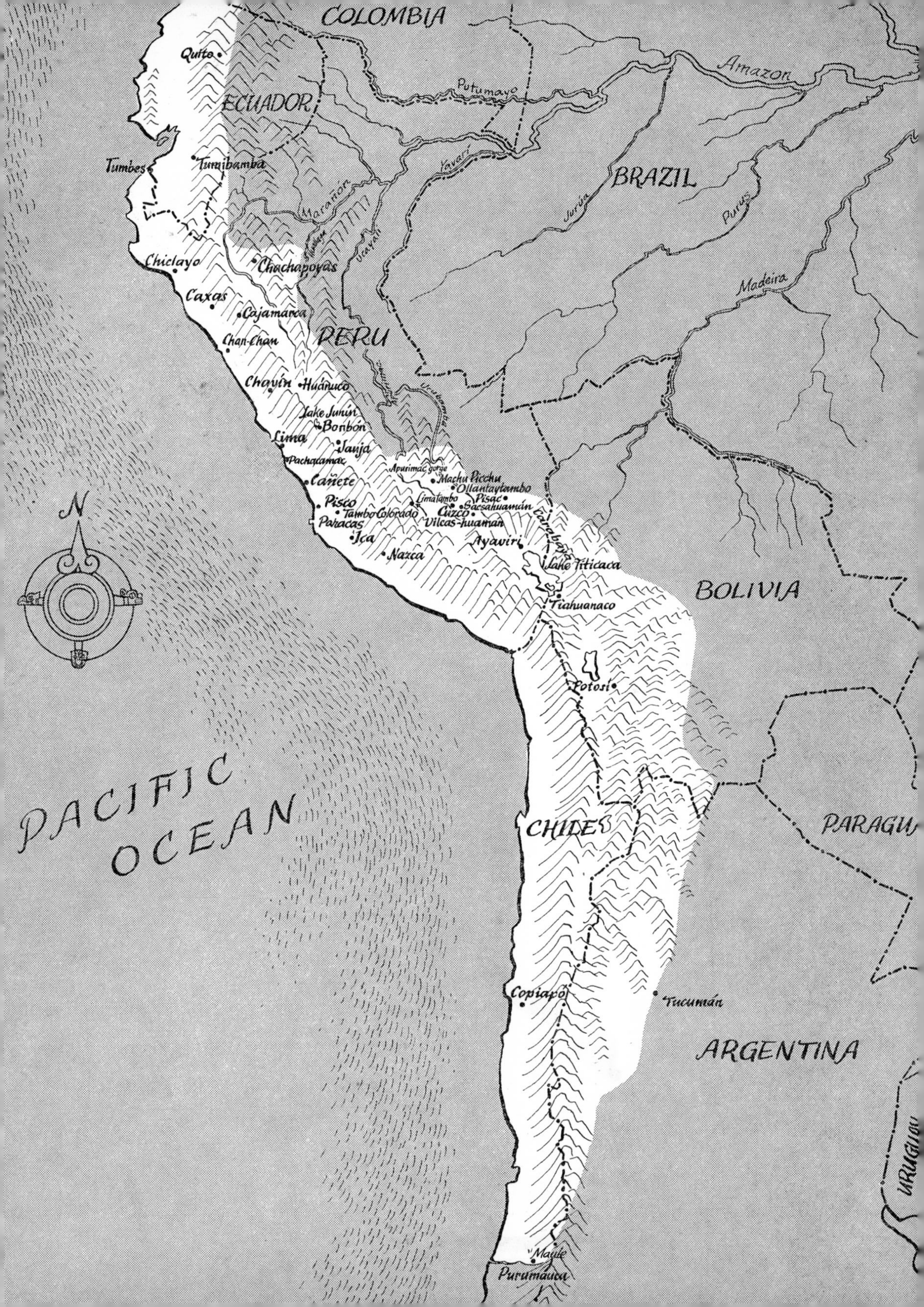

COLOMBIA
Quito
ECUADOR
Putumayo
Amazon
Tumbes
Tumibamba
Yavari
BRAZIL
Marañon
Juruá
Purus
Chiclayo
Chachapoyas
Madeira
Caxas
Cajamarca
PERU
Chan-Chan
Chavín
Huánuco
Lake Junín
Bonbón
Lima
Jauja
Pachacamac
Apurimac gorge
Machu Picchu
Cañete
Ollantaytambo
Pisac
Limatambo
Sacsahuamán
Pisco
Tambo Colorado
Cuzco
Paracas
Vilcas-huaman
Ica
Nazca
Ayaviri
Carabaya
Lake Titicaca
BOLIVIA
Tiahuanaco
N
Potosí
PACIFIC OCEAN
CHILE
Copiapó
Tucumán
ARGENTINA
Maule
Purumauca

The three Perus. *High in the Andes, as in the gorge of the Urubamba river (left) the Incas built fortress cities, roads and irrigation terraces. To the east lay the vast jungle (above), broken only by the rivers which feed the Amazon. On the west, arid desert stretched for 2000 miles along the coast.*

The temperate zone in the Andes lies in the grass areas at a land height above 9,000 feet; it is a region that is capable of sustaining an intensive agriculture. Here in this purlieu, trees were also rare but there was rock, so stone became the source of these Andean peoples' culture. The sun here was the source of life, so the sun became their principal deity.

The deep valleys of the Cordilleras (as the first Spaniards called the mountains) take the run-off of the water and form it into numerous rivers, which emerge into the gigantic rivers Huallaga and Ucayali, both tributaries of the Amazon. This is the jungle, the third of the three Perus.

Actually the forest begins as montaña at 6,000 feet altitude, for it is ceaselessly wetted from the rain-bearing trade winds which collide with the Andean spurs that slant sharply east. The montaña is heavily matted with forest, and wildly plunging rivers; this is the *yungas*, a Quechua word applied both to the hotlands and to the people living there.

The eastern slopes of the mountains are inexorably flattened until they become finally a vast carpeted forest broken only by rivers which flow through the green mansions of trees, propelled by the eastern slant of the land into the Amazon. Here to plant one tree you must first cut down twenty. In this terrifying luxuriance a totally different people lived—fierce, independent, cityless warriors who were armed with poison-tipped darts. They were jungle farmers and resisted any form of organization; only the margins of the jungle yielded to the soldiers of the Inca.

These, then, are the three Perus, and out of these three contrasting geographies—desert, mountain and jungle—the Incas hammered their fabulous realm. No matter what form of society that lived in this ancient Peru—whether it was the effete Chimú, who surrounded himself on the desert coast with gold and ease, or the head-hunters in the jungle—all were brought into the orbit of the Incas.

But what of the long history of the region before the Incas arrived to transform it into the civilization that we know? The story that archaeology tells us in Peru is this: a succession of cultures endured for millennia, and in many instances died out, before the Incas arrived to engulf the whole land and to organize its conquest-acquired inheritance into an empire.

That we have almost no history of many of these pre-Inca cultures other than that which archaeology reveals, we owe principally to the Incas themselves, for in their conquests they snuffed out the others by an effective 'selective manipulation of remembered history.'

For not only were the earth and the peoples in Peru organized by the triumphant Incas but memory as well, and the theme of the Inca as *the* 'civilizer' became their dominant theme. Their thesis was that before their arrival all of South America was a cultural void. And this official history was forced upon all those conquered. Memory of past peoples and cultures was systematically purged and subjected to a 'sort of editing and selective distortion not entirely unlike the tendentious distortion to which the Spanish themselves subjected it [the Inca history] in their turn.' An 'official' Inca history was created, local oral traditions of the tribes whom they had conquered supplanted and allowed to lapse. The official 'rememberers,' who were the Incas' historians, no longer bridged the gap between legendary man and those innumerable pre-Inca cultures, so that this 'selective manipulation of history' which was to represent the Incas as being alone the culture bearers, emerged as *the* history of preliterate Peru. All the rest of the pre-Inca histories were allowed to be lost in oblivion.

What then, and who were all these civilizations, now without name and barely with legend, that preceded the Inca?

The curtain rises at approximately 1200 B.C.: Man has already been on the north desert coast of Peru for a long time. He has had pottery and weaving since 1500 B.C.. He builds structures. He is already growing maize (no doubt with bird guano as fertilizer), and he raises the tuber called manioc. But he is not the first here; there were others long before him, for the remains of their weaving and agriculture, as proven by the carbon-14 tests, show them here as early as 3000 B.C.

The first culture of prominence is *Chavín*; its leit-motif is a ferocious-looking Cat God found on pottery and stonework and in weavings. This motif was to haunt the cosmology of the ancient Peruvians for the next thousand years. Chavín's centre (presumably it was a mecca even during late Inca times) is the site of Chavín de Huantar, which lies in a narrow valley in the Andes beyond the Cordillera Blanca. Here are the remains of impressive buildings characterized by well-laid stone walls and ornamented with stone-carved human and animal heads set into the wall.

Paracas, which lay below Central Peru to the south of Lima near Pisco, is another pre-Inca culture. It is famed for its textiles, among the finest ever loomed. This culture is wrapped in mystery; we do not know its tribal name nor anything more positive about it than the evidence in their caverns found in the brazen desert and close upon the sea on the Paracas Peninsula. In deep subterranean rooms four hundred or more mummy bundles were found: the flexed bodies were adorned with superbly woven shawls, turbans, and robes, all in the most exquisite polychrome embroidery.

By between A.D. 400 and 1000, man has completely dominated his environments of the desert coast and the Andes; he has acquired wit and cities. It is the period of high craftsmanship in architecture, ceramics, and weaving. On the coast the *Mochicas* (we have no idea what they called themselves) are a caste-minded empire; they lord it over the northern Peruvian

The enigmatic remains of a culture *centred on the Paracas Peninsula in Central Peru include magnificent textiles and strange terracotta figurines such as this, just over 3 inches high. 'Of no aesthetic or technical interest,' says one critic; yet the rectilinear patterning and the bold stylization of face and hair seem to point forward to the sophisticated achievements of later periods. The date is early 1st millennium* A.D.

Whistling pots *were among the household goods of the Chimú people, who dominated northern Peru from about* A.D. *1000 until they were conquered by the Incas in 1466. When the vessel, of unpainted black ware, is tilted, air is drawn in and a whistling sound comes from the little flute-player on the side.*

The climax of pre-Inca ceramic art *comes with the Mochicas (about* A.D. *400–1000). An abundance of brilliant pottery has survived, giving us an amazing insight into every detail of their lives. Here a warrior is about to deal a blow with a club held in both hands—and the number of bodies discovered with skull-fractures is some proof of the efficiency of such weapons.*

Nazca pottery *is roughly contemporary with Mochica but shows almost no interest in modelling, though stylized human figures do sometimes occur. The emphasis is on the painted decoration rather than on the shape. As many as eleven soft pastel colours may be used on one vessel.*

The Cat God's face *grins from this silver plaque from Pachacamac, Peru. The Cat God was the chief deity of the ancient Chavín culture (1200–400* B.C.*)*

desert and one can still see the remains of their temples, one of which, called Huaca del Sol, in the Moche Valley is constructed of 130,000,000 sun-dried adobe bricks. This, naturally, suggests a complex social organization to accomplish so effective a construction; the advancement of their society is given further emphasis by their skill in gold casting and wood carving. Their weaving was done on a shop basis, for on one Mochica vase a man, obviously a chieftain, sits under a straw roof and directs rows of women busily engaged in weaving on their back-strap looms. The Mochicas had warriors, messengers, weavers, and 'doctors'; they built roads and organized a courier system, and perfected many a social pattern that appeared later in the political organization of the Inca.

In the five verdant valleys of Nazca, which lie south of Paracas, another culture—the Ica-Nazca—was overrun first by a religio-military cult in the 9th century, and then later, after 1400 A.D., conquered by the Incas, who caused their tribal history to be 'disremembered.' They are now somewhat less of a mystery because of the work done by archaeologists. Fine weaving and excellent ceramics were emphasized, and not too distant in design from those of Paracas. Architecture, however, is not a dominant feature, and little remains to speak of how they lived. Like the others, they are anonymous. The greatest mystery of the Ica-Nazca cultures is the vast network of 'lines,' a fantastic assembly of rectangles and squares that have been etched into the sand and waste gravel. Outsized birds, spiders, whales, and surrealistic figures are also present. These lines, some running for miles in length, have remained in a good state of preservation, showing this land to have been, then as now, a desert of everlasting drought. They are approximately fifteen hundred years old and might be calendary observations, or they could be genealogical symbol 'trees.' What is now positive, at least, is one date: an American archaeologist found a wooden 'sighting' stump at the end of one of the lines and carbon-14 tests have placed it close to the date of A.D. 500.

It is known that sometime close to A.D. 900 a mountain people called the *Tiahuanaco Empire* came to the coast in a religio-military invasion, sweeping down from their stronghold centred either about Lake Titicaca or northward at Huari, a city of Tiahuanacan origin. They had then an interest in astrology, a solar calendar, and, as well, a sort of shadow clock. It is highly possible that the Tiahuanacan culture brought the technique of the 'lines' to Nazca before their cult of the Weeping God.

Whatever the origins of all this, the Incas allowed nothing about them to come down to us. For the 'lines' of Nazca, they had full contempt; those practical Inca engineers ran their 24-foot-wide coastal road directly through them.

Symbols of a forgotten religion.
In the Pisco Valley, home of the Paracas Culture, appear these strange shapes, hollowed out in the dry earth of the hillside. The Spaniards called them 'Tres Cruces'—Three Crosses—but more probably they mean something akin to the Tree of Life. Other 'lines' in neighbouring valleys look more like birds and spiders.

The empire of Tiahuanaco is the dominant civilization between A.D. 1000–1300 in Peru and Bolivia. Like all the other pre-Inca cultures, it has left us only unexplained mysteries. The remains of what must have been the greatest ceremonial centre in all the Andes are still to be seen on the Altiplano in Bolivia, near Lake Titicaca at an altitude of 12,500 feet. Dr. Wendell Bennett has concluded that 'Tiahuanaco is the most elaborate and the purest manifestation of the culture yet to be found up to this time.'

The stonework of Tiahuanaco developed centuries before the Inca and was, until their advent, the best in the Andes. Stones are fitted together with insets and tenons; larger stones are bound with copper clamps. All this architectural megalithic stonework presupposes a social organization, a strong central government which could divert the use of manpower into non-food-producing channels on so large a scale. All this must have been done by a large supply of workers with a long technical tradition.

And yet nothing is precisely known of these people or their empire. They too, like the others, are nameless.

Chan-Chan, capital of the Chimús, *was a spacious city of straight streets, gardens and reservoirs. Its walls were mostly of mud-brick, covered with lively decorations using plant, animal and bird motifs. The designs are small and identically repeated; they were presumably made with moulds and must have been protected from the rain, since the mud is unbaked.*

That this great culture, Tiahuanaco, should have no oral history points more than any other evidence to the success of the Incas (who were, in some stage of their development, doubtless contemporaneous with them) in deliberately obliterating all memory of them. For when Pedro de Cieza de León made inquiries in 1549 about the people who built the ruins at Tiahuanaco, the oldest of the Indians then living could not even recall a single fact, and to these inquiries they replied that it had been built long before the Incas ruled but that they were unable to say who had built it.

Yet the Tiahuanacan cultural conquest penetrated many of the remote corners of Peru. Many of the contemporary cultures, even the early Inca, adopted the symbol of the Sun God. This Weeping God, weeping all manners of zoömorphic tears—condor-head tears and snake-head—and other design motifs, such as the puma, trident, and step designs, are widespread along most of the thousand-mile coast. But that conquest, motivated by religious fervor, was not systematically organized, for the Tiahuanaco left behind them little social impress—only those unmistakable designs on pottery and cloth, and the cult of the Weeping God.

The *Chimú Empire* (A.D. 1000–1466), called the Kingdom of Chimor, also belongs to this period even though it extends beyond it into that of the Incas.

The Chimús were coastal people, workers in plastic mud and worshippers of the moon. Their capital, Chan-Chan (which is near where the Spanish-Peruvian city of Trujillo stands), covered eight square miles, replete with enormous step pyramids, rows of houses, great walled compounds, irrigated gardens, and gigantic stone-lined reservoirs.

From Chan-Chan, the Chimús ruled over six hundred miles of coast from Rimac (now Lima), up to the humid tropics of Ecuador. Indirectly, they ruled over much more territory. Everything here was on a large scale: weaving was on a mass basis; pottery, mostly black ware, was produced in moulds; whistling jars and cooking pots were mass-produced. Their weavers made superb feather tunics and goldworking was also on a large scale, for the amount of gold yielded to their conquerors, the Incas, was staggering and even that which the Spaniards found much later (which was a mere nothing) reached into the millions. The Chimús developed the roads, taken over from their predecessors, the Mochicas; they developed further the courier communication system, and they extended their political alliances beyond the coastal desert far up into the Andes in order to protect their water supply.

The Chimú Empire was the last of the larger cultures to offer opposition to the Incas. That we know a good deal about the Chimú culture is due only to the fact that before the Inca methods of historical selectivity could be brought into full effect to eliminate the Chimús from human memory, the Spaniards arrived.

The listing of these pre-Inca cultures will seem, as it indeed is, foreshortened; there were many others, but only those of the greatest cultural influence in Peru have been named in order to show how steady was the cultural evolution that had been going on for three thousand years in Peru before the advent of the Inca.

Severed human heads, *like head-hunters' trophies, are represented on this carved stele at Cerro Sechin, a religious centre of the Chavin people. A whole avenue of these stelae survives, leading to the ruins of a temple. Chavín religion is still a mystery and Sechin seems untypical of the culture—there are no Cat God figures—but it is clear that human sacrifice was a cult feature in early Peru.*

Many of these civilizations were of the highest level, and from them the Incas drew heavily in order to form the material culture of their own empire. In a sense, and the analogy has often been made, the Incas were like the Romans—inheritors of a vast skein of cultures which became, in the weaving, a complicated tapestry of human progress.

Thus archaeology stands in direct opposition to the form of history which the Incas told of themselves, which is that all of the Andean (and coastal) peoples were savages until the Incas came upon the scene.

'In the year 1000 A.D.,' wrote Pedro de Cieza de León, '. . . in the name of *Tici Viracocha* and of the Sun and the rest of his gods. Manco Capac founded the new City.

'The origins and beginnings of Cuzco was a small house of stone roofed with straw which Manco Capac and his wives built and which they named 'Curi-cancha,' meaning 'Golden Enclosure.''

Pedro de Cieza de León had it from the 'rememberers' of history in Cuzco in the year 1549; it is as good and simple a historical premise as any.

The Inca civilization was built up by an intensification of pre-existing cultural and social patterns. Nothing came from 'without' that changed or modified it. The Incas developed within the valley of Cuzco and as they expanded they liquidated the earlier inhabitants.

This was Andean in pattern. And yet they had something more, an innate sense of organization. War was no longer an elaborate façade to overawe an enemy; war was to be won and conquest was to be organized. The people of the Incas became a disciplined people living within the framework of the Andes, and out of this discipline came the solid base of people, who, born to this type of society and thriving on it, went about the daily business of ordered human lives; and, in so doing, became an empire.

It took time to mould people in this manner, and its passage we must accept; and so we come to that period of Andean history (between the dates of A.D. 1200 and 1438) when their rulers, the 'Incas,' have pushed the expanding realm beyond the narrow confines of their 'origin' valley and have dominated the surrounding mountains.

The Weeping God of Tiahuanaco—*the central figure from the great monolithic gateway, carved in lava, and reproduced here in a fine 19th century lithograph. In each hand he holds a staff ending in a condor-head. His face is ringed with circles and puma-heads; the eyes are blank, with tears dropping from them. More condor and puma heads appear on his body, and from his belt hangs a row of faces, perhaps trophy-heads. Substantially the same image is repeated on innumerable Tiahuanacan objects and was taken over by the Nazcas.*

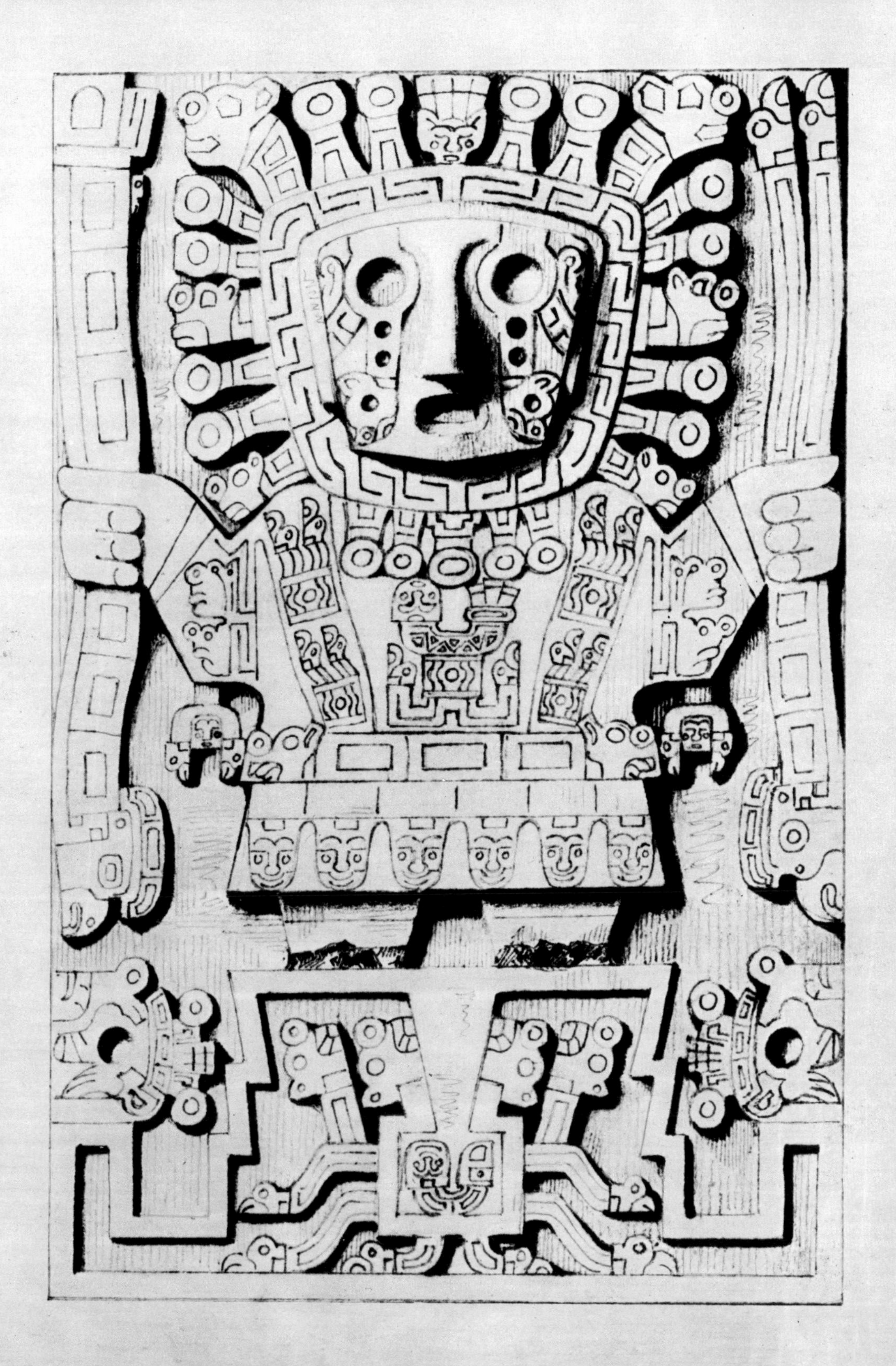

14 Broad Base of the Pyramid: the Worker

THE QUECHUAS, the people over whom the Incas were establishing their rule, were American Indians, and native to the Andes. Although there are marked variations between one tribe and another, there is an underlying appearance and trait in them all which is American. The Quechua was (or better *is*, since there remain some five million of them) of medium height and inclined to be thickset, with large hands, small wrists, a disproportionately large chest (developed for breathing in high altitudes), well-developed legs, and widespreading feet. They are broad-headed, with high cheekbones, prominent aquiline noses, and small, almond-shaped eyes.

The women are smaller and more delicately constructed, yet they wear a false frailty for they are capable of arduous physical exertion; they give birth and return to the fields within twenty-four hours. Many of the Quechua women have delicate features; some could be called beautiful. At least the early Spaniards found them so and married them. The early Spanish portraits of them exhibit very delicate features, and a chronicler, commenting on the women of Chachapoyas, wrote: 'We found them the most fair and good-looking of any . . . seen in the Indies . . . exceedingly beautiful fair and well formed.'

The Peruvian is capable of great physical endurance even in high altitudes. Centuries of acclimatization in the Andes have developed his body so that he can carry on normal functions. His chest, as well as his lungs, are abnormally developed so that the high altitude does not afflict him with shortness of breath; he carries in his organism the hereditary and ancestral *soma* which allows life at these heights.

So it was this man, copper-coloured, hard-working, tireless, robust, and by nature attuned to his surroundings, who became the broad base of the social pyramid which was the Inca Empire.

He was classified as a *hatun-runa* or *puric,* an able-bodied worker; he belonged to an earth-cell commune, and as such was given a head count in the decimal pyramidal pattern of the Inca Empire.

He wore a garment that was like a shortened version of the Victorian night-gown, made by cutting a hole for the head in the woven woollen textile; the edges were then sewn up, leaving large gaps for the arms. It was simple and unpretentious. It was called an *onka,* and made from the wool of the alpaca. He had another woollen cape garment (*yacolla*) which he threw over his shoulders at night or when the day was cold.

The last item of his dress was the breechclout; this was passed between his legs and the two ends held in place by a colourfully woven woollen *chumpi* belt. He assumed this when he was fourteen years of age.

This then, a breechclout, tunic, and rustic cape, was all the Indian had to wrap his body in this frigid Andean clime. When working in the fields, he merely braided his long hair with coloured woollen strings, but when travelling to a market or to a festival he wore a distinctive headgear which distinguished him from other clansmen travelling on the royal road. On festive occasions he had a longer tunic, reaching to his ankles, on which he or his wife expended their finest talent; he usually went shod in sandals.

Woman's dress was equally simple. It was a long rectangular piece of woven alpaca cloth (*anacu*) passed over the head and made wide enough to overlap and be held in place with a sash. It fell to the ankles, almost to her

An obscure Inca-Spaniard, *Felipe Guamán Poma de Ayala, spent nearly forty years collecting information about his people's history and traditions, and illustrating it with his own pen-drawings. When his book was finished, in about 1599, he sent it to the King of Spain, who ignored it. For centuries it was lost and forgotten, but in 1908 it was rediscovered in the Royal Library of Copenhagen, and is now one of our most important sources for the details of ancient Peruvian life. Left: the sixth Inca, with his son; in his left hand he holds a standard. They wear a cape, embroidered tunic and sandals. Right: humbler society—preparing the thread for weaving. Women wore a long piece of alpaca cloth, held in place by a sash. Over this, a cape was secured by a metal pin.*

feet. Over this she had another woollen cape garment woven from the wool of the alpaca, a *yacolla.* This she threw over her shoulders at night or when the day was cold. This costume is well known, having also been drawn by a native artist at the time of the conquest. Over her shoulders a shawl was held together by a copper, silver, or, if fortunate, a golden metal pin; this *topo* was universal with the women and still is. The hair was braided, bound, and tied with woollen ribbons.

The higher men and the 'Incas by privilege,' which included the governing *curacas,* dressed in a style similar to the common Indian, but the quality of the material was sumptuous. They were easily distinguished if not by their tunics then by the massive earplugs, usually in jewelled gold. The Inca himself dressed much as did his people except that his tunics were spun from the finest vicuña wool by his women attendants. While the man of the people seldom took off his tunic, the Inca never wore the same one twice. It was destroyed on the changing. 'And I asked them why,' wrote one of the soldiers. 'They replied . . . because everything touched by the Inca-kings, who were children of the Sun, had to be burned and made to ashes and scattered to the winds so no one else could touch it.'

Model and reality: *a Chimú black-ware pot consisting of a leg wearing a string sandal, with next to it a real sandal from an Inca grave. Clearly the two cultures were very close, even to the details of daily life; the sandal seems an excellent fit for the foot, though they are probably separated in time by a hundred years.*

The peasant subjects of the Incas *were the Quechuas: there are still five million of them, preserving many of the characteristics of their ancestors. This man comes from Hatuntaqui, high in the Peruvian Andes. Life at these altitudes, now as then, is a hard struggle against climate and poor soil.*

The *ayllu* was the basic social unit. It has been defined as a sort of clan, a group of extended families living together in a restricted area with a common sharing of land, animals, and crops. Everyone belonged to an *ayllu*; an Indian was born into it. This commune could be large or small, extending itself into a village or a large centre or even into a complex city; for even Cuzco, the capital, was itself only an aggrandized *ayllu*. This social organization must be emphasized for the entire structure of the Inca society is based on it.

Individually no one owned land; the *ayllu* had a definite territory and those living within it were 'loaned' as much land as was necessary for their well-being. Again, the Incas did not invent or create the *ayllu*—it was already there, part of the long development of primitive Andean society—but the Inca systematized and extended it. An *ayllu* was ruled by an elected leader and guided by a council of old men. A number of these scattered communes came under the dominance of a district leader; these in turn formed a territory, and finally they coalesced into 'one of the quarters of the world' which was ruled by a prefect, who answered only to the Lord-Inca himself.

'The political pattern, and in turn the economic, can be described as a basically decimal pyramidal pattern. At the base of the pyramid was the *puric*, an able-bodied male worker. Ten workers were controlled by a straw boss; ten straw bosses had a foreman; ten foremen in turn had a supervisor, ideally the head of the village. The hierarchy continued in this fashion to the chief of the tribe, reportedly composed of ten thousand workers, to the governor of a province, to the ruler of one of the four quarters of the Inca empire, and finally to the emperor, the Sapa Inca, at the apex of the pyramid.'

For every 10,000 people there were 1,331 officials.

At the age of twenty a man was expected to marry. If he did not find a woman, or the other way round, and had reached marriageable age, marriages were 'arranged'.

The marriage rites of the common Indians were simple: there was a joining of hands, later followed by a charming arcadian ceremony of an exchange of sandals.

Marriage for the lower man was monogamous, and since the woman prepared food and drink the death of an Indian's mate was calamitous. Polygamy existed only for the nobility, the Inca himself having hundreds of concubines. All of the ruling classes as well had plural wives. The first, however, always remained head wife; all the others were secondary. The death of a wife among those blissfully polygamous was not so difficult for the male, except that his secondary wives wept 'noisily and lengthily' hoping by the attraction of sentiment to be upgraded to the position of head wife. Among the upper classes, sons of officials grew up with nurses their own ages who became their concubines until they were ripe for marriage.

Once a year, every autumn, the communal lands of the *ayllu* were divided among the members of the commune. Each couple united by marriage was given by the headman of the village, who presided over it, a *topo* of land, roughly 300 by 150 feet. The distribution of land was based on the amount of mouths to feed; those with larger families were given an increased acreage for each child. After the division, each family was responsible for its own particular piece of land.

The communal land of the *ayllu* was divided thus: first for the people, then for the Inca (that is the state), and thirdly for the Sun religion (call it tithes). Those two parts of the land for state and religion were tilled communally and harvested communally as part of the labour tax.

The peasant's house was a rectangular, windowless room built of field stone plastered with adobe mud or made up entirely of sun-dried adobe bricks. It had one entrance; the 'door' was a woollen drapery. The supports which held up a roof, either gabled or hipped, were made from gnarled poles cut from mountain shrub. The roof was very thickly and beautifully thatched with *ichu* grass. The house had neither chimney nor fireplace; the smoke rising from the cooking was left to find its way out between interstices of the thatch. One can see the houses of rustic stonework at the fascinating ruins of Machu Picchu and observe very clearly this type of house.

The floor was of beaten earth; perhaps skins of llamas or alpacas might have been laid upon it. There was no furniture; only the head of the tribe was allowed a stool. The Indian sat on the mud floor or on an old weaving, or squatted on his haunches. He slept on the ground either upon llama hides or on a blanket. Niches in the wall served as shrines for a local god. Pegs were used to hang extra tunics, robes, shawls, festive cloaks, slings, or if one belonged to a militia, a warrior's fighting tunic, helmet, shield, and distinguishing headgear with the totem mark of the village *ayllu.* Stones were arranged to hold up the clay cooking pots; the kitchen utensils, clay dishes for eating, copper or bronze knives, bone skewers, and a large stone mortar where the Indian women brayed their corn stuffs were in this section. All was simple and expedient.

The village was built on a rectangular plan and laid out, presumably, by professional architects sent out by the state. Three or four rectangular walls formed a sort of common wall, a *cancha,* a form of co-operative backyard; out of this grew the organized village. This type of architecture is still to be seen in the ruins of the village of Ollantaytambo under the fortress of

Stone houses were rare—*they were mostly built of adobe brick—but are all that remain to tell us what the rest were like. This example is at Machu Picchu. The low doorway would have been closed by a curtain, the windows, if there were any, small and uncovered. Inside, the floor was of beaten earth and there was hardly any furniture.*

Growing up in ancient Peru, *according to Poma de Ayala. Below: the baby, aged one month, securely strapped into an elaborate wooden cradle. The boy, aged five, wears a wolf-skin cap and whips a top.*

the same name, which lies on the upper Urubamba River some twenty-four miles from Cuzco.

The round of daily life began at daybreak. The Indian slaked thirst and hunger by quaffing fermented *a'ka,* a mildly intoxicating, thick, malt-smelling beverage. A family had no breakfast as such; they ate what was left of yesterday's evening meal. Then the farmer went to his fields.

In late midday the family gathered for their second meal. Cooking was mostly done by boiling; grease and frying were unknown. Maize was cooked with chili peppers and herbs until it split; this was *mote.* Sun-dried llama meat was made into a soup into which *chuñu* (dehydrated potatoes, reduced to a thick whitish powder) was put to make a stew called *locro.* Popcorn was known and considered a delicacy. Ground maize was made into a paste and baked in the ashes like bread. Bright-eyed *cui* (guinea pigs), which ran about the darkened corners of the house, were raised for food. These types of food, certainly not inspiring to a gourmet, were, with variations, the food of the common Indian.

The evening and final meal was taken between four and five o'clock. Men squatted about the pots laid upon a cloth on the ground, helped themselves from the pot with fingers or quaffed the soup from ceramic bowls; the women sat outside of the circle, their backs to the men. When their *ayllu* was visited by the governor, the people of the commune joined together in long lines facing each other (all having brought their own food), and the *curaca* at the head of the 'table' sat on his golden stool.

At the mature age of twelve, *the young man is entrusted with the care of animals, probably alpacas, though Poma's drawing leaves room for some doubt. A large net, held on two sticks, has been used to catch birds.*

Children were trained from the beginning of their lives for the part they were expected to play in the community. After birth the child was washed at the nearest stream, and on the fourth day placed in a cradle, called a *quirau.* It was carried on the mother's back and put always within easy reach. The child was suckled until two to three years of age, and after that he began to imitate the parent's life. The child was not named for the first two years, being called nothing else than *wawa* (baby); then there was a family festival and the elaborate ceremony of *rutu-chicoy* (hair cutting) took place. The child was given then a temporary name, and the permanent name was given only when he reached puberty.

At the age of fourteen the boy put on his breechclout. Among the upper classes this meant a pilgrimage to the birthplace of the Inca state at Huanacauri up the Cuzco Valley, the sacrifice of llamas with priests officiating, and the smearing of blood on his face. Later he took on the aspect of a warrior, replete with shield, earplugs, and slingshot, and made public avowals to the Inca. Then the boy of the upper classes was given the type of traditional education which fitted him for a later administrative post within the realm.

Young girls became of age about the same time in a charming hair-combing ceremony, and they, too, took their permanent names. Strangely enough, a woman had a chance to leave the *ayllu* and better the existence into which she had been born. If she had special talent in weaving, showed grace, or was very beautiful, she might be selected as a 'Chosen Woman'

August: *men using the foot plough, women breaking up the earth.*

September: *the main crop of the year—maize—is planted.*

October: *a boy guards the young shoots from birds and animals.*

The labours of the months: *Inca agriculture through the year, in Poma de Ayala's naïve but very informative drawings, which give both the farmers' activity and the state of the weather.*

(*Nusta*). Under these conditions she was brought to Cuzco, or some other provincial capital of one of the quarters of the world, there to learn specific things such as weaving, cooking, and rituals of the Sun, the state religion. She might become the wife of a high-placed official, or if fortune favoured her, a concubine of the Lord-Inca himself.

But normally men and women of the realm of the Incas were born, reared, and buried within their *ayllu*. There was no escape from it. It gave them security, but the price of security was absorption into the state.

Under the guidance of the Inca's 'professionals,' the whole of the realm—which included Andes, desert, and Upper Amazon—became a great centre of plant domestication. *More than half of the foods that the world eats today were developed by these Andean farmers*; it has been estimated that more kinds of food and medicinal plants were systematically cultivated here than in any other sizable area of the world! One has only to mention the obvious: maize—(twenty varieties); potatoes (240 varieties); sweet potatoes, squash, beans of infinite variety; manioc (from which come our farina and tapioca); peanuts, cashews, pineapples, chocolate, avocados, tomatoes, peppers, papaya, mulberries; so many and so varied the plants, and so long domesticated in the Old World, one forgets that all of these originated in the Americas.

The potato is the dominant food-plant in the high Andes. Nowhere else are there so many localized varieties or colours of potatoes as in Peru: white-yellow, pink-gray, brown, purple, black, spotted, and streaked; they are planted from the hot coast seemingly to the sky; the *tatu* variety is planted up to 15,000 feet above the level of the sea and is fully able to withstand the heavy frosts.

November: *the maize shoots are irrigated from a reservoir.*

December: *oca, another staple Inca food, is planted.*

January: *weeding and hoeing; in the distance—rain.*

Sara, that is maize, shared the social base with the potato, and it was, as now, the great food staple of the American Indian. Not able to withstand as harsh a climate as the potato, maize reaches its highest limits of cultivation in sheltered slopes about Lake Titicaca, at an altitude of 12,700 feet. *Sara* also has great antiquity; it is found in pre-Inca graves dating back to 3000 B.C.

The Andean farmers' year was divided into two seasons: wet and dry. The wet season began in October and extended to May; the dry season, starting in May, although subject to considerable caprice (hence the Inca's preoccupation with obeisance to the unseen powers), continued into November. The lands were cultivated communally and the produce stored in granaries. These state granaries were stocked, so the early Spaniard remembered, with maize, quinoa, *chuñu, charqui* (dried llama meat), fish, cords, hemp, wool, cotton, sandals, and military arms, stored in hampers, each item in its appropriate warehouse. They were seen by Francisco de Xerez, the first soldier-chronicler of the conquest in 1533, who remembered these storehouses as being 'piled to the roof, with things even as the Merchants of Flanders and Medina make them.'

August was ploughing time, and work in the fields was—like all else—communal. It began with a festival. The nobility took it all most seriously and always participated. 'If,' wrote the Jesuit historian Padre Cobo, 'the Inca himself or his governor or some high official happened to be present, he started the work with a golden digging stick which they brought to the Inca, and following his example all the other officials and nobles who accompanied him did the same.'

They had no plough and no draft animals. Men used, as they still do,

February: *animals raid the ripening maize; rain continues.*

March: *the crop ripens in the rain; a boy frightens birds.*

April: *human pests—a thief begins premature harvesting.*

the *taclla,* or foot plough, which was a thick pole six feet in length with a fire-hardened point; sometimes it was bronze-tipped. There was a footrest near the tip and it was driven deep into the soil by a thrust of the foot and shoulder pressure. The clod of earth was then prized up. The digging stick, like all else in the realm, was a group tool and was seldom used by only one man. His kinsmen of the *ayllu* formed a long line across the field to be ploughed, chanting rhythmically. The men worked backward, the women followed facing them and breaking up the clods with a sort of hoe called *lampa. Sara* (maize) was planted in September, potatoes when the rains began to fall, i.e., between October and November. After ploughing the fields of the Inca, the Sun, and their own, they next turned to those fields of kinsmen who were serving in the army, and then finally to those of the sick and the halt. Their principal tribute (it was part of their tax), said Garcilaso, was 'the working and cultivating and harvesting of the lands of the Sun and the Inca.'

Agriculture was bound up very closely with terracing and irrigation, since the amount of flat land was somewhat limited as most Andean valleys are deep and narrow. The sides of the valleys were wonderfully terraced and these terraces are very exciting when seen for the first time. The rainy season run-off carries away soil; terracing prevented it. Terracing further extended the soil community where the earth surfaces were scant; so the Indians, too, were soil makers.

Under Inca rule, terracing of the Andean valleys was systematic, a method of soil preservation and soil creation. In the greater projects, those, for example, of Pisac—where the terraces stand poised over the heights of the upper Urubamba River—or at Ollantaytambo (where the workers cut into

May: *the maize cobs are picked and plants cut.*

June: *the potato harvest; women do the carrying.*

July: *the crop is stored; chickens and a dog glean what is spilled.*

the living rock), professional architects were sent out from Cuzco to plan them. It was an enormous expenditure of labour. That these terraces still stand after five centuries is sufficient testimony to the the skill of these Inca engineers.

Irrigation was tied closely to terracing and so naturally with agriculture. It was the lifeblood of empire. In the wet season rain does not always fall nor does all this borax-filled earth hold the water, so the Inca engineers harnessed the brawling streams pouring out of glaciers and brought them down in the most careful manner to water fields, even though separated by immense distances from the watercourse. These techniques helped to control the density of population and gave the social body a meticulous balance between population and productivity. Much Inca-directed skill was devoted to irrigation. There were immense water reservoirs in the fortress of Sacsahuamán above Cuzco; water was laid underground in superbly made stone-laid sewers in many widely spaced areas. Rivers were straightened, canalized as one sees the Urubamba River, a few miles east of Cuzco and below the great fortress of Pisac. This type of advanced engineering once extended throughout the empire, but is now only dimly seen since so much has been lost to the insults of time.

Water was so engineered as to be introduced at the top of the terraces, thence it ran down from one gigantic terraced step to another, the whole area being watered by a single stream. Water conduction demands careful design and must be determined by a knowledge of hydrologic conditions, the nature of the soil, and the general conformation of the land. To secure the flow it must run down a slight incline: too fast, it will erode the banks; too slow, it will allow weeds to grow and silt will choke up the channels.

Gigantic terraces covering whole hillsides *preserved the precious water upon which Inca agriculture depended. They are engineering works comparable in scale to anything of that date in the Old World, and must have demanded huge forces of organized manpower. The water was often brought several miles and distributed in carefully graded channels. This aerial photograph shows the country round Pisac, not far from the Urubamba gorge with an Inca road running through it.*

Cotton was known very early in Peru. *It has been found in graves dating back to 2000 B.C., and certainly the Spaniards saw it stacked in the Inca state storehouses. Here an Indian of today picks cotton at Chiclayo, where the river turns the desert into green and fertile land.*

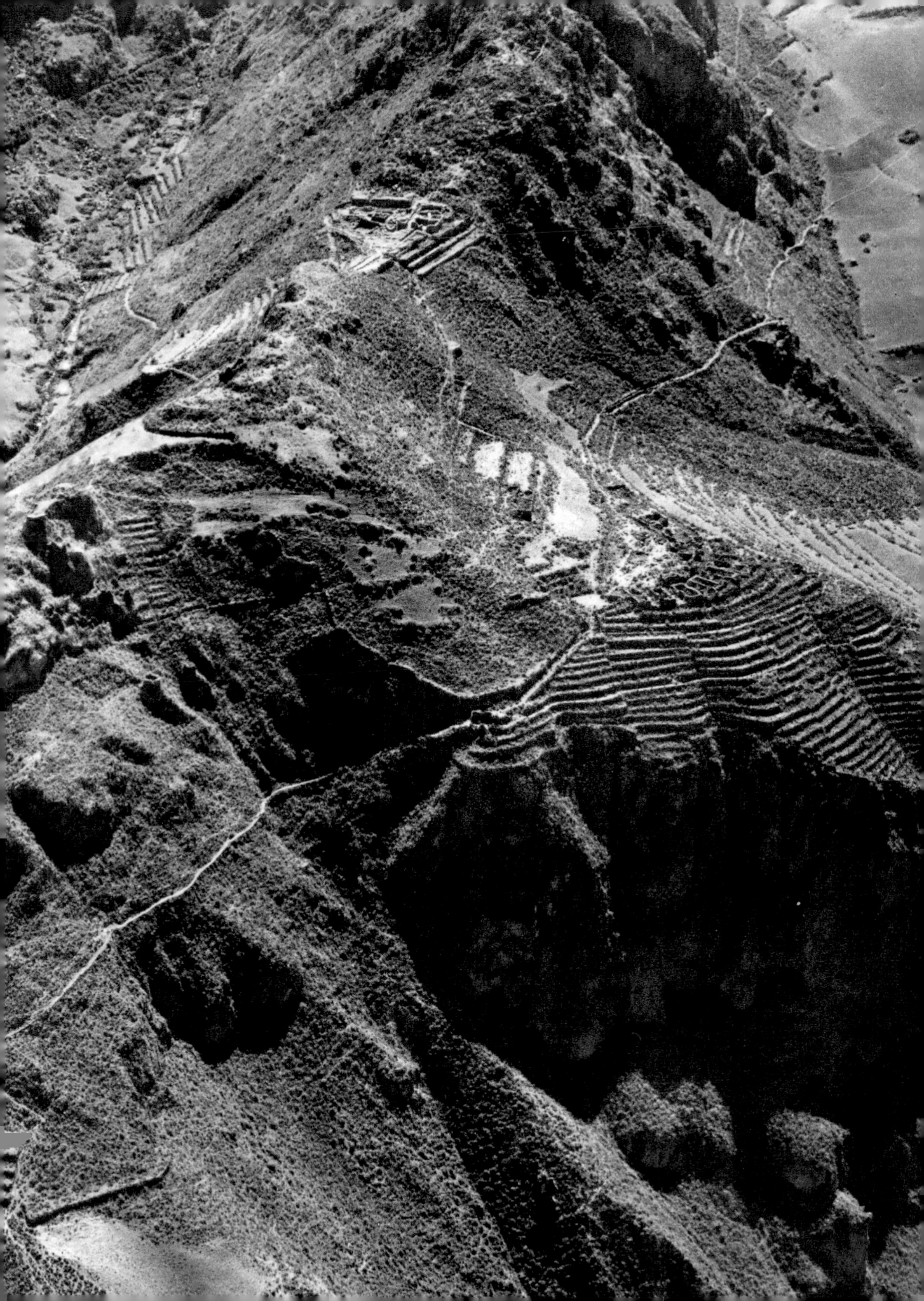

Animals were state property, *and were bred or hunted by royal officials. Llamas provided meat and coarse wool, and their dung was used for fuel. They can carry small loads six to twelve miles a day. The earliest evidence for llamas and guanacos was recently discovered, engraved and painted on a rock face near* San Pedro de Atacama *in northern* Chile *(opposite). Alpacas (left) provided fine wool for clothing and textiles. The vicuña was described by Pedro de Cieza de León as 'a delicate animal with plenty of fine wool'—so fine in fact that it was reserved for the Inca and his circle. Cieza's woodcut, above, was the first illustration to be made of vicuñas.*

It is scarcely surprising that wherever in this variegated globe water conduction has been practiced, the techniques of it are almost identical.

In Peru, after the September planting, especially in those lands unreached by irrigation, October was always the 'critical' month; if rain did not fall, there would be a crop failure. In instances of prolonged drought the Indian fell back on the 'mysteries' and the high priests took over.

Throughout the planted land llamas were sacrificed to the rain gods. If that did not seed the rain clouds, then a man, a woman, perhaps even a child, was sacrificed. The procedure was repeated in Cuzco on a greater scale. The people paraded dressed in mourning; black llamas were tied without food or drink in the belief that the gods could not withstand the plaintive wail of the llama and would send rain to assuage it.

The American Indian had no draught animals, and the llama was the closest he got to a domesticated animal. (Before the coming of the white man,

America had neither horse, nor steer, nor bovines of any form, nor domesticated pigs or goats.) The llama has a camel's head, large eyes, a split nose, a harelip, no upper teeth, and two-toed feet, which look cloven but are not. Its usual gait is as leisurely as that of a *grande dame* entering a salon, but it can leap like a deer. Llamas were, and are, seldom ridden, though there are Mochica ceramics showing Indians mounting them; they are not milked and never used for wheeled drayage. Yet they have, like the camel, an amazing ability for adaptation; they can live in the range of perpetual glaciers, 17,000 feet altitude, or acclimatize themselves to the desert. Normally a llama loaded with half its weight will walk between six and twelve miles a day; if pressed it will travel longer. As the camel was to the Asian, so the llama was to the Inca; its wool was used mostly for heavy blankets, strong cords, sacks for cargo (the wool is very greasy); its dung, like that of the camel, was a fuel and was gathered in their communal voiding places.

15 Products and Pleasures of the People

THE WEAVING skills occupied both men and women, the wool stuffs col-lected by their *ayllu* were divided among them according to their needs, i.e., depending on the number and demands of each member of the commune. The residue was stored in the official storage bins, the precise amounts accounted for by those officials who recorded this on their *quipu* string counters, so that the governor of a given province could know how much wool was available in this district.

Wool, until Inca conquests opened up the channels for trade to obtain cotton fibre, was *the* Andean material. The wool of the alpaca, generally white, but mixed with grays and natural browns, was used for wearing apparel because of its superior fineness and long fibre; llama wool, coarse and greasy, was spun, in a distinctive brown-white colour, as fibre for heavy blankets, durable sacks for llama transport, and ropes and llama halters. Vicuña, soft, silky, the finest in the world, was reserved only for the highest luxury weaving. The wool was dyed before carding and spinning, although where the particular weaving called for the natural colours of the wool they were fully utilized.

After dyeing, the wool was tied to a distaff and spun. The spindle was a straight stick with a piece of ceramic whorl (usually nicely decorated) which one spun between the fingers as one would a top, while the other fingers, well moistened with spittle, fed the fibres from the wool ball on the distaff. This system of spinning is world-wide. Cotton was spun in the same manner.

The looms to spin wool and cotton were of three kinds: the backstrap or belt loom, wherein the upper part is tied to a tree or upright and the belt for tension is passed around the back of the weaver (hence the name); the horizontal loom, put upon the ground, the warp being supported by a forked-stick support a foot above the ground; and the vertical loom, built against the wall, upon the cloth of which the weavers—usually men—worked standing.

What is certain is that the art of the loom was widespread throughout Peru, and that the Incas were inheritors of the techniques that had been thousands of years in the perfecting. Almost all authorities seem to agree that most of the fabrics found in graves came from the backstrap loom;

Brilliant textiles still on the loom *have been recovered from pre-Inca graves. The loom was tied to a wall or post at one end and supported round the weaver's back at the other. The principle of weaving is everywhere the same, the thread of the woof being passed under and over the strands fixed to the loom (the warp)—in this case by the fingers only, not by a needle. The weavers had a superb sense of colour and design; these textiles are now prized as works of art all over the world.*

A housewife's work-basket, *plaited straw on a wooden base, containing spools wound with spun thread and other weaving materials. Together with a mummy and a piece of woven cloth, it comes from a grave of about A.D. 1000 belonging to the Tiahuanaco culture.*

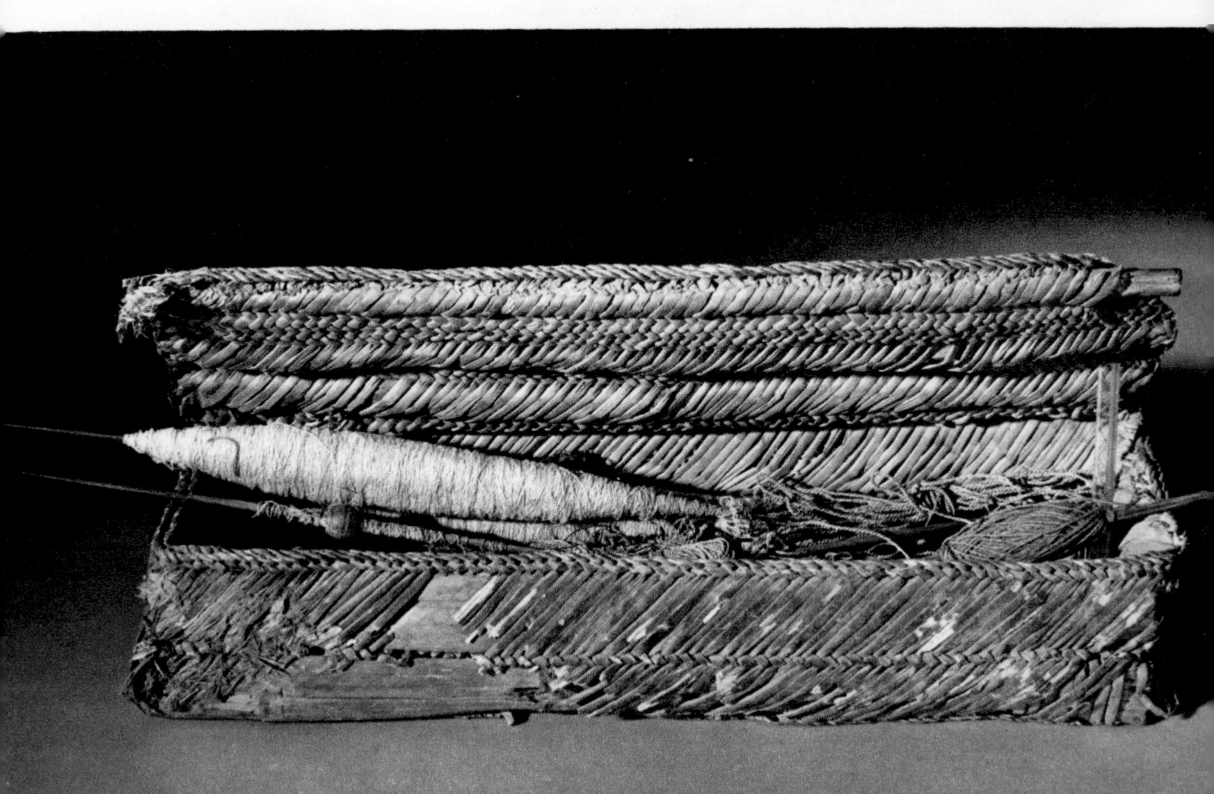

these looms have often been found in graves—usually in that of a woman so that in the netherworld she could occupy herself as she had in this one—and on these backstrap looms cloth is found half completed. By comparing these with the present-day looms of tradition-bound Peruvian communities, one can see that the techniques have changed little in two thousand years.

Weaving has had a long history in Peru; the Incas inherited complete techniques; their notable contribution was to perfect a method of obtaining the wool of the vicuña which was made, as said elsewhere, into weavings of such fineness that they were mistaken by the first Spaniards to be of heavy silk.

As in spinning, so with looms. Those used by the ancient Peruvians (*ahuanas*) are identical with those of other civilizations with which they had absolutely no contact. A form of backstrap loom was used in Egypt, a horizontal loom appears in predynastic Egypt, and the one pictured on the tomb of Khnem-hotep (at Beni Hasan), circa 1900 B.C., is practically identical with those of the Andean and coastal Peruvians.

The weaving methods of the Incas, like all else about them, were functional. Three grades of wool cloth were woven, all distinguished by names. The common was the *awaka* woven material. The finest and most finished (on both sides) was *kumpi.* Many Inca materials were done in tapestry weave, but much of this has perished due to the climate. The thick and heavy weave, *chusi,* was a baizelike material used for bed coverings or door hangings.

Men as well as women were weavers; the latter, however, were entrusted with the finest wools of the alpaca and the vicuña. One of the functions of the Chosen Women was to produce the fabulous vicuña tunics for the Inca—the kind which he never wore more than once before it was destroyed. They also fashioned the feather tunics, a mosaic of jungle-bird feathers put quill-first into the warp of the weaving. 'The lustre, splendour and sheen of the fabrics of feather-work,' said the Jesuit Bernabé Cobo, 'were of such beauty that it is impossible to make them understood, unless by showing them,' and what he said then applies equally now. They are indescribable except to call them feather mosaics. In addition to the feather weaving, other cloth was richly adorned with bangles of gold or tiny bells and golden particles called *chaquira*; there were tunics completely covered with gold, silver, or burnished copper pieces.

Pottery, one of the oldest of skills in the Americas, was made without the potter's wheel. Yet the ancient Peruvians, despite their primitive techniques, produced pottery that is among the world's best. Inca pottery is well made, fine-grained, with a hardness almost metallic. Pottery shaping was made by first rolling clay into sausage form, then building spirally into the projected pot, one hand feeding the sausage-shaped core, the other pressing it into shape. This was then smoothed and moulded by a small flat wooden disk; then it was dried, painted, and fired.

Inca pottery has a wide range of shapes. There are the utilitarian, three-legged pots used by the warriors on campaign, the household pottery, strong and crude red; the enormous, beautifully shaped aryballus (although not like the Greek, from which its name derives)—a bottle-shaped pot with a pointed bottom, which fell to its side when emptied, but was so exquisitely balanced that a jar, capable of holding six to eight gallons of fermented *chicha,* could, when filled, balance on that single point. The Inca aryballus had a long, graceful neck and two band-shaped handles, used for holding a rope passed through them for carrying; it was the most characteristic of Inca pottery.

There were shallow dishes for food, a type of service all seemed to have, and sometimes wonderfully decorated. There were beaker-shaped vessels for drinking, and three-legged braziers, wide and open-mouthed for heating the otherwise unheated rooms.

The designs of Inca pottery are very distinctive: usually elaborate geometric patterns, so unmistakably Inca that they are as easily identifiable as a Roman coin; for Inca pottery, as indeed is equally true of other Peruvian pottery, is a diagnostic for spatial relationships.

Markets under the Inca Empire were frequent and general, but trade was purely local and commerce a government monopoly. The need for markets within the empire was an important element in the economic structure of the realm. 'In order,' wrote Garcilaso de la Vega, 'that labour might not be so continuous as to become oppressive, the Inca ordained that there should be three holidays every month in which the people should divert themselves with various games. He also commanded that there should be three fairs every month, when the labourers in the field should come to the market and hear anything that the Inca or his council might have ordained.' They called these markets *catus.*

This system of using the market as an official decree-dispensing method is remembered in one of the smaller market centres of Cuzco itself; it is known as Rimacpampa, the 'Speaking Place,' where the people gathered to hear the Inca equivalent of 'Hear ye, hear ye . . .'

The jungle people brought feathers for the feather mosaic weavings, *chonta-palm* (an iron-hard wood) much used by the Incas; there were birds, jungle game, and batwings' fur (from which a silklike cloth was made for the Inca), dyestuffs, and many Homeric simples such as quinine, ipecac, sassafras, *guayusa* (used for a febrifuge), rubber, and gum latex from the sapodilla tree, strong tobacco leaf, and narcotics.

The language of pottery *was spoken in ancient South America with many voices, from the earthy humour of the Mochicas to the elegant functionalism of the late Inca style. Illustrations on these pages show Inca pottery in its variety. All were hand-moulded, since there were no potter's wheels, and they all date from the later Inca period before the Conquest, from 1450 onwards.*

Mortar and food-jar, *utility vessels, the latter with a neat lid: height ab out 3 inches.*

An 'aryballus', *used for storing maize-beer, from Cuzco. These come in all sizes—this one stands four feet high.*

Vessels of wood *sometimes echoed pottery forms. This inlaid beaker or 'quero', shaped like a man's head, is from Cuzco. Similar beakers are still in use in the Andes.*

A form of 'aryballus' *from the Chancay culture. This coastal culture was liquidated by the Incas after 1400.*

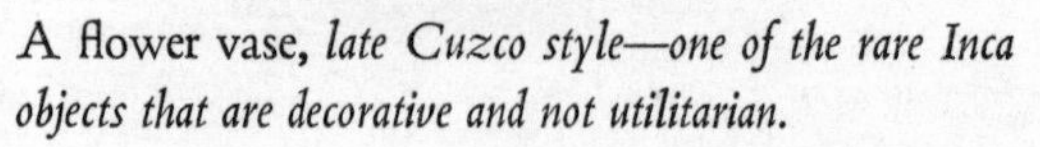

A flower vase, *late Cuzco style—one of the rare Inca objects that are decorative and not utilitarian.*

Jaguar and snake, *unusual Inca motifs, show that this jar was made after their conquest of Upper Amazonia. It was found near Cuzco.*

The Andean people brought to this type of market their excess manufactures: weavings, bowls, carvings, potatoes, *chuñu,* corn—that which they did not themselves consume; and since the empire levied no property taxes, only *mita* labour service, they were free to exchange any accumulated movable property.

Pedro de Cieza de León, that most accurate of observers, tells something about them in 1549, long after the departure of Inca glory. The barbaric pageantry that went with these markets can only be dimly surmised: 'In all parts of this kingdom of Peru we who have travelled over it know that there are great fairs or markets, where the natives make their bargains. Among those the greatest and richest was formerly in the city of Cuzco, for even in the time of the Spaniards its greatness was caused by the gold which was bought and sold there and by the other things of all kinds that were sent into the city. But this market or fair at Cuzco did not equal the superb one at Potosí, where the traffic was so great that among the Indians alone, without including Christians, twenty-five or thirty thousand golden pesos exchanged hands daily. This is wonderful, and I believe that no fair in the world can be compared to it. . . .'

The holidays, which were public ceremonials, were many and elaborate, bound to the markets and to the ceremonial year which was tied up with the agricultural year.

The Inca year was divided into twelve months, each month named after its ceremony. The year began in December with *Capac Raymi,* the 'magnificent festival' month. There were many sports and games attached to the festivals, and the coming-of-age rites were held, with the boys of the upper class receiving the breechclout. There was the month of the 'small ripening' and the 'great ripening'; there were others which were called the month of the 'dance of the young maize,' and later the 'festival of the water'; and so on.

Holidays might last for a day or for a week. There might be public dancing, such as when hundreds of radiantly clothed Chosen Women danced with Huáscar's Chain. There could be games and sports. There was always drinking, for the Indian was expected to get drunk, which he did, quaffing immense quantities of fermented *chicha*; ritual drunkenness was as essential to a good festival as agricultural discipline was to a good harvest.

The musical instruments of the Incas were as limited as the variation of their dance. By their nature they were self-limiting; they were mostly percussion and wind instruments, and strictly bucolic. Drums were made of a hollow log and covered either with llama or tapir hide (they varied from small drums used by women to war drums used by warriors). Whatever the variety, they were beaten by a rubber-knobbed stick, and their drumming

'Fiesta' is Poma de Ayala's word *but of course all Inca festivals were primarily religious ceremonies, mostly concerned with the agricultural year. Here a man and woman are partners in a dance. The men wear little copper or silver bells hanging from their legs, and the one on the right plays reed-made panpipes.*

had nothing of the quality of the sensuous music of the Mediterranean world. A tambourine was used in dances. There were copper and silver *chanrara* bells, attached to clothes and hung on bracelets and dangling from wooden maces. On the dancers' legs were attached anklets of silver bells or shells, and snail-shell rattles.

The most stirring of the trumpets was the *potóto*, made from an enormous conch shell; it is monotonic, but the effects of a massed chorus of these in war ritual must have been stirring. The Incas seem not to have had, or at least did not use, the large trumpets known to the coastal people, which have been found both in metal and ceramic forms.

Flutes were many and varied; the flute, *quena*, made like a recorder, ranged from two to six notes. There were flutes made from the femurs of jaguars and human beings, but the most typical was the syrinx or Panpipes of cane or pottery made in a minor scale. This *antara* is still found throughout the Andes.

Music was bound up with the dance and the dance with religion; all forms of religious expression involved dancing. The dance itself included singing; it was part of the collective hypnotism. The songs were repeated endlessly, monotonously; the evolutions of the dancer, the ornaments, and the furiously rapid movements robbed all of the onlookers of their self-possession and gave them a feeling that their needs—for which the dance was

Percussion and wind-instruments *exhausted Inca musical equipment. Flutes, played by the men on the left, could be of bone, cane or pottery. On the right a woman strikes a tambourine with a stick that could have been rubber-tipped.*

designed—had been supplied. Masks and costumes were important in these dances, and they have survived to a surprising degree among the Andean Indians of the present day. There were dresses in mimicry of animals (and the dancers were always accoutered in the pelt of the animal depicted); there were victory dances limited to warriors who, holding hands and in full military panoply, formed a great circle, moving and writhing as a snake. The drumbeat for this was usually performed on what had been the body of an enemy: the skin of the whole body of a dead man had been flayed and the belly stretched to form a drum; the whole body acted as a sound box, throbbings coming out of the open mouth—grotesque but effective.

There was a farm dance of the common people; here the Indian farmers carried the instruments of their work.

The most elaborate was the *way-yaya*, the formal dance of the Inca family, not much different in idea and substance from the dance of that other Sun King, Louis XIV, which opened the minuet. It was performed very solemnly and in a stately manner, self-limiting and self-sufficing, two steps forward, one step backward, as the line of dancers moved slowly toward the golden stool on which sat the Lord-Inca.

The Inca empire was a functioning theocracy: the Inca being god and man, any crime was at once disobedience and sacrilege.

The people formed a very simple and sensible notion of evil—their

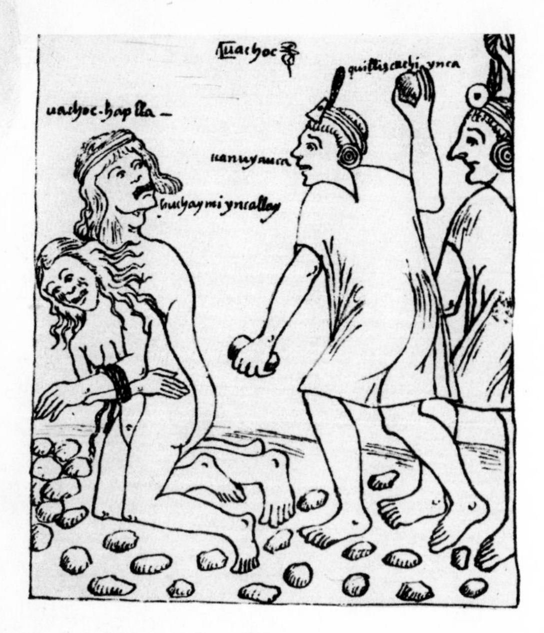

The punishment for adultery *was stoning, seen here in another page of Poma de Ayala's book. Offences against the state were, however, even more serious than private sins.*

Hanging by the hair *over the edge of a cliff was one of the punishments decreed by the Incas for immorality. It is shown here (with a certain artists' licence) in one of Poma de Ayala's drawings.*

functions and natural feelings were tied up with their prejudices. Parental authority was strict, in fact severe. Parents had the respect of their children, and the daily round of the child and its education was by doing; a child had practically no life apart from his parents.

Murder, violence, theft, lying, adultery, and laziness were, since they are human, motivations present in Inca society; all were punishable. Murder was punished by death: hanging, stoning, or merely pushing over a cliff was the method (there are several such execution places known, notably at the site of Ollantaytambo, near to Cuzco). Punishment, however, was mitigated if murder was done in self-defence or in a rage against an adulterous wife. Stealing carried its own prognosis—death. Since one pilfered from a god, taking anything from public property was the most heinous of crimes: breaking into the Inca's storage chambers, destroying bridges, and entering the precincts of the Chosen Women. Stealing was especially peccant since there was virtually no want and so there would normally be no temptation to steal. There was no incentive for the common Indian to accumulate possessions.

The basic honesty of the Indian under Inca rule is attested not alone by learned Spanish judges but by one of the conquistadors, the famous Mancio Sierra de Leguisamo, the one 'who gambled away the sun before the dawn.' In the preamble to his will, filed in Cuzco, he wrote: 'The Incas governed in such a way that there was not a thief, not a criminal, not an idle man . . . the Indians left the doors of their houses open, a stick crosswise in front of the door was a sign that the owner was not in . . . and nobody would enter.'

Theft was regarded as an aberration, and when theft did occur (the machinery of justice was administered merely by accused and accusers telling their sides of the story to a *curaca*) there was a differentiation between robbery from malice and robbery through necessity; if the Indian did so through want, the official was punished for his lack of administration which brought about the crime.

Since laziness deprived the Inca of the Indian's services, this was punished first by public rebuke, then stoning, and, if continued, by liquidation.

Drunkenness was allowed, and was condemned only when occurring at the wrong time, i.e., when the Indian was supposed to be working; then drunkenness was a crime, since it encouraged laziness.

'The Incas,' said Garcilaso de la Vega, 'never made laws to frighten their vassals, but always with the intention of enforcing them on those who ventured to transgress them . . .'

There were, it appears, two forms of justice: Inca law distinguished crimes involving nobles from those concerning the common people, and the upper classes were given more severe punishments than the lower. What was mere public rebuke for the common people became for the noble, when involved, banishment; what was torture for the common Indian, such as having one of his eyes torn out, for the noble was—death.

Death was a preoccupation of the Inca, almost as much as with the Aztec and the Maya.

'Indeed,' said Pedro de Cieza de León, speaking of the immense monuments that surrounded Ayaviri, hard upon Lake Titi-

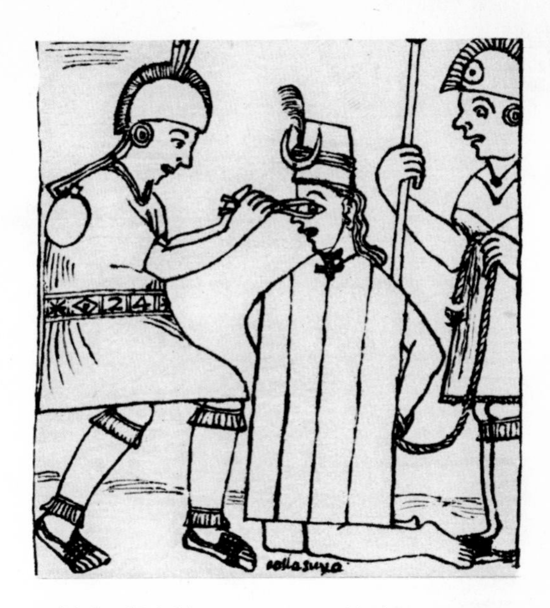

A high official loses an eye. *Had he been a commoner, the punishment would perhaps have been milder, but Inca class-distinctions operated both ways. With power came severe penalties for misconduct.*

Medicine and magic *went together. Witch doctors could summon their demons either for the cure or the doom of the sick man: at the top, the 'maker of dreams'; below, the 'maker of fire' and the remover of poison.*

caca, 'the place is... worthy of note, especially the great tombs, which are so numerous that they occupy more space than the habitations of the living....'

Even death divided the common man from the higher. Death merely continued the dichotomy: the *puric* died almost as he had lived, communally; only for the great were reserved the enormous prestige burials. There has been described the ordinary Indian's way of life, his appearance, dress, language, marriage customs, birth, his round of daily life, his arts and crafts, his markets and his holidays, and the division between the worker and the Lord-Inca was sharply marked in all of these. Clothing (among the lower class) was worn until it became too old to retain; tunics of the Lord-Inca were never worn twice. The Indian had one wife; the Inca had hundreds. The taxpayer had few privileges, the Inca created them. The Inca had considerable education; the Indian found his through the empiricism of his life.

In death, the little man had to be content with the little gods. His end, like his beginning, was a simple ritual. Although he had many gods, only one, the creator-god Tici Viracocha, was very real; Pachacamac led a pantheon of lesser gods, and these gods, like those of the older world, had special functions and powers. The Indian believed in immortality; in fact he believed one never died, for when shrived and flexed the dead body merely became undead and it took on the influences of the unseen powers.

The body of the dead one was flexed, knees up to chin, and shrouded in his own tunic and wrapped in cloth. In the Andes his tomb was under rock eaves; the small catacombs—round, square, or oval—were made of field stone and cemented with adobe mud. Inside the tomb, the sitting body had placed about it food, bowls of *chicha*, and the many small things of his life—if a warrior, the instruments of his trade; if a weaver of note, those artifacts. A woman was given her loom, her colour boxes, and wool to spin.

The dead now became *huaca*, i.e., godlike and mysterious; they exercised a charm so that one had to be careful that none of the *ayllu* offended the dead. The dead were numbered now among the unseen powers and had to be propitiated. Yet in time the dead died, and gradually, unless they were such as the Inca-God (who even when dead, was surrounded by gaudy ritual) were forgotten.

Yet the hold of religion on the Indian was enormous and very real, for life was practical and religion was life, and since all life was controlled by the all-pervading unseen powers, the Indian had to come to a tacit agreement with them for his own well-being. This, then, was the life of the Indian—typical of the unknown number who formed the base of the pyramid which was the Inca realm. At the summit was the Inca.

16 The Royal Inca

Louis xiv, the Sun King of France, actually had to insist that *he* was the state: '*L'Etat c'est moi.*' The Sun King of Peru, the Sapa Inca, never had to over-emphasize—all which lay under the sun was his; it was known to everyone and accepted. He was divine, descended by direct line from the Sun, the creator-god; everything—the land, the earth, the people, gold (the sweat of the sun), silver (the tears of the moon)—belonged to him. He was absolute. He was God. His empire was no theoretical theocracy, it was very real.

The Incas were plenary rulers with their powers held in check only by the influence of ancient customs and the fear of revolt. Beyond his exalted position, there was no final court of appeal; the Inca had merely to lift a hand and with that gesture order death to a renowned general or even to a blood relative who had displeased him.

'I remember,' said Pedro Pizarro, a cousin of *the* conquistador, 'I remember the Lord of Huaylas once asked the Inca [for permission] to visit his estates and it was granted, the Inca giving him limited time in which to go and return. He took rather longer, and when he came back (I was present) brought a gift of fruit and arrived in the Inca's presence. The Lord of Huaylas began to tremble in such a manner before the Inca that he was unable to remain on his feet. . . .'

If this emotional reaction occurred to one of the most powerful *curacas* of the land, what then must have been the effect of the Inca on mere men, on an Indian who was only a unit in the decimal classification of empire? Yet the concern of the Inca for his people, too, was very real; it was not, naturally, as benevolent as that Inca-descended historian, Garcilaso de la Vega, made it out to be when, with the pathos of distance, he wrote his *Royal Commentaries*, nor was it as tyrannical as the Spanish viceroys made it out to be in order to rationalize their destruction of the Inca Empire. The Inca's position and his wealth and his power came from the people and their well-being, for a country does not gain its wealth solely from the numerical quantity of its minerals but from the character and strength of its people. The people and their organization and development within the framework laid down for them were the primary concern of the Inca. All his officials were held to account for maladministration.

The Inca's wife was a *coya* (queen). In the early beginnings of the Inca dynasty the ruler often married into families of other tribes for political alliances. Later, when the Inca was supreme over the land, he married his own sister as his principal wife. The right to marry within the clan belonged only to the Inca. Marriage within the totem group was strictly prohibited. There was an inviolable custom—no one could marry within the first degree. The formal Inca statement was: 'We, the Inca, order and decree that no one shall marry his sister or his mother, nor his first cousin, nor his aunt, nor his niece, nor his kinswoman, nor the godmother of his child, under penalty of being punished and of having his eyes pulled out . . . because only the Inca is allowed to be married to his carnal sister. . . .'

The meaning was obvious: the Incas wanted to insure that their divine descent remained unquestioned, and so from this purity of descent, from the male line of this marriage, came the successor to the 'crown.'

In addition to his *coya*, the Inca, being polygamous, had many subsidiary wives; the ménage of royal concubines numbered into the hundreds, and so out of this fecundity flowed immense numbers of descendants of royal, 'divine' blood. It is estimated that the last Inca before the conquest had in the male line alone five hundred living descendants; from these were

The Inca's sister and queen; *he had many wives and even more concubines, but it was from among the sons of the 'coya' that the next Inca would be chosen. To everyone else incest was tabu. The queen's dress is basically that of other women, but made of richer material and fixed with a gold pin. The 'coya's' attendants are hunchbacks who had their part in Inca court-life.*

formed the Lord-Inca's immediate family, his own royal *ayllu*: 'a useful court circle of educated men trained in the imperial ideology and interested in its perpetuation. The [Lord-Incas] chose their top administrators from this group when possible.'

The Incas (like the Romans, in the latter days of empire), had no clear line of succession; they named as their successor the most competent of those sons from the principal wife, the *coya*. In one sense this was politic, for the oldest son, as history has repeatedly shown, was not always the most competent, but when the supreme crisis occurred in the empire—the arrival of the Spaniards—a lack of a clear line of descent for an heir apparent laid the base, among other things, for eventual disaster.

Pomp and circumstance surrounded the sons of the Lord-Incas from birth. The smallest things, even such as a haircut, or putting on the breechclout at maturity, were clothed in ritual.

At fourteen years, the sons of the nobility assumed the breechclout; a llama was sacrificed, the blood of it smeared on the boy's face. An oath was sworn to the Inca, and the boy received his plaited wool sling, shield, and a silver-headed mace. At the end of the sixth day's ceremony, his ears were pierced, and he became officially a warrior in the Inca's élite guards.

The Child of the Sun *makes his act of homage. The Inca's clothes, of vicuña wool and the most precious metals and jewels, were worn only once; next day they were burnt and he donned new ones, made by the 'Chosen Women'. Poma de Ayala's representation of the sun as a face surrounded by rays is authentic Inca iconography.*

By the time an Inca's descendant was ready to marry, he had as thorough an 'education' as one could have in pre-Spanish America. He had accompanied the Inca on tours of the great empire; he had been with the governors who made their rounds; he had taken part in battles either to defend what the Incas had won by arms, or to suppress those who rebelled. He was soaked in ritual and immersed in Inca history; he had tasted love in various forms, and had no doubt served some sort of apprenticeship in government so as to gain experience in administration.

His dress, as well as that of the other nobles, was not different in style from the ordinary Indian's—only more sumptuous. His ears were pierced and extended with golden ornaments and jewels; his hair was cut in bangs. His tunic was of the finest alpaca, and often vicuña; his sandals were high and well made.

If the young noble in question was the eldest son of the reigning Inca, born of his first wife, the *coya*, and if it was finally decided by the Inca and his council ('twenty of his relatives,' wrote a chronicler, 'old and prudent men, full of experience in the government of the kingdom') that this son would be the Inca apparent, sometime toward the end of the Inca's life the son was so designated. The whole empire went into mourning at the Inca's death. His concubines and his personal servants, as in Egpyt, were expected, following good custom, to accompany him on his journey to the Sun; they were made drunk, danced, and then were strangled. The Inca's body was partially mummified; the entrails were removed and the vacuity stuffed with cloths.

Mummification was a magico-religious act, and its object in Egypt or in Peru was to keep the body as it was during life for the eventual return of the soul. In the humid uplands of Peru mummification was a technical problem; on the desert Peruvian coast it was different, for the heat of the sun and the naturally sterile, porous sand made the conditions for desiccation and mummification of the dead bodies possible.

The mummy of the dead Inca was placed in his house, and a life-size golden statue was made of him; it was served with food as though he still lived. He sat on his golden stool, which was the symbol for a throne. There are few descriptions of these mummies; some were carried away by Manco Capac II when the young Inca rose in revolt against the Spaniards in 1536 and fled into the vastness of Vilcapampa. In 1559 a Spanish official found the mummified bodies of three of the Incas. The Spanish viceroy ordered their removal from Cuzco to Lima, where they subsequently disappeared.

The new Inca, after fasting for three days, was crowned. There were, as on all occasions such as this, pomp, dancing, drinking; obeisance was made to the dead Inca, and the new Lord-Inca started, as was the custom, to build

Big Ears—'Orejones'—was the Conquistador's uncomplimentary name for the high Inca officials. As a sign of rank the ear-lobe was enlarged and jewels or gold disks up to two inches wide inserted in it—many of these ornaments still survive. This illustration from Cieza de León is remarkably accurate: the extended ear-lobes, the 'royal fringe' of llanto and the sandals.

himself a new elaborate house in the centre of Cuzco. (That of his predecessor, the deceased Inca, had become *huaca*, or shrine.) His principal wife, long acquired, now was his *coya*. Secondary wives were acquired, urged on him by other members of the select circle of nobility; concubines came to him from among the Chosen Women. He set the policy of his reign, and acquired many of the honorific titles of his father.

As Inca, his life was governed by elaborate ritual. He ate from gold and silver services, placed upon finely woven mats: his Chosen Women held the plates as he ate. The uneaten food was put aside and stored to be burned later with ceremony, along with his clothes, which he never donned twice. He slept on a raised paillasse covered with colourfully woven woollens, and attended by numbers of his women. As befitted a god, he rarely walked for long distances: when he led a battle he was carried on the royal litter; when he made a tour of the empire, which could well occupy years, he was borne in his royal palanquin. 'They travelled in great majesty,' wrote Pedro de Cieza de León, '. . . seated in rich litters, fitted with loose poles of excellent wood, and enriched [i.e., covered by plate] with gold and silver. Over the litter there were two high arches of gold set with precious stones. . . .'

There is little doubt about the magnificence of these litters, for when Francisco Pizarro, *the* conquistador, entered Cuzco, he found one in the tombs of the mummified Incas; by his contract with the King of Spain he was allowed to select one of these for himself, which he considered the most precious object of his loot.

The Lord-Inca was accoutred as his people: tunic-like poncho, breechclout, sandals, all magnificently woven in vicuña wool by his Chosen Women. His ear spools were immense, gold and jewelled; his hair was cut in bangs and he carried a golden-headed mace. There seems to have been an imperial standard, a pennant stiffened with dyestuff on which a symbol was painted. His crown was a royal fringe made of red wool and worn wrapped around the head. A fringe of red tassels lined with gold lamé hung down before the eyes. An eyewitness to the conquest saw the Inca wearing '. . .on his head a '*llautos*,' which are braids made of coloured wools, half a finger thick and a finger in breadth, made in the form of a crown, rounded and without points, a hand's width, which fitted his head, the forehead a tassel called a borla . . . adorned very subtly with bangles of gold'.

The last Inca before the conquest, Atahualpa (apart from those puppet Incas placed on the royal throne-stool by their conquerors), is the only Lord-Inca whose personal description we have: 'He was well set up for an Indian, of good presence, medium figure, not over stout, comely of countenance and serious withall, his eyes florid... much feared by his people . . .' And fastidious: 'One day as he was eating . . . while raising a piece of food to his mouth it dropped onto the robe he was wearing . . . he quickly rose and retired to the inner chamber and returned wearing an under-robe and a dark brown mantle,' made of bat skins. And of unchallenged power: 'Nor have I seen in all this Peru an Indian like unto this Atahualpa either for this fierceness or for his air of authority.'

There is no doubt about the sumptuousness of the Inca's world; archaeology has confirmed it. The gold that did not disappear into the crucible of the conquistadors confirms all that had been first said about it. Tombs have yielded gold-spangled litters, superb examples of feather weaving and woven tapestries which hang today in the world's most famous museums.

The Incas, just as the common Indians, had their own royal *ayllus*; from them came the Incas by blood. They formed the ruling classes, and from them the Inca chose his administrators. They had their ears pierced. Pierced ears marked the nobility. The small hole in the ear lobe was gradually enlarged until an egg could pass through it; into this the Incas placed a rounded golden and jewelled disk.

The entry of Atahualpa *into the square of Cajamarca—a woodcut published in 1534, only two years after the event. Though crude, some of the details are reliable; Atahualpa sits on a litter and is protected by a sunshade. To the left, meeting him, are Padre Valverde and the Pizarro brothers.*

The second class of administrators were Incas by privilege, those called *curacas*, who were not necessarily born in the royal *ayllus* but whose ability pulled them upward. Because the Incas extended their empire so rapidly, they did not have the number of Incas by blood needed for administrative purposes; often a conquered land had its own chieftain confirmed in his rule, while his sons were whisked off to Cuzco for an orientation course and returned as *curacas*. All were exempt from taxation, i.e., the work tax: they drew their emoluments from the service of the common Indian.

The founding of Cuzco by the legendary first Inca, Manco Capac, is

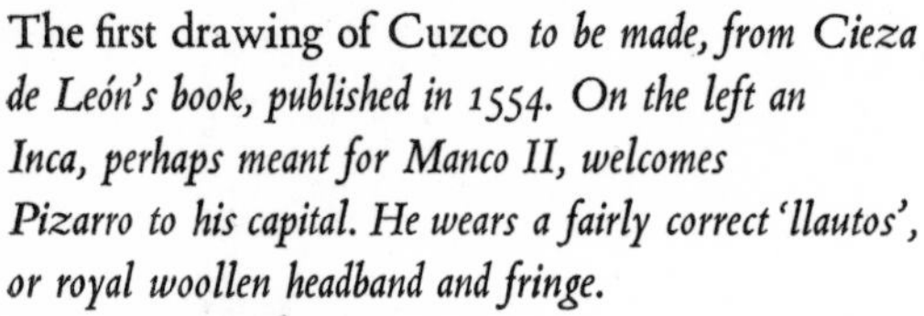

The first drawing of Cuzco *to be made, from Cieza de León's book, published in 1554. On the left an Inca, perhaps meant for Manco II, welcomes Pizarro to his capital. He wears a fairly correct 'llautos', or royal woollen headband and fringe.*

Cuzco lies high in the Andes *at about 11,000 feet. Mountains rise on three sides, to the south-east a widening valley carries two small rivers away. But this 17th century engraving, with its predecessor by de Bry, is no safe guide to the plan of the Inca capital.*

placed circa A.D. 1100. Cuzco was the place where Manco Capac rested after his wanderings from the south and where the golden staff given to him by the Sun God disappeared when he threw it into the ground.

Cuzco lies in the hollow of a valley at about 11,000 feet. On three of its sides the mountains rise precipitously, and at its south-east the valley yawns widely and stretches for miles between a double array of mountains, a succession of fertile plains and bog. Two small rivers flow down into it, and in Inca times these were canalized with finely worked stone; buildings were erected on the banks.

It was divided into two parts: Hanan, or Upper Cuzco, and Hurin, or Lower Cuzco. In the latter part, the capital centre, the nobles had their houses. There were two main plazas from which narrow streets issued. 'It was grand and stately,' wrote one who saw it in its glory, 'and must have been founded by a people of great intelligence. It has fine streets, except that they are narrow, and the houses are built of solid stones, beautifully joined. . . . [Cuzco] was richest of which we have any knowledge in all the Indies, for the great store of treasures was often brought to increase the grandeur of the nobles. . . .'

Cuzco, as a city, emerged in final form when it was rebuilt after A.D. 1400, and it showed good town planning. At this time the two rivers that entered from the north were canalized. There was a gridiron scheme for streets, converging out of two central plazas. The houses of the meaner sort were one-storied, but others, the greater ones, were two-storied, and sometimes three stories in height. The principal buildings were located about the great plaza, and the towering Sun Temple occupied the most prominent part. To retain its purity, water was conveyed with great care through stone conduits laid in the middle of the street.

Out from the principal plaza, called Huaycapata ('Joy Square'), spread the twelve wards of the city, divided roughly into four sections—the four principal directions or quarters of the world which gave the empire its name, Tawantinsuyu. The King of Spain's inspector said that there were 100,000 houses in the city—obviously an exaggeration—he perhaps meant the number of people—yet he affirmed that 'in the eight days [that he was there], I have not been able to see everything.'

The Sun Temple, the edifices of the Lord-Incas, the Chosen Women, and others were constructed by professional architects and were the pride of the realm. They were defined by long reaches of stones elaborately cut and fitted with a precision which has never been duplicated anywhere in the world. The exteriors of the buildings (unlike the Maya or Aztec buildings, which were floriated with design) were seldom if ever decorated; the more important ones were sheathed with gold plate. The first Spaniard to see Cuzco—it seemed ablaze with gold—reported he saw a 'quadrangular building . . . measuring three hundred and fifty paces from corner to corner, entirely plated with gold; of these gold plates they took down seven hundred which together weighed five hundred pesos of gold. . . .' Much of the golden loot from Cuzco was plate torn from the walls: 'These had been taken from the walls . . . they had holes in them showing that they had been secured by nails,' showing that many of the royal edifices in Cuzco had been gold-plated. At least enough to make the high sententious fantasy of the conquistador soar.

Cuzco was certainly magnificently planned. The most fabulous edifice in Cuzco was the Curi-cancha, 'Golden Enclosure,' at the spot where, according to, legend stood the first edifice erected by the first Inca. The conquistadors

'It has fine streets, *except that they are narrow, and the houses are built of solid stones, beautifully joined.' So wrote one of the Conquistadors who saw Cuzco in the days of its glory. It was rebuilt about 1400, on systematic town-planning principles. The straight streets still survive, with modern dwellings built on top of the superb Inca masonry.*

who saw it never tired of telling of what they saw, and after five hundred years archaeologists are still trying to piece together this most stupefying, ancient, and sacred of Inca shrines. The Temple of the Sun adjoined the Golden Enclosure. It was a shrine as well as a centre for the priestly organization. It was presided over by the 'chief priest *Huillac-Umu* who lived in the grand temple,' This complex structure had six major buildings: sanctuaries to the Sun, Moon, Stars, Lightning, Rainbow, and a sort of chapter house for the priests of the Sun; all these various parts surrounded the Inti Pampa, 'Field of the Sun.' A fountain in its vast centre was encased in gold on which was etched the image of the Sun, the same Sun which fell to the conquistador who gambled it away one night. The outside of the building (parts of which can now still be seen as part of the Church of Santo Domingo set on top of it) was covered with gold plate so massive that each sheet weighed from four to ten pounds. Although the roof was thickly thatched with grass, it also had, reportedly, golden straws among the others, which caught the rays of the sun's declension with each day.

To the utter amazement of the first Europeans to see it, the Curi-cancha had in its fields a golden mimicry of plants: maize, actual size, was 'planted' and its stalks cunningly wrought in gold, and Cieza tells of the 'garden where the clods [of earth] were pieces of fine gold, and it was artificially sown with cornfields which were of gold, as well as the stems of the leaves and the [corn] cobs. Besides all this they had more than twenty llamas of gold with their young, and the [Indian] shepherds life-size, with their slings and crooks to watch them... all made of gold.' There is no doubting this report, for the King of Spain's inspector, Miguel de Estete, attached to the expedition to attest officially to the items of loot received, recorded that he saw 'straws made of solid gold, with their spikes just as they grow in the fields. And if I was to recount all the different varieties in the shape of gold my story would never end. . . .'

It strains the imagination, at this distance in time, to accept all this as coming out of the indigenous American cultures, without contact with the old; but a visit to any of the museums which contain ancient Peruvian collections (bearing in mind that the best was melted down in the crucibles of the conquest) will convince even the most sceptical of the organization that this barbaric empire must have had.

But it must be repeated that the form of organization within the four quarters of the empire was only an *intensified* development of the original pre-Inca patterns. This specialization of Indian labour made possible the great achievements of the Inca Empire.

17 'Sweat of the Sun, Tears of the Moon'

GREAT CITIES like Cuzco sprang from traditions and techniques going far back into the pre-history of South America. Architecture, in fact, developed out of the rustic houses of the peasants. This was as true in Peru as it was in Greece. The most awe-inspiring of Inca structures—the cyclopean walls of polished stonework—are only a development of the one-room house of the common Indian, the kind which proliferated at random throughout the Andes at the beginning of the Inca realm.

These houses, placed in a square with a common yard, developed into the rectangular city plan of the Incas, and no matter how imposing the Inca building, it suggests always its humble origin.

The Incas are famed for the quantity and variety of their stone structures, but few have ever emphasized the sheer mass of buildings that existed; it is true that much centres about Cuzco, yet much lies outside it.

At the height of the Inca Empire, say, A.D. 1500, Inca structures spread over an enormous distance—from the Sun temples and fortress of Purumauca on the north bank of the Maule River (35° S. lat.) in southern Chile, north to the Ancasmayo River (approximately 1° N. lat.), which is now in Colombia—3,250 linear miles.

Along this route were large centres, replete with administrative buildings and Sun temples; there were stone-laid palaces, temples for Sun Virgins, official storehouses, and fortresses. Along the entire web of roads, *tampu* way stations appeared every four to twelve miles, so that for the sheer mass of building the empire almost equalled the Roman.

There were no walled cities. Each large city had, if it was built close to a hill, which it usually was, a fortress and within there was a miniature of the city it guarded. When attacked, the people were expected to go up to it with their weapons and from there defend themselves.

All this architecture came from central planning. In the extent of this type of realm, that is, in three thousand miles, there was, and still remains, a great variety of forms of architecture, and enough survives to gain a fair idea of what this civic-military planning appeared to be. To give some of these significant examples, one can begin at *Cacha.* This city stands on the right bank of the Yucay River about forty-eight miles from Cuzco. The temple, one of the most unusual of Inca structures, was dominated by a row of round columns on its two sides. The structure, which has been in the most part destroyed, still has walls of beautifully worked stone at the base, adobe as it rises; it was straw-thatched and must have been equivalent to one of our buildings three stories in height. ('Within it there was a stone idol, the height of a man, with a robe and crown.') Going out from this remarkable structure there are a series of formal streets with houses capped with gabled roofs. Beside it, and plainly to be seen still, runs the royal road, eighteen feet wide. Here appears the architectural impress of the Incas—the trapezoidal niche—and it appears wherever they set foot; it is the dominant architectural decoration and is in effect the leit-motif of the Incas.

Urban centres of formal nature, plazas bordered with Sun temples and palaces (yet changing to fit the geography) are found all along the royal roadway toward Cuzco. There is a formal gateway at *Rumicolca,* twenty-one miles from the capital. The hills about are studded with ruins, Inca and pre-Inca; the sites keep to the plan. And in those intervening miles between the formal entrance and Cuzco itself there are, or were, many others.

They used no nails, no wood, except the poles held together with withes to serve as base for the thickly thatched roof. Although the corbelled arch was known and used in bridges, it was almost never used in the large buildings. The placing of the small niche window and the large stone door is a miracle of proportion and symmetry.

Next in the architectural parade is *Pisac,* twenty-one miles northeast of Cuzco; it guarded the upper Urubamba River. On the pinnacle of a rock massif stands, or better hangs, Pisac and its agricultural terraces. The Inca's engineers took advantage of this natural fortress, separated from the rest of the massif by deep gorges, to construct an amazing series of defensive forts, tunnels, walls, and gateways. Many of the important structures in the sacred part of the city of Pisac, i.e., the part built about the so-called sundial (*Intihuatana,* 'hitching place of the sun'), were built upon the outcrops of the living rock; the marvellously wrought stones fitted, in a perfect concourse, into this living rock, forming what Wright, that demiurge of modern building, called 'organic architecture.' It is the 'nature of an organic architecture to grow from its site, come out of the ground into the light.'

There is nothing quite like Pisac in the entire range of the Inca realm.

Yet, farther down this gorge, is *Ollantaytambo* ('Posthouse of Ollantay'), twenty-four miles northwest of Cuzco and set near to the upper Urubamba

The hallmark of Inca architecture *is the trapezoid, a shape which seems to have held a peculiar fascination for them and which appears all over their vast empire. It was used for doorways, windows and niches, as in this example at Machu Picchu, and in another dimension can even be traced in the plans of their great plazas.*

River. It was first a village; then in 1460 it was rebuilt as a fortress to protect against the incursions of tribes from the Antisuyu (northeastern quarter of the empire) advancing on Cuzco. There is a famous local legend which identifies Ollantay with the lover of an Inca princess, perhaps the best-known example of 'Inca literature'. Since the present-day village is set over the old one, it has been a favourite place for the study of Inca architecture, for the site still is one of the finest examples extant of Inca town planning.

The old part of the city is composed of a large plaza laid out like a gridiron, and rising above is an acropolis of rock with an enormous fortress built on its sides; cut into the living rock itself are agricultural terraces. It was being built when the Spaniards arrived in 1536; work was stopped, and one can still see the immense stones lying where they were abandoned. The present-day village, dating from 1540, was built into and around Ollantay. The streets are narrow, the walls bounded by beautiful lines of masonry, so complete that one can form a fairly clear idea of this type of Inca town planning. Houses constructed of stone foundations and adobe are built into a group and surrounded by a wall, the *cancha,* essential base of all complex Inca architecture. The fortress is built on top of the acropolis and frowns over the city; a massive stone stairway leads to the top. Here there are six famous megalithic stones which were to form the base of the Sun Temple, and a wall behind the fortress (which has a number of dwelling places and storage rooms) completes the fortress acropolis. On the other side of the Urubamba River are quarries; a road zigzags up the steep sides, and from here the Indian miners quarried the rock masses. Still to be seen are the rude houses of the workers, and the valley is full of half-worked stones.

Farther down this Urubamba gorge, high on the top of the V-shaped valley, are a series of stone-laid cities which constituted a veritable chain of fortress-sanctuaries, built, it is believed, to defend the empire from raids of the wilder tribes of the jungles. They are built about fifteen hundred feet above the gorge of the river and seem to be hanging. These fortress complexes, known in succession as Huamanmarca, Patallacta, Winay-whayna, Botamarca, Loyamarca, terminate in the most spectacular one of all—the well-known *Machu Picchu.* All of these are bound together by a stonelaid road. They are approximately ten miles apart. At Machu Picchu the Urubamba River cascades onward and downward to the humid jungles.

Machu Picchu is so well known its story need hardly be repeated. Until its discovery in 1911 by Hiram Bingham, it was never mentioned by Inca or Spaniard. It was as if it had been left by its last inhabitants, so that here we have—almost without parallel in any other culture (if one excepts the ruins of Pompeii and Herculaneum)—an undisturbed picture of what such a corporate village looked like.

Handmaidens of the Sun, *specially selected women who served at the Sun temples, lived in dwelling places apart. On a hillside near Ollantaytambo, away from the town, stand the ruins of one such house. Behind it are agricultural terraces.*

Most spectacular of all Inca sites—*Machu Picchu, on the Urubamba gorge, one of a chain of fortress-cities protecting Cuzco. It occupies the saddle between two peaks and is bordered on either side by steep descents. Temples, plazas, houses and residential compounds cluster together, hanging to the sides of the mountain by means of wonderfully wrought terracing. The view on the right looks towards the peak Huayna Picchu—note the buildings and terraces at its summit. Above is Intihuatana, 'the Hitching Place of the Sun', where the shadow cast by the sun was used to determine the solstices.*

'A large stone seat, *where the Lord-Inca sat to view the dances and festivals.'* *Once gold plated, it stands on the summit of the Sun Temple of Vilcas-huamán (below right), the only surviving stone sun temple in the Inca Empire, though there were once thousands. Behind the stone gate (again trapezoidal in form), thirty-three steps lead upwards. Vilcas-huamán ('The Hawk's Sanctuary') was an important city with a broad plaza and many imposing public buildings. The Incas called it the 'centre' of their realm since it was midway between Quito in the north and Chile in the south.*

The ruins of Machu Picchu lie in a topographical saddle between the peaks of Machu (Old) Picchu and Huayna (New) Picchu. In this saddle is a complex of terraces, gabled houses, temples, sacred plazas and residential compounds. Machu Picchu had one stone entrance, with a massive wooden gate (an eye-bonder projected from the stone lintel to support it), and it had a small perpendicular stone pin to lock the gate. Machu Picchu was a self-sustaining unit. There are here, as elsewhere in the Inca Empire, various styles of architecture: the royal palaces made of well-fitted granite ashlars, crude clan houses for the common people, barracks for soldiers. All houses were thatched with grass roofs, very thick and possibly of long duration; the interiors of the houses were Spartan in their severity. Such is Machu Picchu, the terminus, it seems, of a constellation of hanging cities, joined by a stone-laid road to the centre of the empire—Cuzco.

Northwest of these, in a different valley and on a direct line to Cuzco, is *Limatambo,* lying within full sight of Mount Salcantay, 20,000 feet high. Limatambo was the way station a stop before 'the Great Speaker,' the Apurimac River, one of the royal stations on the great 1,250-mile-long arterial road between Cuzco and Quito. Like the finest buildings of Cuzco, it is constructed in the polygonal style, large, irregularly shaped stones faced according to natural contours, and with such accuracy that the finest blade cannot be pushed between them. What remains of Limatambo again shows town planning.

Still continuing on the royal road and a hundred miles northward is *Vilcas-huamán,* at 11,000 feet altitude. 'The Hawk's Sanctuary' lies on the high Vilcas plateau above the Vischongo River. Here a stone-laid, truncated Sun Temple still stands, the only one of those numbered in the thousands to survive. Vilcas-huamán, although two hundred miles distant from Cuzco, has all of the aspects of Inca architecture, and shows the striking uniformity in Inca town planning. There is an immense plaza ('large enough to hold,' said Pedro de Cieza de León, who had apparently seen it then, 'fifty thousand people'). It is bordered to the west by the Sun Temple, to the east by the palace of the Inca; the House of the Virgins of the Sun occupied another corner, and in another section were the royal storage chambers. The streets were narrow and paved and were lined with houses.

Three roads of empire coming from different directions met in the plaza. The Sun Temple is now as it was described by Cieza de León: 'made of very fine fitting stones with two large doorways (on opposite sides), with two stairways leading up from them with thirty-three steps . . . and on its truncated top one hundred feet above the plaza . . . a large stone seat [once gold-plated], where the Lord-Inca sat to view the dances and festivals . . .'

At *Cajamarca,* five hundred miles farther north (and where the last Lord-Inca Atahualpa was captured, held for ransom, and executed), there was yet another Inca centre, planned as all the rest. Lying at 8,500 feet in altitude, halfway between Cuzco and Quito, it was small as Inca centres go; still the Spaniards who first saw it on Friday, November 15, 1532, found its plaza 'larger than any in Spain,' surrounded by a high wall and entered by two doorways which opened upon the streets of the town. The buildings were long, strongly built, 'three times the height of a man and roofed with straw.'

'They were,' the king's inspector went on, 'the finest we had seen.'

Continuing beyond the confines of what are now the political boundaries of Peru, and into Ecuador and along the royal road, the same careful urban planning of cities continued.

Quito, 1,250 miles from Cuzco, was one of the large cities. Here, too—although Quito and its environs were not fully part of the empire until 1492—the Incas constructed their usual urban centres—and far in advance of anything Europe was doing at the same date. It was in full operation and 'beautifully wrought' even within fifty years of its Inca conquest.

Architecturally we have now seen Inca centres picked at random and described along an approximate 2,000-mile-long stretch, from Lake Titicaca to Quito, at altitudes ranging between 8,500 and 13,000 feet. There are no other people in history who constructed and maintained such complex urban centres at such great heights.

As in the Andes, so with the coast: as they conquered the lands of the desert they modified the structures; when they had their victory, they levelled part of the old city and superimposed their plaza, Sun temples, and administrative centre. When they built anew, they followed a formula almost exactly as had the Romans for their newly conquered territories. On the coast the Inca worked with adobe blocks; at important religious centres—such as the mecca of Pachacamac near Lima—stone was brought down and certain doorways and niches were constructed of it; adobe was used above the stone. At newly constructed sites such as Incahuasi in the Cañete Valley and Tambo Colorado in the adjoining valley of Pisco, the Inca masons worked only with adobe, but fashioned and shaped it as they would stone.

It is now time to see how the builders worked.

Many writers on these problems—and included therein are quite a few archaeologists—take this position, that the cyclopean stonework which one sees in Cuzco and especially in the fortress of Sacsahuamán was pre-Inca, and all this stonework is attributed to some vague and shadowy anterior civilization called by them the 'Megalithic empire.' This position has little archaeological support. The varying styles, it has been abundantly shown by excavation and restoration, are only the evolution of Inca styles themselves, or what is more likely, the difference in building materials and the plasticity of the Inca craftsmen.

And of the stone: when the gigantic size of the stones that form these structures is viewed for the first time, the utter enormity of the task of shaping, transporting them, and putting them into place—the edges so chamfered as to join without even a semblance of joining—is such that the viewer refuses to submit to the inescapable conclusion that the stone was quarried, pulled into place without draft animals, fashioned by stone instruments, and raised by crude leverage. Although such monoliths weighed as much as twenty tons and were variously shaped, they were made and fitted easily without cement. Such structures, except where destroyed by man, have resisted the insults of time.

Quarrying of stone was done in America as the Egyptians and all other earlier cultures did it. Rock was searched for natural faults; after boring, the holes were filled with wooden wedges, swollen with water, and in time this swelling action cracked the huge rock masses. (The Romans, even with the most advanced technology of the ancient world, did it no differently.) Inca quarries are still to be seen on the mountain slopes opposite Ollantaytambo. There, 1500 feet above the river, are the quarries; stone, half-shaped, is still there. Rock shapes are partially formed out of the porphyritic rock, and the place is piled with rock chips. Quarries are also found at Huaccoto (black andesite), eight miles from Cuzco, and others at Rumicolca (*rumi,* 'stone'), twenty-one miles from Cuzco, which yielded the fine rock reserved for the best of Inca structures. Limestone was used for the great fortress of Sacsahuamán, and it was fashioned into the enormous polygonal megaliths that form the base of the fortress. A study of the quarrying techniques of the Egyptians shows that they were almost identical with the techniques of the Incas.

Transport was by manpower. We can only deduce the transport techniques. Although the Indian did not have the wheel, he used wood and stone rollers, and the rock in the rough was pulled by ropes with manpower. He used levers operating on bosses, perhaps sledges for dragging, but had only the most elementary knowledge of dynamics and of methods for handling mass weight.

Sacsahuamán was the great fortress of Cuzco. It is without doubt one of the greatest structures ever erected by man. It was begun by Pachacuti ('Earthshaker') after A.D. 1438, and it employed thirty thousand Indians for the seventy years of its construction. It was completed circa 1500; its fate was not unlike that of the Maginot line—it fell quickly. The principal

How the Inca mason *achieved precision like this is still largely a mystery. The wall on the right is at Cuzco, on the left at Sacsahuamán, the fortress which overlooked it. The Cuzco wall is of relatively small stones, roughly rectangular and laid in courses, (protuberances have been left on some of them to make them easier to move); other walls in the city—see the picture on page 279—are even more regular. Edges are bevelled for artistic effect. In the far bigger work at Sacsahuamán, on the other hand, the blocks are huge, polygonal and irregular. The sheer scale is astonishing—one stone in the fortress is 27 feet high and weighs 200 tons. Somehow the Inca engineers, with only stone hammers and axes, bronze chisels, sand abrasives and wooden crowbars and rollers, managed to quarry these monsters, shape them, transport them distances ranging from nine to twenty miles, and finally place them exactly in position, lifting and setting them down a hundred times until they fitted perfectly on all their sides. No mortar is used, yet there is not a crack for the thinnest blade to be inserted.*

fortifications face north; along this side is an unbroken wall over fifteen hundred feet in length. The cyclopean wall is composed of three massive tiers of stone walls, broken into forty-six parts, each supporting a terrace; the three parapets rising to a combined height of sixty feet are constructed of salients, retiring angles, and buttresses. There were only three doors—three entrances—and one of these still retains the name of the principal architect. There were two square military towers at either end of the front underground passages, an enormous water reservoir with stone-laid conduits in which the water passed from one place to another, a beautifully wrought palace for the Inca, storage places for food and arms, habitations for soldiers and people who would maintain the defence. The first Spaniards who saw it were speechless with astonishment '. . . neither the stone aqueduct of Segovia nor the buildings of Hercules nor the work of the Romans had the dignity of this fortress . . .'

Metals were mined and worked on a scale comparable with the great undertakings in stone. Although gold was found in great quantities, the Incas in fact mined a considerable variety of other metals. Bronze was the most important and was the only metal allowed to be used decoratively by the ordinary Indian. Copper was mined in Mesopotamia as early as 3500 B.C., and it appears first in Peruvian graves sometime after 2000 B.C. The Incas, when they appeared, brought no new techniques, but they did organize the method of obtaining it.

First, all the gold and silver mined and in mines belonged to the Inca. All bullion had to come to Cuzco; no Indian was allowed to leave the city with any of it on his person.

The Incas had precise laws for mining and miners. The mines were only allowed to be worked in the Andes during the four warmest months. In the perpendicular hills that surrounded the terribly humid lands of the Carabaya (east of Lake Titicaca in the Montaña), where the Inca got much of his gold, the hills are terraced for crops and the remains of gold-mining villages are still found there. Gold was mostly secured by panning; another method was to build a series of stone riffles across the bed of a river, and stones which held gold particles were collected after the rains. Smelting of the gold into ingots was done by bringing the gold to the furnaces atop lofty hills; these furnaces, operated with charcoal and bellows, faced east into the wind and gave sufficient draught to obtain the high temperatures needed for melting.

The Inca metallurgists used all the techniques known to metalworking: casting, hammering, soldering, riveting, and *repoussé.* The goldsmiths (who were stationed within Cuzco itself and were exempt from taxes) used the techniques described by Garcilaso de la Vega, 'the Inca,' who was born in

Cuzco in 1539 and no doubt saw them at their bellows and blast furnaces: 'they went round the fire blowing with the tubes.'

Gold, of course, is highly ductile; it is softer than silver—a single grain of it can be drawn into a wire a hundred feet long—and it is universal in appeal. The Incas kept detailed statistics. There were officials at the mines to check on production and miners, but whereas in other lands miners were usually criminals, among the Incas it was carried on by the people as part of their work tax.

Gold belonged to the Inca. No one knows how much gold the empire produced, yet from the accurate *quipu* records which were interpreted to the Spaniards it was believed that gold came into Cuzco at the rate of seven million ounces annually.

After his death, each of the Lord-Incas had a life-sized gold statue made of him, and his palace, which became his tomb, was ornamented with gold.

The gold of Peru *was what fascinated Europe above everything else. Where facts were missing imagination supplied the details, as in this engraving by Theodore de Bry. He knew from a historian that the goldsmiths 'went round the fire blowing with tubes', but he obviously had no idea of Inca art; see the fantastic rococo vase on the bench behind. There were, however, certainly extensive workshops at Cuzco, where gold, the personal property of the Inca, was fashioned into all kinds of secular and religious decoration.*

Even the ruthless Conquistadors *were moved at the sight of Inca goldwork. There were fountains of gold, lifesize human and animal figures, 'goblets, ewers, salvers, vases of every shape and size, ornaments and utensils for the temples and palaces'—sometimes whole buildings were covered in sheets of gold so that they shone like the sun—'Truly, it was a thing worthy to be seen.' Yet this did not prevent the Spaniards from seizing every ounce they could find. After the conquest the Inca goldsmiths were employed for a whole month in the tragic work of melting down the masterpieces that they had created. Hardly anything survives. To gain an idea of what has been lost we have to look not only at the few minor gold and silver objects that have been recovered, but also at the goldwork of near-contemporary cultures that shared some of its splendour.*

Inca gold. *A golden llama, eight inches high, partly cast and partly soldered. It was found in the ruins of Sacsahuamán in 1934. Right, a gold figurine cast in a mould, showing a worshipper; such offerings were buried or hung in the temples.*

A strangely elaborate silver plate *of unknown purpose comes from Cuzco. If water is poured into the aryballus-shaped urn on the rim, it will flow out through the little man underneath into the small bowl in the middle. There are also two deer, one with head missing.*

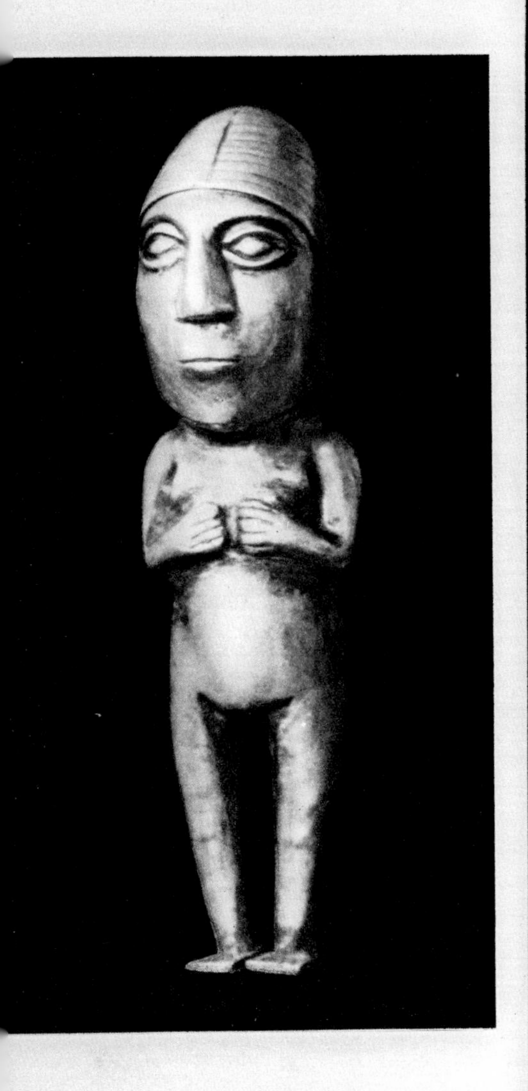

Sacrificial knives, *once used for human or animal sacrifice, have been recovered from graves of the Chimú, a people who for a hundred years formed part of the Inca Empire. The blade is of stone, the handle of gold, representing a demigod: semi-circular head-dress of exquisite filigree, studded with eight pieces of turquoise and with tiny birds hanging on each side; two more pieces of turquoise as earplugs; wings sprouting from the arms; bells dangling from the skirt and legs. The height of the whole is about ten inches.*

Treasure that escaped the Spaniards *and later robbers has recently been discovered in graves at Batan Grande, on the north coast of Peru—the greatest single recorded find of goldwork ever made in South America. The objects on these pages and the gold knife overleaf come from this source. Though Chimú, and therefore pre-Inca, they can be taken as guides to what Inca work was like. Above: Two gold beakers encrusted with turquoise, the bottom section soldered on to the upper; each stone has a graceful beaded setting. Right: gold ornaments to decorate cloth; the bird figures are also common on pottery. The brilliance of the clothes worn by these Chimú aristocrats must have been overwhelming.*

Silver, too, was the Inca's divine property. Silver was a quality rather than a substance, and the tender moonlight lustre of its brilliance caused the Indians to regard it as the tears of the moon. It was plenteous in Peru.

The techniques of Peruvian metallurgy have not been extensively studied. However, we know they used tin alloys, and tin is found in much of what appears at first sight to be pure gold; they employed a formula for combining copper and tin to produce bronze, casting them in one piece and hammering it cold. With such casting techniques they produced mace-heads for war clubs, hard bronze levers, knives, a fairly diverse list of surgical instruments, bolas used for the ensnaring of birds and animals, pins to hold the women's garments together, ear spoons and hair tweezers; the list could be extended, yet it is enough to display the wide application of metallurgy. All of it was overshadowed, of course, by the immense amount of gold and silver ornaments.

The gold and silver which was collected at Cajamarca, brought there by the orders of the Lord-Inca Atahualpa, who was held captive by the Spaniards and who agreed to ransom himself by filling a room twenty-five feet long and fifteen feet wide and 'as high as a white line which a tall man could not reach,' amounted to 1,326,539 pesos of pure gold and 51,610 marks of silver. In terms of art, the value of these objects is incalculable. Naturally, to be transportable and divisible among the conquistadors, these art objects had to be melted down and put into ingots. Although some of the remarkable pieces of goldwork were set aside for the Emperor Charles V of Spain, *not a single object of art survived*; all of it went into the crucibles by reason of a royal edict (February 13, 1535): 'All gold and silver from Peru shall be melted in the royal mints at Sevilla, Toledo and Segovia.'

All we know of this lost art is what the common soldier, touched by what he saw, wrote about these fantastic pieces of goldsmithery, 'In Cuzco . . . they found many statues and images entirely of gold and silver, complete shape of a woman in *natural size* very well wrought, well shaped and hollow; these I believe were the finest that could be made anywhere . . .' Another conquistador wrote of seeing 'many vessels of gold, lobsters of the sort that grow in the sea and on other gold vessels were sculptured with all birds and serpents, even spiders, lizards and sort of beetles . . . carved on the body of gold.' And the conquistador's secretary, who recorded all of the booty before it was consigned to the goldsmiths who melted it down into ingots, saw it all piled high: 'Truly it was a thing worthy to be seen . . . vessels, vases and pieces of various forms in which the [Inca] lords of the land were served . . . there were four llamas in fine gold and very large, ten or twelve figures of women, natural size, all of fine gold and as beautiful and well made it seemed as if they were alive . . .'

18 The Highways of the Sun

CUZCO, although in the heartland of the Andes, actually lies very close to the jungles of the Upper Amazon. It is only a few miles from the upper Urubamba River; four days of an Indian's walk northeast would carry him into the jungles. And directly east, two days' walk would bring an Indian to the Paucartambo, a gigantic river which cascades mile upon mile down into a jungle of towering trees and constant rainfall. Here a bewildering number of fierce tribesmen, 'untamed' Indians, who, with the consistency of ants, were never discouraged by devastating setbacks, kept hacking at the outposts of the Inca's realm. Three of the empire's most gigantic fortresses—Sacsahuamán, which guarded holy Cuzco itself, Ollantaytambo, twenty-four miles northwest of Cuzco (which defended the upper Urubamba River, a natural gateway to Cuzco), and Pisac, another gigantic fortress, which guarded the upper reaches of the same river as well as the pass which led east to Paucartambo—were erected to guard against the incursions of the jungle tribes into the environs of Cuzco.

The Incas were able, in some instances, to win over the tribes here, and they yielded tribute in the form of gold, bird feathers, *chonta* wood, dyes, fruits, animal skins, wood fibres, and jungle-reared cotton. Other tribes, notably the Aguarunas ('water people'), a subtribe of the head-hunting Shuaras, never yielded, and the Inca's troops were decimated in the humid jungles where the tactics of mass attack and envelopment were of little value. Most of these jungle Indians knew of copper and bronze instruments, which they had through trade with the Incas.

For one hundred years the Incas made war upon the coastal tribes, and lateral roads, wonderfully built, were made to cling to the sides of the gorges of the rivers which ran west; almost every valley had such roads. War occupied the affairs of the *apo* or governor of this quarter until about 1476, when the Incas finally conquered the Chimú Empire. This effectively ended all opposition on the coast.

In the Inca dominions, the lives of both men and women were fully controlled. Women were subject to a head count, and all girls above ten years of age were classified. Young girls who possessed beauty, grace, or talent were brought to the attention of the visiting *curacas*, singled out, and brought to Cuzco to become Chosen Women. Those not selected were known as 'left-out girls.' The Chosen Women were placed under supervision (they might be likened to nuns), trained to weave, and were attached to the rituals attending the religion of the Sun. Those so trained were 'Handmaidens of the Sun,' and were established throughout the empire wherever there were Sun temples. Their dwelling places, out of reach of ordinary men, were placed high in some inaccessible spot, such as one can still see at the ruins of Ollantaytambo or at Incahuasi in the Cañete Valley.

There were as many as fifteen thousand such Chosen Women, and those who were not connected with the rituals pertaining to the Sun were either taken in royal concubinage or else as wives by famous generals. Later, if unmarried, the Chosen Women assumed the titles of *mamacuna* and became the instructresses of the newly arrived Chosen Women. They wove garments exclusively for the use of the Lord-Inca and his *coya.*

It was these women, quartered at Caxas in the Sun Temple in northern Peru, that the Spanish soldiers raped in the first days of the conquest. This so enraged the Inca that he planned their annihilation, which only his capture prevented.

If a conquered tribe was recalcitrant and refused to accept the Inca's ways, its people were decimated, or if too large, they were moved out of their own lands and a reliable, 'safe' Quechua-speaking people were put into the voided land. These *mitimaes* played the same rôle in the newly conquered quarter as the Roman soldier had played in his conquests. Their mission was to teach Inca cultural ways, so they were in their way the 'civilizers.'

The administration of so far-flung an empire depended on its communications, and as the great plaza of Cuzco was the demarcation of its four sections, so too was the plaza the starting point of its roads—the web of communications which bound the realm together.

In the main there were two sections of roads. The royal road, called *Capac-ñan,* moved through the Andes from the border of the empire at the Ancasmayo River (1° N. lat.), down through Ecuador, Peru, Bolivia, and thereafter into Argentina (coming to an end at Tucumán), and then into Chile, where it ended at the Rio Maule (35° S. lat.). There the Incas built a fortress and their most southern station at Purumauca. The coastal road, beginning at Tumbes (3° S. lat.), the frontier city which marked the coastal end of the Inca realm, ran southward through the brazen desert, the entire length of Peru; thence down deep into Chile, connecting at Copiapó with the road coming over from Argentina and continuing down to the Maule in Chile, which marked its end.

The Andean royal road was 3,250 miles in length (making it longer than the longest Roman road—from Hadrian's Wall in Scotland to Jerusalem); the coastal road was 2,520 miles in length.

Greater freedom of expression *is evident in Peruvian textile design. The fabric shown on the right is from a pre-Inca Chancay grave and is remarkable in that it is a series of designs invented by some master-weaver which were to be copied by other weavers. In this textile of natural brown and white cotton there are no less than ten distinct patterns: variations of the zig-zag, spiral and Greek-key combine with forms based on animals and birds (is it fanciful to see cats and llamas in this example?) until an astonishing complexity is reached, as in the second row from the bottom.*

A woollen doll, *simple and appealing, shows that the looms produced unpretentious articles for everyday use as well as the more highly finished work. It was found in a late pre-Inca grave at* Caqui *in the* Chancay Valley.

In addition to these arterial roads, there were numerous laterals, careering down the sides of the V-shaped valleys and connecting the mountain roads with the coastal one; there were special gold roads, such as those which moved into the rich gold areas of Carabaya, east of Lake Titicaca, and there were especially wide military roads such as the one built from Huánuco to Chachapoyas, stonelaid in its entire length of four hundred miles in order to undertake the conquest of an escaped tribe of Chanca Indians. Roads also pervaded the jungle. They were built at the highest altitudes ever used by man in constant travel; the highest Inca road recorded (17,160 feet) is the one behind Mount Salcantay.

The standard width of the Inca coastal road was twenty-four feet. It is not known, as yet, why so wide a standard was set or what precise measurement determined it, but from hundreds of measurements made upon the road by the von Hagen Expedition along one thousand miles, this was the standard gauge; it only departed from it when some immovable obstacle prevented this 'official' width from being obtained. The Incas had no wheel and no draught animals; the common denominators were the foot of the Indian and the hoof of the llama. There was no need for the deep roadbed of the Roman roads which were solidly constructed to accommodate vehicular traffic. And it is known historically that *nowhere did prepared surfaces appear on ancient roads* until wheeled transport came into general use.

On the coast the natural hard-packed surfaces of the coastal llanos were sufficiently hard to support traffic without a surface. When the road passed over a bog it was raised high like a causeway; when it moved down steep inclines it became a step road. When the roads entered the larger coastal cities and their environs, they were often paved for short distances.

The consistent twenty-four-foot width is the architectural feature which distinguishes the Inca roads from those built by anterior civilizations. Another feature of the Inca road is the side wall to keep out the sand drift, to mark the road, and to keep the soldiers, who mostly used it, within the bounds of the road. This was one of the first things noted by the Spaniards. 'Along this coast and vales the Caciques and prime men made a road ... with strong Walls on both sides ...' These walls can still be seen in many

The dazzling colour-schemes of Peruvian textiles *were achieved by using a wide range of dyes, mostly vegetable but including a few of chemical and animal origin. They had jet-black, indigo and scarlet, cochineal red and Tyrian purple (from a mollusc related to that used by the Romans). In all 190 different hues have been distinguished. Wool was normally dyed as yarn, since dyeing tends to tangle the threads, but the dyeing of woven cloth was done at times. This example from a Chancay grave is a textile pattern of a master weaver.*

places marching across the naked desert, which is devoid of everything else save this remarkable road.

The road was marked along its entire length by *topos* (road markers), 'with the distance between them,' said Cieza de León, who interested himself in such things, 'a Castillian league and a half,' i.e., $4^1/_2$ miles. (The Romans, it will be recalled, put up road markers computing the distances in number of miles from the Forum in Rome; more than four thousand have been found.)

The coastal road, twenty-four feet wide along its length of 2,520 miles, was connected by lateral roads with the royal road in the Andes. Eleven such laterals have been explored, but there are doubtless many more. Every valley of consequence had these lateral communications. Many were pre-Inca roads (not as well engineered and lacking the overall master plan of width and construction) and these the Inca engineers either disregarded or else in time-honored fashion built theirs on top of the older ones. At first these were Inca conquest roads, brought down from the Andes into various valleys to overwhelm the enemy by mass attack. One lateral, typical of all of them and the best preserved, is that road which connects the two arterial roads through the valley of Cañete. The Incas had built New Cuzco (now called Incahuasi), the largest coastal structure there, and their road alongside it. They preferred to build their road against the canyon walls; it was chipped away, terraced, and the sides built up with dry-laid stone. Drainage, when the roads reached the wet zone, was important, and it was provided for every rivulet, for here streams and rivers shift their banks with callous ease. They excluded water, that wanton destroyer of communications, completely from their roads. They dealt with water as the Romans did: they out-witted it by making sure that it was not there. This particular Cañete Valley lateral moved up from sea level across and up over a land height of 15,600 feet, stone-paved a good portion of the way, to emerge 125 miles beyond in the valley of Jauja (a great Inca centre in the later days of the realm); there it became connected with the royal road of the Andes.

The 3,250-mile-long road commenced beyond Quito, close to the natural bridge across the Ancasmayo river (now Colombia), made its way down the Andean valleys, then over the treeless *puna*, and, as has already

The Bridge of San Luis Rey, *the most famous and perhaps the finest of all Inca bridges, spanned the precipitous gorge of the Apurimac river. The cables—plaited and twisted rope as thick as a man's body—were 148 feet long, with another forty feet embedded in the rock on each side. These were renewed every few years. More cables formed the floor of the bridge and were covered with wooden planks. There was no way of steadying it in the wind, and the early Spaniards crossed it in terror. First built in* A.D. *1350, it continued in use until 1890.*

Through the arid desert *that covers most of South America's western sea-board the Inca coast road ran for 2,500 miles without a break. Where the terrain permitted, the Inca engineers, like the Roman, built in straight lines. The road was 24 feet wide and marked on either side by twin rows of low stone walls.*

Connecting the coast with the mountains *are numerous lateral roads, most of which have been explored. One of the most impressive and best preserved comes down the Cañete valley and joined the Andean mountain road with the coastal road. In this picture the modern and ancient roads run side by side (with a modern irrigation ditch between them). Inca roads were kept high to avoid water.*

The mountain road, *hardest of all to build, and a magnificent testimony to ancient Peruvian engineering. In some places it was made into a causeway; in others, where the ground was swampy, it was paved. On the right is a 'gold road,' entering the village of Tambillo in the rich gold area of Carabaya, east of Lake Titicaca.*

Where the steep rocks *of the Andes make a smooth surface impossible, the Inca road breaks into long flights of steps, and since it never had to carry wheeled vehicles of any kind this was no drawback. Llamas are used to negotiating paths like these, nor were they any obstacle to the armies, for whose quick movements the whole great network of roads was primarily conceived. This section is on the way to Huánuco.*

been described, moved down toward South America's southern tip. This was, until the nineteenth century, the longest arterial road of history. Its width varies between fifteen and eighteen feet, suggesting that either the coastal twenty-four-foot road was a later development or that the Andean road was a compromise with geography; it was difficult to maintain so wide a road except under unusual circumstances in this perpendicular land. Like its coastal counterpart, it was unpaved except where there was unavoidable water; then it was made into a causeway as at Anta, near to Cuzco, built circa A.D. 1300. It is twenty-four feet wide and *eight miles long* and stands eight feet above the wide-spreading quagmire; it is more or less as Pedro de Cieza de León saw it in 1549, a 'great swamp which could only be crossed with difficulty, had the Inca not built a wide-paved causeway.'

It was evident that the builders were instructed from a master plan; the engineering of the bridges, the step road, constructed when perpendicular mountains were to be crossed, drainage, and terracing show general uniformity throughout this long stretch of road.

The empire did not need so elaborate a network of roads for economical reasons, since most of the provinces had considerable economic independence; for the north-south axis such a road designed for pure commerce was superfluous. In the main they were roads of conquest. Once a territory was conquered, the roads were important for control over the newly annexed territory. Prescott was correct when he wrote: 'Not an insurrectionary movement could occur, not an invasion on the remotest frontier, before the tidings were conveyed to the capital and the imperial armies were on the march across the magnificent roads to suppress it. . . .'

Since the object of battle was to win, roads were built to get the warriors into battle in the fastest possible time. This was the *reason* for the Inca's roads.

The bridge, an integral part of the road, was one of the proudest of Inca achievements. So sacred was the bridge that death was decreed for any who tampered with one.

There were many types of bridges: suspension, pontoon, cantilever; clapper types (for crossing small streams), permanent and of stone slabs. All had their special names, but the generic name for bridge was *chaca*. The greatest of these *chacas* was the one that crossed the formidable gorge and river of the Apurimac. It has entered literary immortality as *The Bridge of San Luis Rey*; it was the greatest and without doubt the most outstanding example of native engineering known in the Americas.

Vital links in the chain of roads *were the bridges. In the great days of the Empire there must have been hundreds of them, for Peru is one of the most mountainous countries in the world, and deep gullies and canyons are frequent. The bridges were of three types—suspension, pontoon and corbel-arched. The third type is shown here, in the Carabaya area. Its total span is 30 feet. In spite of all their achievements, the Incas never discovered the true arch, and this was about the greatest distance they could span a cantilever bridge.*

When the Incas broke out of the traditional territory that was Inca, they first had to bridge the Apurimac River in order to be able to move northward. This occurred circa A.D. 1350 and the bridge was built by the Lord-Inca Roca.

The Andean Indians had no wood readily available; they did not know the arch; they knew and often used the cantilever type of bridge, but this could only be used to bridge rivers not much more than forty feet in width; so they perfected the suspension bridge. The Incas reversed the arch curve and gave it wings—and it became the hanging bridge. First in construction—the cables; those of this particular bridge were accurately measured by an American in 1864; they were 148 feet long (add an additional forty feet for imbedding). They were as thick as a man's body, plaited and twisted as rope cables are, made in fact from the same material as modern rope is—the *cabuya* (a plant related to the *agave*, the fleshy-leaved century plant). The cables were spun at the edge of the river to be bridged, and then taken across to the other side. They were then buried deep in the earth and held by six wooden beams ('as thick as oxen' says Garcilaso 'the Inca'), then raised onto tall stone pillars which supported the cables. The action was repeated on the other side. Three other cables, tied to the base of the stone towers, formed the 'floor' of the bridge; the suspension cables and the floor cables were then held together by additional cables and the floor of the bridge had wooden supports. The middle of the bridge sagged from its own

A bridge of boats *crossed the Rio Desaguadero, the only river that flows out of Lake Titicaca. Boats made of balsa and reeds were placed side by side, and linked by a thick cable which in turn was held by stone towers on each side. A grass floor was then laid over it. This drawing is by the American traveller E. George Squier, who saw it just before it was demolished in 1875.*

Upon the cyclopaean foundations of the Incas *stands a modern suspension bridge crossing the Urubamba river. The size of the stones gives a good idea of the scale of the ancient work. Formerly cables would have been slung between the two stone abutments and a precarious road of wooden slats suspended above the stream. There were more than 40 large suspension bridges along the route of the royal roads and over 100 smaller ones.*

weight, and there were no guy ropes added to steady it so that in the high winds it swayed dangerously. The early Spaniards crossed it with fright and terror, and their letters are filled with their plaints about it.

This bridge, built circa A.D. 1350, endured for over five hundred years; it lasted through the entire Inca regime, was kept up by the Spaniards during the entire colonial epoch (ended 1824), and it continued in use during the republican government. It was finally abandoned about 1890.

At many places along the road there were two suspension bridges, hanging side by side—one for the higher men, the other for the lower, who paid tolls to cross it. Hernando Pizarro, on his march to the coast from the Andes to hurry up the flow of gold for the Inca's ransom, first described an Inca bridge on January 14, 1533, after coming down the step road to Piga, where they came to a canyon (Santa River): 'It was spanned by two bridges close together made of network . . . They build a foundation near the water and raise it to a great height, and from one side of the river to the other there are cables . . . thick as a man's thigh. By one of these bridges the common people cross over and a guard *is stationed to receive transit dues* [italics added].' Later on, during their return over another road, at the great city of Huánuco they crossed another bridge, 'over a torrential river [the Vizcano] made of three thick logs and where *there are guards who collect a toll as is customary among these Indians* [italics added].'

Permanent bridges of stone or of wood were used over small streams (many are still to be seen), and where minor traffic did not justify labour expenditure there was another type, called *oroya*, two cables stretched between stone towers, with a basket attached to one of the cables and drawn to either side by means of additional ropes.

Another bridge type, which also struck the first Spaniards as ingenious, was the balsa pontoon bridge. The most notable was the one that crossed the only river that drains Lake Titicaca. These were built as all pontoon bridges, except that here the pontoons were balsas, straw boats made of *totora* grass. These craft were placed side by side, linked by a thick cable, which in turn was held by stone towers on the opposite shore; a grass floor was laid over the grass balsa boats. As this type of grass boat becomes waterlogged, the pontoons were replaced every two years; it was the duty of the village of Chacamarca ('Bridge Village') to replace these as part of their *mita* (labour tax). This bridge endured for over eight hundred years; it was used until 1890.

Along the roads and over the bridges travelled the Inca convoys. The only draught animal, as we have seen, was the llama, which was principally employed to transport cargo, either for war or commerce; as many as twenty-five thousand might be sent on a single convoy. Averaging eighty pounds of cargo each, they could travel about twelve miles a day. Man can outlast any animal, including the horse, especially in this up-and-down world of Peru, and can carry more than a llama and go longer distances; thus transport on the roads was shared between man and llama.

The litter as a means of transport seems to be world-wide. Some of the oldest illustrations of Mesopotamia, for example a relief from Ur dated 2500 B.C., shows bearers carrying a litter. Models of palanquins from Crete are dated 1600 B.C., so it is not surprising to find that the Incas were carried along their royal roads in litters. The use of litters was confined, however, to the highest nobility.

'When the Incas visited the provinces of their empire . . . they travelled in great majesty,' says Cieza de León, 'seated in rich litters . . . enriched with gold and silver.' There were curtains to be drawn during long journeys or to protect against sun or rain, '. . . round the litter marched the Lord-Inca's guard . . . in front went five thousand slingers.' There were

Planche XVI. pag. 109
N. Guerard fecit
A. Plan dune Balse faite de peaux de loups marins cousues et pleines d'air.
B. Indien sur une Balse vüe de Coté. C. autre vüe de front
D. Trauerses pour rassembler les deux moitiez de la balse E trou pour
lenfler et la remplir d'air. F. maniere de Coudre les peaux
G. Loup marin a terre H Pingoüin.

Inca boats, *frail craft of reeds and balsa wood, have all vanished without trace, but it is possible to reconstruct their appearance both from representations in pottery and from later examples. This engraving, published in 1737, shows a form of boat in use at that time in the south—two walrus-skin floats held together by transverse struts. They are so light that they can easily be carried overland if necessary.*

eighty litter-bearers, men drawn from the rugged Rucana peoples, clothed in special blue livery; they ran beside the litter in teams and took turns carrying. The royal road even had resting platforms where litter-bearers could pause on steep ascents.

Water transport was minor for such a thoroughly land-based people. The largest vessel known in the Americas was the balsa raft made from the logs of the balsa tree (*Ochroma*), which grows in humid Ecuador. These logs, sun dried and naturally buoyant, were lashed together with vines. The raft had a large square sail, a crude deckhouse with palmleaf roof, and forward of that a hearth for the preparation of food. It used the centreboard for tacking of sorts; it had no pseudo bow. There is, as Means remarked, 'a conspicuous lexical poverty in Quechua or any other pre-Inca coastal language on sailing, and is a reflection of the general ineptitude of the people for seamanship as a whole.' The name for rafts was *huampus*.

In addition to this large raft, the coastal people (as well as the mountain people on navigable lakes) had a vessel, made of straw, called by the Spaniards (with no little humour) 'little horses of the sea' in reference to the way they were used: the Indians mounted them astride. These *huampus* (also now called balsas) were made from a tubular reed which grows eight feet tall and a half inch in diameter. It grows in the shore swamps, and is dried and fashioned into four cigar-shaped bundles. Two of these bundles, tied with grass rope, form the prow. The other two, laid on top and off centre, form its sides, and it is thus a vessel with tapering prow and square-cut stern. The sail, operating like a venetian blind, propels the boat; when there is no wind, the paddle or punt is used. Generally these boats, as shown by the old illustrations taken from Chimú or Mochica pottery, showed one, or at most three, fishermen in the boat, but on the surface of Lake Titicaca rush boats were made sufficiently large to hold forty people.

To construct their transport systems and to regulate the economy of the country, some way of keeping accurate records was essential. How was this done? The *quipu* (pronounced 'kee-poo'), which means simply 'knot,' and which the couriers passed from hand to hand, was as close to writing as man got in South America; the *quipu is not writing*, and, moreover, the device is not even an Inca invention. It is simply a mnemonic device to aid the memory and its knotted strings are based on a decimal count. Moreover, all *quipus* had to be *accompanied by a verbal comment*, without which they would have been unintelligible.

The *quipus* have been thoroughly studied and described. It was a simple and ingenious device, consisting of a main cord (ranging from a foot to many feet in length) and from this cord dangled smaller coloured strings which had at intervals knots (*quipus*) tied into them. It has been shown most conclusively by those who have studied them that the strings were used to record numbers in a decimal system, and that there was a symbol for zero, that is, a string with an 'empty space'; this allowed them to count to over ten thousand. Knots were tied into string to represent numbers; if a governor was visiting a newly conquered tribe and the Inca wanted to know how many able-bodied Indians there were, these were counted and the number tied into the *quipu*. It may be that there was a certain symbol or heraldic device for 'men,' but if there was one it is not known. There was attached to the governor an official knot-string-record interpreter known as a *quipu-camayoc*, whose duty it was to tie in the records. He then had to remember which *quipu* recorded what: numbers of men, women, llamas, etc., in the

On the waters of Lake Titicaca, *the Uru fishermen still eke out a poor livelihood by paddling craft that have hardly changed from those used by their ancestors 500 years ago. The bundles of rushes and reeds will rot after a few months but are easy to replace. The big wooden ring is the frame for a net, which is dipped into the water like a giant shrimp-net.*

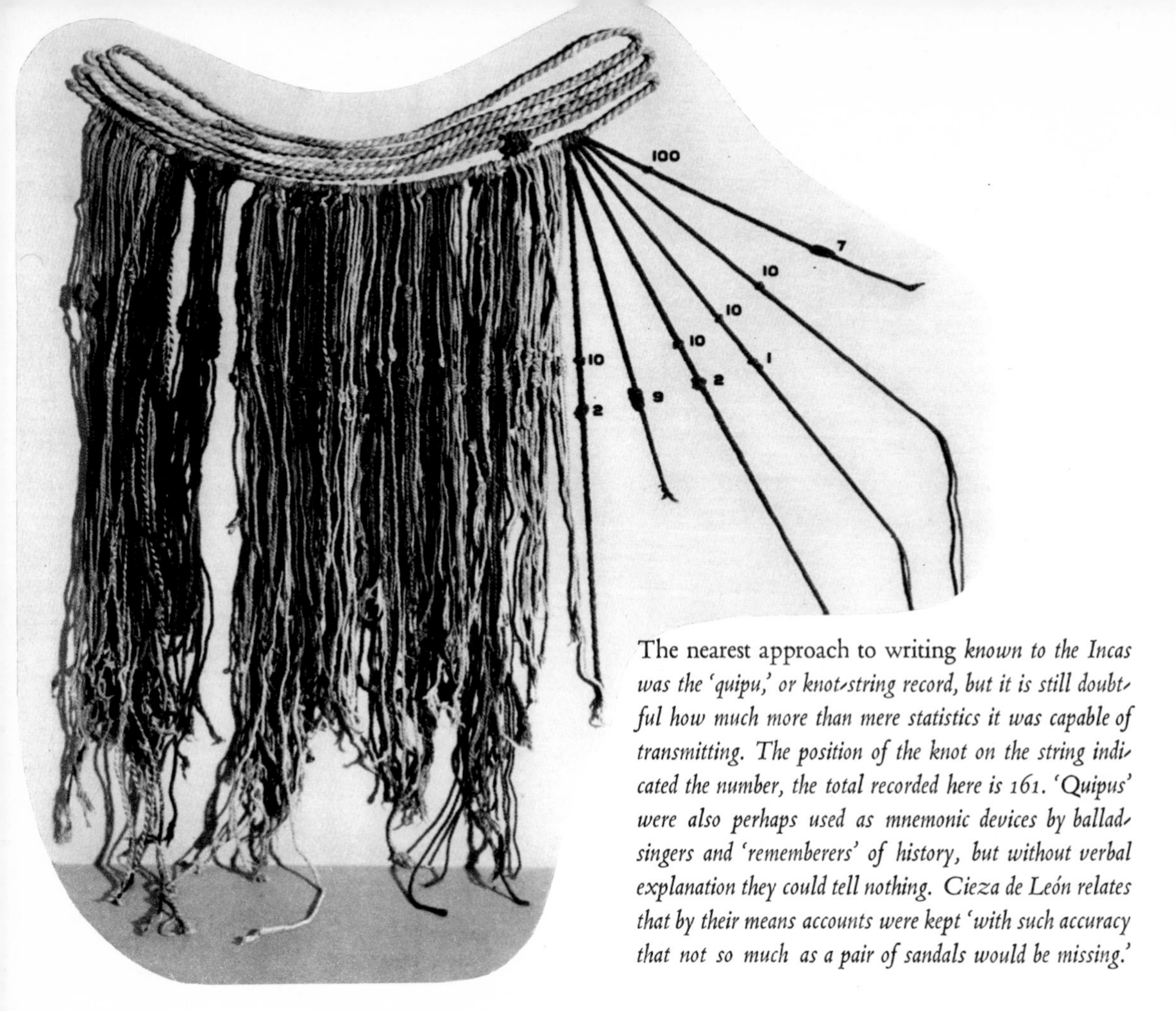

The nearest approach to writing *known to the Incas was the 'quipu,' or knot-string record, but it is still doubtful how much more than mere statistics it was capable of transmitting. The position of the knot on the string indicated the number, the total recorded here is 161. 'Quipus' were also perhaps used as mnemonic devices by ballad-singers and 'rememberers' of history, but without verbal explanation they could tell nothing. Cieza de León relates that by their means accounts were kept 'with such accuracy that not so much as a pair of sandals would be missing.'*

newly conquered lands. When a governor had an audience with the Inca he could, with this knot-string record plus the 'rememberer,' recite the facts as gathered. It was a surprisingly efficacious method of counting and one that their Spanish conquerors much admired.

The different colours of the wool threads apparently had meaning; the mode of intertwining the knot or twisting the thread or the distance of the knots from each other gave nuance. With these *quipus* the Inca had the numbers of tribes, llamas, women, old people. Beyond mere numbers the colours, the smaller threads, the green, blue, white, black and red colours, could, it is believed, express meanings and even, it is asserted, abstract ideas. When Pedro de Cieza de León in 1549 talked to some of the old 'rememberers' they explained that these 'knots counted from one to ten and ten to a hundred, and from a hundred to a thousand. Each ruler of a province was provided with accountants, and by these knots they kept account of what tribute was to be paid . . . and with such accuracy that not so much as a pair of sandals would be missing.'

Swift runners *were perpetually travelling the Inca roads with official messages. information and special delicacies for the Inca. All the way along the route were stations where relief runners were on duty day and night. Each courier ran a mile and a half in an average time of ten minutes, and then handed on his 'quipu' to the next. Indeed early chroniclers agree that a message could be sent from Quito to Cuzco, a distance of 1250 miles, in five days (and nights). It was the fastest communication system the world had seen, not excepting the Roman.*

Like all preliterate peoples, they had good memories. While the *quipu* itself could not be read without verbal comment to make all the entanglements and knots understandable, it did (this much is certain) go beyond mere compilation of statistics; it was used as a supplement for the memory of historical events.

When a Lord-Inca died and his burial ceremonies were over, a council of *amautas* was called into session to decide 'what of his memory should be forever preserved.' Having decided this among themselves, they composed their history and then called in the *quipu-camayocs* and gave them the official history; then those skilled in rhetoric and the use of words—and they knew how to narrate the event in regular order like ballad singers—were brought in, and *thus they were instructed* what to say concerning the deceased Inca, and if they treated of wars, they sang in proper order of the many battles he had fought.

The wholesale destruction of the 'archives' of *quipus* by the crusading padres in the seventeenth century (in their zeal to stamp out idolatry, believing naively that the *quipus* 'were books of the devil') and the gradual dying out of the 'rememberers,' the interpreters of the *quipus*, were the twin disasters to Andean history. With the destruction of one and the passing of the other there was lost that history of the whole Andean area which now can be bridged only by archaeology. The *quipus* now found in graves tell us nothing; they are only lifeless strings.

The army of the Incas was actually an agrarian militia. Every able-bodied Indian was liable for military service, trained in the use of such arms as were used in battles. The only professional army was the Inca's body-guard, an unknown number but thought not to have been many more than ten thousand; these served as a sort of cadre for the militia.

Arms were supplied by the state, and there were depositories for this equipment which were seen by the Spaniards at strategic places in the realm.

When he became a warrior, the *puric*, called from his farm, kept his regular clothing except that he put on a distinctive helmet made either of wood or plaited cane and painted with a totemic device; it had red wool fringes, and the same type of red wool fringe was put about the ankle. He wore a quilted cotton jacket for body armour (similar to that worn by the Aztecs). And around the back of his neck, slats of iron-hard *chonta* wood were hung, covering the spine, to protect him from attack. The soldiers carried shields, round or square, made from wood or toughened tapir or deer hide. These were painted with geometric devices which marked their war grouping.

The soldier's primary weapon was the sling for long distance, and the star-headed mace for close infighting. They were not bowmen. It is a curious parallel between the Roman and Inca fighting men that both of these land armies fought the same way: the Romans did not have the bow, but they had the pilum, a spear six feet long, hurled at the enemy when ten paces away; then they closed in with the short sword.

The Inca spear was six feet long with either metal-tipped or firehardened point. The long-range weapon was the sling. Made from plaited llama wool, measuring from fourteen to twenty-eight inches when doubled, it was fearfully and simply made; it had a sort of egg-size cradle for the stone. The sling was whirled about the head, an end released, and the stone shot forward to its mark with great accuracy; it could dent a steel helmet at fifteen yards, stunning the man in it (as the Spaniards could testify); without the protection of a helmet, the injury inflicted by the sling-tossed stone was fatal. The closing-in weapon was the mace, a three-foot-long wooden shaft, topped with a heavy bronze or stone star-shaped piece at its 'business end.' Its effectiveness is borne out by the number of crushed skulls found which had been operated on to relieve the pressure on the brain from such blows. In addition, the Incas used a sort of double-edged sword made from *chonta* wood and used like the two-handed broadsword of the sixteenth century. These were their weapons.

When war was decided upon, the word went out. Warriors were summoned and, on arrival, placed in companies corresponding to their *ayllus*. Each wore the totemic device of his clan. All warriors were, of course, classified by the decimal system. It is related how the Lord-Inca Huayna Capac (died 1527) made war. He was 'a man of few words but many deeds, a

Military power *was the foundation of the Inca, as it was of the Roman, Empire. This drawing by Poma de Ayala shows a general on his way to war. He wears a distinctive helmet of wood or cane painted with heraldic devices, and a woollen fringe round the knees and ankles. In his left hand he carries a square shield made of wood or deer hide, also painted with an emblem connected with his place in the line of battle; and in his right a sling, the main long distance weapon, which could hurl an egg-sized stone fifty yards with accuracy.*

severe judge who punished without mercy. He wished to be so feared that his Indians would dream of him at night.' He set out for the conquest of Quito with 300,000 soldiers; roads were made ready, the enemy ahead was scouted, the *tampus* along the roads filled with food, the llamas assembled to carry, supplemented by thousands of human carriers. The army on the march was severely disciplined. No warrior was allowed off the road to steal or bother the civilians; penalty, death.

Now the reason for the wide, well-kept roads is fully apparent—conquest.

When the enemy was sighted, the Inca's troops did what all their enemies did, they blew their horns, shouted insults, trying to overwhelm them in a chaos of sound; for this reason their Spanish enemy characterized them all as 'brown and noisy.'

Battle began with the slingers tossing their hail of stones, while those armed with the *macanas* advanced. Spears were thrown at short distances; then the warriors closed in with the mace. Once battle was joined, it was a formless mêlée. They used ambush and the burning of grass to force the enemy into positions to be attacked by mass. If they attacked hilltop fortresses, they advanced under a canopy of hides shaped into shields to protect them from the slingshot missiles. If the enemy took refuge in a building, fire-hot stones were hurled to burn the grass thatch and force them out into the open. The formlessness of Inca battle, once it was joined, was a tactical error that the Spaniards exploited to the full, and that is why a Spanish *capitán* could boast: 'I took no more notice of a hundred armed Indians than I would have of a handful of flies.'

There was another traditional weakness in Inca warfare which they practised, like all Andean people. They launched most of their attacks on the advent of the full moon and they kept to a twenty-day rhythm of battle. They rarely fought in mass at night. All these ritual tactics, when understood by their Spanish enemy, were used with marked effect against them.

Yet the Incas learned quickly. After their swift initial defeat by the Spaniards in 1532, they made defence against the horses, they learned to fire the arquebus, they put captured Spanish munitions makers to work; some of them learned to ride horses. In the neo-Inca state (1537–72), operating out of the sanctuary of Vilcapampa, the surviving Lord-Incas and their warriors waged a guerrilla warfare for thirty-five years, and had not the last Inca, Tupac Amaru, been seduced by 'honied words' they might have prevailed.

Once the Incas decided on the conquest of a given territory, no force in the Andes could resist them; the Incas never lost a battle of importance after 1437, and the violence, from all surviving accounts, was sufficiently awesome. There was a wholesale slaughter of the defeated in the field and a ceremonial slaughter later. A warrior was decorated for killing (one man killed, one of the warrior's arms was painted black; two killed, his chest was painted; three killed, a black mark was painted across the face between both ears; etc.). The Incas were not as bloodthirsty as were the Aztecs, but captives were taken, led in triumph through Cuzco, and forced to lie prone in front of the Sun Temple as the Inca trod upon their necks, symbolizing the victory. Heads were taken from the more ferocious of the enemy and made into drinking cups (as with the Vikings). If the enemy was especially hated, they flayed the captives alive, then stuffed their skins in a ridiculous mimicry of life, making the stomachs into drums which they beat when warming themselves up for battle. A sort of museum of these stuffed skins of the Chanca tribe—hereditary enemies of the Inca who had the temerity to attack sacred Cuzco in 1437—was seen by the Spaniards when they entered Peru. Yet the Inca policy generally was: conquer by arms, reconcile by kindness.

The Incas were masters of organization. They turned conquest into empire. They began their political life, circa A.D. 1100, in the limited orbit of the Cuzco Valley. At this time the whole of the Andean and coastal

The largest vessel known in the Americas *was the Peruvian balsa raft, seen here in a coloured drawing by Alexander von Humboldt (1803). It has a mast with a square sail, a large deck-house with a palm-leaf roof, and forward of that a hearth for the preparation of food. The logs of which it was made were lashed together by vines. There is no evidence that Inca sailors ever ventured out of sight of land, but Thor Heyerdahl used a replica of this kind of craft—the Kon-Tiki—to sail from Peru to Polynesia.*

The Inca Atahualpa was judicially murdered *on the 29th August, 1533, after a mockery of a trial at which he was accused of idolatry, immorality and treason to his lawful sovereign, the King of Spain! This old painting, now in Cuzco Museum, is an attempt by a rather imperfectly informed artist to show his last hours. In the middle, under a rainbow and a star-spangled vault, the Emperor sits—headless (he was actually garrotted). At the top, his body is being carried to the prison chapel. Underneath that is the tribunal that condemned him, with Pizarro presiding. There are also portraits of his mother, father and brother, while at the bottom Spanish troops are despatching the last of the Inca's soldiers with muskets.*

areas of the land which one day was to be Inca were broken into an almost unbelievable number of small and great tribes of different tongues and customs. By 1500, the Incas had absorbed every one of these tribes—conservatively estimated at over five hundred—into their empire which stretched all the way from Argentina to Colombia, from the shores of the Pacific into the Upper Amazon. It was one of the great empires of all time, totaling 350,000 square miles, equivalent to the land mass comprehended in the Atlantic seaboard states of North America. The conquests were gradual: first the immediate territory was taken around Cuzco, then beyond to the south, then to the west, then to the north; only when they were fully tested did the Inca's armies try to come to grips with the people of the jungle to the east.

No sooner had the new territory fallen into their conquering maw than a census of all the people was taken by means of the *quipus*. Local customs and dress and language were respected; the local language was allowed, but officials had to learn Quechua.

The Sun replaced all other religions, yet if their local gods were efficacious they were adopted into the Inca pantheon. Local chieftains either were put to death, or sent to Cuzco as hostages and trained to the 'new order,' then sent back and allowed to keep their titles. A relief model, clay or stone, was made of the territory and taken to Cuzco along with a census of people, animals, agriculture. If the principle of the *ayllu*, the earth cell, was not already in operation, it was established on Inca lines. The roads which had been built up to the border of the territory to be seized were now extended through the conquered lands, which were integrated into the empire. Professional architects were sent out from Cuzco and directed the building of a new urban centre, and especially the Temple of the Sun. If the whole population was irreconcilable, then they were moved out bodily—as the Soviets do today—and the vacuum filled by *mitimaes*, Quechua-speaking peoples loyal to the Inca. They were moved into the conquered lands, often many hundreds of miles from their original homes; population transference was an important part of Inca policy.

By peopling thinly populated regions, by placing *mitimaes* in regions devoid of population so that the roads would be kept open, the bridges repaired, etc., the Incas welded the land into empire.

'One of the things for which one feels envious of these Lords-Incas,' wrote that wonderful observer Pedro de Cieza de León, 'is their knowledge of the way to conquer . . . and to bring them by good management into empire. I often remember when in some wild and barren province outside of these kingdoms [of the Incas] hearing Spaniards themselves say, 'I am certain that if the Incas had been here the state of things would be different . . .'

And to this day, in every part of the territory ruled by the Incas, one is hourly conscious of the ghost of the Inca's supremacy manifesting itself in a score of ways: through speech, customs, and material culture.

Thus stood the realm of the Incas on that fatal day of 1527, when a small Spanish caravel, no more than ten tons burthen, sailed into Tumbes.

Why and how did such a benevolent despotism fall so quickly? How was it possible for only 130 foot soldiers and 40 cavalry with but one small falconet-cannon to penetrate the Andes, seek out the Lord-Inca surrounded by fifty thousand warriors, and then in one skirmish—which lasted precisely 33 minutes—psychologically reduce by that bold action this great realm of the Incas? The question has been asked over and over again through the centuries, and no one has yet come up with a satisfactory answer, just as there have been thousands of books to attempt to explain the decline and fall of Rome. There are, however, some historical details which might help explain this decline and fall of the Inca Empire.

By 1493, when Huayna Capac was 'crowned' Lord-Inca, the Inca Empire had almost reached its greatest heights. After a series of setbacks in his attempt to bring some of the jungle Indians in northern Ecuador and Colombia under control, he finally set the limits to the most northern realm at the Ancasmayo River (1° N. lat.) in the mountains, and Tumbes (3° S. lat.) on the coast. Like the Roman Emperor Hadrian, this last great Inca attempted to set limits to his realm.

There is a natural limit to conquest, and that is the power of assimilation. Time gnawed at the bones of the old Inca, who had to consider whom among all his hundreds of male heirs would be named Inca. The first years of this 'setting bounds to the fields' were ones of inward peace within the Inca realm, but in the later years of the reign of Huayna Capac there was disquieting news from without. The later years were full of gloom and evil portent. In defeating a tribe in the Chaco region there had been reported the presence of a strange man, white and bearded, among the enemy. There were further reports, vague and contradictory yet persistent, of other white men sailing in large ships down the Pacific coast.

There was no direct contact between the great American civilizations; they were, so far as we know now, in complete unawareness of each other's existence. If there had been such contact, then that terrible catastrophe of the Conquest of Mexico in 1521 would have been transmitted to the Incas, and they would have put themselves into a state of defence against a doom which could have been foreseen. Yet they must have received vague rumours, through trade that passed from hand to hand coming down from Mexico to Panama, Colombia to Peru, of something that was occurring, and vague foreboding settled over the land. A pestilence at this time came to Peru, and, although it cannot be positively identified, it was new in their experience and could have been one of the diseases, perhaps smallpox, brought by the Spaniard.

Then, toward the end of Huayna Capac's reign, an Inca outpost in the Chaco was attacked by Chiriguano Indians led by a white man. That man we now know was a Spaniard named Alejo García, who, captured by Indians in Brazil, had become their captain. The time was 1525.

Two years later, Francisco Pizarro arrived at Tumbes with his famous 'thirteen men of Gallo'; they embraced the natives, traded gewgaws, shot off guns, skirted the Peruvian coast, and then took Indians aboard to train them as interpreters for their contemplated return. Pizarro left behind for future use two Spaniards, one named Alonso de Molina, and a Negro, Gines. All these strange marvels were transmitted to the Inca, who in 1527 lay on his death bed.

Then Huayna Capac died without naming his successor. As will be recalled, when discussing the Inca state, there was no fixed rule of descent; the Inca chose with advice from his council the most competent of his sons born of his principal queen, the *coya*. Now that son whom most considered would be made Inca was Huáscar, who resided in Cuzco, and in default of a clear line of descent he was proclaimed Inca; but the deceased Inca had among his numerous subsidiary offspring one named Atahualpa, who was born in the region which is now Ecuador and who travelled much with Huayna Capac in his later years, and was personally known and much liked by the principal generals of the army.

The result of this dispute for Inca-ship was a devastating civil war between the two brothers which lasted five years, corresponding precisely with the intervening years when Francisco Pizarro was in Spain organizing for his conquest of the Kingdom of Gold.

In the final battle Huáscar was captured, his generals killed, thousands of Indians slaughtered, and Atahualpa's generals were sent to Cuzco to put to death as many of Huáscar's family as they could apprehend, and also to prepare the capital for Atahualpa's entry into Cuzco to be proclaimed Inca.

At this precise moment Francisco Pizarro arrived with his small army at Tumbes; the date: May 13, 1532.

Atahualpa (who was to be proclaimed Inca) was at this time taking the hot sulphur baths at Cajamarca, a place then of no great importance in the Inca realm. He was awaiting the reports from his *chasquis* from Cuzco about the preparations for his triumphant entry. He was surrounded by his battle-tried warriors, men who had fought this terrible fratricidal war for five years. He was the master now of everything, everyone in the domain; he could lop off the head of his most famous general merely by raising his hand;

The end of the Inca Empire *came at Cajamarca, a relatively minor town, but popular because of the hot springs a few miles away. Its large plaza had buildings on three sides and a stone wall on the fourth, and was entered by two main roads north and south and two more roads leading to the town. Further away was a strong fortress defended by three walls. When Pizarro arrived from the north, with his 167 Spaniards, on November 16th, 1532, the town was deserted. Atahualpa with all his forces was encamped in a meadow on the other side of the city. Pizarro occupied the town and sent an embassy to Atahualpa requesting that he should visit him there the next day. The Inca innocently agreed and arrived with about 6,000 attendants, all unarmed. Pizarro had meanwhile hidden his troops in the streets and buildings surrounding the plaza. At an appointed signal they rushed forward and in a few moments the square was strewn with corpses. The wall on the fourth side (left in the picture) collapsed and the remnants escaped into the country.*

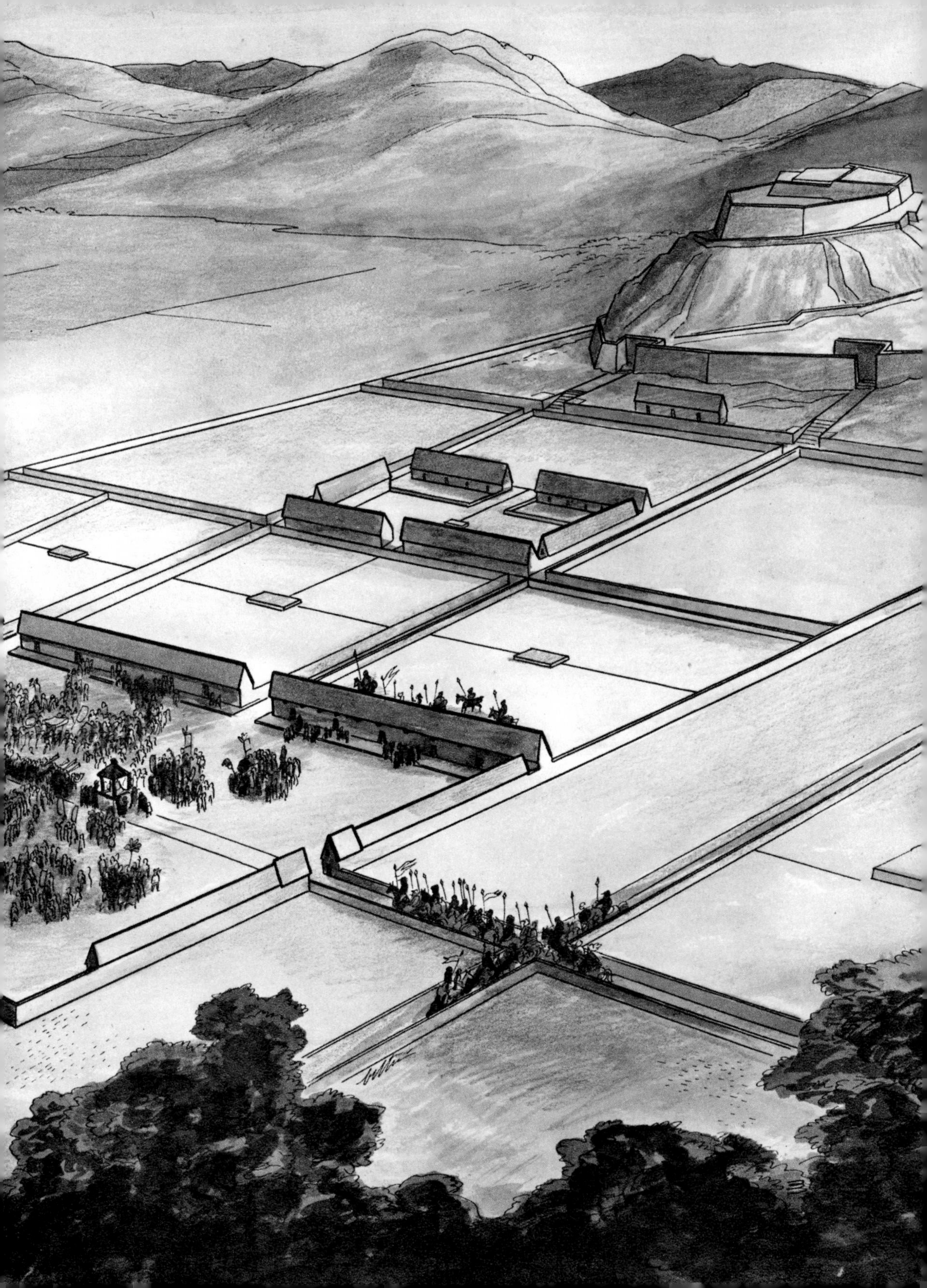

The capture of Atahualpa *is shown here by Theodore de Bry as if it occurred outside the town in the midst of battle. The general effect, however, is fairly truthful, though the Imperial troops did not themselves use the bow. The two falconets in the foreground did comprise Pizarro's 'artillery,' though they were actually placed in the fortress of Cajamarca overlooking the town. We know too that the Inca was sitting on a gold throne and wore a collar of emeralds. Father Valverde, holding up the cross, did in fact preach a long sermon to him before the attack began. Atahualpa was seized alive by Pizarro himself, after which all resistance ceased and the Inca army dispersed. The Peruvians were unarmed; there were no Spanish casualties. 'One of the most atrocious acts of perfidy on the record of history,' is the judgement of Prescott.*

he could do it even by long distance via a messenger. It was then at this moment that he received messages from the coast of the arrival of the Spaniards.

His intelligence was exact; the *quipus* counted out the number of men and animals (so strange that no one could give them a name except that they thought man and beast were one). It was the *interpretation* of this intelligence that was faulty: the animals had feet of silver (the horseshoes gave that effect), they were impotent at night; if the rider fell off the animal that ended both. As for the guns which spouted fire, they were only thunderbolts and could only be fired twice. One of the coastal chieftains, so the report said, poured a libation of corn *chicha* into a barrel of one of the guns so as to solace the thunder god. Moreover, the steel swords of these bearded men were as ineffectual as women's weaving battens. From all this it is clear that the Inca had absolutely no advance notice of the white man. It is true that at first Atahualpa thought that they were returning gods, for it was legend that the Inca's creator-god, Tici Viracocha, who had helped bring civilization to them, had been dissatisfied with his handiwork and sailed away and would someday return (this is a persistent legend throughout the Americas about ships returning over the ocean sea, and must somewhere have substance).

It was at vespers during the early evening of November 16, 1532, when the Inca, carried in his litter and surrounded by an unarmed bodyguard, moved into the plaza of Cajamarca. There was, if one will recall reading Prescott's *Conquest of Peru*, an unintelligible parley between Christian priest and Inca god, then that one cannon belched out its thunder into the ranks of brown bodies, and with the cry of 'Santiago!' and 'At them!' the Spaniards ambushed the hapless Inca.

The rest is history.

Chronology

of the Ancient Sun Kingdoms

AZTEC

MAYA

INCA

EUROPE AND NORTH AMERICA

BC

c 2000
Greeks active in Troy.

850
Age of Homer.

776
First Olympiad held in Greece.

753
Legendary founding of Rome.

431–404
Peloponnesian Wars.

331
Alexander the Great defeats Darius at Arbela.

c. 240
Eratosthenes computes the size of the earth.

146
Romans capture and destroy Carthage.

AZTEC

c 2000
'Tepexpan Man' valley of Mexico; bones associated with mammoth elephants.

800–A.D. c. 600
Olmecs. La Venta culture in Mexico hotlands.

c 500
Tlachtli (a form of basketball) invented by Olmecs. Spreads to tribes from Arizona to Nicaragua.

O L M E C

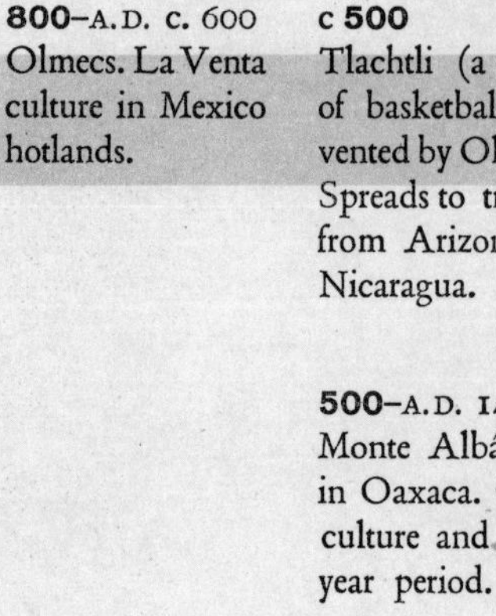

500–A.D. 1469
Monte Albán. Large stone temple-city in Oaxaca. Goes through five stages of culture and growth over two thousand-year period.

200
First evidence of Toltec culture in the valley of Anáhuac.

MAYA

c 2000
Proto-Maya. Widely scattered settlements of people of Maya speech. Huastecs, a tribe of Maya speech separated from main body of Maya. They carry on different form of culture, about Rio Panico in Tampico, but retain physical characteristics.

M A M O M

2000–500
Mamom ('Grandmother') stage of Maya development. Early pottery, strictly utilitarian, widely scattered. Figurines moulded by hand.

500–A.D. 300
Chichanel ('Concealer'). Transitional period in Maya culture. Polychromic pottery appears; human form is painted realistically. Pottery is often glyph dated.

C H I C

c 200
Dzibilchaltún in northern Yucatán functioning as city. Endures to A.D. 1500.

INCA

c 2500
Coastal Indians at Chicama engaged in agriculture.

1200–400
Chavín de Huantar culture, central Andes.

C H A V Í N

750
Coastal cultures: Virú, Cuqisnique, Gallinazo. Formative period in many Peruvian coastal cultures.

400–A.D. 400
Paracas (Caverna) I. Peru, south coast on dry shores of Paracas Peninsula (Pisco).

P A

272
Carbon-14-dated appearance of Mochica culture.

400–A.D. 1000
Nazca, south coastal culture.

N

4
ssassination of
lius Caesar.

AD

79
Volcanic Destruction of Herculaneum and Pompeii.

c 117
Roman Empire at its greatest extent.

c 235
Roman Empire begins to decline.

337
Death of Constantine.

400–800
The Mound Builders: Wisconsin to Gulf of Mexico.

410
Alaric sacks Rome.

632
Death of Mohammed.

1
irst known dated
lmec monument. Inventors of
yph writing,
hich spreads
roughout Mexi-
 and Maya
untry.

O L M E C

c 100
Sun Temple at Teotihuacán is built (Chimalhuacan phase).

c 200
Monte Albán (Period I) in Oaxaca.

c 400
Monte Albán rebuilt, extended (Zapotec period).

510
Toltecs begin to build temples of the Sun and Moon at Teotihuacán.

770
Teotihuacán Period II. Mitl-Tlacomihua, chief of Toltecs, builds temple to Quetzalcoatl.

I A N E L TZAKOL T E P E U H

c 150
Maya ceremonial centres spring up in various regions.

162
The Tuxtla jade piece. The earliest known authentically dated Maya inscription.

317–650
Tzakol ('The Builders'). Maya classic period. The rise and florescence of the great Maya ceremonial centres and temple-cities. Dated monuments.

650

642
Palenque, in Chiapas, is built in a rain forest.

765
Copán holds 'astronomical congress' to adjust Maya calendar.

MAYA CLASSIC PERIOD

R A C A S

400–800
Paracas (Necropolis) II.

M O C H I C A

A Z C A

400–1000
Tiahuanaco Empire (Andean).

700 Gate of the Sun, Tiahuanaco carved. Erected from a single immens
piece of stone.

EUROPE

800
Imperial Coronation of Charlemagne at Rome.

871–899
Alfred, king of Wessex and of England.

900
Golden Age of Arabian power in Spain.

c 985
Vikings settle Greenland.

1066–87
William I (the conqueror), king of England.

1189–92
Third Crusade, Frederick Barbarossa, Richard the Lion Heart and Philip II.

AZTEC

c 890
Great drought. Period of decline of Teotihuacán.

900
Xochicalco, a temple-city (south of Cuernavaca), built by the Toltecs. Tula, new centre of Toltecs, is built.

967
Ce Acatl Topiltzin takes name of the god Quetzalcoatl, rules Tula for 20 years.

987
Quetzalcoatl, exiled from Tula, moves south-west toward Yucatán with large body of warriors.

1156
Tula destroyed by Chichimecs. Another migration of Toltecs results. They settle at Xicalango.

1168
Aztec history begins. Migratory tribes enter valley of Anáhuac.

MAYA

800
The murals of Bonampak (founded 540) are painted.

T E P E U H

879
Kabah founded.

889
The Maya cities of Uaxactún, Xultun, and Xamantun erect dated stelae; last dated monuments.

890
First American book. Mayas produce a 72-page illustrated book (The Dresden Codex), a copy of an earlier document.

987
Chichén Itzá refounded. Occupied by Maya-Itzás and Quetzalcoatl with Toltec warriors.

987
Maya renaissance: Uxmal and Mayapán founded; League of Mayapán begun.

1000
Tepeuh ('Conqueror') period ends. Interior cities of Mayas culturally dead. All Maya activity now concentrated in Yucatán and adjacent territories.

1194
Cocoms, heade[d] by Huanc Ce[el] expel other May[as] from Chichén Itzá with aid o[f] Toltec mercenaries. Mayapán b[e]comes dominan[t] capital from 120[0–]1441.

INCA

900
Chanapata period in Cuzco. Pre-Inca occupation of valley of Cuzco.

M O C H I C A

1000
End of Mochica coastal empire.

c 1100
Cuzco founded by legendary historical figure of Manco Capac. First Lord-Inca.

N A Z C A

1000
Tiahuanaco Empire, either from regio[n] about Titicaca or Huari, sweeps dow[n] upon the coast in religio-military co[n]quest.

800 Huari – Tiahuanaco. An offshoot of the ceremonial centre about Lake Titicaca. Province of Huanta.

T I A H U A N A C O

27
…eath of Genghis …han.

1275
Five-year drought in American Southwest.

1347
Black Death spreads through Europe.

1386
Chaucer composes the Canterbury Tales.

1415
Henry V defeats French at Agincourt.

1431
Joan of Arc burned at the stake.

1450–55
The Gutenberg Bible.

1453
Fall of Constantinople.

…50
…ztecs, called Tenochas, living in …a about Chapultepec close to …ake Texcoco.

c 1325
Aztecs occupy two islets in Lake Texcoco. Tenochtitlán, 'Place of the Tenocha,' is founded.

1375
Acamapichtli, first historical 'king,' or Chief Speaker, of the Tenochas.

1395
Huitzilhuitl, second in line, begins to enlarge his capital.

1414
Chimalpopoca elected Chief Speaker by the noble tlatoani, the electors of Aztec rulers.

1428
Izcoatl, born a slave, rises to leadership. Tenochas assume Aztec civilization. Izcoatl orders all previous historical picture paintings to be destroyed. Begins systematic wars on all neighbouring tribes.

1440
Moctezuma I elected Chief Speaker.

1441–56
Drought. Crop failures, snow, frost.

1250
Mayas spread into Mexico. Their canoes trade from Tampico to Panama. Age of metals, gold, copper, silver.

1300
Cocoms and Tutul Xius jointly ruling Mayapán compel all local chieftains to reside in the capital of Mayapán.

1300–1400
Period of Maya trade expansion. Seagoing canoes sail southward.

1400
Mayas expand trade with Mexico through trading centres of Xicalango located in Laguna de Términos 'the land where the language changes.'

1441
Fall of Mayapán. Tutul Xiu clan murder leaders of their rivals the Cocoms. First and only known central capital of the Mayas disintegrates. Itzás make mass migration to El Petén, set up independent kingdom.

1250
Inca culture in and about Cuzco Valley.

1300
Tiahuanaco coast invasion collapses. Many other cultures spring out of its ruin. Chimú, Mochic-speaking people as were the Mochicas, rise and form an immense empire; rivals of Incas.

1350
Incas begin expansion. Inca Roca, 6th Inca, builds bridge across the Apurimac. Quechua becomes official language.

1390
Chimú, kingdom of Chimor, rules 600 miles of land, completes capital Chan-Chan.

1437
Viracocha, 8th Inca. Cuzco is besieged by Chanca tribe.

1438
Inca troops under Yupanqui, son of Viracocha, defeat Chancas. Proclaimed 9th Inca, he takes name of Pachacuti.

1450
Chimú influence felt from Lima to Tumbes.

1450
Pachacuti enlarges Inca Empire by series of local wars.

EUROPE

1469
Union of ruling houses of Castile and Aragon through marriage of Ferdinand and Isabella.

1483
Richard III, last of Plantagenet kings of England, begins reign.

1492
Columbus discovers America.

1498
Columbus discovers mainland of South America.

1497
North America discovered by John Cabot.

AZTEC

1469
Axayacatl succeeds his father Moctezuma I. Extends conquest to Isthmus of Tehuantepec. Campaigns into Tarascan territory, suffers sharp defeat.

1481
Tizoc succeeds his brother Axayacatl. Begins construction of great temple to Huitzilopochtli, the Aztec War God.

Great sacrificial stone carved. Calendar stone set up. Recovered in 1790.

1486
Ahuitzotl succeeds his brother Tizoc. Dedicates temple to Huitzilopochtli by immolating 20,000 sacrificial victims. Extends conquests down into Pacific side of Guatemala. Pochteca merchants in Honduras, Nicaragua.

1503
Moctezuma II, grandson of ot of same name, elected Chief Speaker.

MAYA

1467
Great hurricane. Destroys cities, houses, people.

1482
Pestilence (yellow fever) decimates cities of the Mayas. Abandonment of whole areas.

1502
Christopher Co lumbus on his fourth voyage makes first Euro pean contact wi Mayas at Guanaj one of Bay Islan off Honduras.

INCA

1463
Pachacuti directs war of extermination against Lupaca and Colla tribes centred about Lake Titicaca in the ruins of Tiahuanaco Empire.

1466
Chimú Empire is overrun by troops of Incas.

1471
Topa Inca, 10th Lord-Inca. State reorganized. Era of road-building.

1480
Inca army under Topa Inca builds roads leading into Chile, preparatory to conquest.

1485
Topa Inca is supposed to have marshalled a fleet of balsa rafts and sailed to the Galapágos Islands.

1492
Topa Inca conquers all of Chile to the Maule River. Establishes Inca fortress called Purumauca.

1493
Huayna Capac, 11th Lord-Inca. Completes coastal road from Chile to Tumbes.

1498
Huayna Capac extends conquest beyond Quito into Colombia. Completes Andean highway, Quito to Talca (Chili), 3,250 miles.

1500
Huayna Capac undertakes final conquest of Cha chapoyas.

1513
Juan Ponce de León discovers Florida.

1519
Death of Leonardo da Vinci.

1519
Magellan begins circumnavigation of the globe.

1529
First siege of Vienna by the Turks.

1534
Church of England established.

1539–42
Hernando de Soto explores the Mississippi.

1507
New Fire ceremony. Columbus' presence in 1503 reported. Priests believe end of world is near.

1519
Cortés enters Tenochtitlán. Captures Moctezuma.

1520
Moctezuma stoned and killed by own people.
Cuitlahuac is made Leader, dies in mêlée as Spaniards fight their way out of Tenochtitlán.

1521
Cuauhtémoc is named last Chief Speaker. Defends Mexico against Cortés. Tenochtitlán falls to conquistadors.

1525
END OF AZTEC EMPIRE

1524
Cortés marches through Tabasco, Campeche, into El Petén in order to subdue an unauthorized Spanish colony in Honduras.

1511
Gerónimo de Aguilar and Gonzalo Guerrero are captured on Cozumel Island, kept as slaves.

1519
Hernándo Cortés arrives at Cozumel. Sails to Vera Cruz and thence to Mexico.

1518
Juan de Grijalva explores coast with flotilla of ships. Discovers all the coastal towns including Tulum.

1527
Francisco de Montejo arrives in Yucatán. Occupies walled city of Xelha and Tulum.

1535
Montejo defeated by the Mayas, sails to the south. Not a single white man remains in Yucatán.

1542
Montejo the Younger renews conquest. Spaniards destroy inland town of T'ho, build their own capital of Mérida.

1513
Vasco Nuñez de Balboa discovers the Pacific. The Incas become aware of white man's presence in South America.

1519
Atahualpa (age 19) destined to be last independent Inca, takes part in military campaigns.

1522
Pascal de Andogoya on an expedition of small ships down toward Darien is made aware of the Kingdom of Gold.

1527
Francisco Pizarro makes first landing.

Death of Huayna Capac.

Civil war between Huáscar, crowned 12th Inca, and Atahualpa, who dominates the north. Huáscar defeated in 1532.

1532 (Nov. 16)
Atahualpa captured by Pizarro in Cajamarca, held captive, agrees to ransom himself.

1533 (Aug. 29)
His ransom completed, Atahualpa is executed for crimes against the Spaniards.

1535
Inca Empire completely subjugated. Manco II crowned 'Inca' by the Spaniards.

1537
Manco II retires with large force into sanctuary of Vilcapampa. Establishes Neo-Inca state.

EUROPE

1547
Death of Henry VIII.

1565
Ivan the Terrible of Russia initiates reign of terror.

1579
Francis Drake explores California coast.

1588
Defeat of Spanish Armada.

1620
Plymouth Colony established in Massachusetts.

1748
Excavations at Pompeii begin.

1776
Declaration of Independence by the Thirteen Colonies.

AZTEC

MAYA

1546
Maya rising against the Spaniards marks the end of resistance in Yucatán.

1566
Diego de Landa finishes his 'Account of the Things of Yucatán.'

1576
Diego García de Palacio discovers the ruins of Copán.

1622
Failure of the first Spanish attempt to conquer the Itzá-Mayas living in El Petén.

1697
Martin de Ursua takes Tayasal, the Itzá-Maya capital, puts chiefs to death.

END OF MAYA EMPIRE

INCA

1551
Antonio de Mendoza named first Viceroy to Peru.

1553
Pedro de Cieza de León publishes (Seville) epoch-making First Part of the Chronicles of Peru.

1572
End of the Neo-Inca state. Tupac Amaru executed.

1595
Sir Walter Raleigh explores lower part of Orinoco River in search of El Dorado.

1780–1
Revolt of Andean Indians led by José Gabriel Condorcanqui, styled Tupac Amaru II. He is defeated and executed.

1781
END OF INCA EMPIRE

Select Bibliography

ANONYMOUS CONQUEROR, *Narrative of Some Things of New Spain and of the Great City of Temestitan,* trans. by Marshall H. Saville. New York, 1917.
ARTHAUD, C. and HÉBERT STEVENS, F., *The Andes.* London, 1956.
BENNETT, Wendell, *Ancient Arts of the Andes.* New York, 1954.
BENNET, Wendell and BIRD, Junius B., *Andean Culture History.* American Museum of Natural History, Handbook Series, no. 15. New York, 1949.
BINGHAM, Hiram, *Lost City of the Incas: the story of Machu Picchu and its Builders.* New York, 1948.
BUSHNELL, Geoffrey, *Peru.* London, 1956.
CATHERWOOD, Frederick, *Views of Ancient Monuments in Central America, Chiapas and Yucatan.* New York, 1844.
COE, Michael, D. *Mexico.* London, 1962.
COVARRUBIAS, Miguel, *Indian Art of Mexico and Central America.* New York, 1957.
Mexico South: The Isthmus of Tehuantepec. London, 1947.
DÍAZ DEL CASTILLO, Bernal, *The Discovery and Conquest of Mexico, 1517–1521,* trans. by A. P. Maudslay. New York, 1956.
GAGE, Thomas, *Travels in the New World,* ed. by J. E. S. Thompson. Oklahoma, 1958.
GANN, Thomas and THOMPSON, J. E. S., *The History of the Maya.* New York, 1931.
GROTH-KIMBALL, Irmgard, *The Art of Ancient Mexico.* London, 1954.
Handbook of the American Indians, Smithsonian Institution of Washington.
KELEMEN, Pál, *Medieval American Art,* 2 vols. New York, 1943.
MASON, J. Alden, *The Ancient Civilisations of Peru.* Harmondsworth, 1961.
MAUDSLAY, A. C. and A. P., *A Glimpse at Guatemala.* London, 1899.
The Maya and Their Neighbours. New York, 1940.
MEANS, Philip Ainsworth, *Ancient Civilizations of the Andes.* New York, 1931.
Fall of the Inca Empire and the Spanish Rule in Peru: 1530–1780. New York, 1931.

POMA DE AYALA, Felipe Guamán, *Nueva Coronica y Buen Gobierno.* Paris, 1936.

POSNANSKY, Arthur, *Tiahuanacu, the Cradle of American Man,* 2 vols., trans. by James F. Shearer, New York, 1945–57.

PRESCOTT, William H., *History of the Conquest of Mexico.* London, 1922. *History of the Conquest of Peru.* London, 1908.

PROUSKOURIAKOFF, T. A., *An Album of Maya Architecture.* Carnegie Institution of Washington, Pub. 558. Washington, D. C., 1946.

SAHAGÚN, Bernardino de, *A History of Ancient Mexico,* trans. by Fanny Bandelier. Nashville, 1932.

SOUSTELLE, Jacques, *Daily Life of the Aztecs.* London, 1962.

SQUIER, E. George, *Peru: Incidents of Travel and Exploration in the Land of the Incas.* New York, 1877.

STEPHENS, John Lloyd, *Incidents of Travel in Central America, Chiapas and Yucatan,* 2 vols. New York, 1841.

THOMPSON, J. E. S., *Mexico Before Cortes.* London, 1933.
The Rise and Fall of Maya Civilization. London, 1956.

VAILLANT, George C., *The Aztecs of Mexico.* Harmondsworth, 1956.

VON HAGEN, Victor Wolfgang, *The Aztec and Maya Papermakers.* New York, 1943.
Jungle in the Clouds. New York, 1940.
South America Called Them: La Condamine, Humboldt, Darwin, Spruce. New York, 1945.
Maya Explorer: John Lloyd Stephens and the Lost Cities of Central America and Yucatán. Oklahoma, 1947.
Frederick Catherwood, Architect. New York, 1950.
The Four Seasons of Manuela. New York, 1952.
Highway of the Sun. New York, 1955.

WALDECK, J. F. de, *Voyage Pittoresque at Archéologue, dans la Province d'Yucatan . . . Paris,* 1838.

WISSLER, Clark, *The American Indian.* New York, 1938.

Sources and Acknowledgements

The sources of illustrations are listed below followed by the numbers of the page on which the illustrations occur. Author and publishers gratefully acknowledge the necessary permissions

Aerofilms and Aero Pictorial Ltd: 19
American Museum of Natural History: 113
M. Angrand, from *Tiahuanaco, Gateway of the Sun,* 1837, courtesy Bibliothèque National, Paris: 239
'Anonymous Conqueror', 1534: 275
Ferdinand Anton: 17
Claude Arthaud: 228, 315
Ayer Collection; courtesy The Newberry Library, Chicago: 134
Alberto Beltrán;
maps and plans: 20–21, 74–75, 123, 227, 324–325 (adapted from the reconstruction by Emilio Harth-Terré)
drawings: 22 (after Codex Boturini), 48, 69, 73, 136 (right), 144 and 147 (right) (after Codex Tro-Cortesianus), 146, 147 (left: after Dresden Codex), 156–157 (after J.E. S. Thompson), 161 (left: after Bonampak Murals), 162, 172
Robert Woods Bliss Collection on loan to the National Gallery of Art, Washington D.C.: facing 14, 41, facing 97, facing 193
Theodore de Bry, *America Suie Noui Orbis,* 1596: 56–57, 121, 225, 295, 326–327
Pablo Carrera after J. L. Quíroz: 83
Frederick Catherwood, *Views of Ancient Monuments in Central America, Chiapas and Yucatan,* 1844: facing 10, 119, 127, 199
Bodil Christensen: 59 (right)
Pedro de Cieza de León, *Parte Primera de la Chronica del Peru,* 1553: 254 (right), 273, 276
Codex Dresdensis, Förstermann facsimile: 212
Codex Fernandez Leal: 59 (right)
Codex Magliabecchi, facsimile edition, 1904: 38, 60, 64, 66, 102, 103, 115
Codex Mendoza, facsimile edition, 1904, courtesy Bodleian Library, Oxford: facing 11, 37, 39, 43, 47, 68, 69 (left), 71 (below), 108, 109, 114
Codex Nuttall, facsimile edition, 1901: 59 (left)
Compañia Mexicana Aerofoto, S. A.: 85, 179
Guillelmo Dupaix, *Antiquités Mexicaines,* with illustrations by Castañeda, 1834: facing 81
Amedée François Frezier, *Relation du Voyage de la Mer du Sud aux côtes du Chily et du Pérou,* 1716: 313
Irmgard Groth-Kimball: 28, 62, 63, facing 80, 186, 203, 204
Abraham Guillén: 232, 233 (right above), 261, 262 (left, right below), 296, 297, 298, 299
Hans Helfritz: 255
Keith Henderson from *The Conquest of Mexico,* W.H. Prescott edited by T.

A. Joyce, by courtesy of Chatto and Windus: 48, 49
George Holton: 188 (above), 207
Alexander von Humboldt, *Nouvelle Espagne Atlas,* 1810: facing, 209: *Vues des Cordillères et Monuments des Peuples Indigènes de l'Amérique,* 1810; facing 320
Illustrations for Sahagún's *Historia de las Cosas de Nueva España,* 1905: 34, 44, 45, 53, 65, 70, 71 (above), 77, 98, 99 (left), 101, 111, 118
Inca Highway Expedition: 307, 308
Instituto Nacional de Antropología e Historia, Mexico D.F.: 61, 83, 106–107, 161
La Preclara Narratione di Ferdinando Cortese, 1524: 79
Libreria Universitana, Universidad Nacional Autonoma de Mexico: 137, 161 (right)
Lienzo de Tlascala, facsimile edition, 1892; courtesy the American Museum of Natural History, New York: 23
José Limón: 26 (right), 27 (left), 54, 201, 221
Dr. Eva Lindemann: 286
Luis Limón: 35
H. Mann: 229 (above), 236, 237, 243, 279
Sir Clements Robert Markham, *Cuzco: A Journey to the Ancient Capital of Peru,* 1856: facing 305
Ann Axtell Morris; courtesy the Carnegie Institution of Washington: 142–143, 211
Musée de l'Homme, Paris: 27 (right), 202 (bottom right)
Museo Arqueologico, Cuzco: 260 (right), 261, 262 (left, right below), 296, 297 (left), facing 321
Museo de Tula: 32
Museo Nacional, Mexico D.F.: 54, 93, 96, 105, 203
Museum für Völkerkunde, Vienna: 99 (right), facing 96, 112
National Museum of Archaeology, Lima: 232, 233 (right above, below), 260 (left), 297 (right), 298, 299
Peabody Museum of Archaeology and Ethnology, Cambridge, Mass.: 205, facing 208
Felipe Guamán Poma de Ayala, *Nueva Coronica y buen gobierno*; courtesy The Royal Library, Copenhagen: 241, 246, 247, 248–249, 250–251, 264, 265, 266, 317, 319
Tatiana Prouskouriakoff; courtesy the Carnegie Institution of Washington: 168–169; courtesy the Peabody Museum of Archaeology and Ethnology, Cambridge, Mass.: 171
Rod Rawlins collection, Ica: 233 (left)
Professor Alberto Ruz: 221
Robert E. Smith (after) in M. Covarrubias, *Indian Art of Mexico and Central America,* 1957: 153
Smithsonian Institution, Washington: 316
E. G. Squier, *Peru, Incidents of Travel and Exploration in the Land of the Incas,* 1877: 310
Richard H. Stewart; courtesy the National Geographic Society: 25
Antonio Tejeda; courtesy the Peabody Museum of Archaeology and Ethnology, Cambridge, Mass.: 158–159, facing 208
Thames and Hudson archive: 34, 37, 38, 39, 43, 44, 45, 47, 50 (top and bottom right), 53, 56–57, 60, 64, 65, 66, 68, 69 (left), 70, 71, 77, 92 (Edwin Smith), 95 (Eileen Tweedy), 97 (Scotty Sapiro), 98, 99 (left), 101, 102, 103, 108, 109, 111, 114, 115, 118, 119, 142–143, 145 (left), 150 (left, above right), 168–169, 171, 185, facing 193 (Scotty Sapiro), 199, 202

(Eileen Tweedy), 212, 225, 254 (right), 273, 276, 295, 326–327

Thompson, J. E. S. (after) *The Rise and Fall of Maya Civilization:* 215

Trustees of the British Museum: 50 (top and bottom right), 94, 95, facing 80, 145 (left), 150 (left, above right), 200, 202

Victor von Hagen: facing 10, facing 15, 26, 27, 29, 31, 32, 49 (above), 84, 88, 89, 91, 124, 125, 129, 131, 136, 141, 163, 167, 173, 175, 177, 181, 182, 183, 184, 187, 188 (below), 189, facing 192, 194, 195, 197, 216, 217, 229 (below), 232 (below), 233 (left), 235, 245, 252, 253, 254 (left), 257, 277, 283, 285, 287, 288, 289, 292, 293, 302, facing 304, facing 305, 306, 307, 308, 309, 310, 311, 313, facing 320, facing 321

Hasso von Winning: 51

University Museum of Archaeology and Ethnology, Cambridge: 50 (top and bottom left), 139, 145 (right), 202 (right above), 232 (above), 242, 257, 262 (right below), 267, 270, 271, 303 (left)

University Museum of the University of Pennsylvania: 150, 151, 198

J.F. de Waldeck, *Voyage Pittoresque et Archéologue dans la province de Yucatan,* 1838: 134, 185

We would also like to thank Routledge and Kegan Paul Ltd for permission to quote from *The Discovery and Conquest of Mexico* by Bernal Diaz del Castillo and *Five Letters* by Hernando Cortés

Index

Page references to illustrations are shown in italic numbers

Adobe, 39, 140, 172, 244, 282, 284, 290
Ah Puch, 213, *213*
A'ka, 246
Almuchil, 192
Alpaca, 241, *241*, 245, *247*, *254*, 256, 258, 272
Amaranth, *45*
Amatl, 30, 36, 52, 58, *59*, 115, 116, 138
Amazon, river, *227*, *229*, 230, 248, 301, 321
Anáhuac valley, 18, 19, 20, *20*, *22*, 24, 29, 39, 53, 73, *74–75*, 83, 330, 332
Ancasmayo, river, 281, 302, 305, 322
Andes, 12, 16, 46, 226, *228*, 230, 231, 235, 237, 238, 240, 248, 281, 290, 294, 301, 302, 305, 311, 320, 322, 330
Anklets, 264
'Anonymous Conqueror', 65
Anta, 308
Antilles islands, 9
Apurimac, river, *227*, 288, *facing 305*, 309, 310, 333
Aqueducts, 47, 76, *79*, 81
Argentina, *227*, 302, 321
Armour, 22, 108–109, 148, 212, 318
Arrows, 22, 58
sacrifice by arrow ceremony: *59*, 213
Aryballus, 259, *260*, *262*
Astrology, 68, 138, 139, 144, 222, 234
Astronomy, 102, 104, 138, 144, *facing 209*, 214–215
Atahualpa, 274, *275*, 290, 300, *facing 321*, 323, *324–325*, *326–327*, 328, 335
Atl-atl, *91*, 170, 210
Aviary, 47, 72, 80, 98–99
Ayavari, *227*, 267
Ayllu, 36, 138, 243, 244, 245, 246, 247, 250, 256, 268, 271, 274, 275, 321
Azcapotzalco, *74*
Aztecs, 120, 137, 143, 154, 159, 162, 170, 206, 212, 214, 220, 223, 278, 318, 332–335
pre-Aztecs, 24–32, 83–90
physical features, 33
clan organisation, 36
daily life, 40–43, 46–52
agriculture, 44–46
government, 67–72
architecture, 81–83
art, 96–99
religion, 100–101

Ball courts, 28, 39, 61, 62, *62*, 77, 78, 87, 133, 161–162, *162*, 168, 173, 183, 190, 195, 213
Ball games, *see tlachtli, pok-a-tok*
Balsa boats, *310*, 312, *313*, 313, *facing 320*, 334
Batabobs, 133, *facing 208*
Batan Grande, *298*, *299*
Beans, 40, 46, 145, 156, 248
Bee-god, *146*, 157
Bells, 9, *27*, *66*, 140, 159, 258, *264*, 264, *297*
'Big Ears', 165, *263*
Blood letting, 163, *200*, 213
Boats, *see* Balsa boats, canoes, *huampas*
Bolivia, *227*, 235, 302
Bolonchen, *127*
Bonampak, *123*, *137*, 180
murals 15, 110, 135, 148, *158–159*, 159, *161*, 166, 180, *facing 208*, 209, 332
Bonbón, *227*
Bone, 245
Books, 9, 10, 11, 14, 22, 115, 120, 145, 207, 209, 220, 222
see also amatl, codices, paper, writing
Bows, 22
Brazil, 9, *227*
Brazilwood, 124, 143
Breechclout, 33, *34*, 69, 134, 241, 247, 271
Bricks, sun-dried, 77, 226, 234, 244
Bridges,
Aztec, 73, 79
Maya, 174
Inca, 13, 266, 282, 308, 309, *309*, 310–312, *310*, *311*
Bridge of San Luis Rey, *facing 305*, 309
Bronze, 245, 250, 294, 300, 301
Bry, Theodore de, *56*, *225*, *276*, *295*, *326–327*
Buct-zotz, *123*, 219
Burial, 65–66, *66*, 141, 164, 179–180, 268

Cacao, 40, 62, 72, 78, 111, 126, 143, 153, 154, 155, 156, 164, 176, 248
Cacha, 281–282
Cajamarca, *227*, 275, 290, 300, 323, *324–325*, *326–327*, 328, 335
Calakmul, *123*, 124
Calendar, 234
Aztec, 10, 53–59, 70, 102–104, *102–103*
Maya, 24, 26, 128, 130, *156–157*, 178, 214–216, *215*, 331
Toltec, 30, 86
Inca, *248–251*, 249–250
Calendar stone, 13, 14, 78, 103, *105*, 334
Calixtlahuaca, *20*, 82, *84*, *88*
Calpulli, 36
Campeche, 26, *123*, 126, 154, *facing 193*, 206, 335
Canals, 22, 73, 76
Cancha, 245, 284
Cañete valley, *227*, 290, 302, 305, *306*
Canoes, 22, 41, 42, *43*, 46, 78, 82, 113–114, *114*, 154, 219–220, 333
Carabaya, *227*, 294, 304, *307*, *309*

Caracol at Chichén Itzá, *188*
Carbon 14 tests, 231, 234, 330
Caso, Dr Alfonso, 26, 97
Cat God, 231, *233*
Catherwood, Frederick, *facing 10*, 14, *119*, 122, *127*, *184*, 191, *199*
Catoche, Cape, *123*, 219
Causeways, 21, *74*, 76, 78, *79*, 113, 132, 174, 196, 197, *216–217* 216–217, 218, 304, 308
Caxas, *227*, 302
Cedar, 124, 219
Cempoala, *20*, 86–87, 115, 220
Cenotes, 126, *127*, 144, 190
  at Chichén Itzá, 148, *160*, 170, *171*, 192, 193, *194*, 195, 197, *205*
Ceremonial cannibalism, *53*, 53
Chabalam, 218
Chac, 144, 145, 188, 191, 192, *199*
Chaca, see Bridges, Inca
Chacamarca, 312
Chachapoyas, *227*, 304, 334
Chac-Mool, 32, *56*, 101, *facing 192*, 194, *195*, 196
Chacmultun, 192, 208
Chalco, *74*
Champotón, *123*
Chanapata period, 332
Chan-Chan, 81, *227*, *236*, 236–237, 333
Chancay culture, *262*, *303*, *facing 304*, 333
Chapultepec, 73, *74*, 76, *79*, 333
Charles III, 13, 122, 178
Charles V, 10, 11, 12, 20, 52, 80, *facing 96*, *99*, 99, 220, 300
Chasqui, 114, 323
Chavín culture, *227*, 231, *233*, 330
Chavín de Huantar, 231
Chetumal, *123*, 219
Chiapas, *123*, 128, 178, *202*, 331
Chicama, 330
Chicha, 259, 263, 268,328
Chichén Itzá, *21*, 30, *83*, *123*, 126, *131*, 132, 141, *142*, 148, 155, 156, 160, *160*, 164, 169, 170, *183*, *184*, 190, 192–196, *facing 192*, *194*, 197, 217, 220, 224, 332
  reconstruction, *168–169*
  murals, 208–209, *211*, 219, *142–143*, 195
  see also Temple of Kukulcan, Temple of the Warriors, Caracol
Chichimecas, 30, 35, 170
Chiclayo, *227*
Children, *41*, 41–42, *43*, 247, 271
Chile, *227*, *255*, 281, 302, 334
Chili peppers, 40, 50, 145, 246
Chimor, *see* Chimús
Chimús, 81, 113, 115, 230, *232*, *236*, 236, *242*, *297*, *298*, *299*, 301, 314, 333, 334
Chinampas, 36, 46, *73*, 76
Chocolate, *see* Cacao
Cholula, *20*, 28, 50, 115
'Chosen Women', 247–248, 258, 263, 266, 273, 274, 278, 301–302
Chultunes, 126, 144, 190, 191
Chuñu, 246, 263
Cieza de León, Pedro de, 236, 238, *254*, 263, *273*, 273, 280, 289, 305, 312, 316, 321, 336
Clothing, *facing 11*, 33–34, *34*, *35*, *48*, *49*, 49, 134–135, 180, 241, *241*, 268, *270*
Coatlicue, 90, *92*
Cobá, *123*, 196, 197, 216, 218
Cochineal, 148, 154
Coclé, 220
Cocoms, 170, 171, 332–333
Codices, 144, 145, 222
Codex Florentino, 34, 76, *98–99*
Codex Magliabecchi, *60*
Codex Mendoza, *facing 11*, *39*, 41, *71*, *114*
Codex Peresianus, 222
Codex Tro-Cortesianus, 222
Coiling technique in pottery, 149, *150*, 258–259
Colombia, 14, 72, *205*, 220, *227*, 281, 305, 321, 322, 334
Cólon, Cristóbal, *see* Columbus
Colour symbolism, 48, 100, 147–148
Columbus, Christopher, 9, 70, 117, 120, *121*, 124, 154, 219, 222, 334, 335
Copal, 125, 153, 154
Copán, *facing 10*, 120, 122, *123*, 130, *134*, 152, 161, 168, 176–178, 213, 215, 331, 336
  Jaguar stairway, 176
  Reviewing stand, 177
  Hieroglyphic stairway, *177*, 177, 214
Copiapó, *227*, 302
Copper, *66*, 91, 111, 140, 154, 207–208, 235, 242, 245, 258, 264, 294, 301, 333
Corbelled arch, 132, 173, *175*, 178, 184, 195, 282, *309*
Cordilleras, 230, 231
Corn, *see* Maize
Cortés, Hernan, 9, 10, 22, 23, *23*, 29, 33, *48*, 52, 62, 64, 67, 73, 76, 80, 86, 87, 98, *99*, 99, 112, 113, 114, 117, *118*, 118, 120, 154, 155, 223, 224, 335
Cotton, 33, *48*, 48, 52, 72, 78, 111, 126, 128, 140, 147, 153, 154, 156, 249, *252*, 256, 301
'Council of Four', 67, *69*, *71*
Couriers, 114, 234, 237, 317
  see also chasqui
Coya, 270, *270*, 271, 272, 273, 302, 323
Coyoacán, 74, 76
Cozumel Island, *123*, 192, 196, 219, 335
Cremation, 65, 164
Cross-eyes, 134, *136*
Crystal skull, 91, *95*
Cuauhtitlán, 58
Cuernavaca, 30, 87, 332
Cuitlahuac, *74*, 335
Culhuacán, *74*
Cuqisnique, 15, 330
Curacas, 242, 267, 269, 275, 301
Cuzco, *facing 15*, 77, 78, 81, 170, 212, *227*, 238, 246, 250, 252, 254, 259, *260*, *261*, 263, 266, 272, 275–280, *276*, *277*, *279*, 281, 282, 288, 289, 290, 291, *293*, *295*, *296*, 300, 301, 302, 308, 320, 321, 323, 332, 333

Dances, 160, *161*, 263, *264*, 264–265, 289
Desaguadero, river, *310*
Desert coast of Peru, 226, *229*, 231, 237, 272, 290, 301
Díaz del Castillo, Bernal, 21, 22, *23*, 23, 34, 52, 53, 63, 76, 78, 82, 86, 87, 96, 97, 98, 108, 109, 116, 117, 124, 134, 155, 219, 220
Digging-stick, *44*, 45, 129, 144, 145, 249, 250
Disks, gold, 170, *171*, *273*, 274
Divorce, 38, 140
Dog, 129
Doña Marina, *23*, 33, 155
Drama, 160
Dresden Codex, 14, 122, 132, 158, *facing 209*, *212*, 213, 222, 332
Drums, 40, 60, *61*, 110, 157–158, 263, 265
  from Malinalco, *83*
Dürer, Albrecht, 10, *79*

Dzibilchaltún, 123, *129*, 206, *216–217*, 218, 330

Eagle Knights, *17*, 58, 66, *77*, 78, 82, *83*, *94*, 108
Ear piercing, 133, *137*, 165
Ecuador, *227*, 237, 290, 302, 322, 323
Education, 42, *43*, 247–248
Ekab, *123*, 154, 219
El Petén, 124–125, *125*, 129, 152, 217, 224, 333, 335, 336
Emeralds, 72, 220
Europe, 9, 11, 24, 58, 80
Ex, 134, 135

Feathers, 52, 62, 72, 78, 111, 154, 156, 301
Feather ornaments, 9, 21, 34, 52, 62, 72, 78, 148, 154, 160, 166, *facing 208*, 210, 259
  Aztec headdress, *facing 96*, 99, 117
  Aztec shield, *99*
Feather working, 22, 97–99, *98–99*, 258, 274
Festivals:
  Aztec, 52–59
  Maya, 156–157
  Inca, 263, 289
Figurines, 51, 100, *139*, *145*, 149, 152, *161*, 206, 330
  see also Jaina figurines
Fishing, 154, 219
Flint, *56*, *94*, 129, 154, 210
Food, 37, 40, 41, *66*, 141–144, 246–247
Frescoes, 28, *142–143*, 170, 208, 209, *211*
  see also murals

Gallinazo, 330
Games, 61–64, 263
  see also tlachtli, patolli, pok-a-tok
Gautemala, 24, 29, 72, 90, 111, *123*, 132, 153, *202*, 223, 224, 334
Glyphs, 110, 115, 116, 130, 132, 133, 137, 145, 177, 214, *221*,
Gods and Goddesses, *41*, 45, 46, 47, 48, 51, 53, *54*, *55*, 56, 58, *60*, 64, 65, 100, *101*, 138, *147*, *212*, 212–213, *213*, 268
Gold, 9, 10, 11, 21, 34, 52, 61, 64, 72, 78, 91, 96, 97, *194*, *205*, 207–208, 230, 234, 242, 258, 269, 273, 274, 278, 280, 300, 301, 304, 331
  Mixtec, 90, *96*, *facing 97*
  Inca, 294–295, *295*, *296*, *297*
  Chimú, *297*, *298*, *299*
'Great Descent', 120, 153, 193
Guanaja, island of, 154, 334

Halach Uinic, 165–166
Head deformation, 133
Headdress, *139*, 165–166, *198*, *203*, *facing 208*, 210
Healy, Giles G., 180
Hemp, 249
Holactún, *123*, 192
Honey, *146*, 153, 154, 157
Honduras, 61, 113, *123*, 126, 132, *135*, 154, 171, 176, *202*, 209, 219, 223, 334, 335
Houses, 86
  Aztec, 38, *39*, 39–40, 62, 77–78, *79*, 81
  Maya, 128, 140–141, *141*, 172–173, *173*, 191, 192, *210*
  Inca, 244–246, 281
Huaca del Sol, 234
Huaccoto, 291
Huallaga, river, *227*, 230
Huampas, 313–314, *315*
  see also Balsa boats
Huanacauri, 247
Huánuco, *227*, 304, *308*, 311
Huari, 234, 332
Huastecs, 18, *20*, 29, 155, 330
Huitzilopochtli, 100, *101*, 101, 106, *107*
  see also Temple of
Humboldt, Alexander von, 13, 122, *facing 209*, *facing 320*
Huntichmool, 192
Hunting, 129, 144
Hun Uinic, 138, 144

Ica-Nazca culture, *227*, *233*, 234, 330–332
Incas, 12, 37, 39, 46, 67, 71, 72, 77, 78, 81, 83, 112, 113, 115, 132, 138, 159, 165, 170, 172, 212, 223, 333–336
  pre-Incas, 230–237
  origins, 238
  physical features, 240
  social organisation, 243–244
  daily life, 246–248, 256–263
  agriculture, 248–250
  architecture, 245, 281–290
  government, 269–275
  religion, *see* Sun Worship
Inca Empire, 226, 240, 265, 269, 271, 275, 278, 280, 281, 288, 308, 321, 322
Incahuasi, 290, 302, 305
Intihuatana, 282, *286*
Irrigation, 13, 46, 146, 226, 237, 250–251
Itzamná, 134, *136*, 213
Itzás, 169, 170, 176, 193, 194, 208, 224, 332, 333
Ixtaccihuatl, *20*
Ixtapalapa, *74*
Izamal, *119*, *123*, 192, 216

Jade, *facing 14*, 21, 22, 28, *41*, 97, 124, 137, 153, 164, 165, 180, 193, *202*, 210, 214, 331
Jaguar friezes, *131*, 194, 196
Jaguar Knights, 58, 82, *83*, 108
Jaina, island of, *123*
  figurines, *139*, 149, *facing 193*, 206–207
Jalisco, 30, *63*
Janja, *227*
Jauja valley, 305
Jewellery, 9, 65, 96, *facing 97*, 97, 98, 133, *137*, 165, 180, 242, 247, 264, 272, 274, 300
Jicaque Indians, *135*
Jungle, 124, 125, 196, *229*, 304
Justice, 38, 64–65, 69, 163–164, 265–267

Kabah, *123*, *175*, *182*, *186*, *188*, 190, 191–192, 217, 332
Keuic, *123*, 192
Kickmool, 192
Kilns, 149, 176
'Kings', Aztec, 47, 67, *68–69*, 166, 333–335
Kingsborough, Viscount, 14, 122
Kukulcán, 170, 194
  see also Temple of

Labná, *123*, *184*, *187*, 191–192, 216, 217, 218
Lacandon Indians, 158
Laguna de Términos, *123*, 154, 219, 333
Landa, Diego de, 11, 115, 121, 125, *126*, 133, 134, *135*, 135, 137, 138, 139, 140, 144, 154, 155, 156, 157, 158, 159, 160, 161, 162, 163, 166, 170, 174, 195, 197, 205, 206, 207, 216, 222, 335

La Venta, *21,* 24, 61, 330
League of Mayapán, 136, 169–170, 180, 191, 332
Lima, 58, *227,* 237, 272, 290, 333
Limatambo, *227,* 288
Lime mortar, 172, 176
Litters, 21, 113, *115,* 219, 273–274, *275,* 312–313, 328
'Little Descent', 192
Llama, 245, 246, 247, 249, 254–255, *255,* 256, 263, 271, 280, *296,* 300, 304, 312, 314, 316, 318, 319
Llautos, 166, *273,* 274, *276*
Long-nosed god, *see* Chac
Loom, back-strap, *43, 48,* 48, 129, *147,* 148, 234, *257,* 258
 horizontal, 256
 vertical, 256
Lord-Inca, 52, 67, 68, 69, 166, *225, 241,* 242, 243, 244, 247, 248, 249, 265, 266, 268, 269–274, *271,* 278, 289, 295, 302, 312, 314, 317, 318, 319, 322, 323, 328
 see also Atahualpa

Macehualli, 33, 35, 38
Machu Picchu, 39, *227,* 244, *245, 283,* 284, *286, 287,* 288
Maguey, 30, 33, 34, 42, 52, 100
Maize, 12, 22, 40, *44,* 44–46, 47, 48, 124, 126, 128, 138, 141, 142, 144–145, *145,* 154, 156, 212, 231, 245, 246, 248, *248–249,* 249, *250–251,* 250, 263, 280
Malinal, *see* Doña Marina
Malinalco, *20,* 82, *131*
Manco Capac, 238, 272, 275, 332
Maní, *123,* 155, 222
Manioc, 231, 248
Maps, 78, *79,* 112, 138, 154, 219
Markets,
 Aztec, 22, 23, 46, *51,* 51–52, 78, 111
 Maya, 155–156, 196
 Inca, 159
Marriage, *37,* 37–38, 139–140, 244, 270
Masks, 24, 91, *92,* 97, *119, 159,* 165, *202,* 207, 265
Maudslay, Alfred, 14, 15
Maule, river, *227,* 281, 302, 334
Maya blue, 148, 209, 213
Mayas, 11, 12, 15, 16, 24, 25, 38, 39, *59,* 69, 70, 83, *84,* 87, 90, 102, 110, 111, 267, 278, 330–336
 settling, 120–128
 origins, 128–130
 physical features, 133–134
 clan organisation, 137–138
 daily life, 141–143, 147–156
 agriculture, 143–146
 government, 165–166
 architecture, 172–197
 art, 197–209
 religion, 212–213
Mayapán, 30, *123,* 149, 169–171, 217, 332, 333
Mayathan, 136
Menché, stone lintel from, *100*
Merchants, 64, 154, 156
 see also pochteca, ppolms
Mérida, 11, *123,* 212, 216, 223, 335
Mesetas, 15, *19*
Metalwork, 91, 96, 97–98, 207–208, 294–300, *295*
Metatl, 40, 124
Mexico, 9, 11, 13, 18, *19, 20–21,* 24, 26, 27, 29, 35, 39, 44, *59,* 70, 82, 83, 87, 90, 91, 101, 112, 114, 115, 117, 162, 196, 223, 322, 330, 333, 335
Mexico City, 13, 18, *19,* 29, 105, 196 *see als* Toenochtitlán
Milpas, 44, 44–45, 100
Mitimaes, 71, 302, 321
Mitla, *20, 49, 84, 89,* 90
Mixtecs, 14, 15, *20,* 28, *84,* 87, *87, 88,* 90, *facing 97,* 115, 154, 220
Moche Valley, 234
Mochicas, 115, 231, *233,* 234, 237, 255, 314, 330–332, 333
Moctezuma II, 21, 22, *23,* 23, 40, 53, 62, 64, 67–71, *69, 71,* 78, 96, *facing 96,* 97, 98, 99, 115, 117, 166, 334, 335
Moctezuma's Book of Tribute, *facing 11, 47,* 48, 49, 97, 115
Monogamy, 139, 244
Montaña, 230, 294
Monte Albán, *20, 26,* 26, 27, 28, *84,* 87, 90, *96, facing 97,* 97, 330–331
Montejo, Francisco de, 11, 120, 223, 335
Mosaic serpent, *94*
Mosaic skull, *facing 80*
Mummies, 65, *66,* 231, 268, 272, 274
Murals, 48, 86, 120, 137, 145, 192, 195, 213
 see also Bonampak, Chichén Itzá
Musical instruments,
 Aztec, *60,* 60, *61*
 Maya, 157–159, *158–159,* 180
 Inca, 263–265, *265*
Musicians, *60,* 158, *158–159,* 265
Muzo, 220

Nahuatl, 35–36, 111
Nazca, *227,* 234
 see also Ica-Nazca culture
Nemontemi, 60, 102, 104
Neo-Inca state, 224, 320, 335, 336
Neolithic, 36, 72, 128, 138, 172
New Year, Maya, *157,* 157, 215
Nicaragua, 35, 40, 72, 111, 132, 334
Nito, *123,* 154

Oaxaca, *20,* 24, 26, 87, 90, 101, 115, 208, 330, 331
Observatories, *188,* 193
Obsidian, *facing 14,* 22, 34, 41, 48, 91, 97, 109, 111, 124, 129, 147, 153, 154, 176, 210
Octli, 37, 40, 58
'Old Empire', 130, 144, 192
Ollantaytambo, 39, *227,* 245, 250, 266, 282, 284, *285,* 291, 301, 302
Olmecs, 18, *21,* 24, *25, 26,* 27, 28, 29, 61, *84,* 87, *202,* 330–331
Omoa, *123,* 176, 219
Omens, *70–71,* 70, 117
Orejones, see 'Big Ears'
Orinoco, river, 336

Pachacamac, *227,* 233, 290
Palace of Moctezuma, *71,* 78–79, 116
Palenque, 13, 15, 21, 120, 122, *123,* 134, 144, 152, 168, 178–180, *179, 185,* 186, *203,* 206, 220, 221, 331
 see also Temple of the Sun, Temple of the Inscriptions
Panama, 9, 72, 132, 208, 219, 220, 322, 333
Paper, 16, 52, 115–116, 130, 160, 220, 222
Paracas, *227,* 231, *232,* 234, *235,* 330–331
 textiles from, 231
Paraguay, 40, 45, *227*
Patolli, 62, 64, *64*
Paucartambo, river, 300
Pearls, 21, 164, 180, 220
Peru, 12, 39, 46, 71, 77, 81, 109, 112, 114, 117, 148, 223, 224, 226, *227, 228, 229,* 230, 231,

235, 263, 281, 290, 300, 302, 312, 320, 330
Petén, Lake, *123*, 155, 176
Piedras Negras, *123*, 144, 152, 193
Pisac, *facing 15*, *227*, 250, 251, *252–253*, 282, 301
Pisco valley, *227*, 234, *235*, 290, 330
Pizarro, Francisco, 12, 117, 223, *225*, 274, *275*, *facing 321*, 323, *324–325*, *326–327*, 335
Pizarro, Hernando, 311
Plough, 248–249, *251*
Plumed Serpent, 15, 16, 87, *88*, *89*, *184*, 194, 195, 196, *197*
Pochteca, 53, 72, 73, 87, 110–111, *111*, 154, 334
Pok-a-tok, 161–162, *162*
Polé, 192
Polygamy, 69, 244, 270
Poma de Ayala, Felipe Guamán, *241*, *246–247*, *248–249*, *266*, *267*, *271*, *319*
Popocatepetl, *20*, 70
Popol Vuh, 128, 152, *153*, 162
Portrait urns, 164
Portuguese, 9
Potato, 46, 246, 248–249, 250, *251*, 263
Potosí, *227*, 263
Pottery, 48, *51*, 111, 164, 231
  Tarascan, *26*, *62*
  Zapotec, *27*
  Tabascan, *27*, 149
  Totonac, *29*
  Aztec, *50*, 50–51, 52
  Toltec, *50*, *150*
  Cholula, 50
  Jalisco, *63*
  Maya, 120, 128, 129, 130, 148–153, *150*, *151*; phases, 152–153, *153*, 330–332
  Chimú, *232*, 237, *242*, 314
  Paracas, *232*
  Mochica, *233*, 234, 314
  Nazca, *233*, 234
  Inca, 258–259, *260*, *261*, *262*
  see also figurines
Pottery moulds, 149
Ppolms, 154–155
Prescott, William H., 14, 67, 122, 309, 328
Priests, 48, 77, 78, 101–102, 104, 138, 140, 213, 214
Pulque, 30, 50
Punic, 240, 243, 268, 318
Punishment, *facing 11*, 42, *43*, 64–65, *65*, *266*, *267*, 266–267
Purumauca, *227*, 281, 302, 334
Puuc region, 132, 172, 180, 190, 192, 193, 208, 217
Pyramids, 28, 39, 78, 83, 168, 173, 174, 176, 180, 193, 237
  see also Teocalli

Quarries, 291
Quechuas, 71, 226, 240, *243*, 302, 321, 333
Quetzal bird, 16, 48, *facing 96*, *99*, 117, 124, 137, 153, 165, 179, 207, *facing 208*, 210
Quetzalcoatl, *27*, 28, 32, 68, 70, 78, *83*, *89*, *facing 96*, 99, 117, 170, 193, 195, 331, 332
Quintana Roo, *123*, 132
Quipu, 256, 295, 314, 316–317, *316*, *317*, 321, 328
Quiriguá, *123*, 178, 206
Quito, *227*, 288, 290, 305, 334

Rain gods, *see* Tlaloc, Chac
Raleigh, Sir Walter, 336
Reservoirs, 126, 144, 146, 174, 218, 237, 294
Roads,
  Aztec, 47, 64, 72, 112, *112*, 114–115
  Maya, 112, 133, 134, 155, 216–218
  see also sacbeob
  Inca, 13, 109, 112, 234, 237, 281, 288, 289, 301, 304–307, *306*, *307*, *308*, 319, 321, 334
  Royal road, 12, 282, 290, 302, 305, *306*, 308, 312
  coastal road, 234, 302, 304–305, *306*, 308, 334
  step road, 304, *308*
Rubber, 61, *62*, 72, 111, 158, 160, 161, 259, 263
  effigies from Chichén Itzá, *160*, *194*
Rumicolca, 282, 291

Sabacche, 192
Sacbeob, 112, 125, 133, 190, 191, 216–218, *216–217*
Sacrifice, 45, 48, 53, 54, *56*, 58, *59*, 72, *80*, 101, 104, 117, 132, 146, 148, 180, *194*, *195*, *201*, 208, 213, 254, 334
Sacrificial knives, *56*, *94*, *296*
Sacrificial wells, *see cenotes*
Sacsahuamán, *227*, 251, 290, 291–294, *292*, *296*, 301
Sahagún, Bernardino de, 32, 34, 61, *65*, *98*, 162
Salt, 52, 53, 126, 154, 156, 219
Sandals, 34, 43, 46, 52, 69, 135, 165, 241, *242*, 249, 272, *273*, 274
San José, *123*
Santa Lucia, *123*, *201*
Santa Rita, *123*, 209
Sapodilla, 125, 173, 174, *207*, 259
Sayil, *123*, *182*, *186*, 192, 217
Seville, 9, 12, 23, 116, 196, 300
Schools, 36, 42, 68, 102
Sculpture,
  Totonac, *28*, 29
  Olmec, *25*
  Aztec, *facing 14*, *17*, *35*, 90–91, *92*, *93*, *95*, *105*, *106–107*
  Maya, 173, *177*, 178, 180, *197*, *199*, *200*, *201*, *202*, *203*, *204*, 206–207
  see also figurines, *stelae*
Shell, 156, 213
Shields, 22, *47*, 98, *99*, 109, 154, 212, 245, 247, 318
Silver, 12, 21, 52, 91, *233*, 242, 258, 264, 269, 272, 273, 295, *296*, 300, 333
Skull-racks, 61, 77, 78, *80*
Slaves, 40, 62, 137, 155, 210
Sling, 245, 318, *319*, 319
Soap, 146
Soliman, *123*, 196
South America, 13, 91, 113, 159, 220, 226, 230, 281, 308, 314,
Spaniards, 9, 20, 23, 26, 51, 62, 69, *70*, 86, 90, 110, 114, 157, 166, 174, 178, 195, 212, 224, 237, 240, 249, 271, 274, 284, 290, 294, 300, 304, 318, 319, 320, 321
Spanish Conquest, 10, 11, *19*, 117–118, 120, 124, 155, 222–224, 322–328, *324–325*, *326–327*
Spindles, *48*, 48, 51, 147, 256, *257*
Spindle whorls, *48*, 48, 51, 147, 256
Squier, E. George, *310*
Stages, 160–161, 174, 196
Steam bath, *38*, 40, 140, 142, 174, *183*
Stelae,
  Maya, *facing 10*, *129*, 130, *135*, 174, 177, 180, 191, 192, 197, *198*, 206, 207, 222, 332
  Olmec, 24, 331
Stephens, John Lloyd, *facing 10*, 14, 15, *119*, 122, *127*, 177, *184*, 191, 192, 217

Stonework, *facing 15*, 125, *172*, 172, 235, *245*, 277, 278, 279, 284, 288, 290–291, *292*, *293*, *311*
Stucco, 178, 180, *184*, *186*, 197, *203*, 206, 214
Suicide, 164, *213*
Sun-God, *56*, *101*, *236*
see also Tonatiuh
Sun Worship, 244, 248, 280, 301, 321
see also Temples of the Sun
Sweet Potato, 46, 142, 146, 248

Tabasco, *20*, 24, *24*, *123*, 126, 155, 169, 219, 335
Tajín, *20*
Talca, 334
Tambo Colorado, *227*, 290
Tampico, *20*, 128, 220, 330, 333
Tampu, 13, 218, 281, 319
Tamuín, *20*
Tancah, *123*, 196
Tarasco, *20*, *26*, 333
Tattooing, 134, 165
Taxes, 46, 47, 71, 77, 244, 250, 275, 295
Tayasal, 224, 336
Tehuantepec, Isthmus of, 90, 128, 334
Temples, 11, 26, 27, 28, 29, 32, 39, 41, 64, *70*, *facing 81*, 87, 132, 133, 138, 213
Temple of Huitzilopochtli, Tenochtitlán, *56*, 76, *77*, 101, 334
Temple of the Inscriptions, Palenque, 179–180, *203*, 220
Temple of Kukulcán, Chichén Itzá, *131*, *168–169*, *184*, 193, 194, 195, 217
Temples of Quetzalcoatl,
Tenochtitlan, 78
Calixtlahuaca, 82
Teotihuacán, 86
Xochicalco, 87, *88*
Temples of the Sun, 281, 282, 290, 302, 321
Teotihuacán, *31*, 83, *85*, 86, 331
Palenque, 178, *179*, *186*
Cuzco, 278, 280, 320
Ollantaytambo, 284
Vilcashuamán, 288–289, *288*, *289*
Temple of the Warriors, Chichén Itzá, *142–143*, 155, *168–169*, *183*, 195–196, *197*, 208–209, *211*
Tenayuca, *75*
'Tenochas', 19, 20, *22*, 24, 67, 68, 333
Tenochtitlán, 10, *facing 11*, 18, 19, 20, *20*, *22*, 23, 29, 36, 38, 40, 47, 61, *70*, 71, 72, *73*, *74–75*, 76–80, *77*, *79*, 81, 82, 98, 101, 104, 110, 112, 115, 155, 170, 333, 335 *see also* Tempel of Huitzilopochtli, Temple of Quetzalcoatl
Teocalli, 78, 81, 83, 107
Teotihuacán, *20*, 30, *31*, *50*, *75*, 83, *85*, 86, 91, 193, 331–332
'Tepexpan Man', 330
Tepeyac, *75*, 76
Terracing, *facing 15*, 46, 250–251, *252–253*, 282, 284, 294, 308
Texcoco, Lake, 20, 69, 70, 73, *74*, 333
T'ho, *see* Mérida
'Thousand columns', Chichén Itzá, 155–156, *168–169*, *183*, 195
Tiahuanaco, 115, *227*, 234–236, *239*, *257*, 331–333, 334
Tici Virachocha, 268, 328
Tikal, *21*, 29, *59*, 120, *123*, 124, *125*, 126, 130, 141, 143, 146, *151*, 152, *167*, 168, 172, 174, 176, 191, 193, *198*, 207, 216, 218, 219, 224
Tilmantli, 33, *37*, 37, *47*, 62, 69
Tin, 300
Titicaca, lake, *227*, 234, 235, 249, 268, 290, 294, 304, 312, 314, *315*, 332, 334
Tizoc, stone of, *77*, 78, *106–107*, 107, 333
Tlachtli, 61–62, *62*, 330
Tlacopán, *74*, 66, 78
Tlaloc, 45, 46, 53, 58, 66, 77, *88*, *101*, 111
Tlaltelolco, 22, *74*, 76, *79*
see also Tenochtitlán
Tlatoani, 39, 67, 330
Tlazolteotl, *41*
Tobacco, 52
Toltecs, 15, *20*, 28, 29, 30, 35, 83, *85*, 86, 87, *88*, *89*, 132, 154, 155, 162, 169, 170, *182*, *183*, 191, 193, 194, 195, *195*, 196, *201*, 208, 214, 330–332
Tonatiuh, 13, *facing 14*, 103
Totonacs, 9, 18, *20*, 28, *29*, 29, 115, 154, 220
'laughing faces', *28*, 29
Toys, 51, 112, *113*, *303*
Trade, 72, 106, 111–112, 130, 132, 138, 153–155, 210, 218, 333
Trapezoidal niche, 282, *283*
Tres Zapotes, *21*, 24
Tribute, 22, 46, *47*, 52, 69, 72, 73, 83, 87, 97, 250, 301
Tucumán, *227*, 302
Tula, *20*, 30–31, *83*, *89*, *91*, *131*, 162, 170, 193, 194, 195, *195*, 196, 332
Tulum, *21*, *123*, *182*, 196–197, 206, 209, 335
Tumbes, *225*, *227*, 302, 322, 323, 333, 334
Tumibamba, *227*
Turquoise, 61, 62, *facing 80*, 97, *297*
Tutul Xius, 170, 180, 333
Tzintzuntzán, *20*

Uaxactun, 24, *123*, 124, 130, 174, 208, 217, 332
Uayeb, *156*, *157*, 157, 214, *215*
see also Calendar, Maya
Ucayali, river, *227*, 230
Uinal, 145
see also Calendar, Maya
Urubamba, river, *facing 15*, *227*, *228*, 246, 250, 251, 282, 284, 301, *311*
Usumacinta, river, 128, 154, 178
Uxmal, *21*, *123*, 132, 169, *175*, 180, *181*, 190–191, 192, 196, 217, 332
Nunnery, 38, *141*, 172, *173*, 181, 190–191, 199
Temple of the Dwarf, *181*, 190, *204*
House of the Governor, *188–189*, 190, 191
'Queen of', *204*

Vaillant, G. C., 36, 38, 58, 90
Vega, Garcilaso de la, 259, 267, 269, 294, 310
Venezuela, 164, 220
Vera Cruz, *20*, 24, 29, 86, 96, 99, 112, 114, 115, 117, 152, 154, 335
Veragua, 208
Vicuña, 242, *254*, 256, 258, 272, 274
Vilcapampa, 320, 335
Vilcashuamán, *227*, *288*, 288–289, *289*
Virús, 330
Volador, *59*
von Hagen Expedition, 304

Waldeck, J. F. de, 122, *134*, *185*
War, 47, 71, 72, 100, 101, 104, 105,

106–110, 210–212, *211*, 238, 317–320
War dresses, *47*, 108, 210
Warriors, 33, 42, 58, 104, 105, *108*, *109*, 210, 213, *233*, 245, 247, 263, 268, 318, *319*
warrior figures at Tula, *91*, 194
Wattle and daub, 38, *39*, 76, 77
Weapons, 42, 46, 109, 110, 132, 153, 210, 320
Weaving, 34, *43*, *48*, 48–49, *49*, 50, 90, 147–148, *147*, 153, 231, 234, *241*, 248, *257*, 257–258, 263, 303, *facing 304*
Weeping God, 234, 236, *239*
Wheel, 9, 27, 51, 80, 112–113, *113*, 128, 146, 291, 304
Whistling jars, *232*, 237
Wood carvings, 173, 174, *183*, 195, 196, 197, *207*, 207, 210, 214, 226, 234, *261*
Wool, 240, 241, 242, 244, 249, 255, 256, 258, 268, 274, *facing 304*, 316
Writing, 27, 331
Aztec, 68, 102, 110, 114–117
Maya, 26, 130, 132, 178
Toltec, 30

Xamantun, 332
Xampala, *facing 81*
Xcalcumkin, 192
Xcalumpococh, 192
Xelha, *123*, 196, 197, 223, 335
Xicalango, *21*, 26, 117, *123*, 154, 155, 170, 178, 208, 219, 332, 333
Xipé, 53, *54–55*, *77*, *92*, *96*
Xochicalco, 13, *20*, 30, 87, *88*, 332
Xochimilco, *74*
Xochiquetzal, 48
Xultun, 332

Yacatecuhtli, 53, 100, *101*
Yache, 192
Yaxchilán, *123*, 124, 144, 180
Yaxuná, *123*, 217
Yucatán, 30, 32, 44, 90, 115, 117, 120, 121, *123*, 124, 125, 126, 128, 132, 135, 136, 144, 152, 154, 159, 164, 169, 170, 180, *182*, 192, 196, 207, 208, 217, 223, 224, 330, 332, 335, 336
Yucay, river, 281
Yum Kaax, 213, *213*

Zapotec, 14, 21, 26, *27*, 27, 28, *84*, 87, *89*, 115, 331
Zip, *156*
Zumpango, 75